DIVAS AND LOVERS

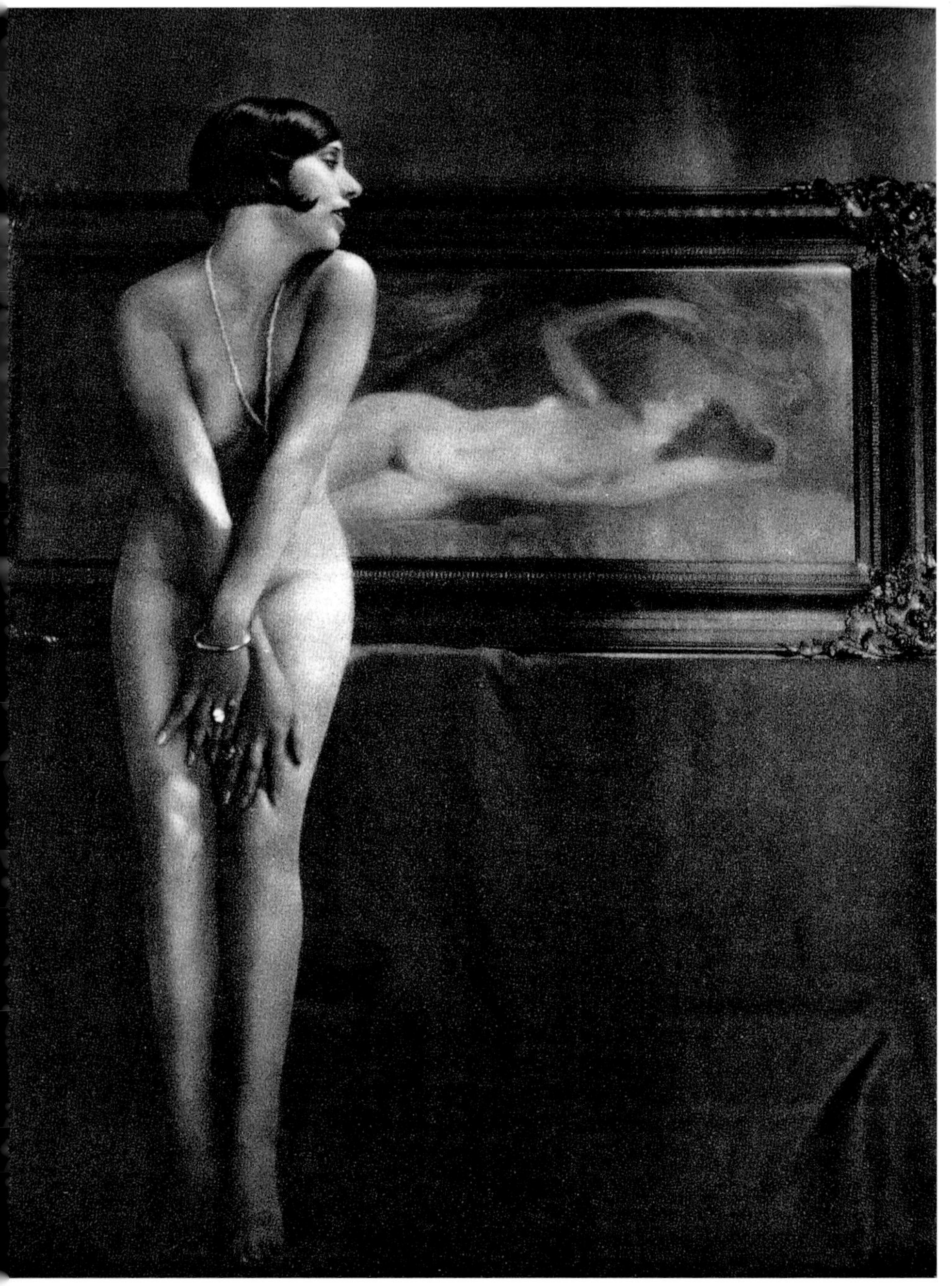

DIVAS AND LOVERS

THE EROTIC ART OF STUDIO MANASSÉ
STORY BY D. H. LAWRENCE
ESSAY BY MONIKA FABER

TRANSLATED BY
MARGOT BETTAUER DEMBO

UNIVERSE PUBLISHING

The stars were marvelous when it came to [posing for] stills. ... They were fascinating, full of sex appeal, exciting. We lived our lives as if we were in a big novel, a romantic fantasy world. We were talented. We had work. We earned money and had no doubts whatsoever that it would always go on like this. We didn't torment ourselves the way people do today. We were much too busy living it up. We were the children of the gods.

George Hurrell

One day the film star's demonic nature will leave her and all that remains will be her bangs. Thus existence crumbles because there is nothing holding it together any longer. The photographic archives have collected in their likenesses reflections of the remaining vestiges of the alienated nature of what was.

Siegfried Kracauer, 1927

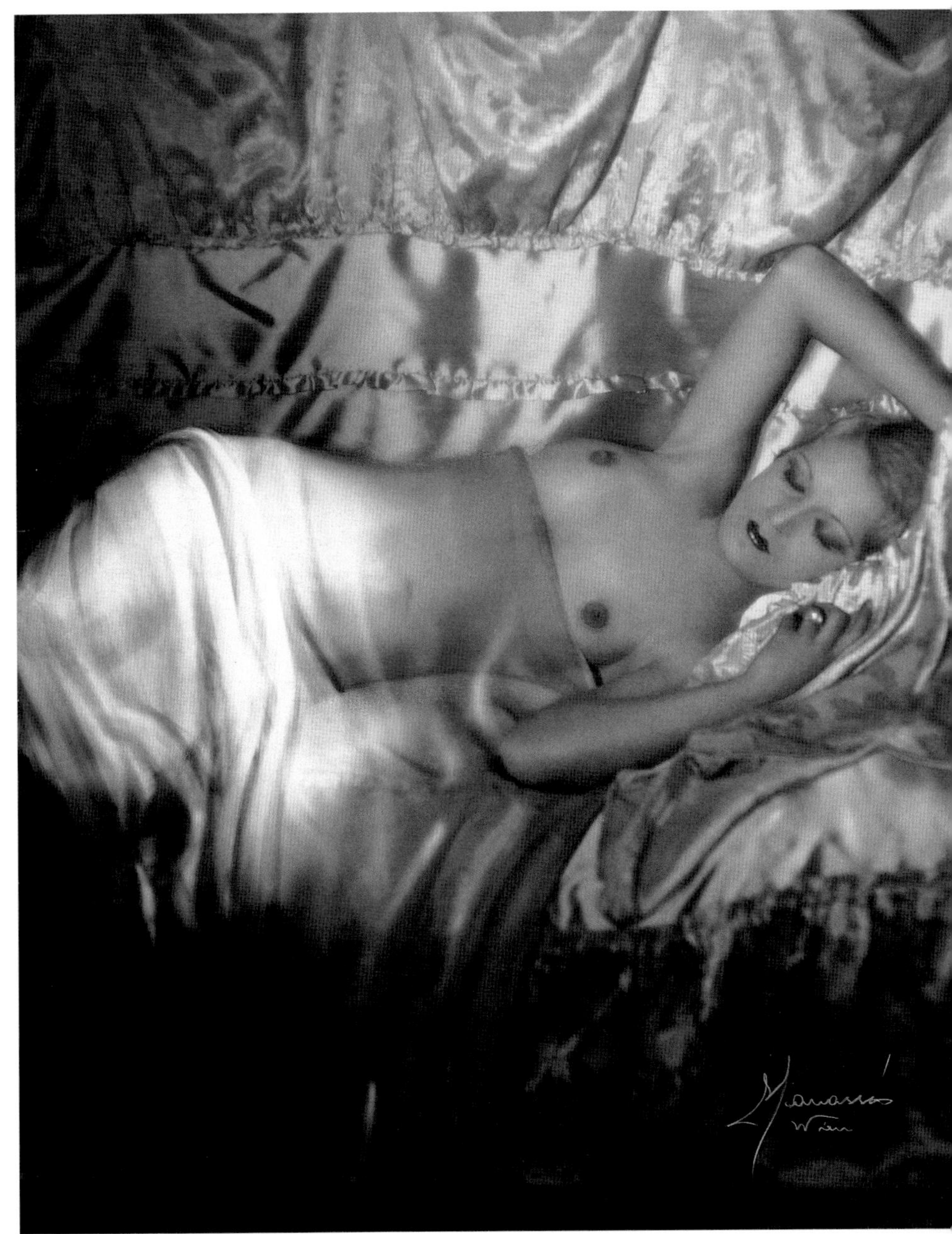

Study, c.1926

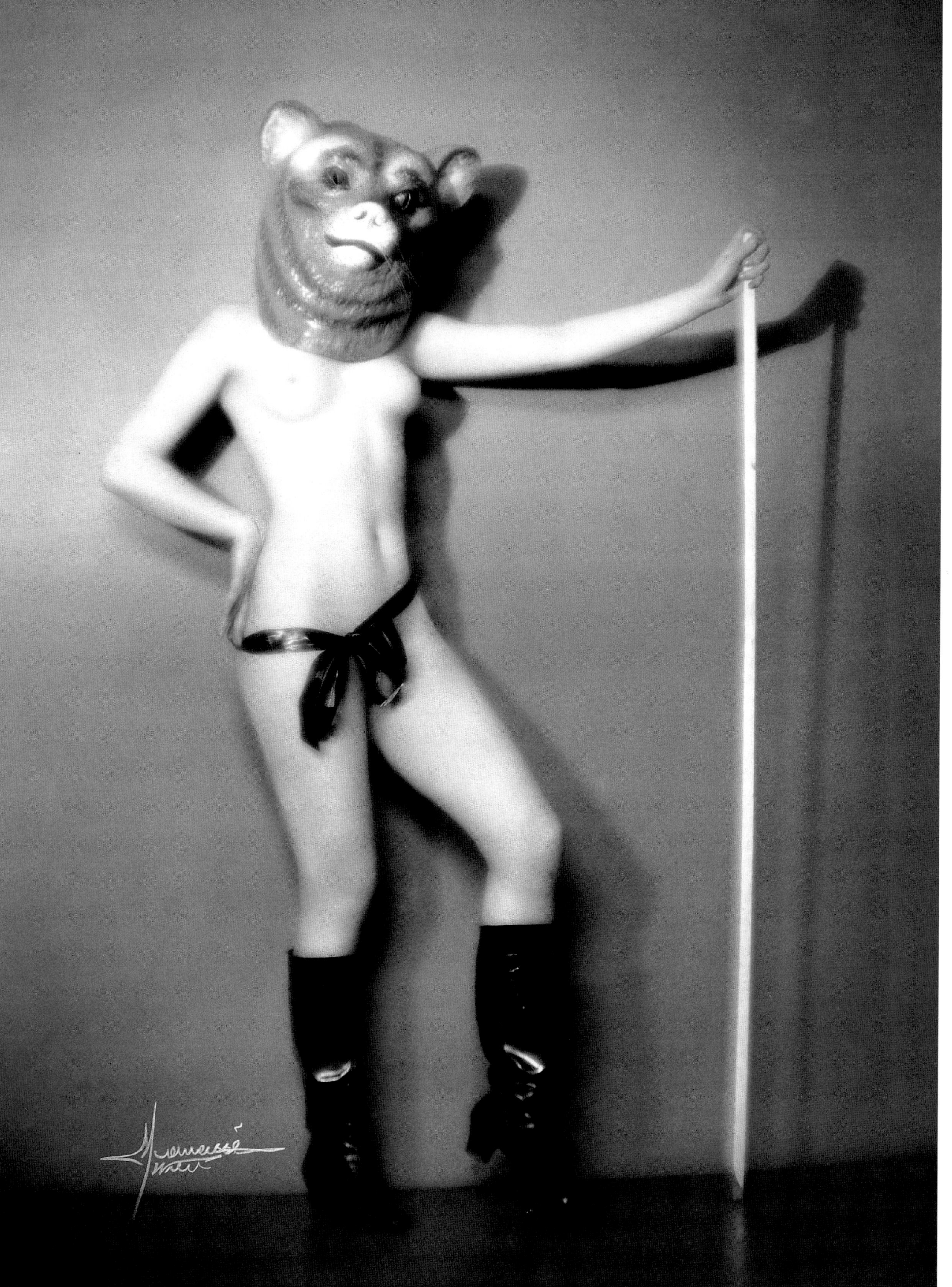

D. H. LAWRENCE
GIVE HER A PATTERN

The real trouble about women is that they must always go on trying to adapt themselves to men's theories of women, as they always have done. When a woman is thoroughly herself, she is being what her type of man wants her to be. When a woman is hysterical it's because she doesn't quite know what to be, which pattern to follow, which man's picture of woman to live up to.

For, of course, just as there are many men in the world, there are many masculine theories of what women should be. But men run to type, and it is the type, not the individual, that produces the theory, or "ideal" of woman. Those very grasping gentry, the Romans, produced a theory or ideal of the matron, which fitted in very nicely with the Roman property lust. "Caesar's wife should be above suspicion."—So Caesar's wife kindly proceeded to be above it, no matter how far below it the Caesar fell. Later gentlemen like Nero produced the "fast" theory of woman, and later ladies were fast enough for everybody. Dante arrived with a chaste and untouched Beatrice, and chaste and untouched Beatrices began to march self-importantly through the centuries. The Renaissance discovered the learned woman, and learned women buzzed mildly into verse and prose. Dickens invented the child-wife, so child-wives have swarmed ever since. He also fished out his version of the chaste Beatrice, a chaste but marriageable Agnes. George Eliot imitated this pattern, and it became confirmed. The noble woman, the pure spouse, the devoted mother took the field, and was simply worked to death. Our own poor mothers were this sort. So we younger men, having been a bit frightened of our noble mothers, tended to revert to the child-wife. We weren't very inventive. Only the child-wife must be a boyish little thing—that was the new touch we added. Because young men are definitely frightened of the real female. She's too risky a quantity. She's too untidy, like David's Dora. No, let her be a boyish little thing, it's safer. So a boyish little thing she is.

There are, of course, other types. Capable men produce the capable woman ideal. Doctors produce the capable nurse. Business men produce the capable secretary. And so you get all sorts. You can produce the masculine sense of honour (whatever that highly mysterious quantity may be) in women, if you want to.

There is, also, the eternal secret ideal of men—the prostitute. Lots of women live up to this ideal: just because men want them to.

And so, poor woman, destiny makes away with her. It isn't that she hasn't got a mind—she has. She's got everything that man has. The only difference is that she asks for a pattern. Give me a pattern to follow! That will always be woman's cry. Unless of course she has already chosen her pattern quite young, then she will declare she is herself absolutely, and no man's idea of women has any influence over her.

Now the real tragedy is not that women ask and must ask for a pattern of womanhood. The tragedy is not, even, that men give them such abominable patterns, child-wives,

Study, c.1931

little-boy-baby-face girls, perfect secretaries, noble spouses, self-sacrificing mothers, pure women who bring forth children in virgin coldness, prostitutes who just make themselves low, to please the men; all the atrocious patterns of womanhood that men have supplied to woman; patterns all perverted from any real natural fulness of a human being. Man is willing to accept woman as an equal, as a man in skirts, as an angel, a devil, a baby-face, a machine, an instrument, a bosom, a womb, a pair of legs, a servant, an encyclopaedia, an ideal or an obscenity; the one thing he won't accept her as is a human being, a real human being of the feminine sex.

And, of course, women love living up to strange patterns, weird patterns—the more uncanny the better. What could be more uncanny than the present pattern of the Eton-boy girl with flower-like artificial complexion? It is just weird. And for its very weirdness women like living up to it. What can be more gruesome than the little-boy-baby-face pattern? Yet the girls take it on with avidity.

But even that isn't the real root of the tragedy. The absurdity, and often, as in the Dante-Beatrice business, the inhuman nastiness of the pattern—for Beatrice had to go on being chaste and untouched all her life, according to Dante's pattern, while Dante had a cosy wife and kids at home—even that isn't the worst of it. The worst of it is, as soon as a woman has really lived up to the man's pattern, the man dislikes her for it. There is intense secret dislike for the Eton-young-man girl, among the boys, now that she is actually produced. Of course, she's very nice to show in public, absolutely the thing. But the very young men who have brought about her production detest her in private and in their private hearts are appalled by her.

When it comes to marrying, the pattern goes all to pieces. The boy marries the Eton-boy girl, and instantly he hates the type. Instantly, his mind begins to play hysterically with all the other types, noble Agneses, chaste Beatrices, clinging Doras and lurid *filles de joie*. He is in a wild welter of confusion. Whatever pattern the poor woman tries to live up to; he'll want another. And that's the condition of modern marriage.

Modern woman isn't really a fool. But modern man is. That seems to me the only plain way of putting it. The modern man is a fool, and the modern young man a prize fool. He makes a greater mess of his women than men have ever made. Because he absolutely doesn't know *what* he wants her to be. We shall see the changes in the woman-pattern follow one another fast and furious now, because the young men hysterically don't know what they want. Two years hence women may be in crinolines—there was a pattern for you!—or a bead flap, like naked negresses in mid-Africa—or they may be wearing brass armour, or the uniform of the Horse Guards. They may be anything. Because the young men are off their heads, and don't know what they want.

The women aren't fools, but they *must* live up to some pattern or other. They *know* men are fools. They don't really respect the pattern. Yet a pattern they must have, or they can't exist.

Women are not fools. They have their own logic, even if it's not the masculine sort. Women have the logic of emotion, men have the logic of reason. The two are complementary and mostly in opposition. But the woman's logic of emotion is no less real and inexorable than the man's logic of reason. It only works differently.

And the woman never really loses it. She may spend years living up to a masculine pattern. But in the end, the strange and terrible logic of emotion will work out the smashing of that pattern, if it has not been emotionally satisfactory. This is the partial explanation of the astonishing changes in women. For years they go on being chaste Beatrices or child-wives. Then on a sudden—bash! The chaste Beatrice becomes something quite different, the child-wife becomes a roaring lioness! The pattern didn't suffice, emotionally.

Whereas men are fools. They are based on a logic of reason, or are supposed to be. And then they go and behave, especially with regard to women, in a more-than-feminine unreasonableness. They spend years training up the little-boy-baby-face type, till they've got her perfect. Then the moment they marry her, they want something else. Oh, beware, young women, of the young men who adore you! The moment they've got you they'll want something utterly different. The moment they marry the little-boy-baby face, instantly they begin to pine for the noble Agnes, pure and majestic, or the infinite mother with deep bosom of consolation, or the perfect business woman, or the lurid prostitute on black silk sheets: or, most idiotic of all, a combination of all the lot of them at once. And that is the logic of reason! When it comes to women, modern men are idiots. They don't know what they want, and so they never want, permanently, what they get. They want a cream cake that is at the same time ham and eggs and at the same time porridge. They are fools. If only women weren't bound by fate to play up to them!

For the fact of life is that women must play up to man's pattern. And she only gives her best to a man when he gives her a satisfactory pattern to play up to. But today, with a stock of ready-made, worn-out idiotic patterns to live up to, what can women give to men but the trashy side of their emotions? What could a woman possibly give to a man who wanted her to be a boy-baby face? What could she possibly give him but the dribblings of an idiot?—And, because women aren't fools, and aren't fooled even for very long at a time, she gives him some nasty cruel digs with her claws, and makes him cry for mother dear!—abruptly changing his pattern.

Bah! men are fools. If they want anything from women, let them give women a decent, satisfying idea of womanhood—not these trick patterns of washed-out idiots.

(D. H. Lawrence, *Give Her a Pattern*. In: *Assorted Articles*)

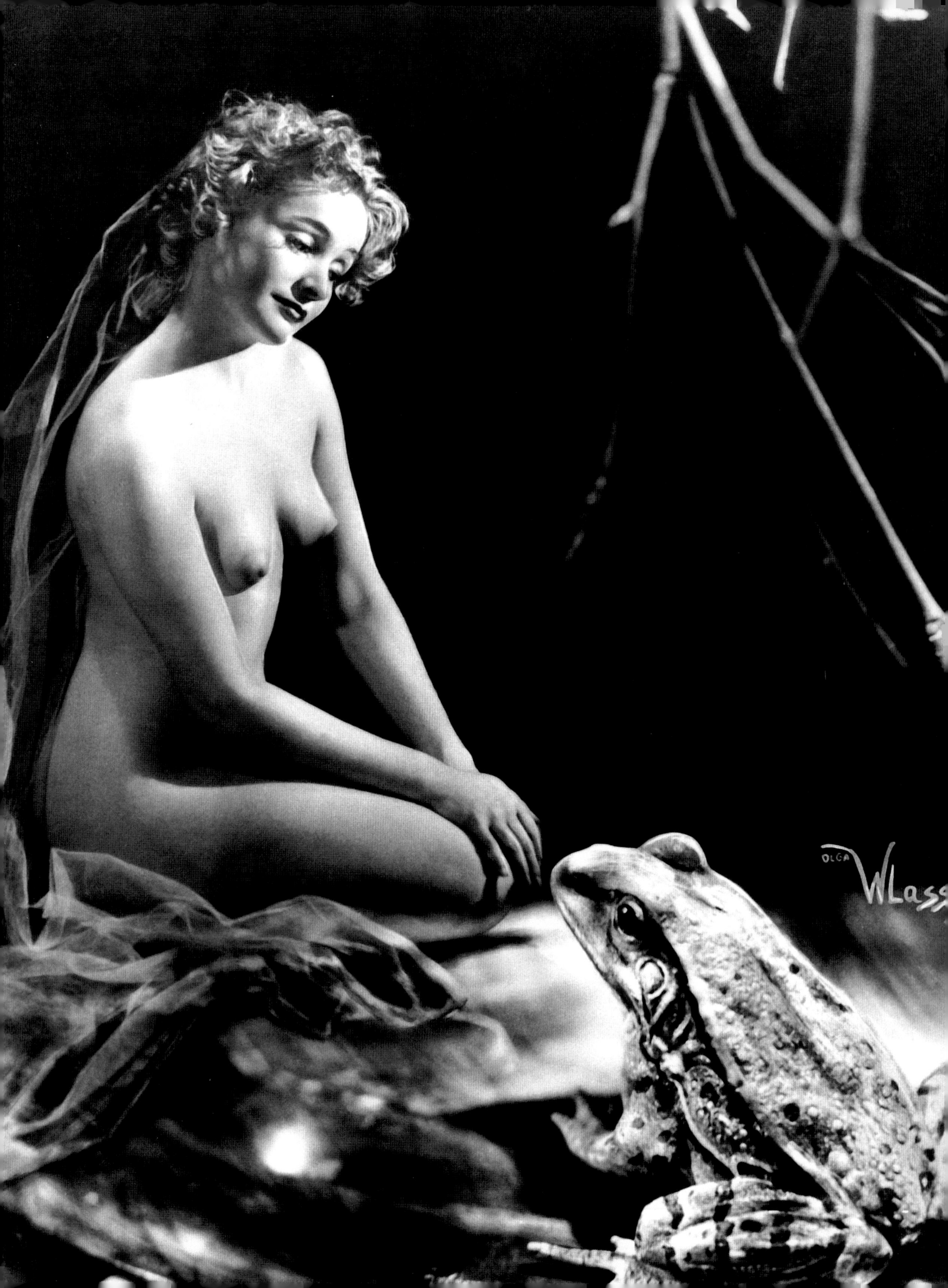
OLGA
WLass

A FAIRY TALE

Once upon a time there was a young man of noble birth who wanted to be an artist. He moved from his native village to a large city, applied for admission to an art school, and passed the entrance examination with flying colors. However, the daily routine did not match his bohemian ideas, and he left the school almost immediately. Following the course prescribed by his family history, he joined his country's royal army and fought with death-defying bravery in the war that soon broke out. He was wounded several times and was decorated for bravery. When he returned home, he met an extraordinarily pretty girl with a bow in her hair and married her. ...

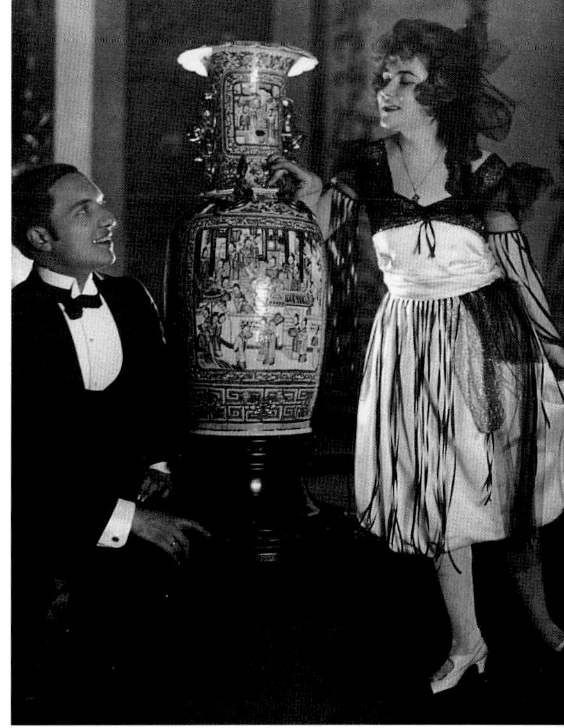

Since we're dealing here with a twentieth-century fairy tale, the young man with shining eyes did not move to a castle with his bride but to a big city near his native village. There he combined his artistic leanings with his social aspirations in a profession. He and his wife, who had appropriate training, established a photography studio and gave it an Old Testament name. Their studio was frequented primarily by people who were as beautiful and young as its owners—or at least seemed to be in photographs produced there. In the wake of the sad decline of the aristocratic milieu of our hero, there is no doubt that these people belonged to the sort of world that brought much-needed sparkle and glamour into a bleak everyday life marked by economic crisis: the world of film, theater, and vaudeville.

With their eyes on Hollywood and a fairy-tale world behind them, the young couple steadily sold pictures to the illustrated magazines that were booming at the time. Now they could afford to pattern their lives along similar lines to those shown in their photographs and photomontages. In their work they coupled a tendency toward the exotic, the romantic, and the latest fashion with the technological ability to improve, rapidly and almost without a trace, everything that was less than perfect by prevailing standards. The marble-like bodies of their models, from which all womanly voluptuousness was removed, along with pubic hair by some well-placed brush strokes, often obscured the fact that our photographers had far exceeded the limits of obscenity in presenting the human body. This was certainly a plus, enabling them to comply with the wishes of female clients for self-portraits while satisfying the erotic fantasies of magazine readers without being caught too often by the censor.

Even when an ominous new regime threatened to make things difficult and dangerous, our couple did not lose courage. They were firmly convinced that a mix of elegance, eroticism, and wit would always be received well everywhere. Instead of leaving the country like many others in their business, they sold their studio on the periphery of the new Reich and moved directly into the lion's den, the hub of events. Yet they had somehow misjudged the

Study, c.1947; Olga and Adorján Wlassics, c.1930

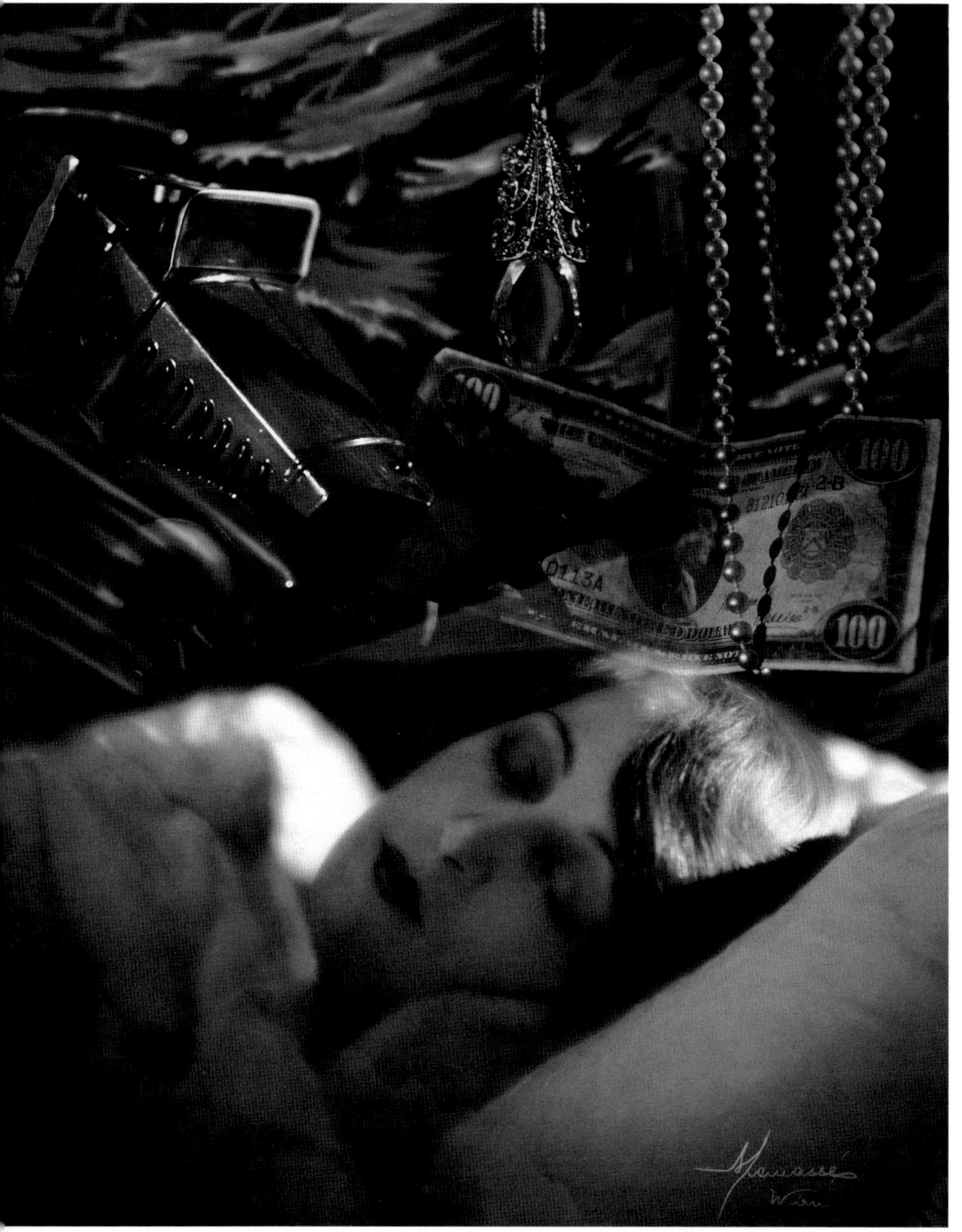

pulse of the time, however. True, noble cleanliness and sublime blondness did begin to appear in their pictures, but they didn't make the right contacts. Then shortly after the collapse of the great Reich, our hero also died.

His widow continued producing photographs and even found a new partner in both her private and professional life. Her business contacts had evaporated however, the war and racist madness having caused too many losses among artists and publishers. In addition, print media that dealt in this type of material had fallen into the hands of new management. Gradually the flow of her productions gave way to the cheap comic magazines of the fifties. And toward the end, our heroine painted pictures of flowers.

That is what happened—at least something like this is all we have been able to piece together about the lives of Adorján and Olga Wlassics, founders of Studio Manassé. The little we know comes from family documents: descriptions of Adorján's World War I military service, a chronicle written by his mother, and several other source materials collected in 1939 to prove the family's Aryan ancestry. Some of the most unlikely sounding statements in our fairy tale are direct quotations. For instance, an official assessment of the young officer in 1915 says, "... When the attack on the enemy was imminent, he boldly put himself at the head of his company and with death-defying courage breached the enemy position so that the enemy—their skulls bloodied—scattered, suffering great losses. ..."

Like all historical research documents, the few available sources tell as much or as little about the writer as about the people being written about. Official praise of his heroic military performance or his mother's hymnic descriptions of Adorján's artistic talents are not the only things that make one wonder. The accuracy of copies of birth, marriage, and

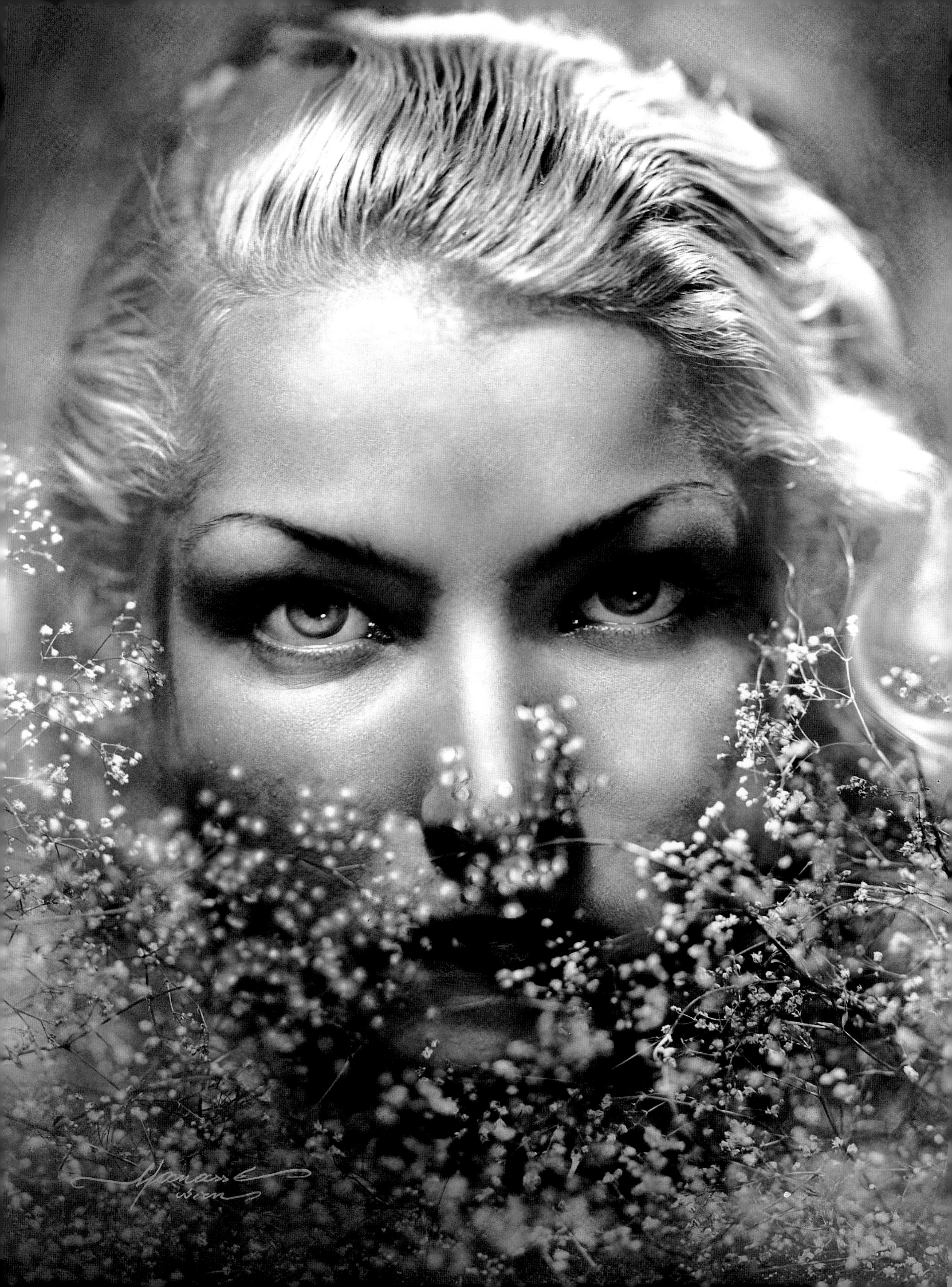
Manassé
Wien

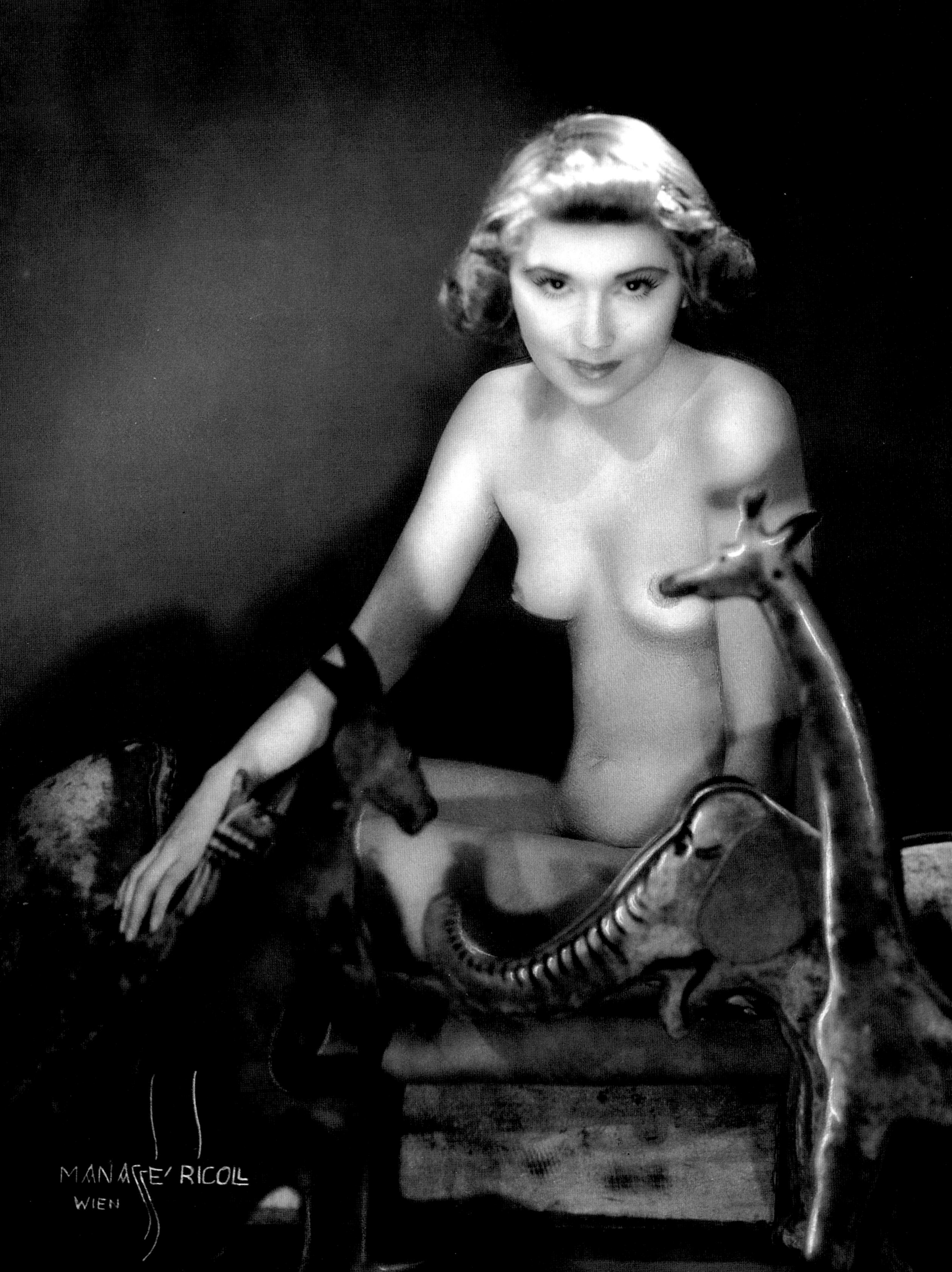
MANASSE' RICOLL
WIEN

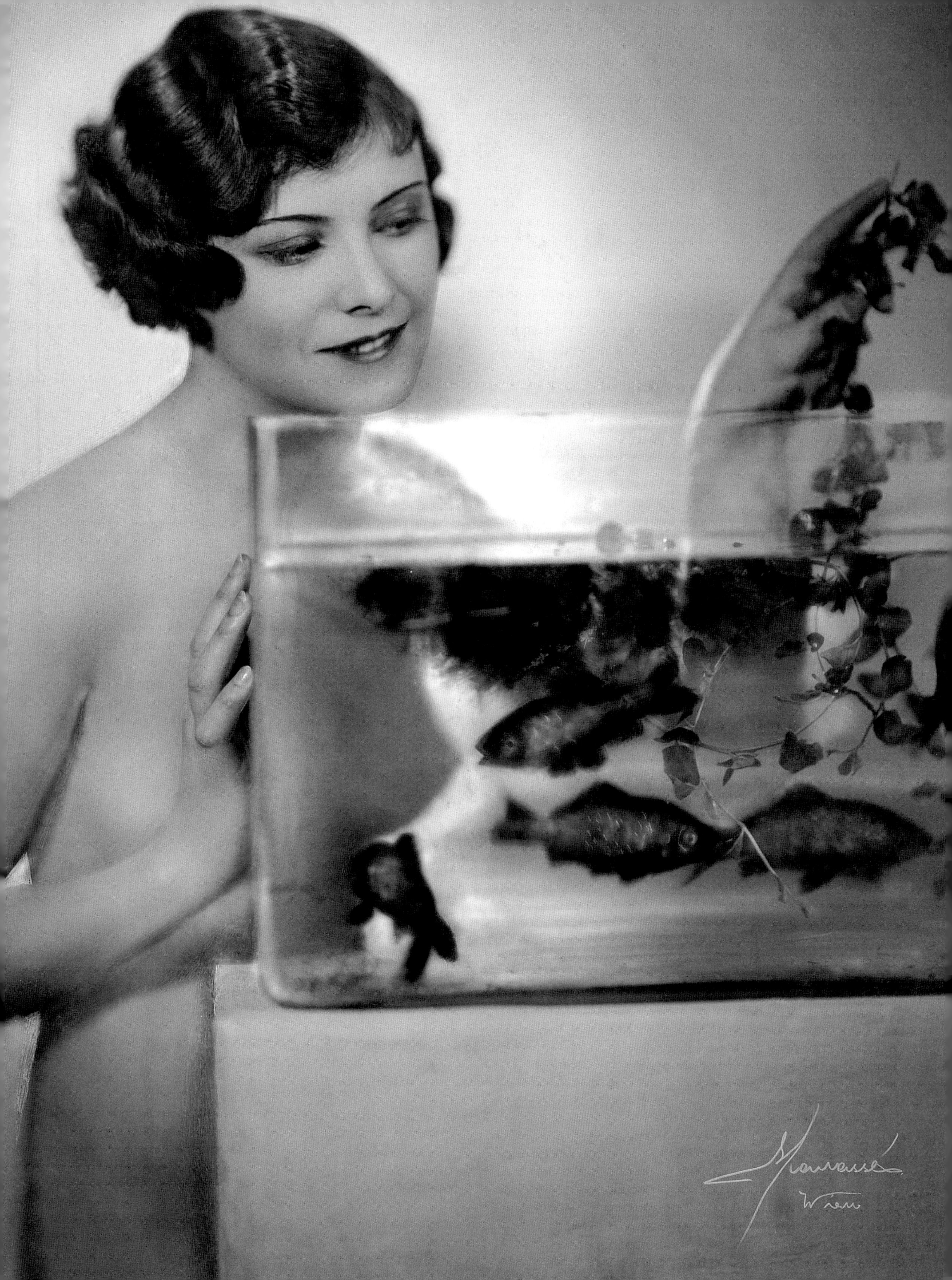
Manassé
Wien

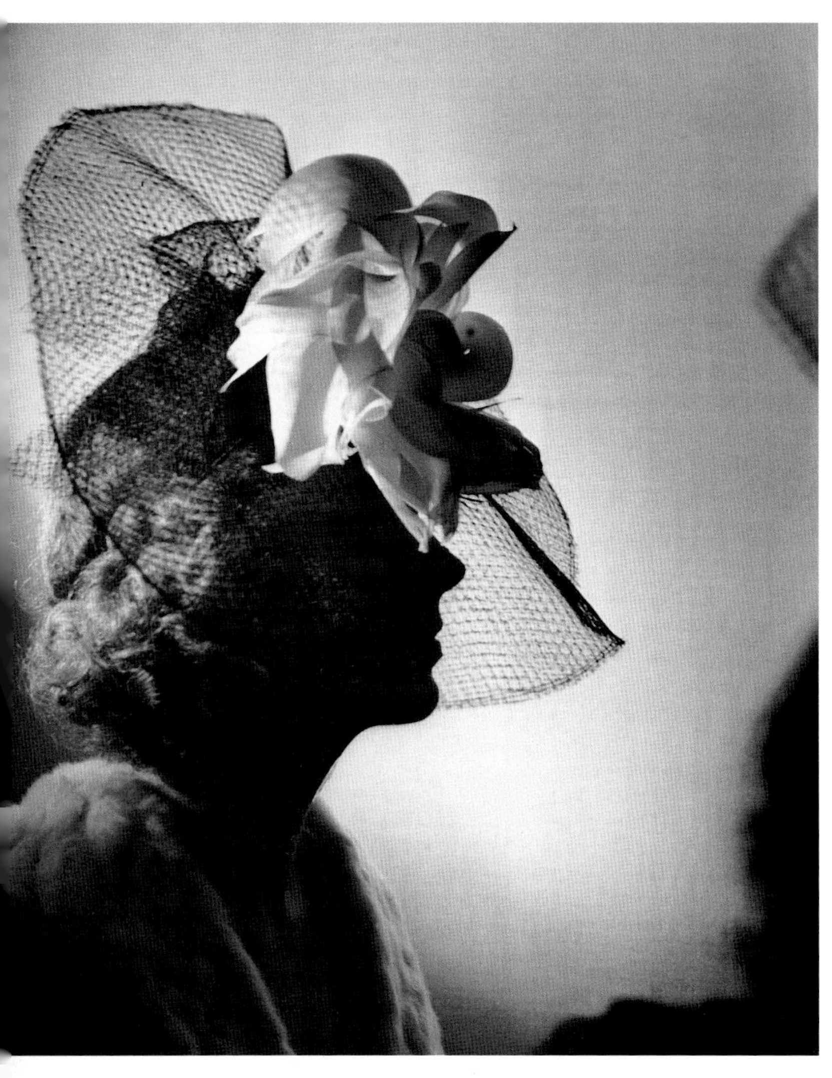

death certificates that various Austrian, Hungarian, and Slovakian communities provided to the photographers in Berlin may also be in doubt. Dates of birth and spelling of names vary a great deal. The time and place of the entry determine whether it was a Magyar, Slavic, or German version of the name; spelling varies from Vlasits to Wlassics, from Spolarics to Spolarich (Olga's maiden name). Were their forbears really all Roman Catholic as indicated in the materials collected in 1939? In those days when Olga and Adorján were living in Berlin, any other religious affiliation would have been worse than inconvenient for them. In the early twenties in Vienna, however, they invented the name *Manassé* for their studio—a name that sounded less than Aryan. It may even have been a francophone variation of an Old Testament name; Manasseh was the deceased husband of Judith, the woman who saved her homeland by decapitating Holofernes, general of the Assyrian armies. A reference to the Judith theme was perhaps entirely in keeping with the spirit of the times (1922) in a city where the films *Samson and Delilah* and *Sodom and Gomorrah* had just been produced with unprecedented extravagance. (The latter was the biggest Austrian film production of all time, reportedly with up to 14,000 extras.) All of this is pure speculation. We have few solid facts concerning the photographers and their studio.

Atelier WOG: Fashion photograph, c.1940; Study, c.1935; next two pages: Indian Ballet Raymonda, c.1931; from the Raymonda Ballet, c.1931

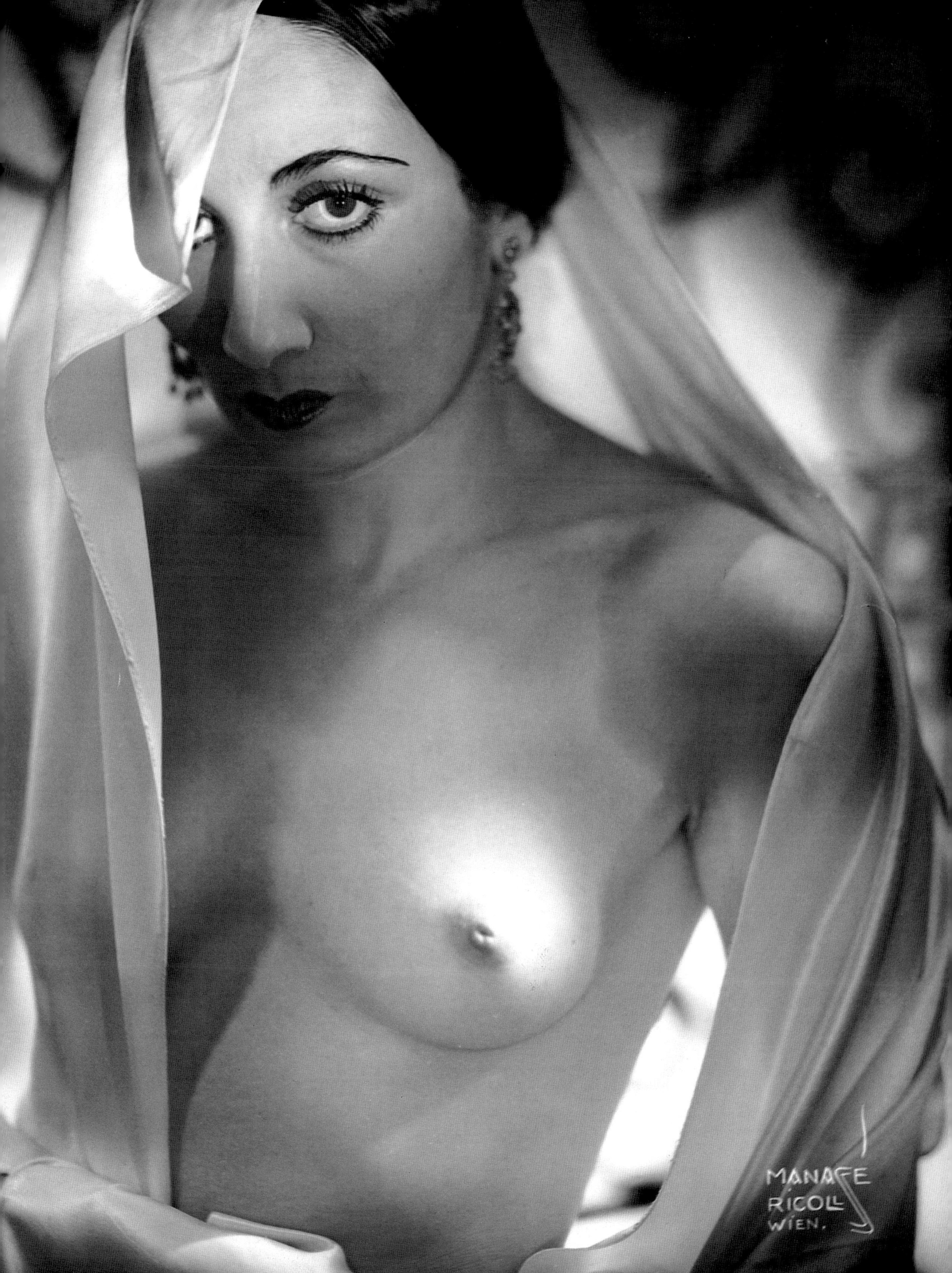
MANASSE
RICOLL
WIEN.

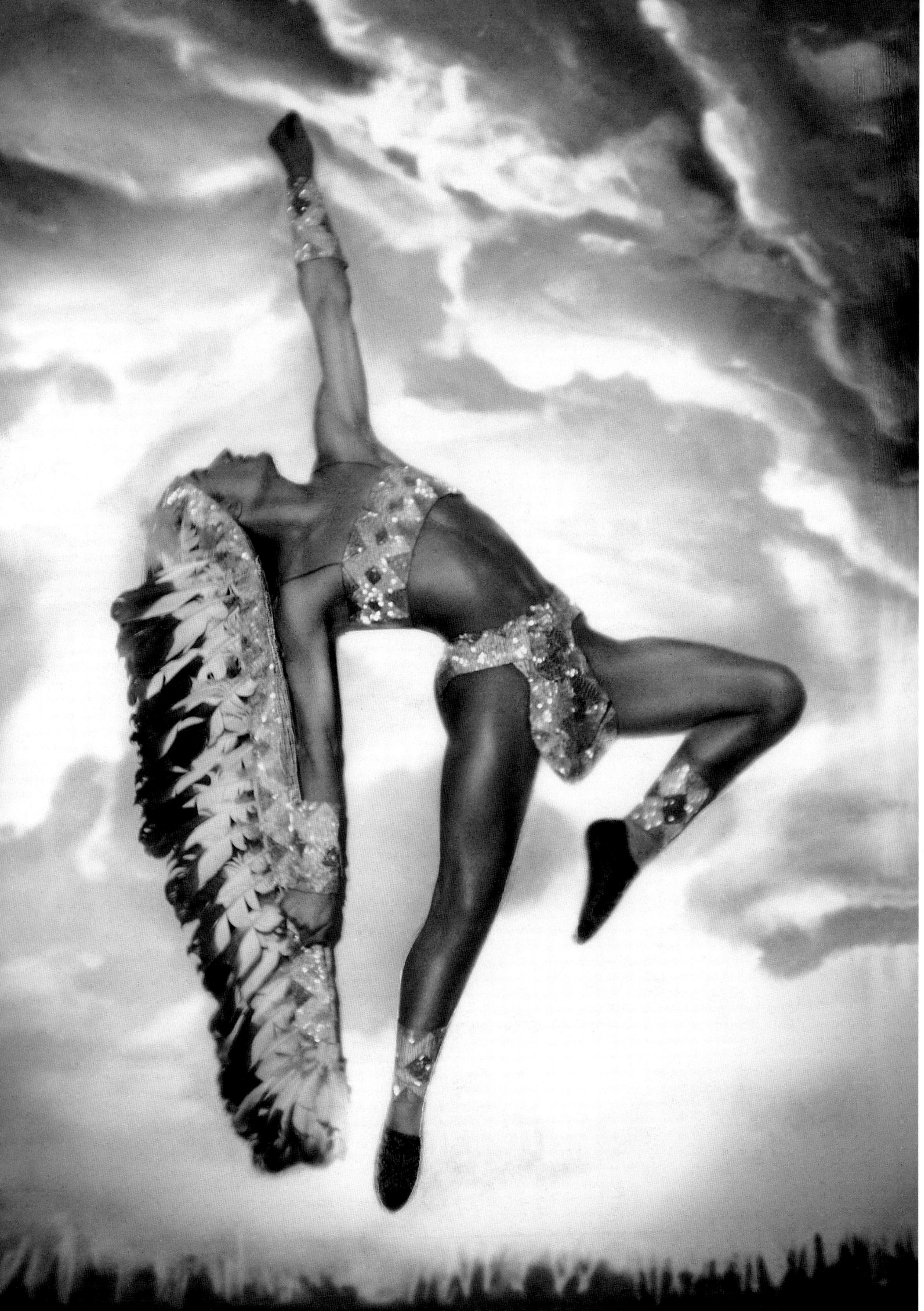

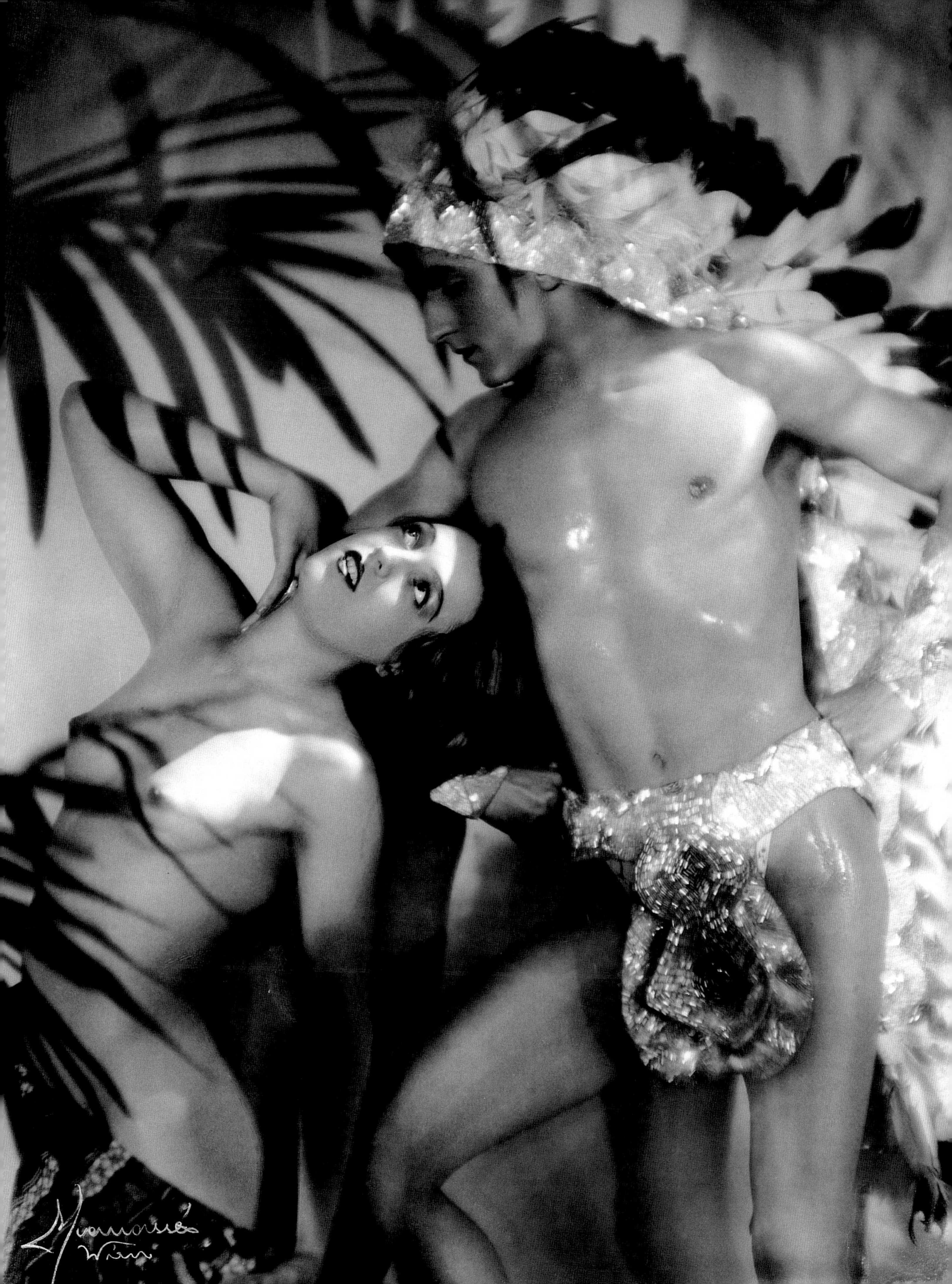
Manassé
Wien

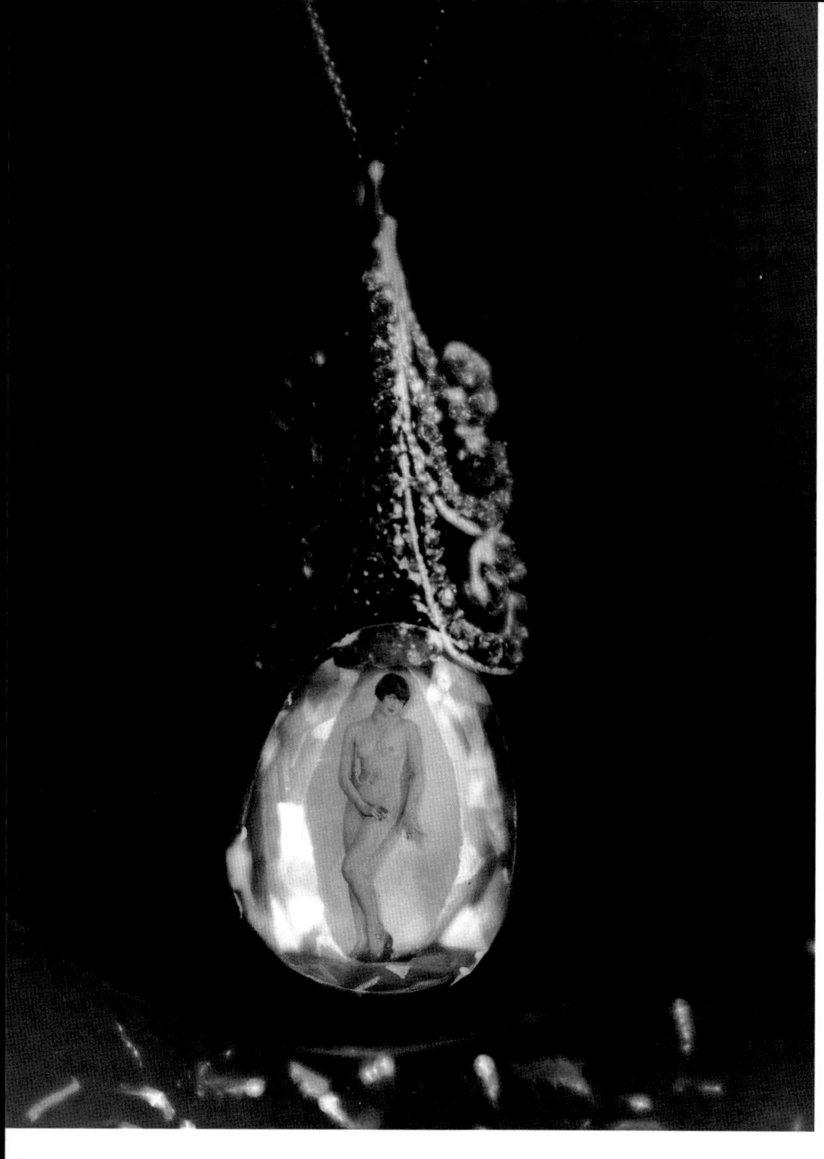

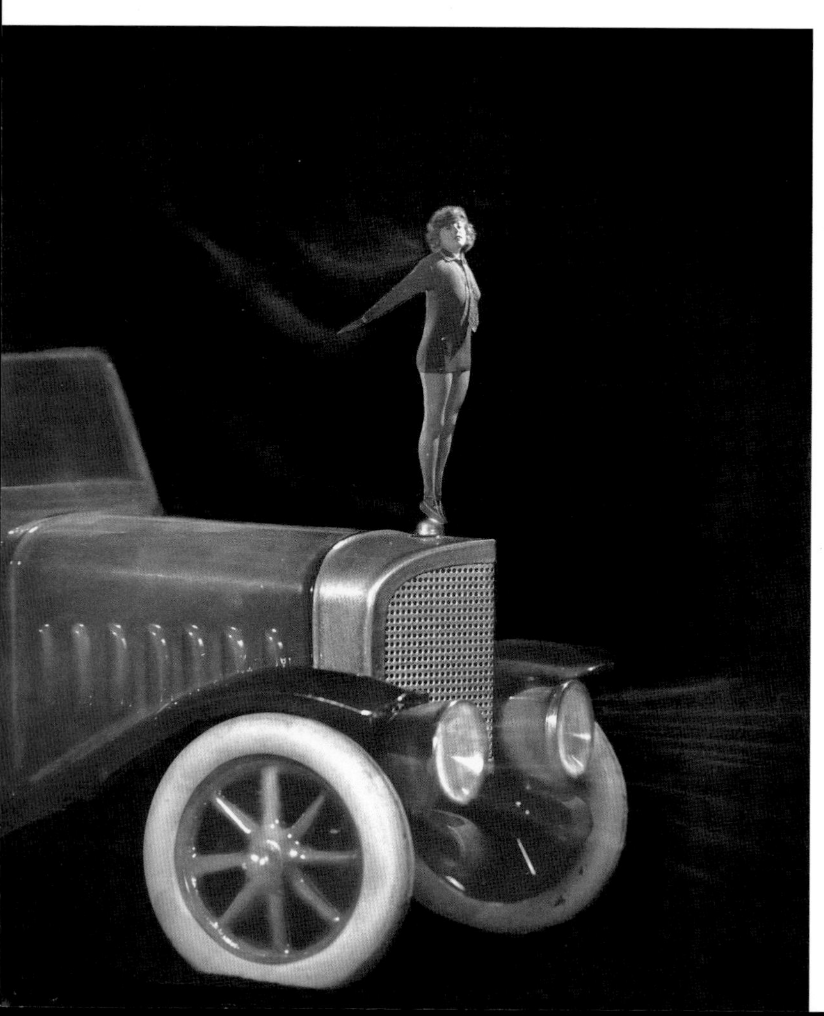

Study, c.1926; Study, c.1924; The Cry, c.1947

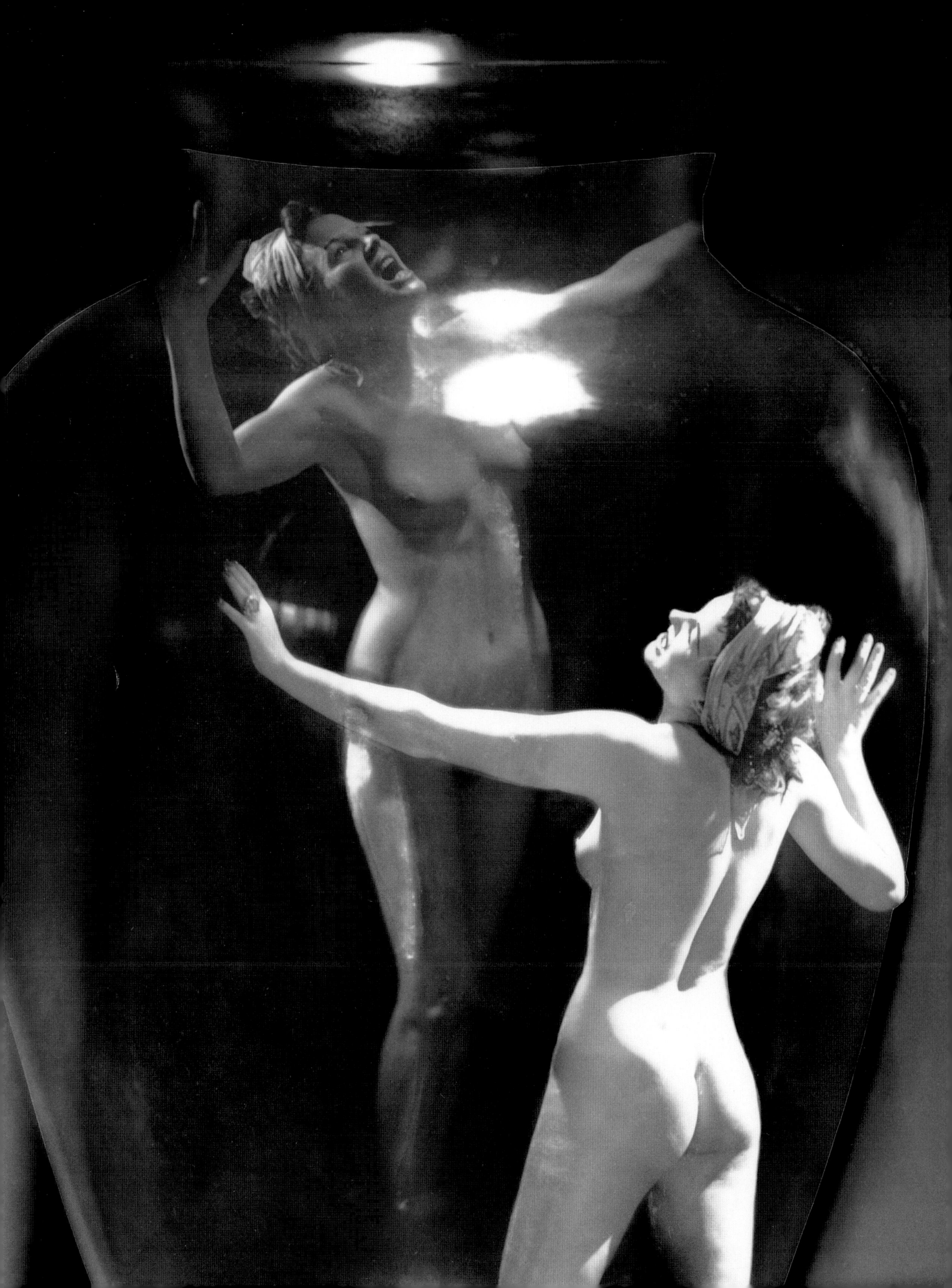

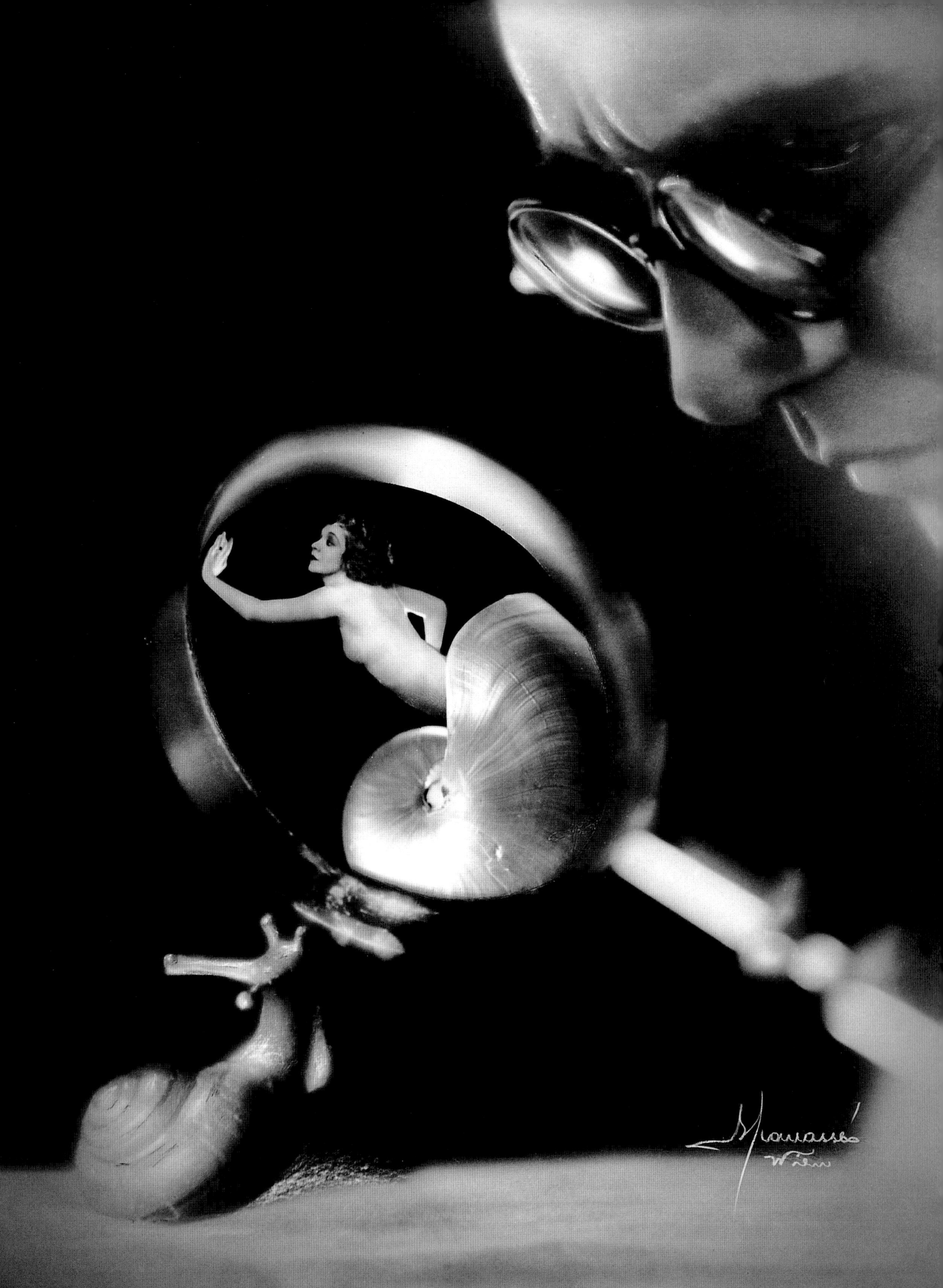
Manassé
Wien

My Snail, c. 1930; Study, c. 1935

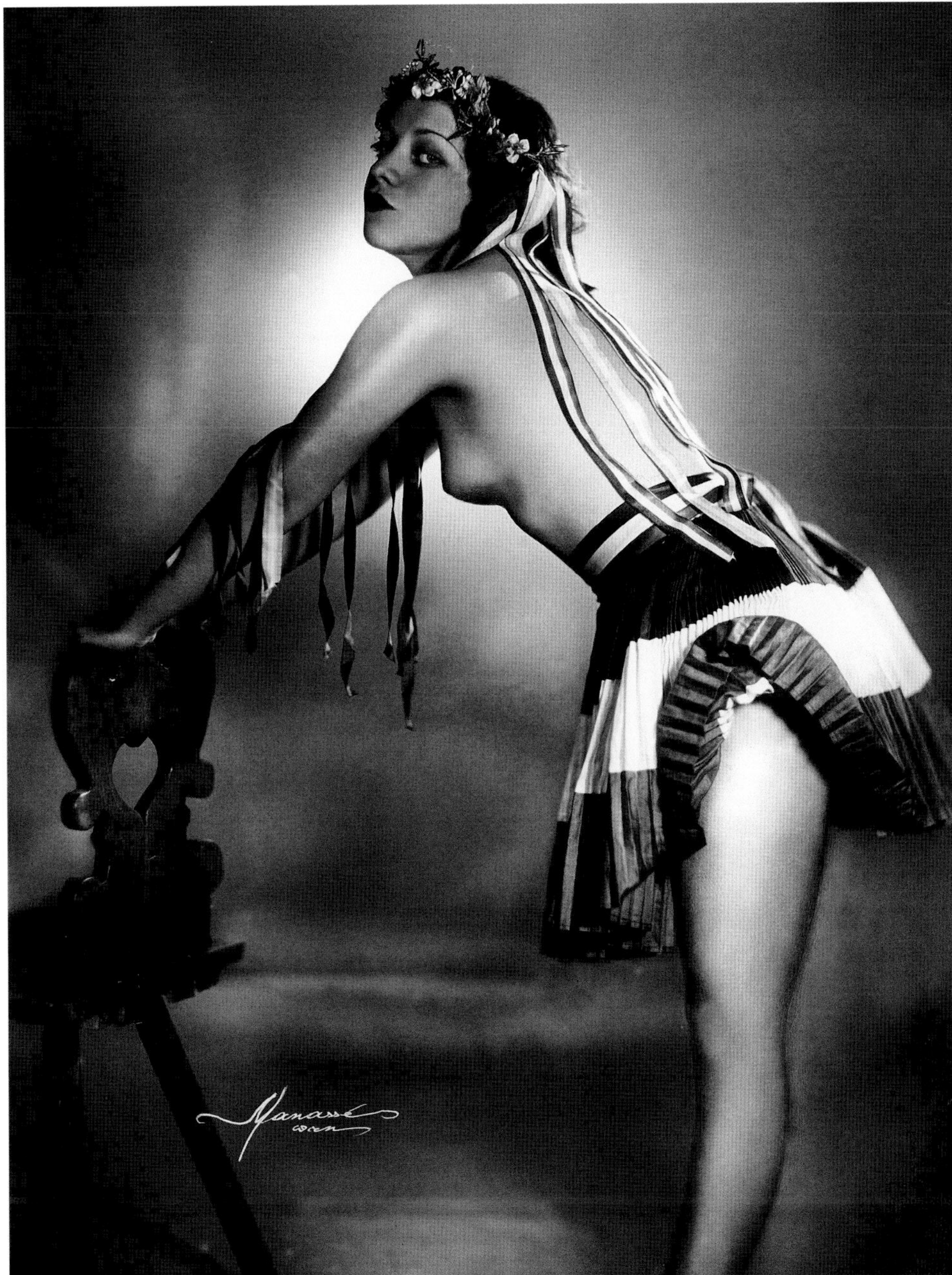

Olga Wlassics (this is how the name is spelled in the Vienna municipal directory from 1925 on) was born May 6, 1895. Both her father, Vilmos Spolarics, and her mother, Anna Pavlidesz (or Pavlidosz?), were from Tolna, a small town south of Budapest on the Danube River. In 1927, Olga posed in Tolna for a photograph with her husband, Adorján, and a younger sister. We know nothing else about her family.

Adorján or Adorian Franz Marie Vlassics (the spelling *Wlassics* does not appear until after 1914) was born April 27, 1893, in the vicinity of Vesprim, an old fortified town west of Lake Balaton. His father, Karl von Vlassics, descended from generations of officers who had served in the Austro-Hungarian Army, and his mother, Rozsa Szabadi, came from the area. Shortly after the birth of Adorján, whose younger brother died in childhood, the family moved to Temesvar in Transylvania (at the time part of Hungary, today in Romania), where the father became "Royal Subdistrict Judge." After his death in 1906, the family probably moved first to Szeged and then to Budapest. Adorján served in World War I as a lieutenant in the First Infantry Regiment and received several commendations. As early as December 1918, he was issued a license to work as a photographer in Budapest.

Olga Spolarich and Adorján Wlassics were married on November 22, 1920, in Vienna. They opened a studio at 19 Opernring under the name *Wlasics [sic]* and lived not far from there at 4 Barnabitengasse in the Mariahilf district. The change of the studio's name to *Manassé* cannot have occurred much later, for there are some photographs bearing that name and the early address. In 1924, the first Manassé illustrations appeared in a magazine, and the studio is listed in the classified pages under its new name at 16 Getreidemarkt in 1925. At this time the Wlassics lived in the center of Vienna at 1 Elisabethstrasse, but in 1930, they moved

Study, c.1936; Study, c.1935

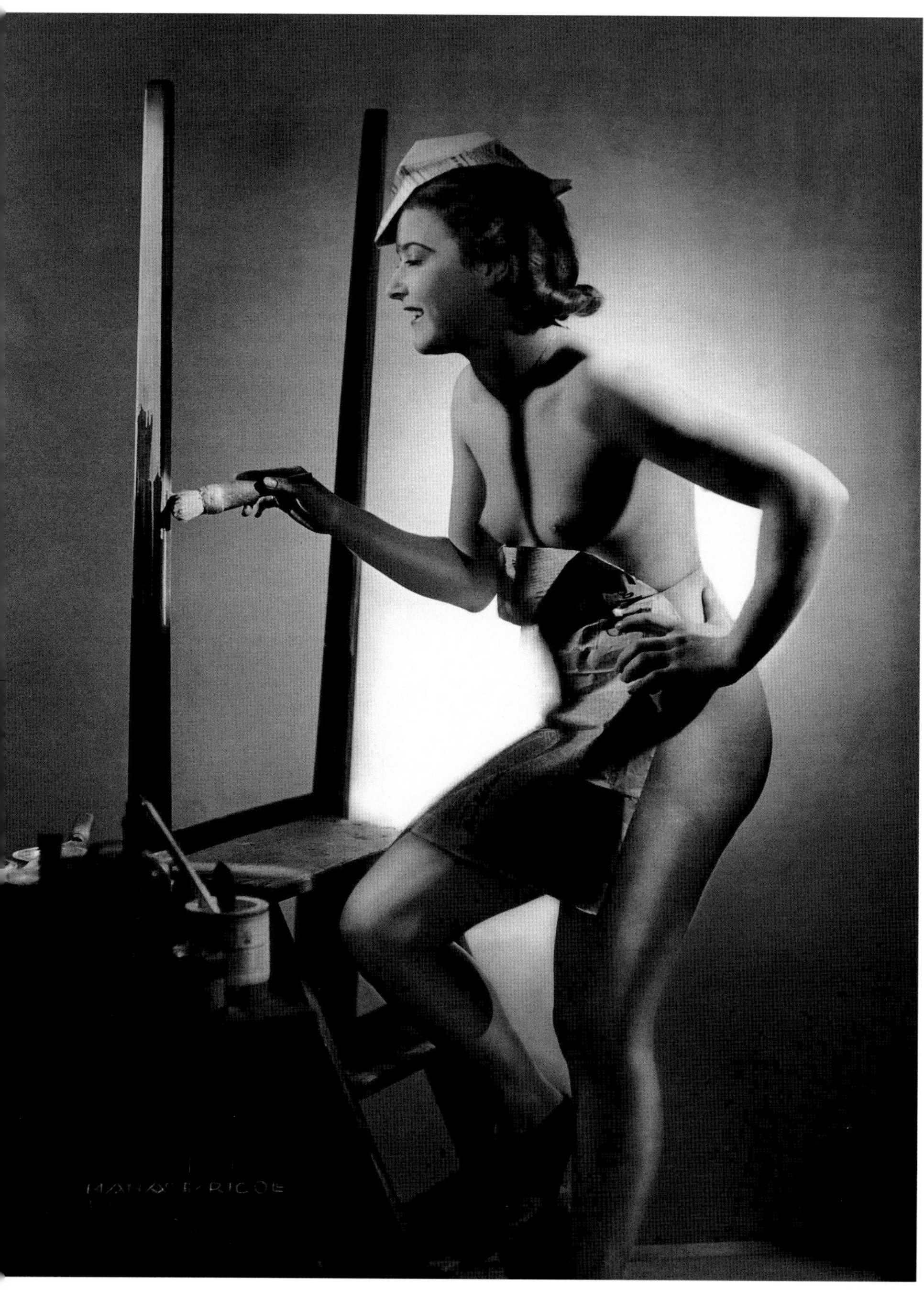

back to 15 Kärntner Ring, only two houses away from their very first studio. Here they combined business and living quarters that featured ultra-stylish furnishings, which they proudly photographed (fig., p. 30a). In 1935–36, they also ran a studio in Bucharest and then opened Studio WOG (Wlassics/Olga/Geschke) in Berlin. The business in Vienna, Atelier Manassé-Ricoll, was managed more and more by associates. They sold the firm's name in 1937–38 to Josef Cebin, the son of a photographer who lived just outside the center of Vienna. (Even as late as the fifties there was a photography studio by this name in the city, and today a framing store there bears the same name.) Olga and Adorján moved to Berlin in 1940, but after suffering air-raid damage, they returned to Austria and at the end of the war were living in Baden near Vienna. The "artist," as he was called in his obituary, died in 1947 after "a brief but serious illness." From 1948 on, Olga Wlassics again ran a studio at 4 An der Hülben in central Vienna. Called *Foto Wlassics,* a name they had occasionally used as early as 1937–38, this studio is where most of the documents cited here and several negatives were preserved. Olga married Hans Rothen, who had a studio in Baden and whose few published photographs scarcely can be distinguished from the Wlassics' pictures of that time. Some documents that have survived from the late fifties indicate that Olga Wlassics devoted herself to painting as she got older, was a member of the Künstlerbund (Artists' League), and exhibited her work in group shows in 1957 and 1958 at the Wiener Kunsthalle on Zedlitzgasse. However, to date none of these paintings has been found. Olga Wlassics Rothen died in Vienna in 1969.

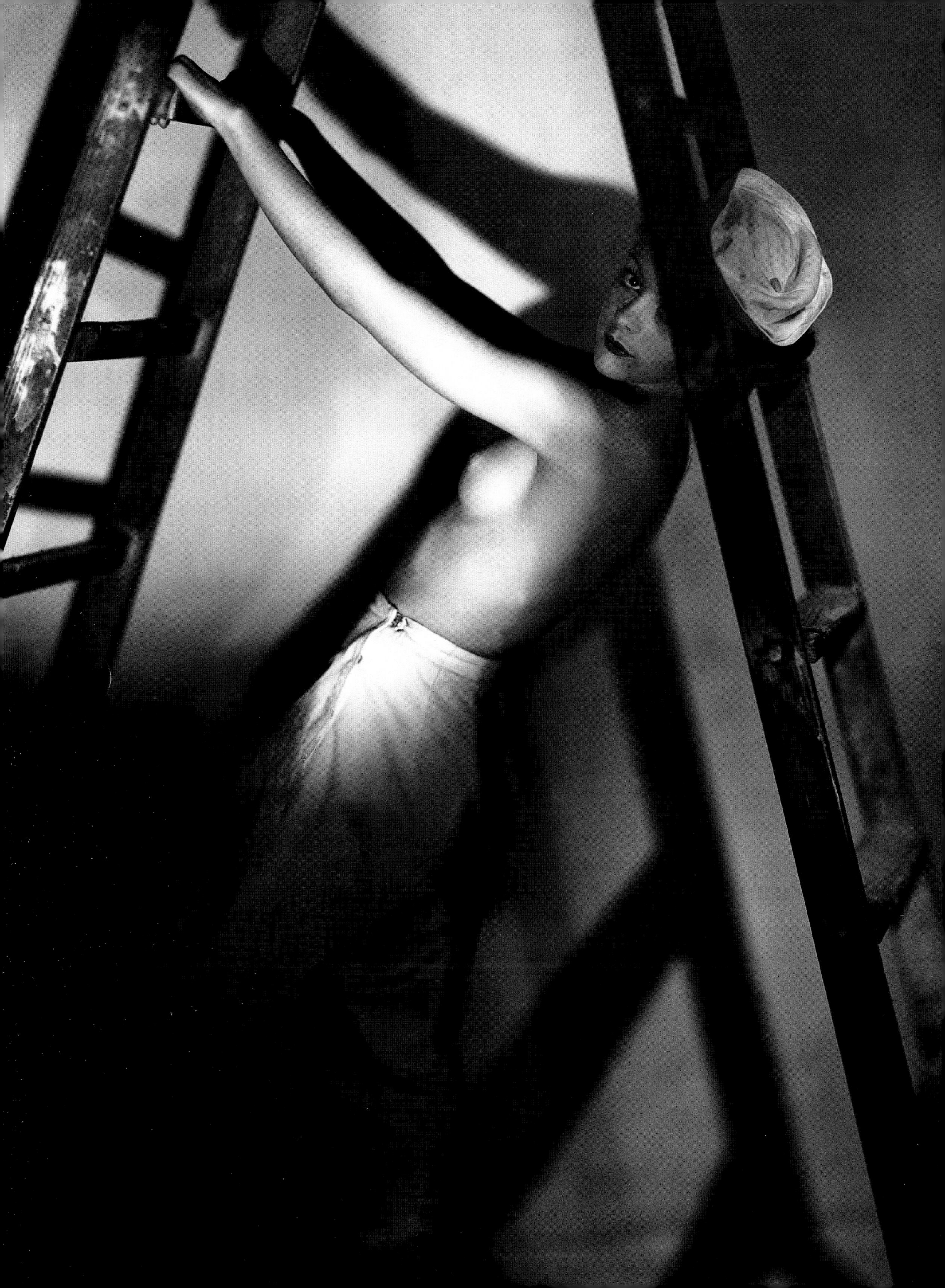

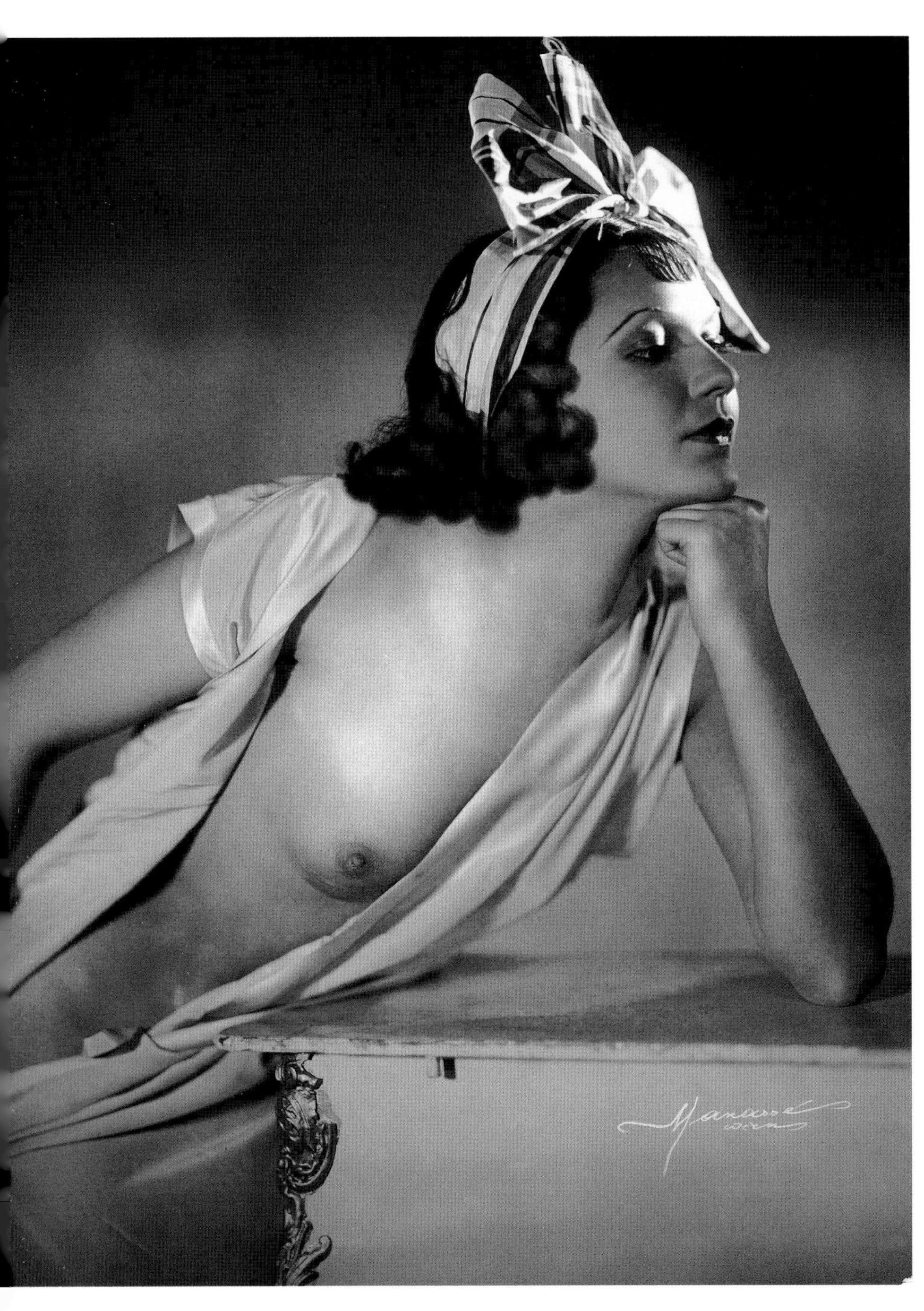

Study, c.1934; Olga Wlassics, c.1926; Olga and Adorján Wlassics, c.1926; Olga and Adorján Wlassics, before 1933

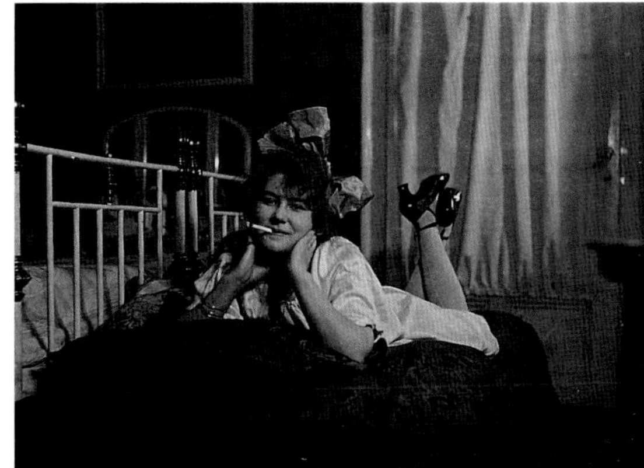

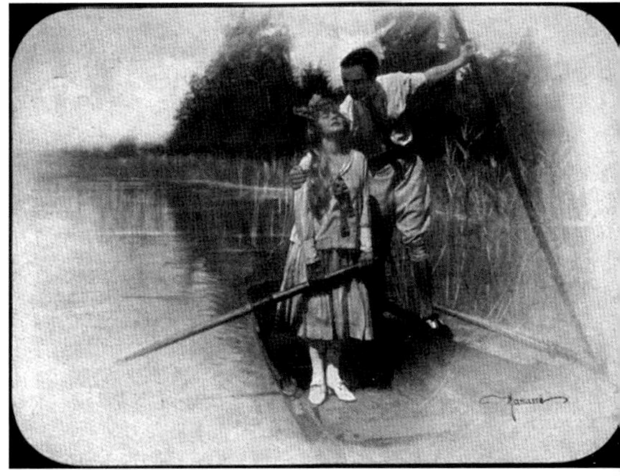

These facts are not only sketchy—there are almost no indications that the two studio owners could have had any training; and one can only guess the reasons for the many changes of residence, etc.—but also they seem dry in that you can scarcely reconstruct any personal details about these two people. Their private lives and their attitudes toward their profession remain totally obscure. However, a visual legacy that leaves the field wide open to interpretation and all sorts of speculation (see my fairy-tale fantasy) compensates in part for this lack of written documentation. In Olga Wlassics Rothen's last studio and in the Provincial Photography Museum of Upper Austria in Bad Ischl, a few photographs have survived, along with negatives, old prints, and documents from the estate of Hans Frank, who was personally acquainted with Olga Wlassics. They show Mr. and Mrs. Wlassics together and Olga by herself. These photographs are all different, ranging from small-format prints bearing private handwritten notations (most in Hungarian, such as "In the spa park with green silk dress" and similar things) to large, signed and stamped photos, printed postcards, and touched-up photographs.

These differences in finished products seem to correlate with the degree of public exposure that Olga and Adorján Wlassics intended for these pictures. For instance, the portrait of Olga with the doll (fig., p. 31) was found in a bundle of material in the Schostal Agency's archive, which confirms that it was available for publication. Among the surviving photographs, two are worth mentioning: The first is one of the few examples I know of in which the two photographers themselves appear in a picture published in one of the publications they supplied with material, *Wiener Magazin*. In this photo they adopt a "leisure look" in bathing suits with parasol and give no indication of their profession (fig., p. 27). This sort of unpretentious self-portrayal is very rare. In another issue of the same magazine there is a picture of Olga Wlassics alone, in the sort of get-up we are familiar with from her glamorous portraits: the décolletage could hardly be lower, her skin is retouched to the point of total uniformity, her curls are manneristic, her eyes almost closed—a vamp, a star. The caption reads: "A member of Viennese Society: Mrs. Olly von Wlassics" (fig., p. 40). There is no indication that the person portrayed here owns half of Studio Manassé. Could this be merely the capricious whim of a picture editor or part of the business strategy of an enterprise that derived a measure of its success from the fact that its owners were part of "high society"? (Translation of text within image: "The Most Famous Colleagues of Wiener Magazin: Mr. and Mrs. Adorján von Wlassics, who under their company name Manassé, have attained world reknown and are the discoverers of international female beauties.")

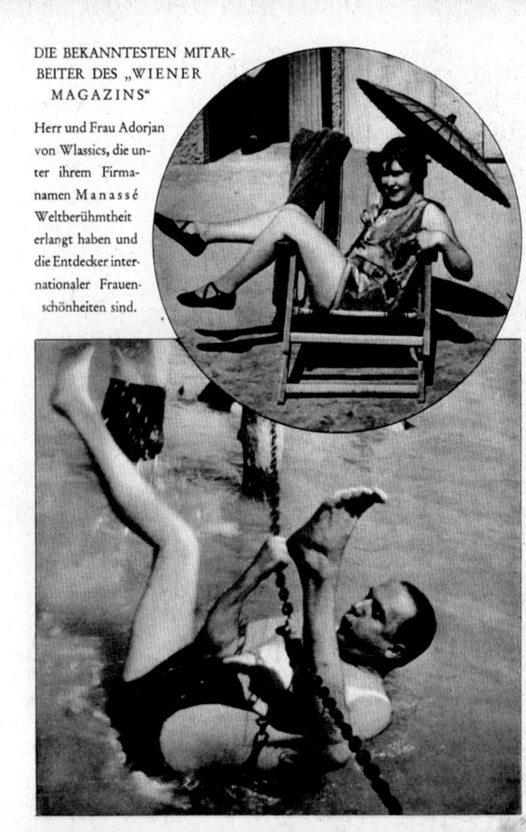

DIE BEKANNTESTEN MITARBEITER DES „WIENER MAGAZINS"

Herr und Frau Adorjan von Wlassics, die unter ihrem Firmanamen Manassé Weltberühmtheit erlangt haben und die Entdecker internationaler Frauenschönheiten sind.

I intend to use the term "self-portrait" in a general way to denote those pictures that allow one to ask the most interesting questions about the way the Wlassics

Olga Wlassics, c.1926; Harold Dean Carsey Studio: Clara Bow, c.1926; Ninon Darville, c.1931

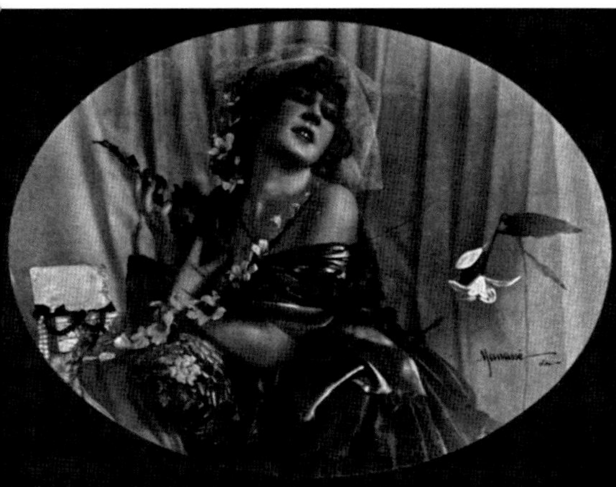

saw themselves photographically, whether both partners appear in the pictures or only Olga. (The matter of who did what in the studio will be considered elsewhere.)

In one of the pictures Olga is lying on a sofa facing out, a bow in her hair, wearing shoes with laces that encircle her ankles (fig., p. 27a)—a classic, cliché embodiment of young innocence, except for the cigarette in her mouth, which belies the initial impression. This technique of gathering together the many characteristics of a certain type of woman (the naïf, the star, the vamp, or any other types who existed in the twenties) and then countering the image with more or less minor contradictions (in this case turned against Olga herself) was a method the Manassé studio often employed, even in their commercial photographs. Features used to characterize these different types of women—huge bows in the hair, a cigarette, different kinds of shoes or slippers—are all part of a large reservoir of popular coded attributes that the Wlassics used, often conforming to conventions, but sometimes contradicting them.

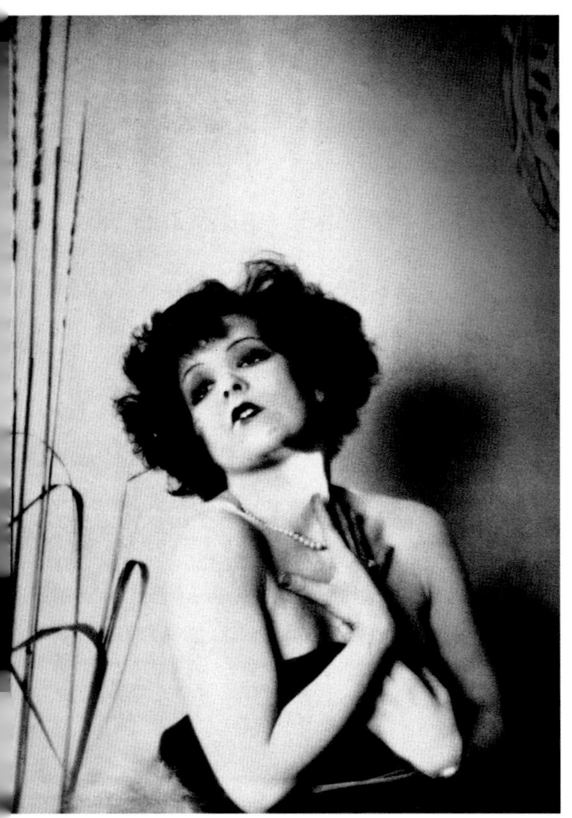

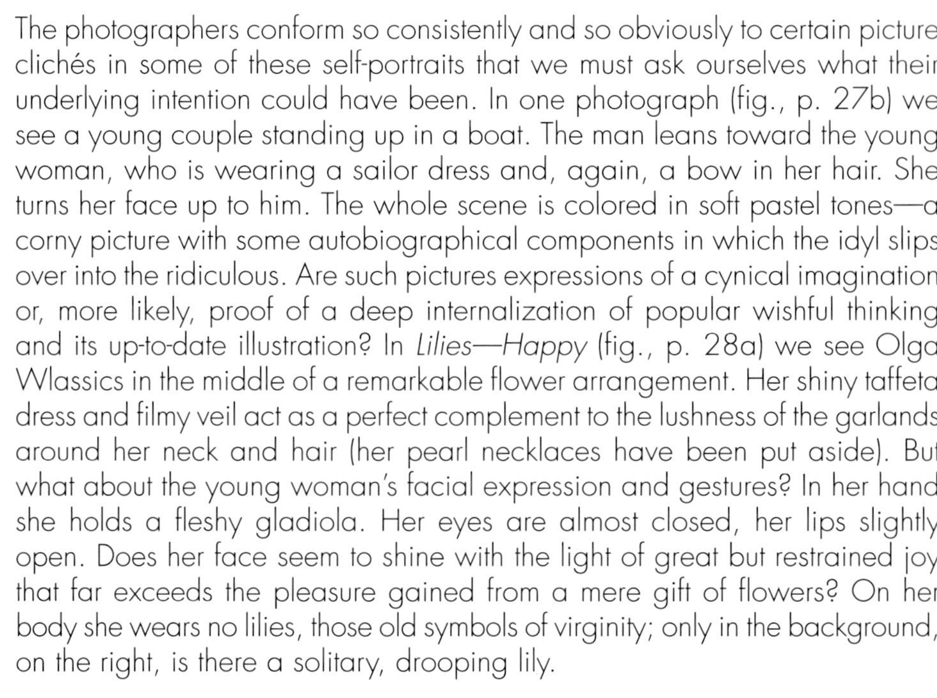

The photographers conform so consistently and so obviously to certain picture clichés in some of these self-portraits that we must ask ourselves what their underlying intention could have been. In one photograph (fig., p. 27b) we see a young couple standing up in a boat. The man leans toward the young woman, who is wearing a sailor dress and, again, a bow in her hair. She turns her face up to him. The whole scene is colored in soft pastel tones—a corny picture with some autobiographical components in which the idyl slips over into the ridiculous. Are such pictures expressions of a cynical imagination or, more likely, proof of a deep internalization of popular wishful thinking and its up-to-date illustration? In *Lilies—Happy* (fig., p. 28a) we see Olga Wlassics in the middle of a remarkable flower arrangement. Her shiny taffeta dress and filmy veil act as a perfect complement to the lushness of the garlands around her neck and hair (her pearl necklaces have been put aside). But what about the young woman's facial expression and gestures? In her hand she holds a fleshy gladiola. Her eyes are almost closed, her lips slightly open. Does her face seem to shine with the light of great but restrained joy that far exceeds the pleasure gained from a mere gift of flowers? On her body she wears no lilies, those old symbols of virginity; only in the background, on the right, is there a solitary, drooping lily.

Lilies—Happy and the picture of the couple in the rowboat are printed color postcards, the originals of which were painted photographs. (The common designation"colored photographs" would not be appropriate here because of the comprehensive treatment given the subject.) They must have been intended for wider distribution than the silver prints. Was there perhaps an attempt to start a postcard business, which did not succeed and was dropped? Besides these two examples, which were probably made about 1925, no other postcards published by the studio have been preserved. Printing may have been assigned to firms that specialized in such things, for Studio Manassé did not do such printing again until 1936. *Portraits of 10 Stars* (the original title of the leaflet) were combined with texts of songs by well-known composers, such as "Frauen sind zum Küssen da" (Women are meant to be kissed) by Hermann Leopoldi and "Ich lass mir meine Träume nicht verbieten" (I won't let anyone keep me from dreaming) by Richard Tauber. They then produced in Berlin a brochure without text called "Kunst und Anmut" (Art and Charm) in which the women looked more devoted than self-assured. (fig., p. 50)

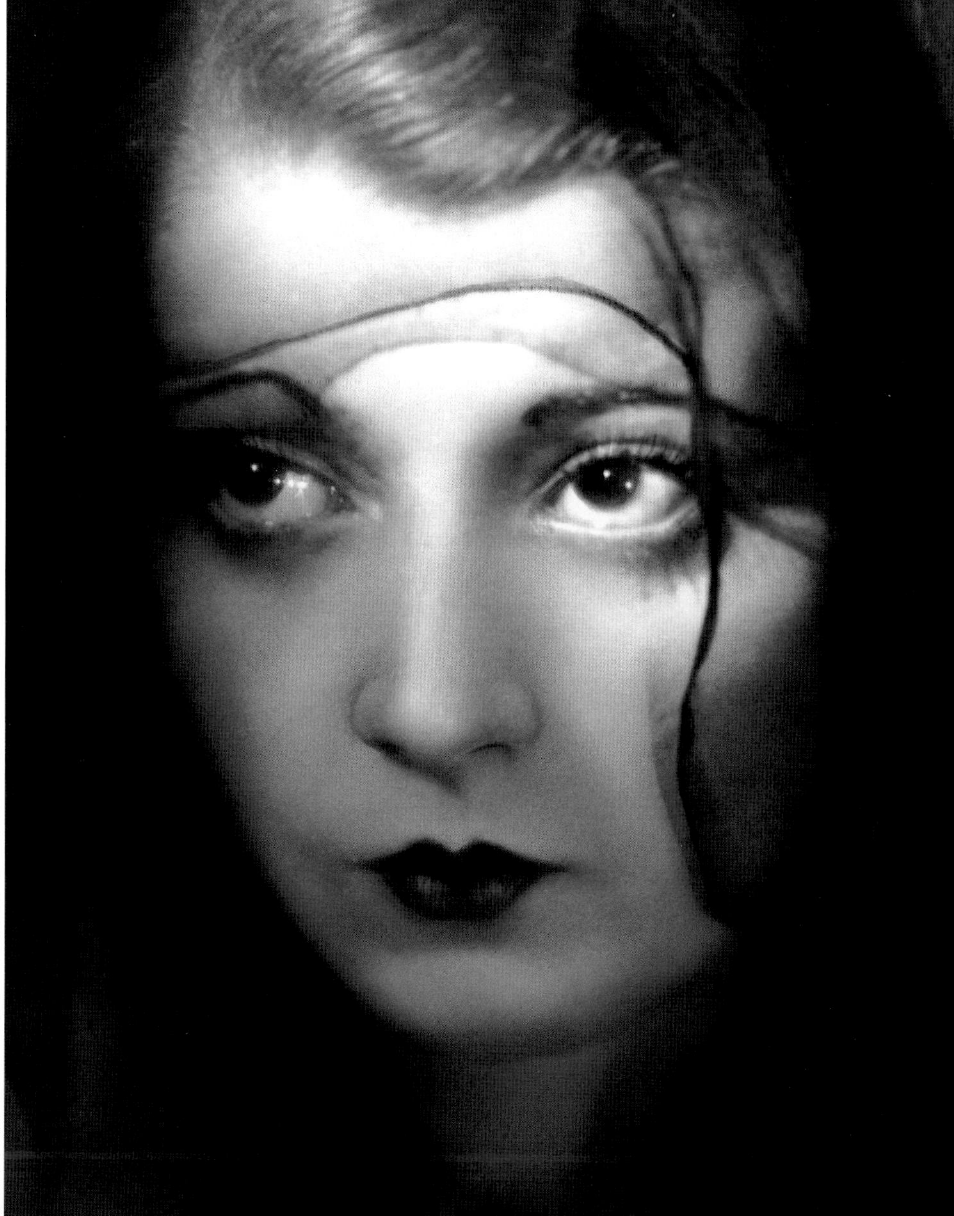

Although not reprinted here, there is a picture also in postcard format of Olga Wlassics wearing a modified peasant costume and a fluttering kerchief, lost in thought before a wayside cross. Is this an early example of a bizarre fashion photograph, evidence of deep religiosity, or a satire of one or the other? Someone looking at these pictures at the end of the twentieth century is led into reflections about trash and ludicrousness, cynicism or absurd humor. At the time these pictures were taken, however, they did not seem out of the ordinary. Considered in the context of photography that is shown and published as art today, these photographs from Studio Manassé must seem strange. Our astonishment and their ambiguity become relative, however, in the context of the pictorial universe from which they come and of which they remain a part. A closer look at pictures and texts in illustrated periodicals of the twenties and thirties (and in certain pseudoscientific books that played a considerable role in the photographs produced by the Wlassics) shows a similar tone in both tragedy and comedy, instruction and satire. Indeed, glamour and kitsch are close neighbors. Many of the films from that period also

Bedroom in the studio-cum-apartment, 1930; The Polarbear Skin, c.1930; Olga Wlassics, 1930

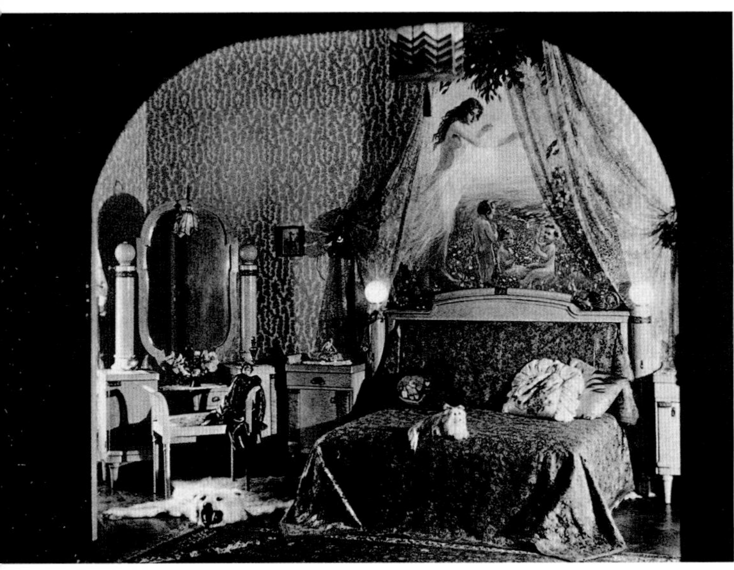

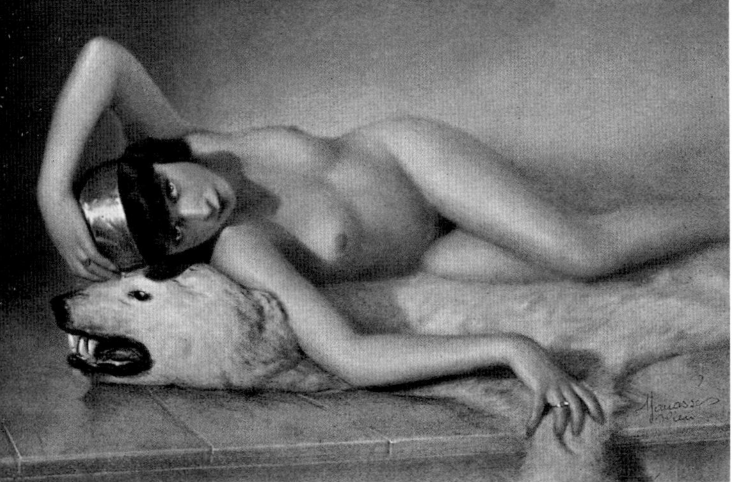

reveal the exaggerated gestures and looks that occur so frequently in the photos.

Silent film created its own constraints and developed special conventions that compensated for the lack of the spoken word. These conventions spilled over into the medium of photography. For example, *Lilies—Happy* appears to have been inspired by a photograph of the silent film actress Clara Bow (fig., p. 28b). From the position of her head and the melting expression on her face to the affected spread of one hand, both the Viennese photographer and the famous Hollywood star ("The It Girl") hold the same pose, yet in mirror image, a pose that seems to be taken directly from one of Clara Bow's flapper films. The difference, which is crucial to the overall effect, is in the decor. It is very restrained and economical in the American picture, while it absolutely engulfs the subject in the Manassé version. This added decoration not only diminishes the presence of the subject but, with its more or less explicit symbolism, also destroys the mysterious glamour that radiates from the portrait of the actress.

To our eyes the Wlassics themselves seem to be exposed to a similar proliferation of decorative elements in their surroundings. Photographs of 1930 that show the interiors of the Manassé studio-cum-apartment on the Kärntner Ring in the center of Vienna present us with the same problems as the self-portraits. The little Empire table and baroque chair, the Rocaille wallpaper, and the shaft of a Greek pillar serving as a flower stand—this frilly display and ornate extravagance in their reception room can be attributed to the expectations of a clientele who had certain notions of continuing and perhaps even surpassing the elegance and luxury of a vanished aristocratic world. A glance into the couple's bedroom proves that this style of furnishing is not only perpetuated here but also carried to extremes. Above the bed the curtain-draped painting of a copy of Philip Otto Runge's *Sunrise* makes the kitschy postcards from the Manassé studio seem dull. Yet we are dealing here with only a copy of the decorating style that Michael Kertész (the name was later changed to Curtiz) popularized in his 1925 film *Das Spielzeug* von Paris (Red Heels) and that Erich von Stroheim memorialized as typical of the more elegant Vienna in *The Merry Widow*, which also dates to 1925. This bedroom and certain pieces of furniture and decorative items in it also served as the setting for a series of photographs by Manassé. For instance, the polar bear skin is an important element in one of a number of the studio's illustrations—many retouched—that appeared in a book called *Die Erotik in der Fotographie* (Eroticism in Photography), published in Vienna in 1931.

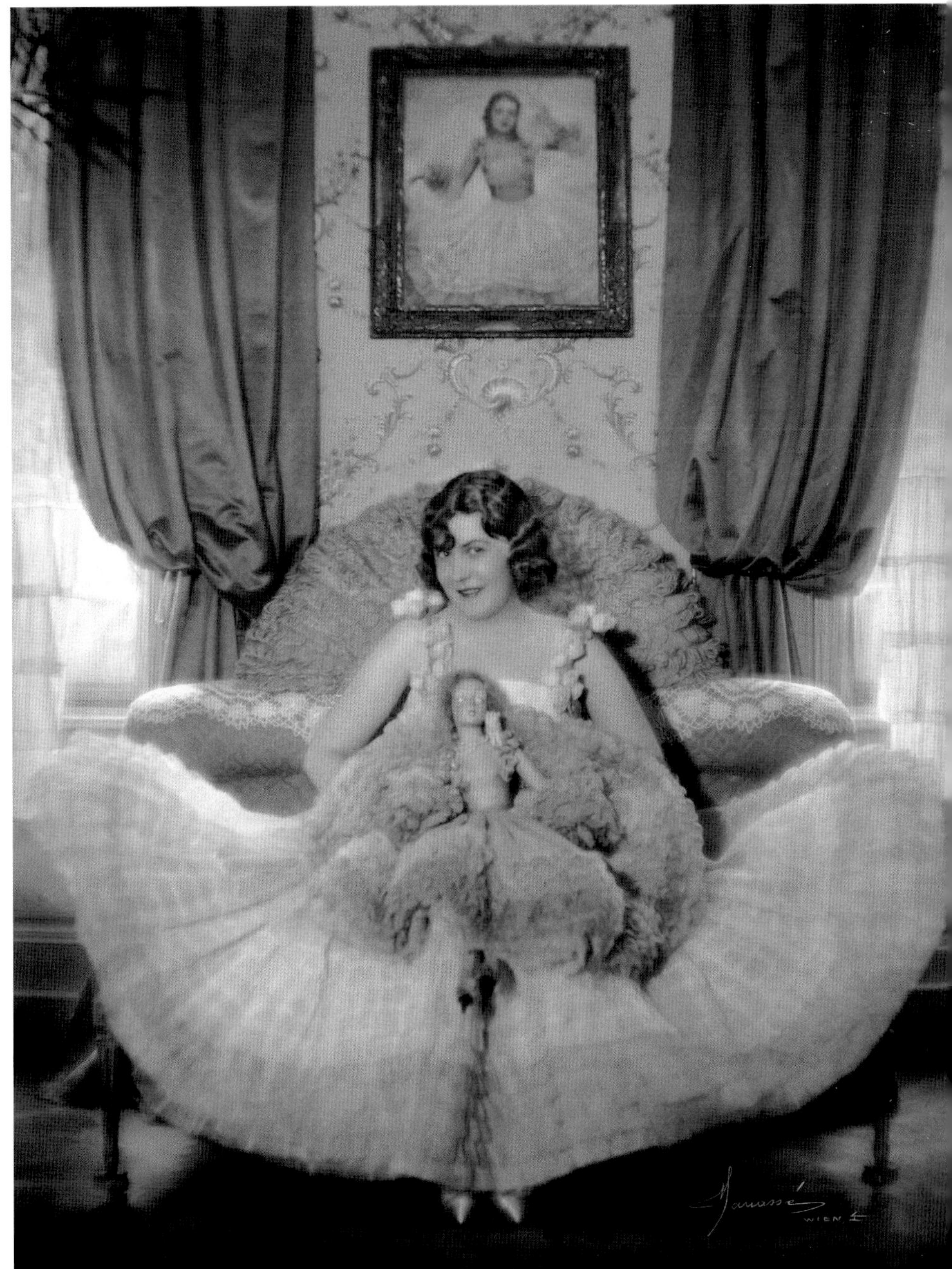

The combination of a remunerative profession and a private obsession seems obvious, but perhaps one should not judge too quickly here either. Some of the Manassé pictures in the book are called "photographic jokes," a type of picture considered a Wlassics "specialty." Nevertheless, one can't help thinking that there was something quite serious behind some of these "jokes." On one hand, Olga and Adorján Wlassics understood the important role of the person behind the camera and his or her intentions; on the other hand, they could distinguish among different levels of representation and often directly implemented their ideas about photographic portraits into their settings. One of Olga in her salon is an example of this (fig., p. 31). Here she sits on a plush sofa, ruffled skirt spread out about her, a ruffled doll in her lap. Above her head hangs a picture of a woman wearing a ruffled skirt. The three-fold repetition of the same motif can either be interpreted as simply a superficial joke or as an enigmatic irony.

In art of the period between the wars, the multiple possibilities of the doll motif as metaphor for female manipulability and disposability are known. However, the commonplace identification of woman = doll generally prevails in the Manassé photographs. Comparison with a picture by another Viennese studio, also reproduced in *Die Erotik in der Fotografie*, demonstrates this. The photograph (fig., p. 32) is called *Zwei Puppen* (Two Dolls). In 1928, Siegfried Kracauer also pointed out this cliché as one of the common examples of bad taste in the films produced that year: "Thus, for the sake of a putative joke, young, chic women in close-ups are always associated with rag dolls that are intended as counterparts of their mistresses." Can we look at the Manassé

Atelier Willinger: Two Dolls, c. 1930; Fortuna La Creole, c. 1934

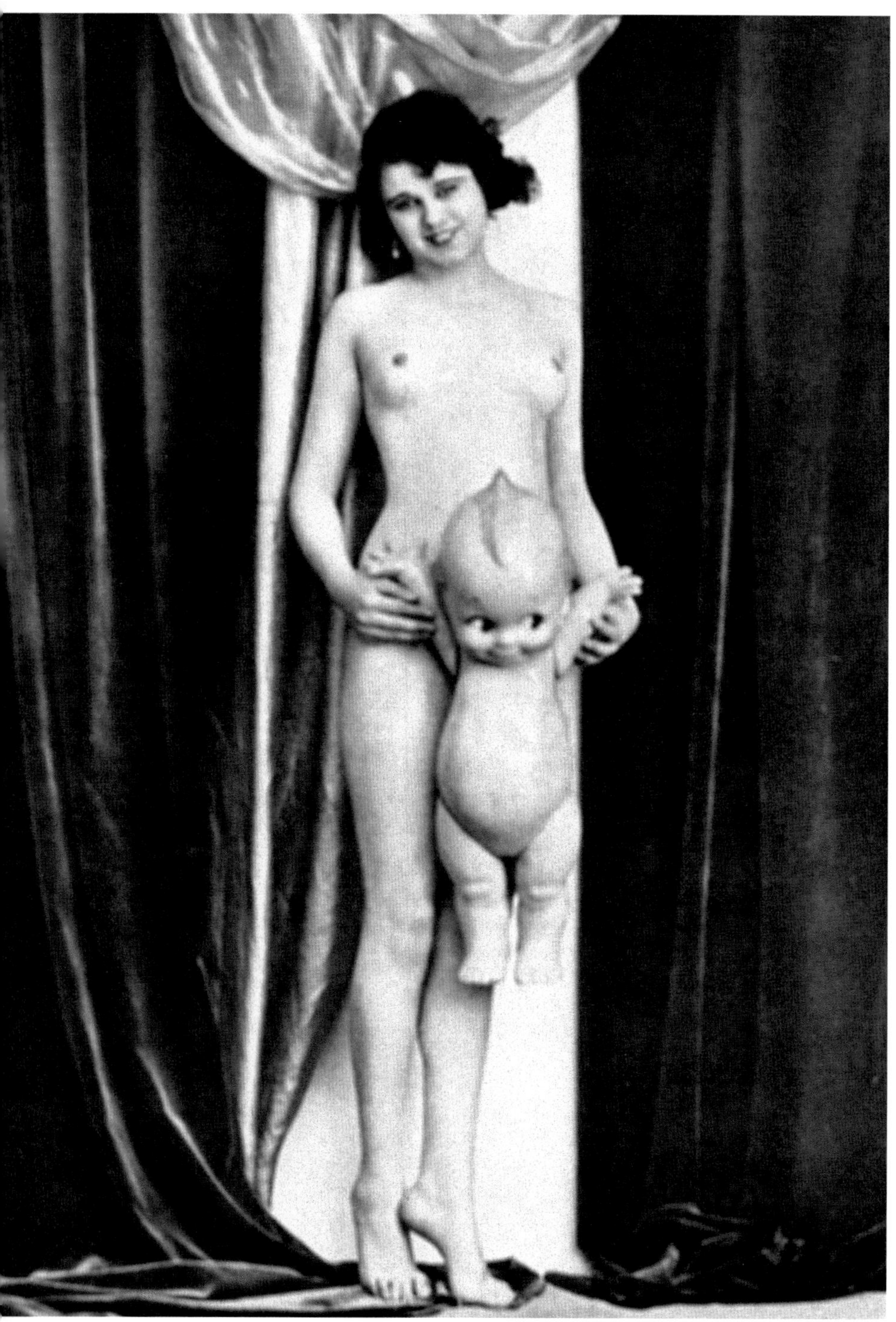

photo of a laughing dancer named Fortuna La Creole holding a monkey doll (fig., p. 33), without sensing a trace of racism behind the humorous facade?

If it were not for the fact that there is also the painting (or is it an overpainted photograph?) hanging over the model's head, one would have to assign a similar banality to the picture of Olga with the doll. However, the doll, the woman, and the subject of the painting can be interpreted as being on three different levels of reality or reproduction of the same motif. No attempt is made to establish which of these variants is to be taken as the starting point of the imitation game. Is Olga copying her doll in dress and pose? Is the picture in the background a portrait of Olga in the same dress, or is it a model she is emulating? In any event, the old-fashioned romantic dress worn by this "Lady of Viennese Society" (fig., p. 40), who is usually attired in the latest style—or perhaps not clothed at all—seems to support the interpretation that it is a mockery of current clichés.

The ambiguity present in this three-level picture perhaps could also be considered a parallel to the multifaceted role the Wlassics played in their extensive photo enterprise. A variety of reasons turned them into imitators as well as creators in the presentation of female roles. The way they saw themselves personally and socially was drawn from the universe of their models, whom they in turn portrayed in their pictures as creatures who presented the public with daydreams instead of reality.

Today's Ideal of Beauty (the title used for one of the first Manassé photographs that appeared in the magazine *Die Bühne* in 1925) represented both the starting point and the final objective in their picture production. Therefore—in addition to the studio's

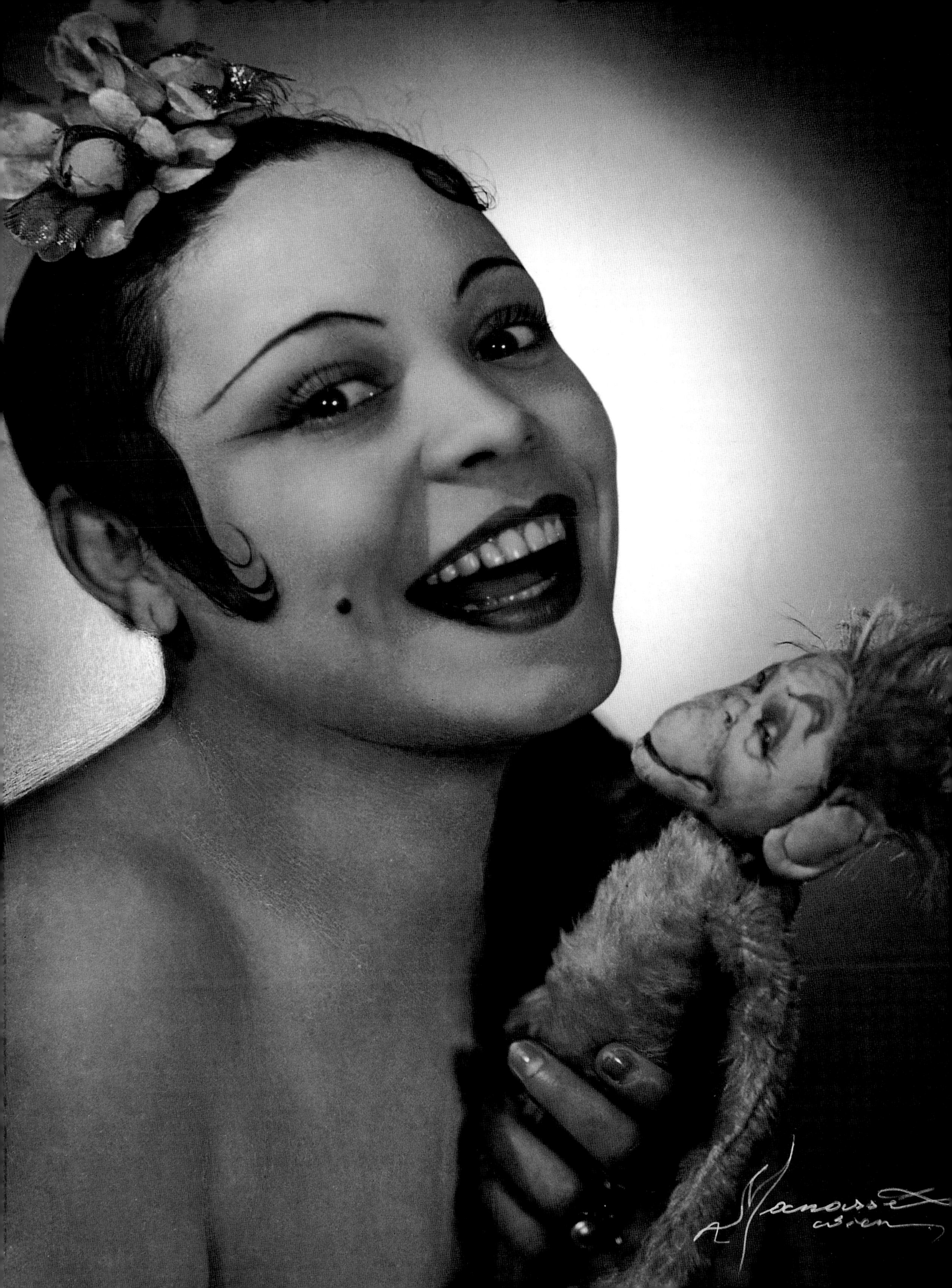

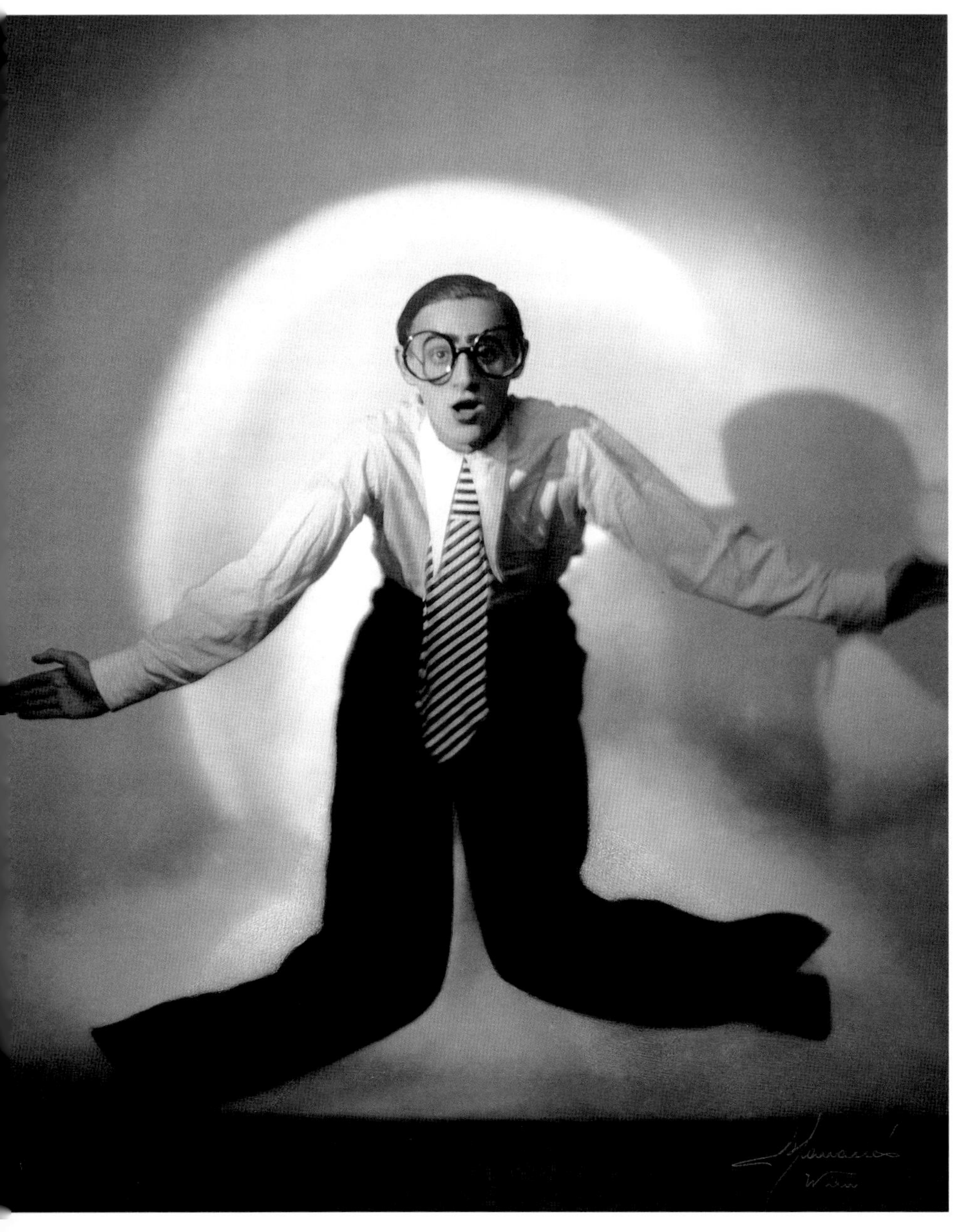

extraordinary consistency in motifs and photographic arrangements—we can also trace the more or less fluidly evolving changes in this ideal of beauty in the period between the early 1920s and 1938. We are dealing here with an interrelated combination of dress, hair styles, and accessories; the facial expressions, gestures, and pose of the model; and last but not least the composition, lighting, cropping or trimming of the photograph. The same magazines that published the Manassé

Sindaire, c.1930

pictures also published the material that quite obviously fed these changes: First there were articles on the theater, revues, dance, and silent film; then, later, more and more were about 'nature' and sports. And so the time approached when 'beauty' turned into 'charm' and all suggestions of the ironic, openly funny, or slightly risqué were banned from the Manassé pictures in favor of, whenever possible, a beauty even more 'smoothly' retouched, elegantly proportioned than before (cf. fig., p. 50).

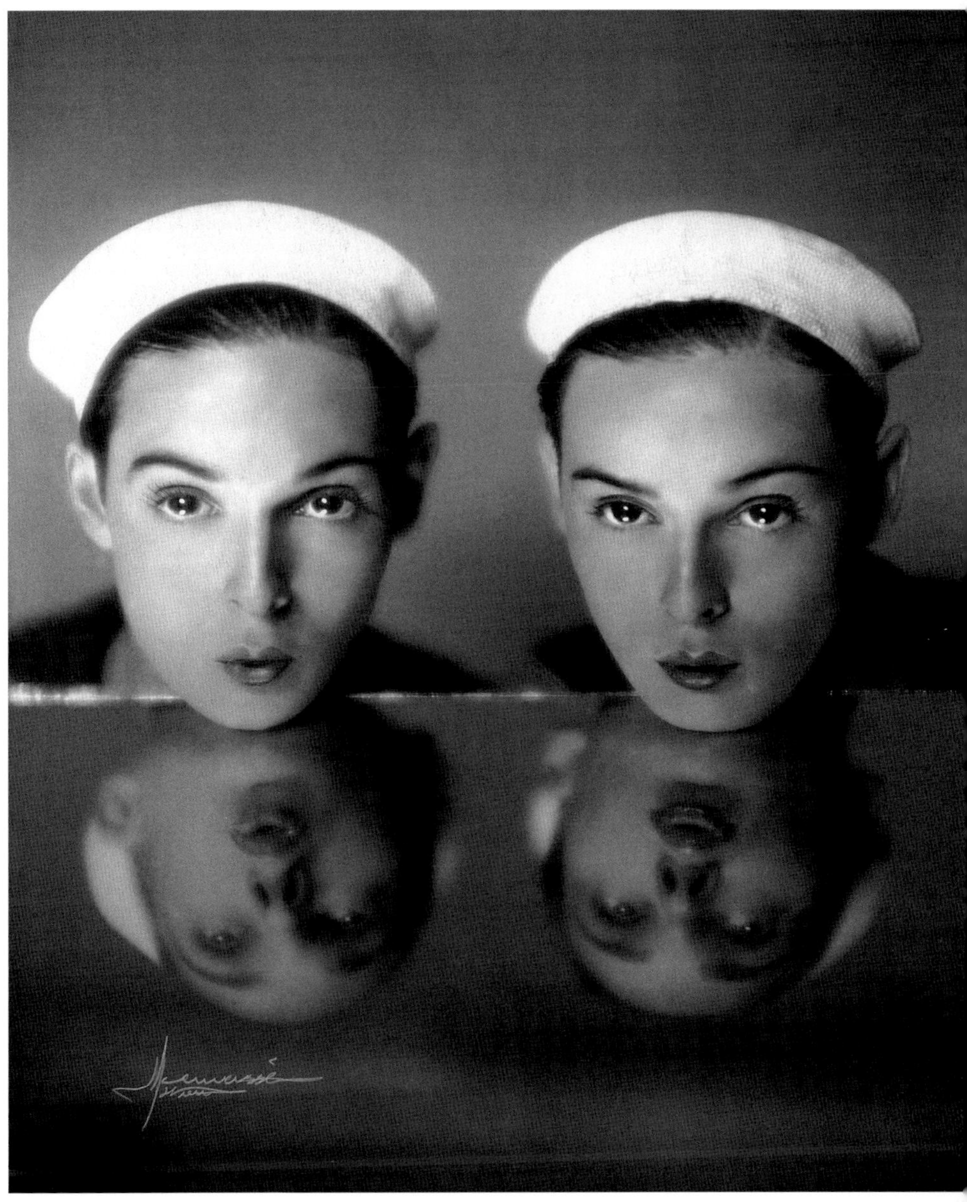

The Rocky Twins, c.1927

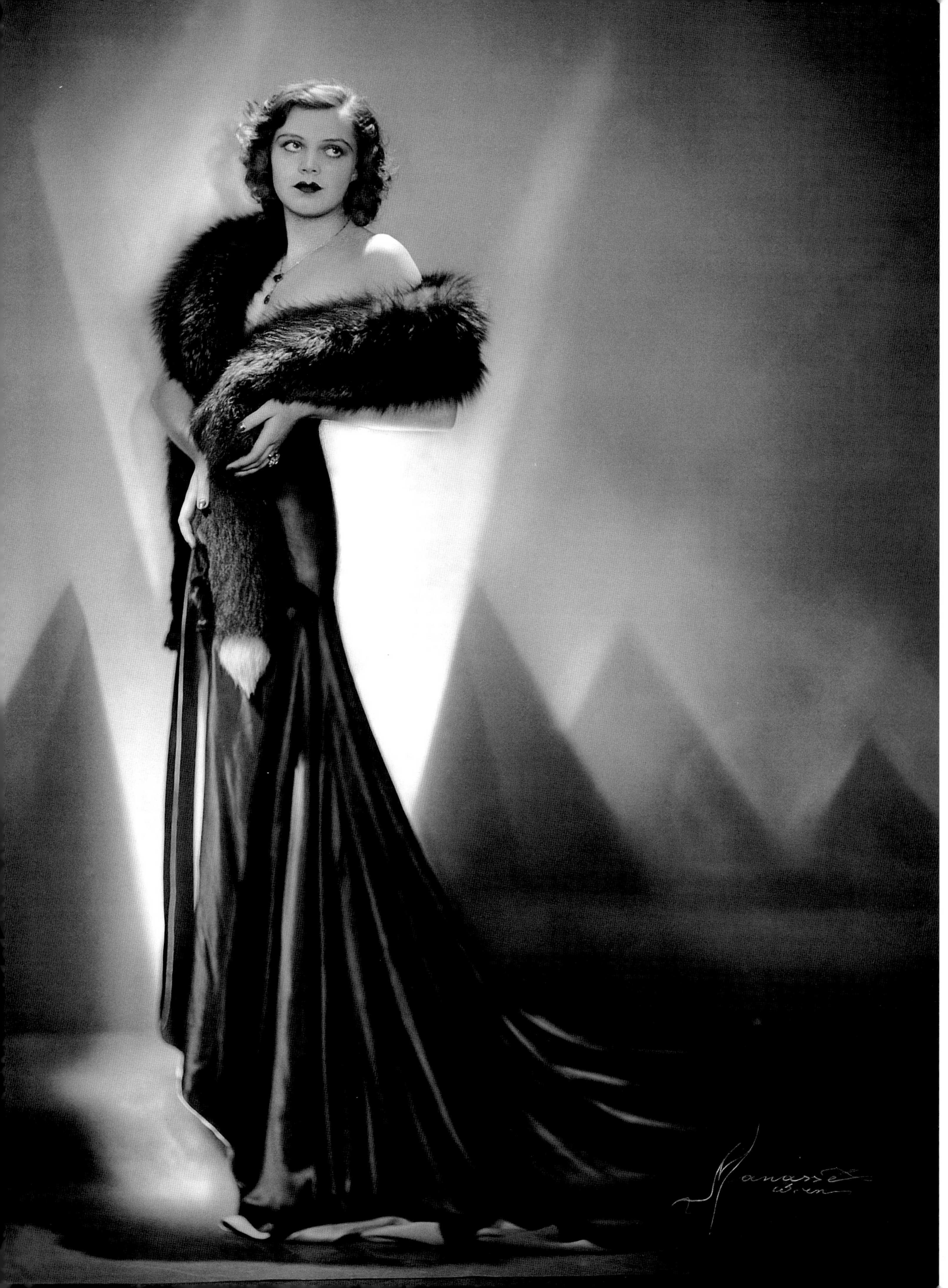
Manassé
Wien

MANASSÉ TRADEMARK:
THE COMPONENTS OF A PHOTOGRAPHY BUSINESS

For the Wlassics interaction between photographers and their models, between their perception and staging in accordance with prescribed production guidelines, between playing roles and visual clichés, occurred only in the studio. Every landscape and all backdrops were either constructed there or later painted into the negative. These pictures, made in an enclosed space that could be totally controlled, were for the most part intended for publication. Occasionally, however, pictures were also produced at Manassé for customers to use for private purposes, such as "Picture of a Lady," an illustration for a magazine advertisement. But the main body of material that has survived indicates that, at least until they moved to Berlin, they ran a business that flourished doing private work for clients during the time between the wars. Studio Manassé was one of those specialized enterprises that prospered at the tip of the huge iceberg in the German-speaking realm in the 1930s.

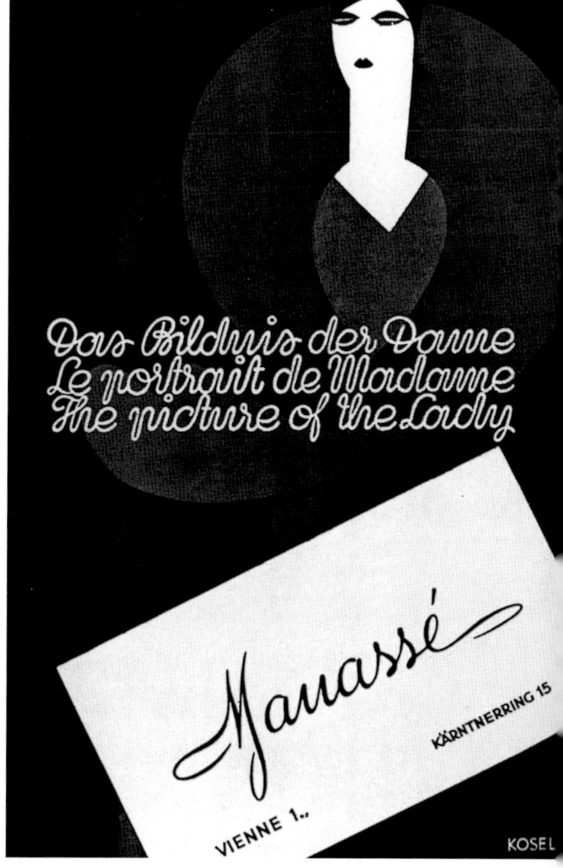

Martha Steiner, c.1934; Announcement in *Wiener Magazin*, 1931

The Wlassics served a clientele in professions related to the theater, vaudeville, and film. These clients valued pictures that were somewhat unconventional because such photos were important in cultivating their image. The nineteenth-century custom of supplying one's fans with original photos, individually dedicated and signed or combined with the portraits of others in a portfolio with an elegant cover, had by now lost some of its importance. Instead, a growing number of artists' agencies used portrait and casting photos to land new engagements for clients. In the Vienna Theater Museum, a collection of material left behind by such an agency (Koller) comprises several thousand sample stills. These show that the average quality of photos was shockingly poor: careless, unflattering, and old-fashioned in every way. With vast competition in the marketplace, it must surely have been an enormous advantage to have one's promotion and publicity pictures, whether for personal or agency use, made by a high-class studio. In the bundle of papers left by the Koller agency, the Manassé pictures stand out conspicuously from the rest. No doubt they were much more expensive than those made by smaller and less well-known studios, and many artists simply could not afford them. These disadvantaged performers thereby lost an added chance to become better known, a chance that Studio Manassé offered them by having their pictures published in specialty magazines. (Greta Garbo was one of the best-known examples of the value of this kind of exposure. Hollywood producer Louis B. Mayer had not been impressed by her when they met, and he did not recognize her when she appeared on the cover of *Vanity Fair* in 1925, in a photo by Arnold Genthe. Yet he immediately wanted to hire the woman in *that* photograph.) The wording of a printed Manassé release form that has survived comes as no surprise: "To the firm Foto-Kunst, 'Manassé.' I herewith affirm with my signature that I have given you permission to use the photos

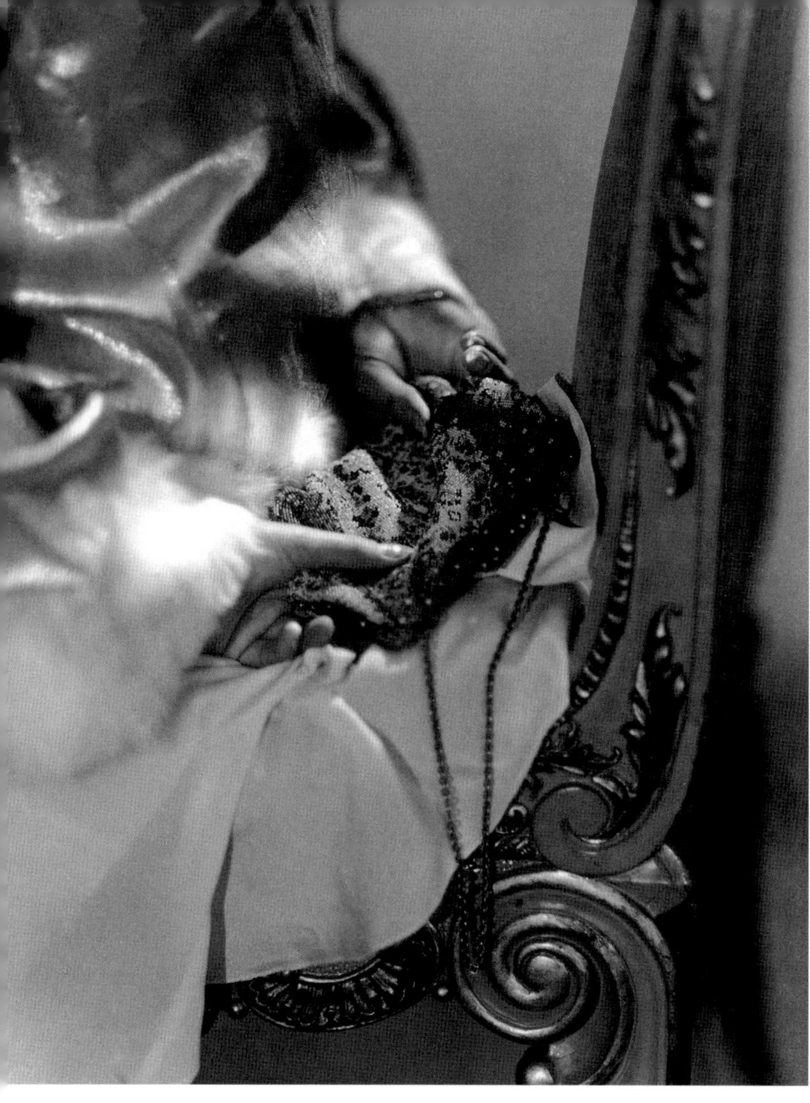

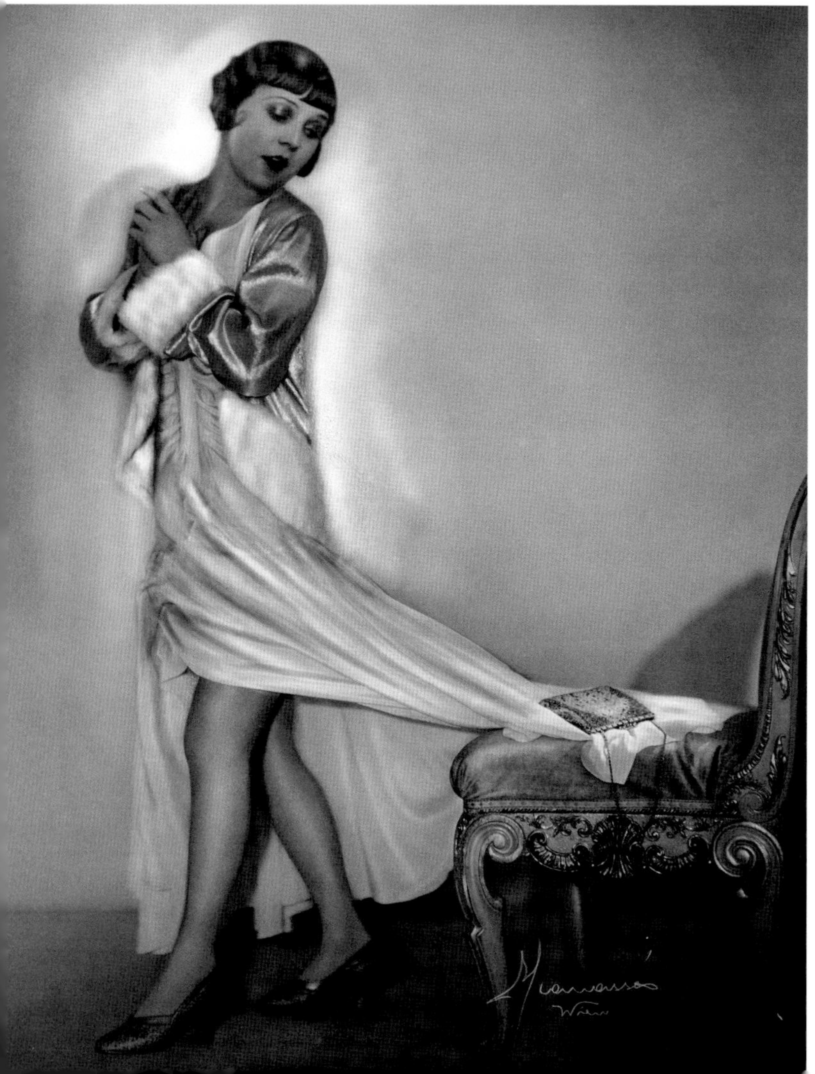

Handbag Trick to Show Beautiful Legs (two parts), c. 1931; Gerty Gert, c. 1932

and/or pictures you have made of me, without valuable consideration to me, for purposes of reproduction and advertising."

As an essential secondary prong of their business, the Wlassics maintained connections with a series of Austrian, German, and some foreign language magazines. These publications were customers for such pictures because portraits of prominent personalities were an integral part of their contents. There are obvious similarities with present-day practices, from Helmut Newton to Annie Leibovitz. Although today, seventy years later, magazines and photographs have a different look and new media have joined what was even then a complex game, the fundamental economic patterns have not changed. The two primary components of this business—the stars (as well as those who want to become stars) and the media (in those days, the illustrated magazines)—form an integral unit.

This partnership first appeared in the glamour-hungry culture following the First World War. Between 1918 and 1930 (the year that marked the end of silent film production in Vienna), almost 700 short- and full-length feature films were made in Austria. There was also a booming business in magazines. More and more publications that aimed at satisfying public hunger for stories about the world of the performing arts and provided new pictures of actors and actresses were coming on the market. These glimpses into the world of glamour were generally scattered among articles about gossip (with pictures of "society ladies"), old and new fashions, descriptions of the excesses and advantages of "modern" life, and shocking, melodramatic or witty reports about various subjects of interest to readers, ranging from murder and sports to etiquette at the Egyptian courts. Humorous short or very short stories, a genre that came into being just for this special medium, were also a popular feature. These literarily undemanding stories provided occasions for using illustrations, often photographs of more or less provocatively dressed or undressed women. Such pictures might also appear

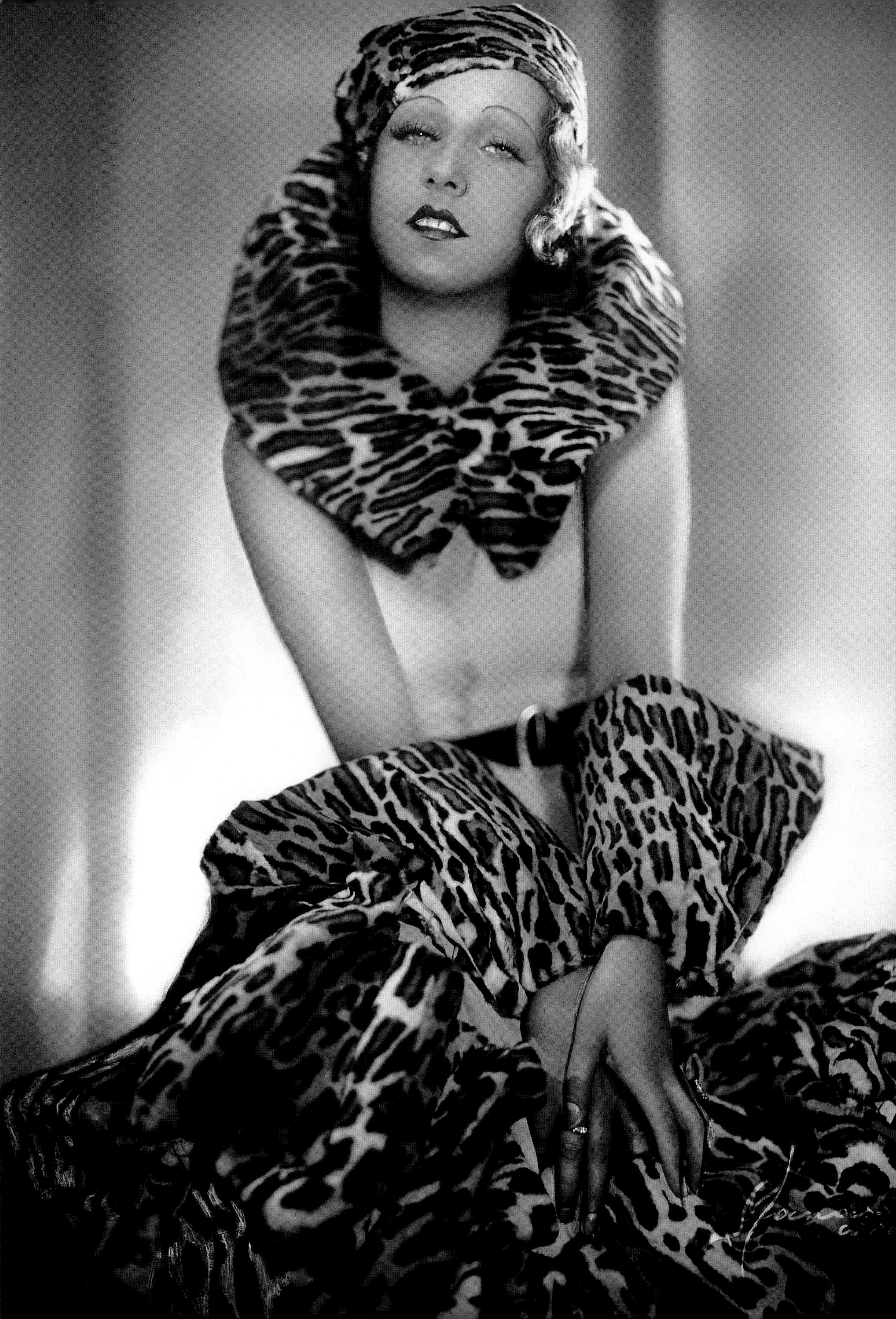

Olga Wlassics, 1928; Study, c.1931; next two pages: Gry Dorescu, c.1928; Study, c.1930

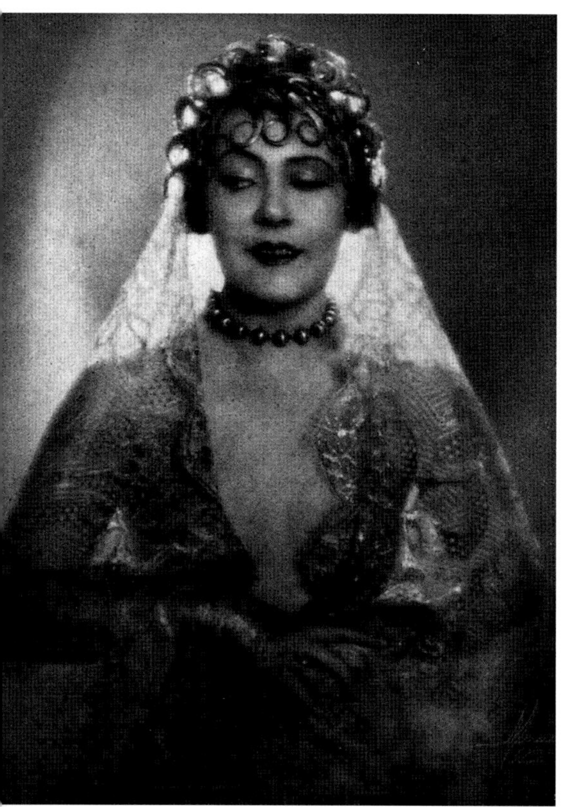

without having any connection to the text, or they could even furnish an excuse for a playful little story. On seeing some Manassé photographs in the *Revue des Monats* in 1928, Hubert Miketta, one of the pioneers in magazine publishing in Berlin, "philosophized" about baskets as follows: Fruit basket, wash basket, rooster in a basket, figurative basket. (Of course each basket had its attractive female accompaniment.) Hans von Bueren, in a 1931 piece called "Zündkerzen" (Spark Plugs), babbled on about the "sparking effect of sex appeal" with the help of décolletage and leg photos by Manassé.

Around 1930 there were some 30, mostly small-format, illustrated magazines in Austria and many times that number in Germany. The largest bundle of Manassé photographs (more than 500 pictures) survived in the archive of an international picture agency, the Schostal Agency, also called Wien-Bild or Wiener Photo Kurier. In business from 1927–28 until 1941, it worked primarily out of Vienna with branch offices in Milan and Paris and, for a time, also in Berlin, Stockholm, and Warsaw. Pictures by photographers whom Schostal represented appeared in periodicals far beyond the borders of the German-speaking area. In Austria, Schostal also represented the large American Keystone Agency, which still exists today. Schostal had on file thousands (a million, if one is to believe an agency prospectus from the mid-thirties) of pictures to be used "for press and publicity or advertising purposes" (according to a stamp on the back of the photographs). These were either directly supplied to newspapers and magazines or forwarded to other sales agencies, such as Bildervertrieb Schröder in Berlin or Globe Photo in New York.

Studio Manassé was only one of many suppliers of pictures. Its most prominent Viennese competitors were d'Ora (Arthur Benda and Dora Kallmus who worked in Paris later on and were also represented there by Schostal) and Trude Fleischmann. There were also such press photographers as Lothar Rübelt and Wilhelm and Laszlo Willinger. Among the best-known business associates of the Schostal Agency abroad were Lotte Jacobi, Germaine Krull, and YVA in Berlin. Jacobi, Kallmus, and Krull were represented by the agency in the German market even after 1933, when Jewish photographers were forced to emigrate.

Manassé pictures form the largest single group in the still extensive Schostal archive, which came to light again only a few years ago. Most items are marked on the back with numbers, making it possible, among other things, to compare dates of publication and changes in the studio name and to determine an approximate chronology of the studio's output during the Viennese period. In other holdings, such as those in the Austrian Theater Museum, there are photographs of stars with dated dedications to their admirers. These also help to fill in chronological gaps. In addition to portraits of famous people, numerous fashion photos, and various nude pictures—so-called "studies"—this group

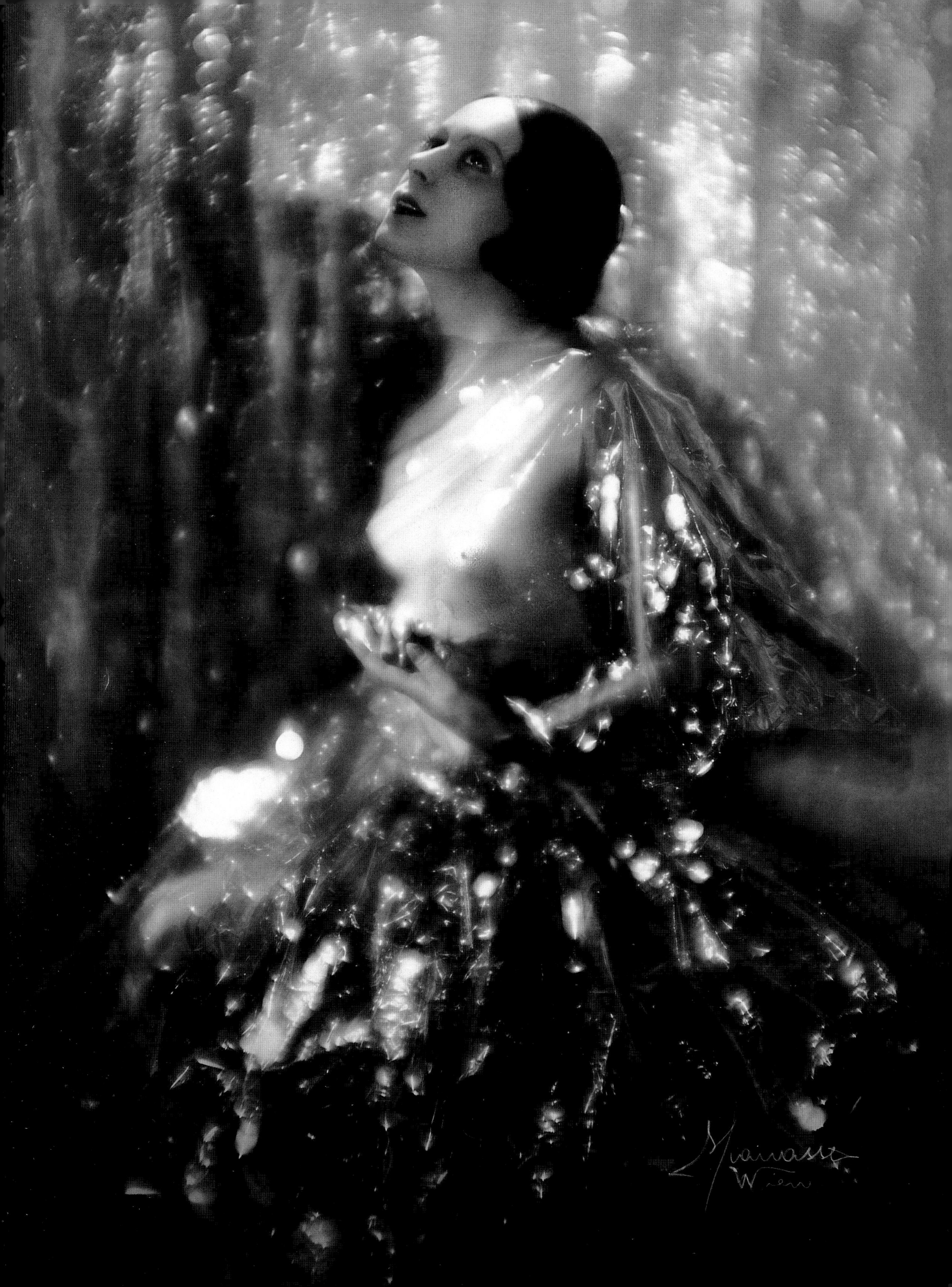
Manassé
Wien

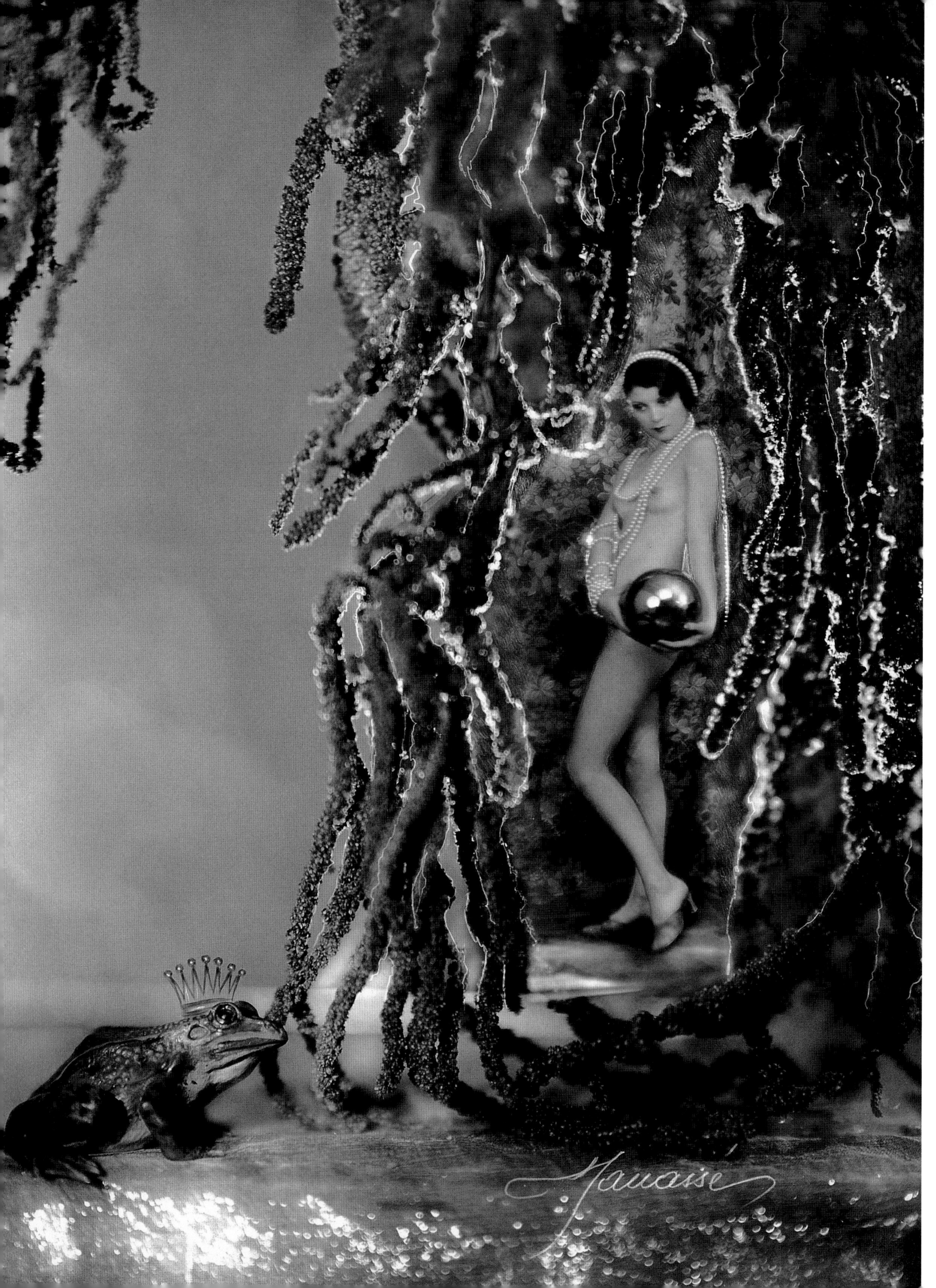
Manasse

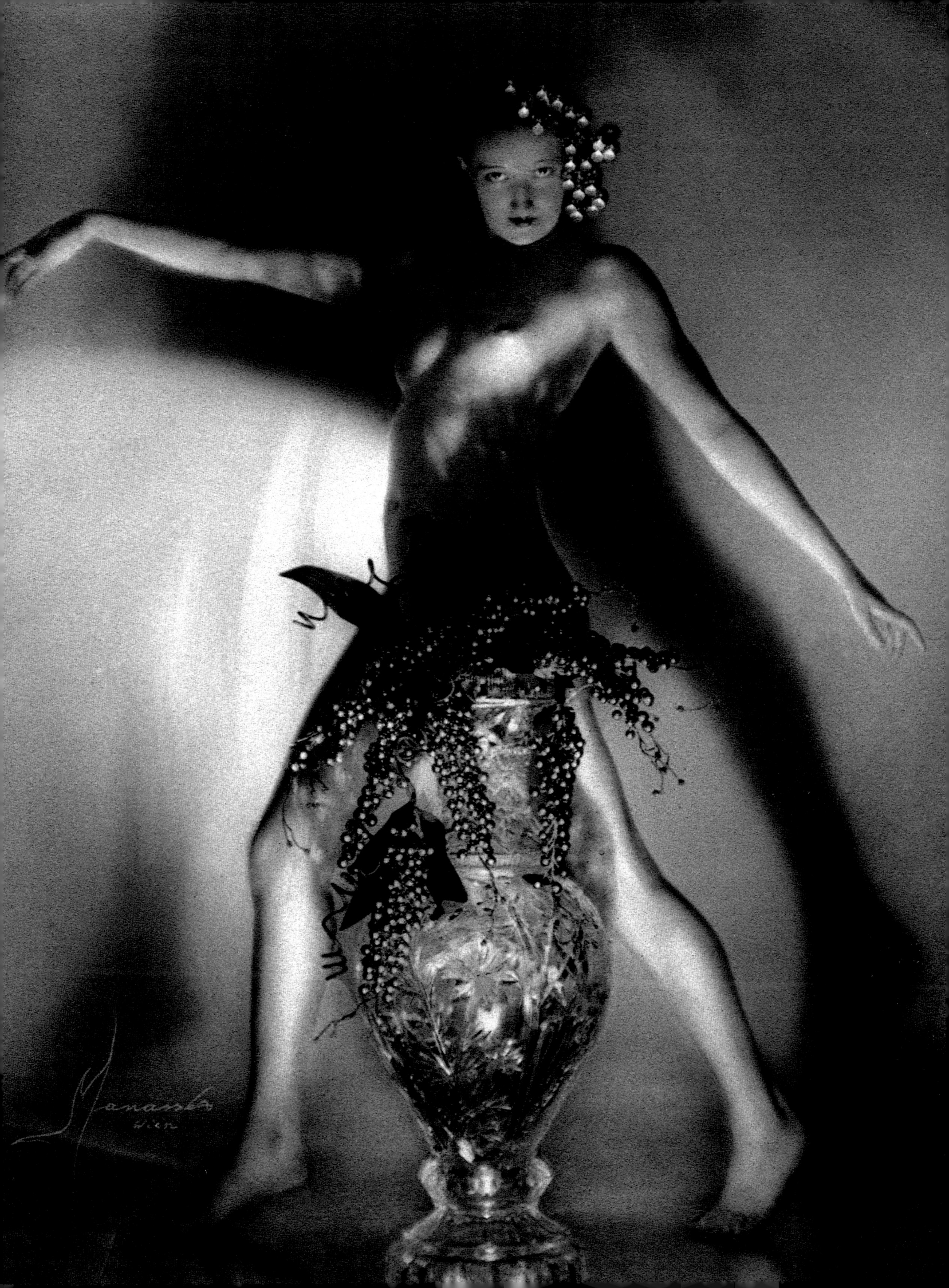

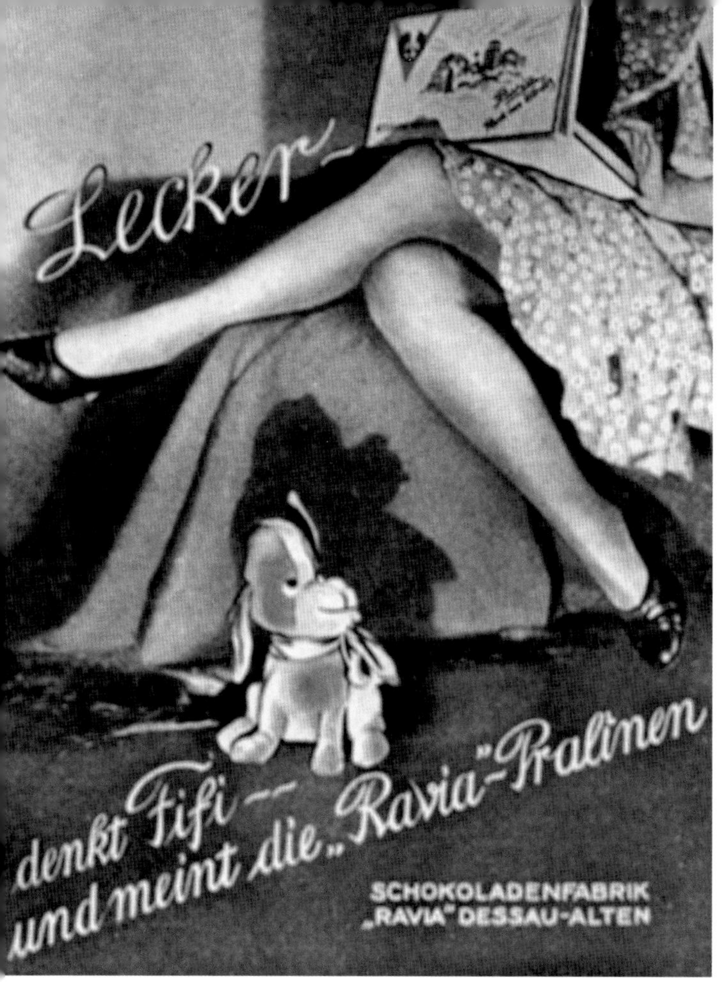

Unknown photographer: Advertising photo from Die Erotik in Der Fotografie 1931; Study, c.1934; Study, c.1930

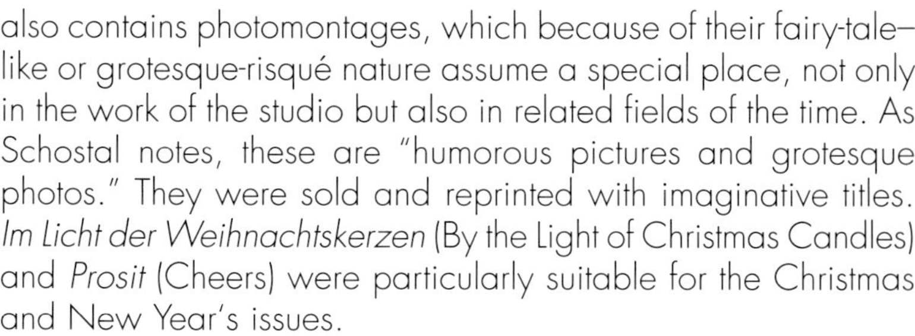

also contains photomontages, which because of their fairy-tale–like or grotesque-risqué nature assume a special place, not only in the work of the studio but also in related fields of the time. As Schostal notes, these are "humorous pictures and grotesque photos." They were sold and reprinted with imaginative titles. *Im Licht der Weihnachtskerzen* (By the Light of Christmas Candles) and *Prosit* (Cheers) were particularly suitable for the Christmas and New Year's issues.

The Schostal agency also had an advertising department where—according to their own ads—one could buy "*a finished picture* to advertise all concepts, for every sort of illustrative purpose." Some photographs preserved in the Manassé bundle were apparently intended to be used for this purpose. They certainly do not conform to guidelines for avant-garde advertising that were being formulated at this time by the Bauhaus. Rather they aimed at a wittier form. "Eros as advertising chief" was the avowed motto of these photographs, and they represented the prevailing pattern well. A contemporary writer commented laconically about examples similar to the Manassé products in the previously cited *Die Erotik in der Fotografie:* "A male viewer, looking at pictures of such women in scanty dress, probably thinks first and foremost about the sweet kernel she encloses." Even in the rare case when a "pure" Studio Manassé photograph has survived, because of its lavish use of painted-in lines and shading in the background of the technological products being touted, it is more like art-deco wallpaper than the functional advertising photos developed in the environment of the German Bauhaus (fig., p. 48).

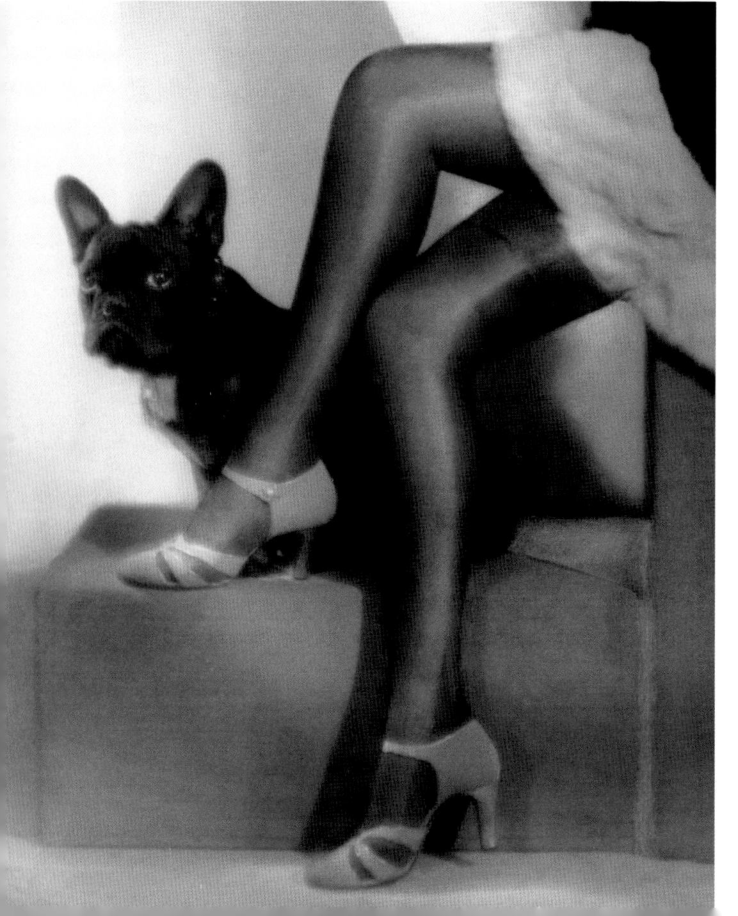

Not all of Manassé's contacts with the public were through Robert Schostal. For many years the studio worked directly with several periodicals, demonstrating the Wlassics' flexibility in picture production as well as in marketing strategy. They supplied the *Salonblatt*—a relic from the days of the monarchy, which, even at the end of the twenties, still dealt almost exclusively with "social happenings" in aristocratic circles—only with proper and, for today's taste, extraordinarily dull portraits. Other publications were supplied with visual "spice." The first Manassé illustrations appeared in the Viennese periodical *Muskete* in 1924, long before the founding of the Schostal agency. This magazine's humorous iconographic style probably had considerable influence on the production of the newly founded

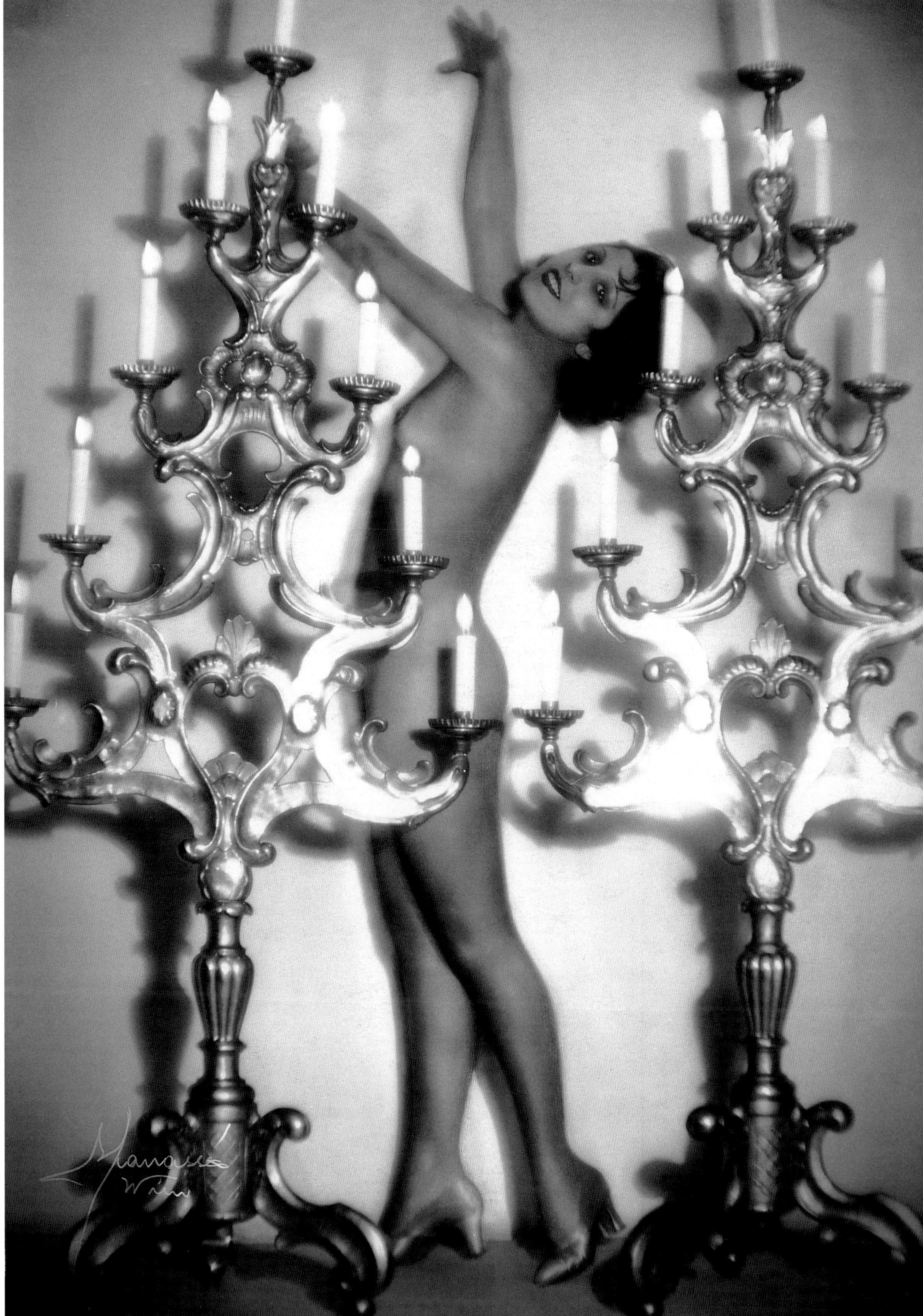
Manassé
Wien

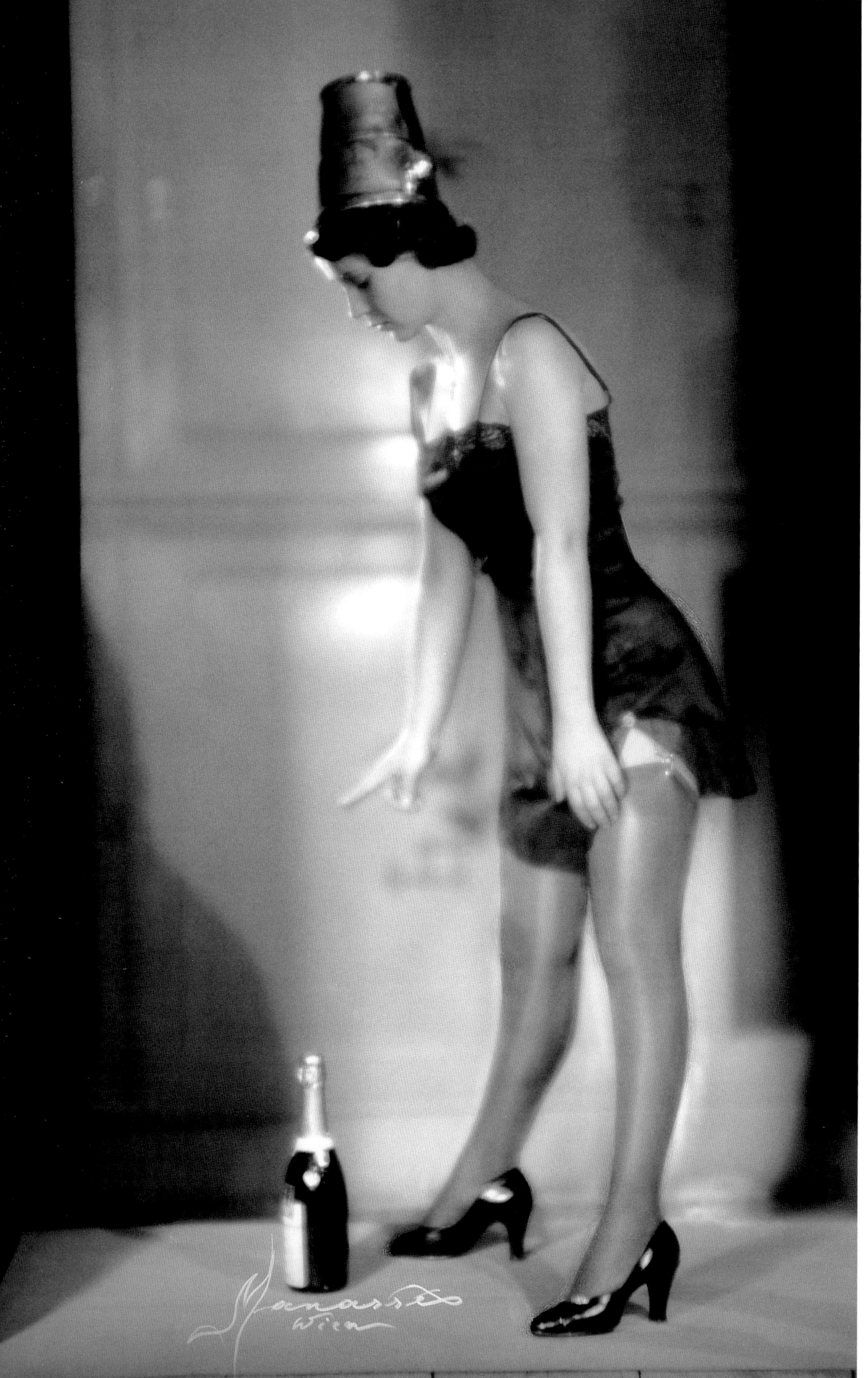
Manassé
Wien

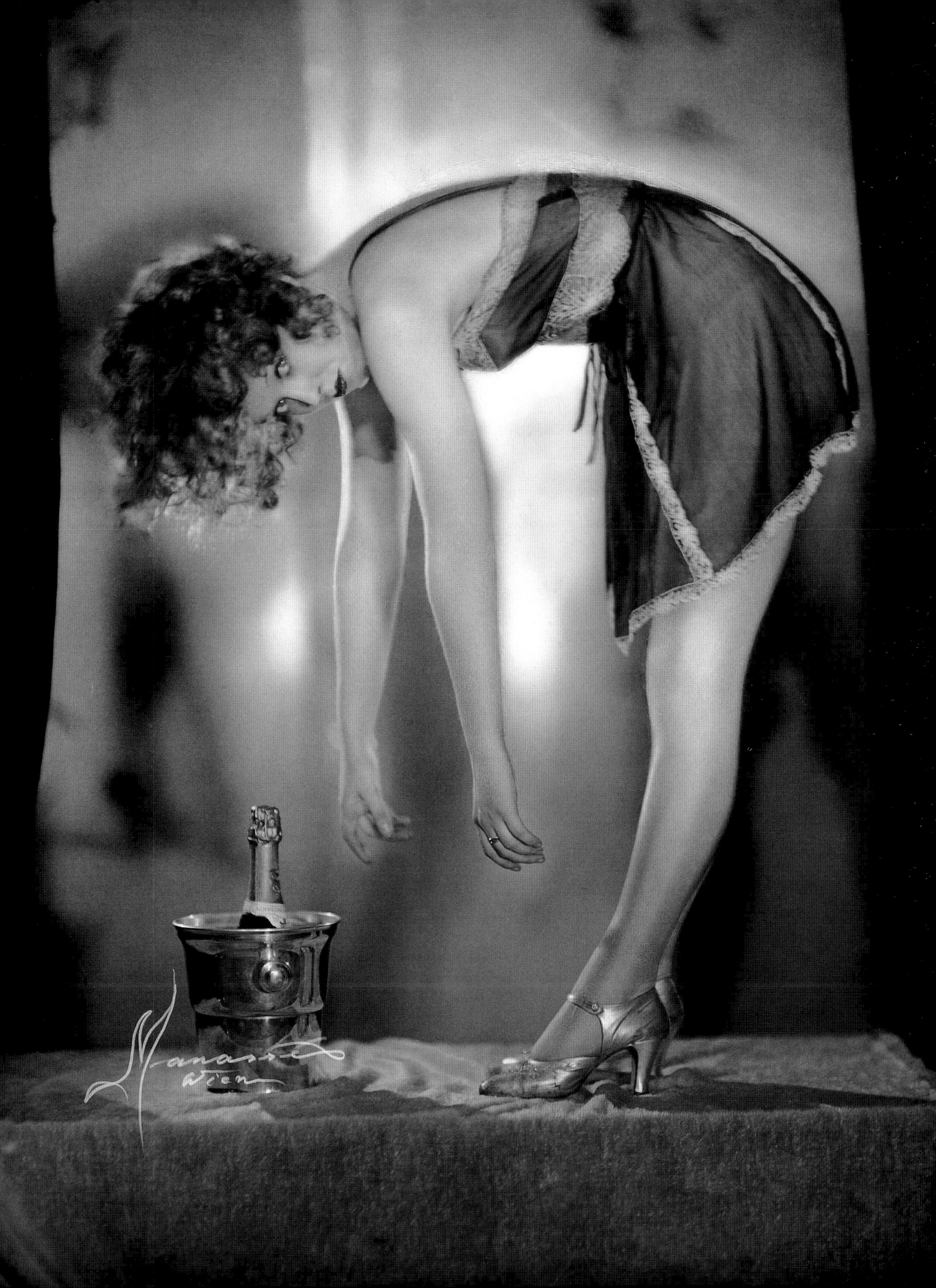
Manassé
Wien

Previous two pages: Hansi Prinz, c.1932; Anita Knauer, c.1932; these pages: Ballbearing, 1933; Darmora, c.1927

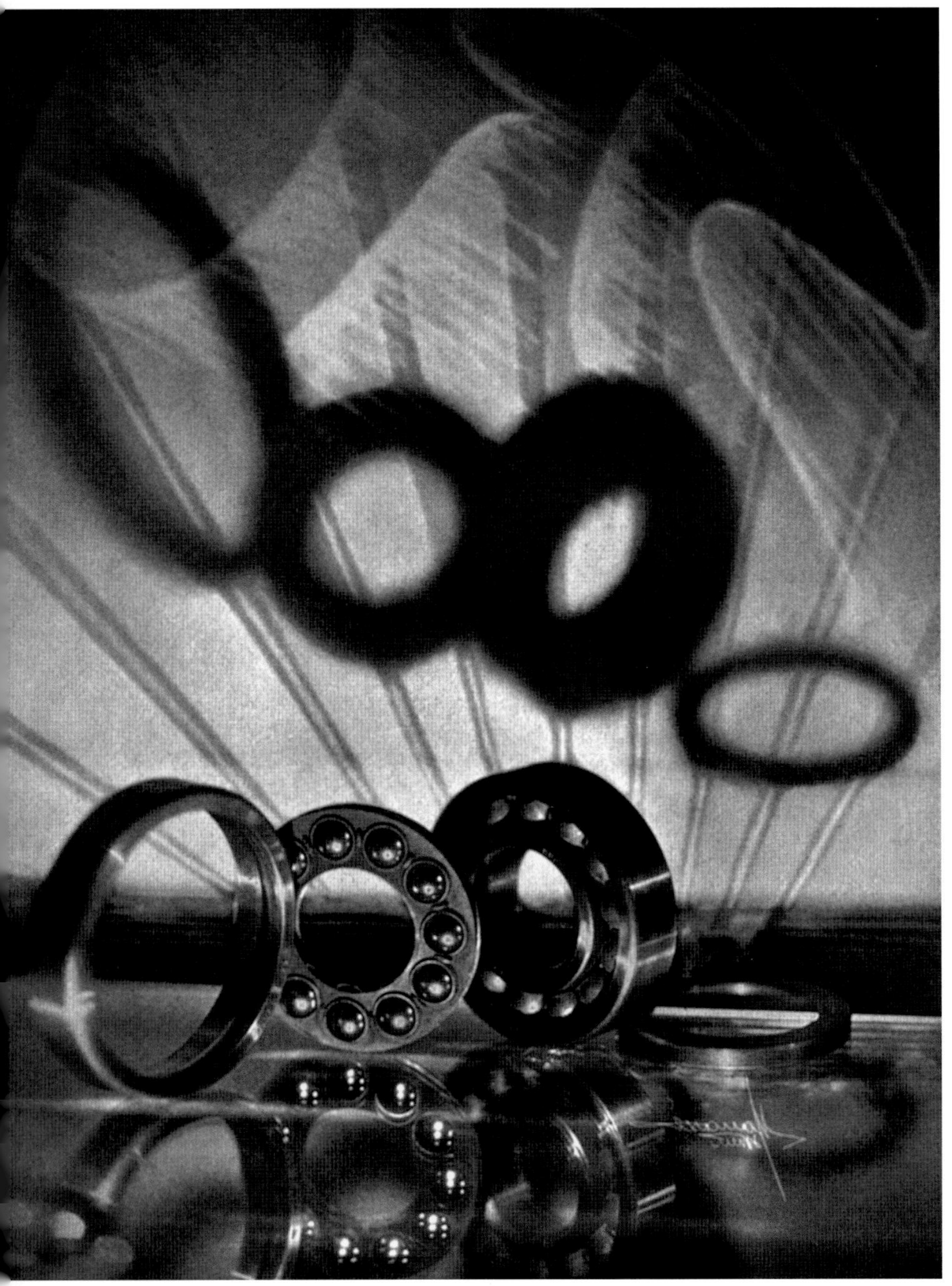

studio, while several of its painted illustrations or covers appeared to be direct copies of Manassé jokes.

Olga and Adorján Wlassics readily adapted to the long-standing and well-proven magazine concept and, after a meager beginning, became major suppliers. From *Wiener Magazin's* first issue in November 1927, they regularly produced numerous text illustrations for it as well as cover pictures, each a painting based on a photograph. In exchange, for many years the magazine carried a full-page ad for their photo studio (fig., p.37). In addition to pictures from other Viennese studios (such as Edith Barakovich, Arthur Benda, Kitty Hofmann, Franz Löwy) and from Berlin studios (Studio Binder, Schlosser and Wenisch, Walther Jäger, etc.), material from Hollywood played a special and important role and was avidly copied in Viennese pictures. Manassé photographs, which represented the bulk of the illustrations until 1936, when they were replaced by Manassé-Ricoll and then WOG pictures, stand out partly because of their extraordinary heterogeneity. In addition to subjects mentioned before, the Manassé studio also published landscape photographs in the moderately modern style that flooded the scene after the avant-garde exhibition *Film und Foto* in Stuttgart in 1929. (The show was seen in Vienna the following year.) There were also photographs of cute, impish young girls, pictures that already went beyond the bounds of what is acceptable in today's popular magazines. Several Christ studies in these otherwise far from religious pages were equally disconcerting. Only a few years earlier the same magazine had shown a picture (entitled *Mysterium*) of a nude wearing a hint of a nun's habit. It seems not to have mattered whether the illustration was a landscape, a picture of Christ, or a glamour shot; Olga and Adorján Wlassics probably would have agreed with a statement made by Laszlo Willinger, one of the star photographers for the Hollywood studios who

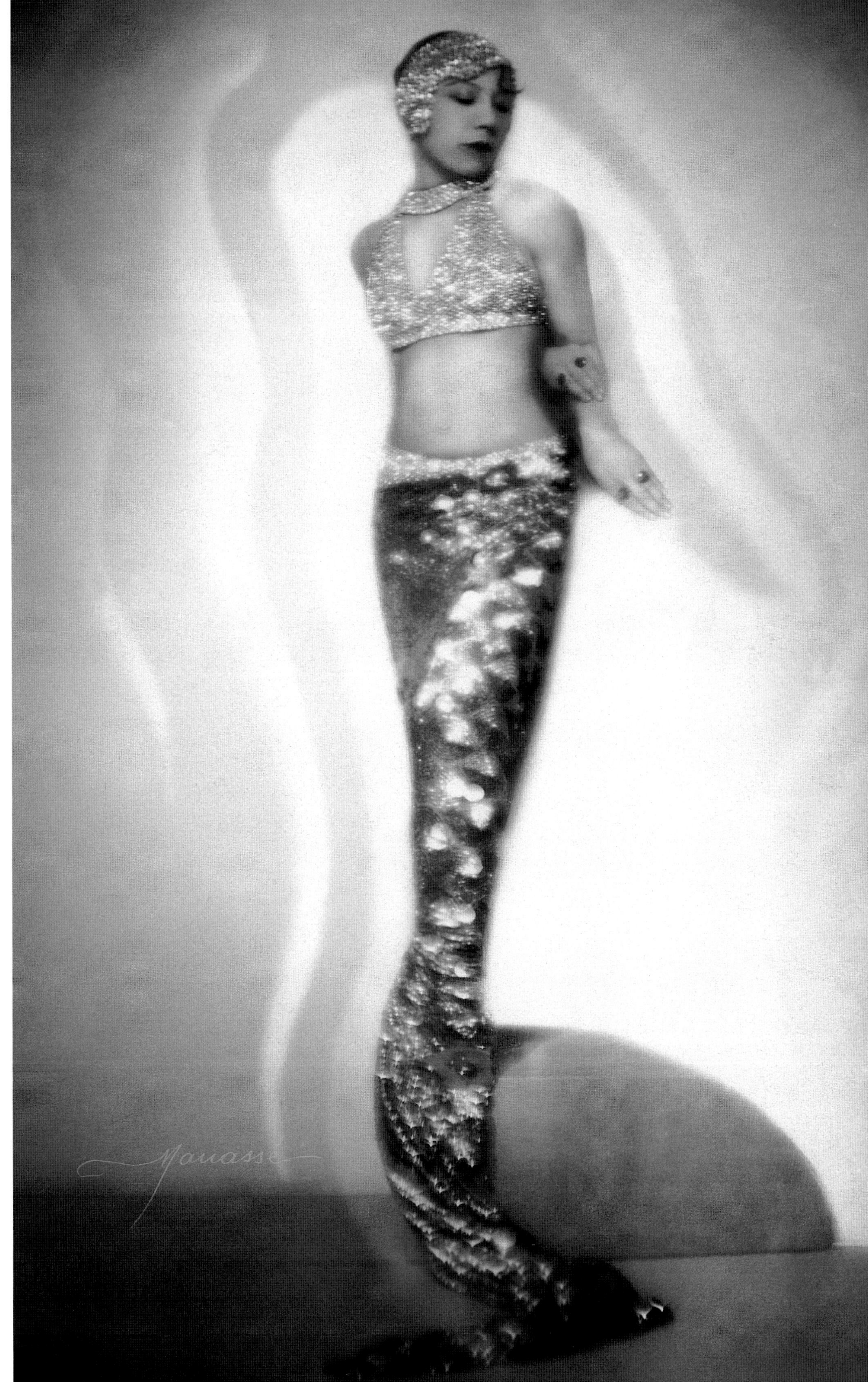
Manasse

Atelier WOG: Brochure, c.1940; Passion, 1932; Little Red Riding Hood, c.1928

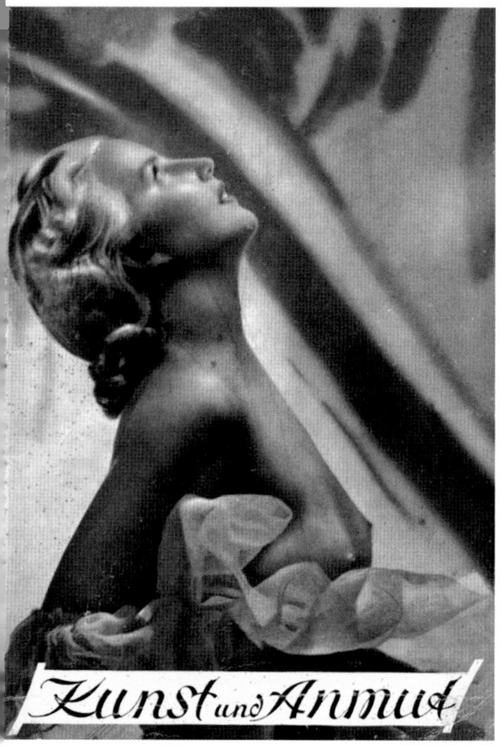

Wiener Magazin
DEZEMBER 1932
VI. JHRG. • VERLAG ALEXANDER & CO. • NR. 12
Phot. Manassé
Passion

had also been born in Budapest around 1900, then worked in Vienna for Schostal, and probably knew the Wlassics. Looking back on those days, he said, "I never forget that a photograph has a goal independent of its subject, whether it's a film star or a matchbox: it must sell itself. I never lose sight of this basic fact. There are an awful lot of photographers who are full of their own importance and take photographs only for their own pleasure—a nice sport that I could never afford."

The importance of the entire range of Manassé illustrations to *Wiener Magazin* was recognized in an extraordinary gesture by its editors: a full-page picture, with text, dedicated to the "best-known contributors to our magazine." The form and content of the page illustrate the sense of irony and humor of the photographer couple as well as that of the magazine's editors. Who really likes to "take a bath" in connection with his profession (fig., p. 27d)? After the 1934 political putsch in Austria, the nature of pictures in *Wiener Magazin* changed rapidly. Instead of Hollywood stars, German actresses now predominated; nude photos, although not reduced in number, were less lascivious; and models were more often pictured out-of-doors rather than in a studio setting. The glitter is gone. For the first time, Manassé lovelies appear in sweaters. The clean German girl is no longer distant. What was still possible in 1930, now became totally unthinkable—for printed material of an erotic nature to be openly advertised in *Wiener Magazin*. These materials, though thinly disguised as having educational value or containing "health care information for the people," scarcely left any erotic desires unfulfilled, however. The publications included material by the Institut für Sexualforschung (Viennese Institute for Sexual Research) published by the Verlag für Kulturforschung, as well as the previously mentioned two—volume *Die Erotik in der Fotografie* (Eroticism in Photography) and a multivolume work about the "erotic typology of women." In most of these volumes there were photographs by the same studios that were also represented month after month in *Wiener Magazin*—although they were pictures of a somewhat different kind.

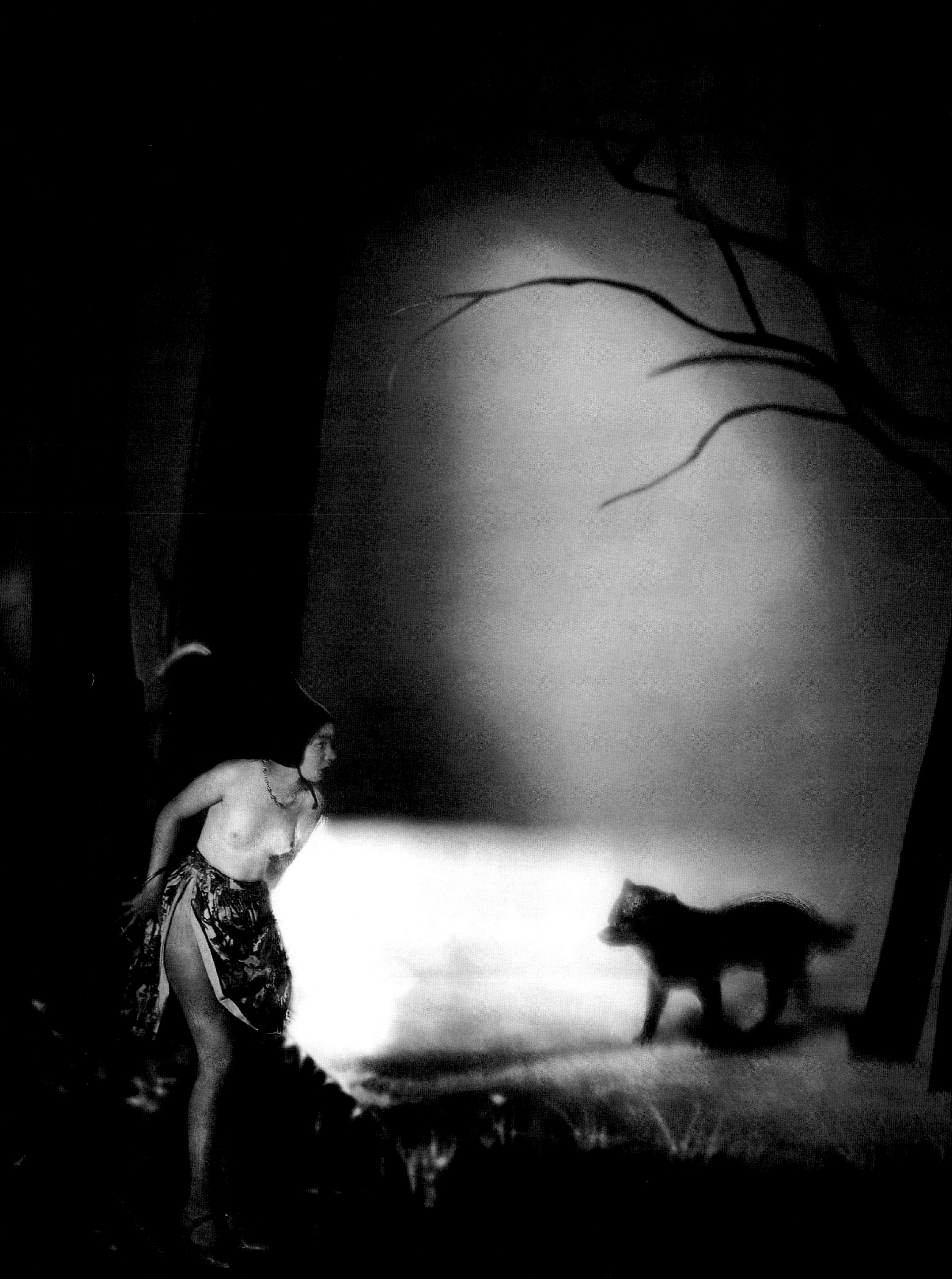

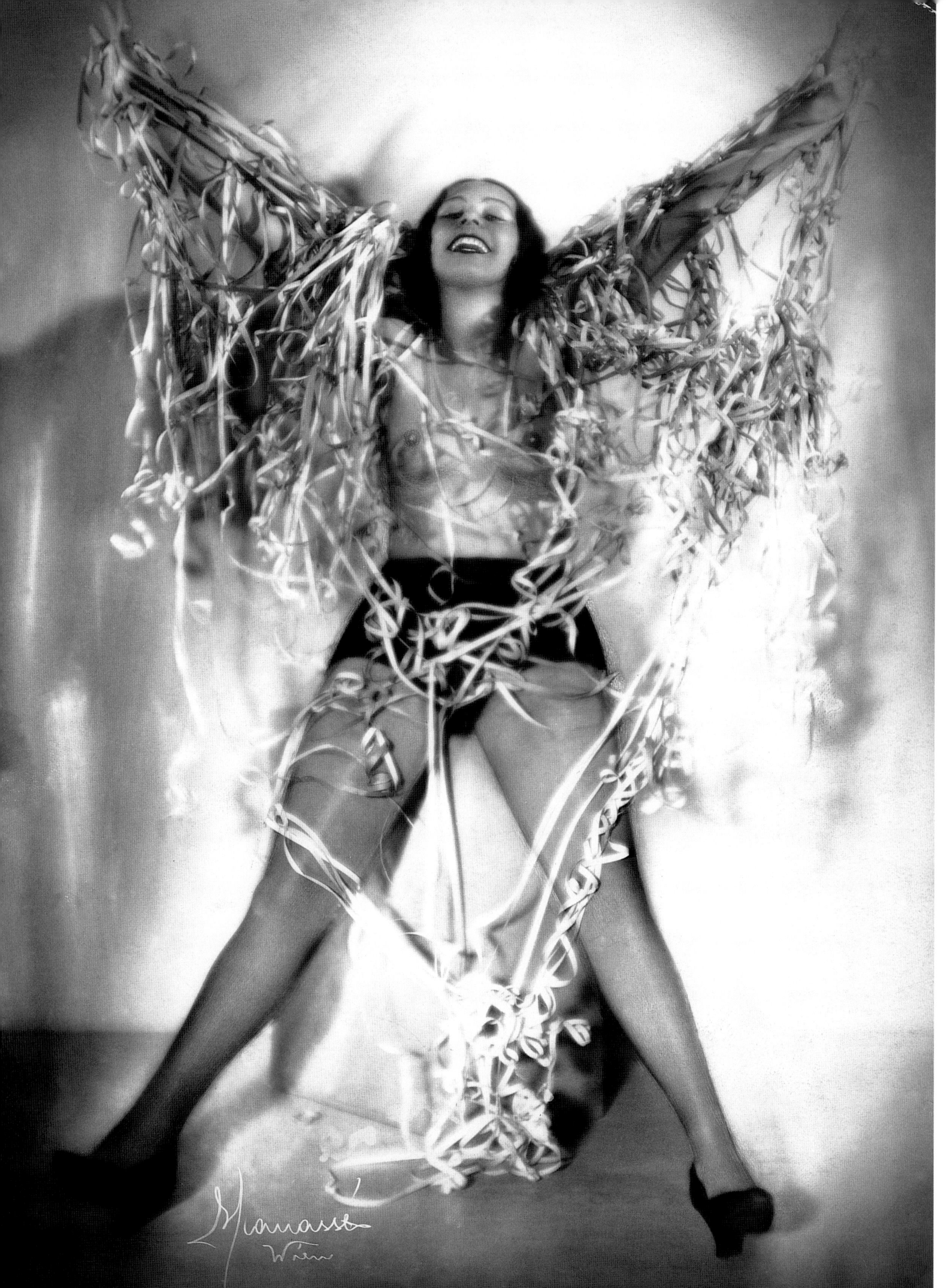
Manassé
Wien

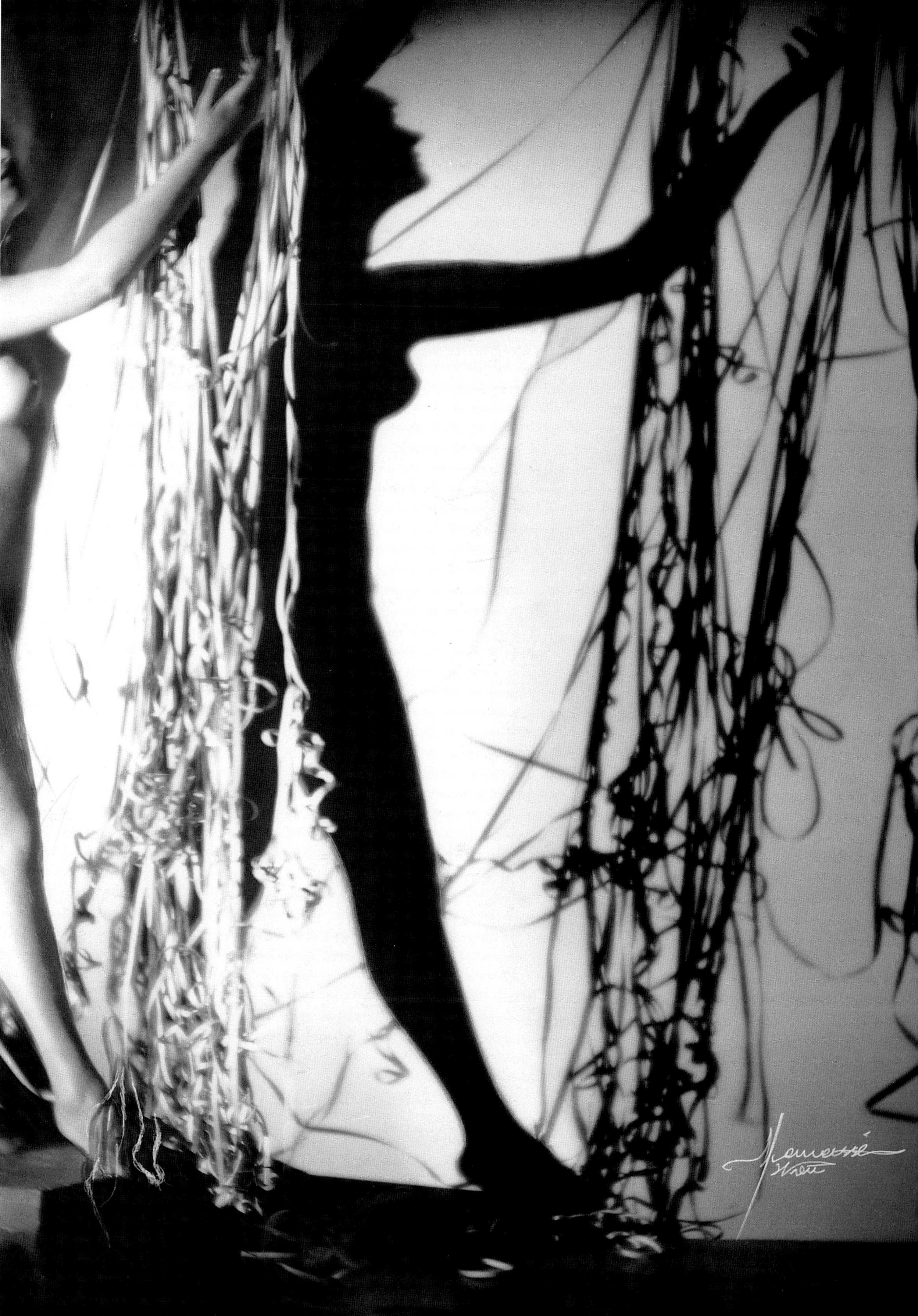

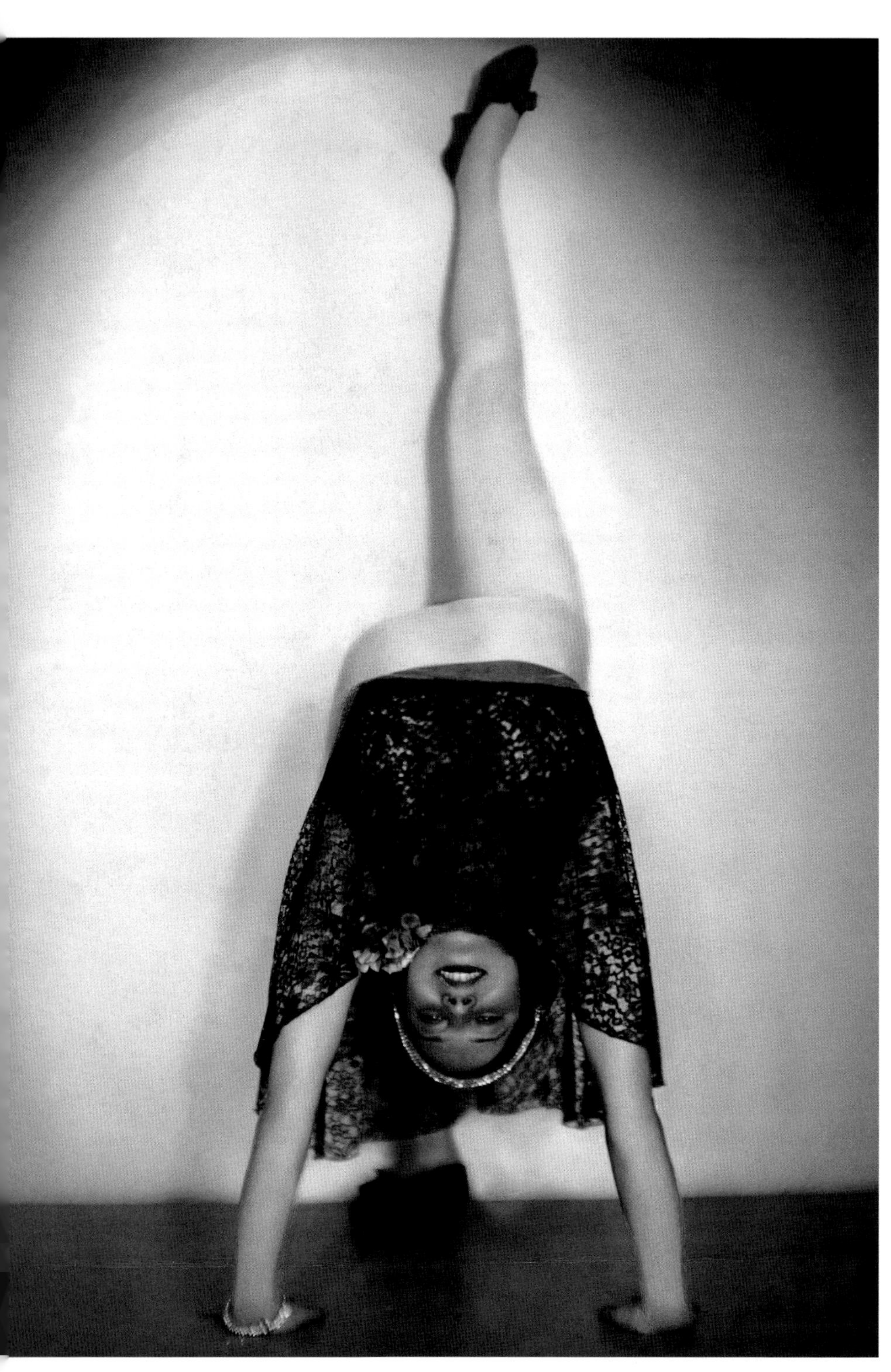

Previous two pages: Study, c.1931; Study, c.1926; this page: Hildegard Thiele, c.1928

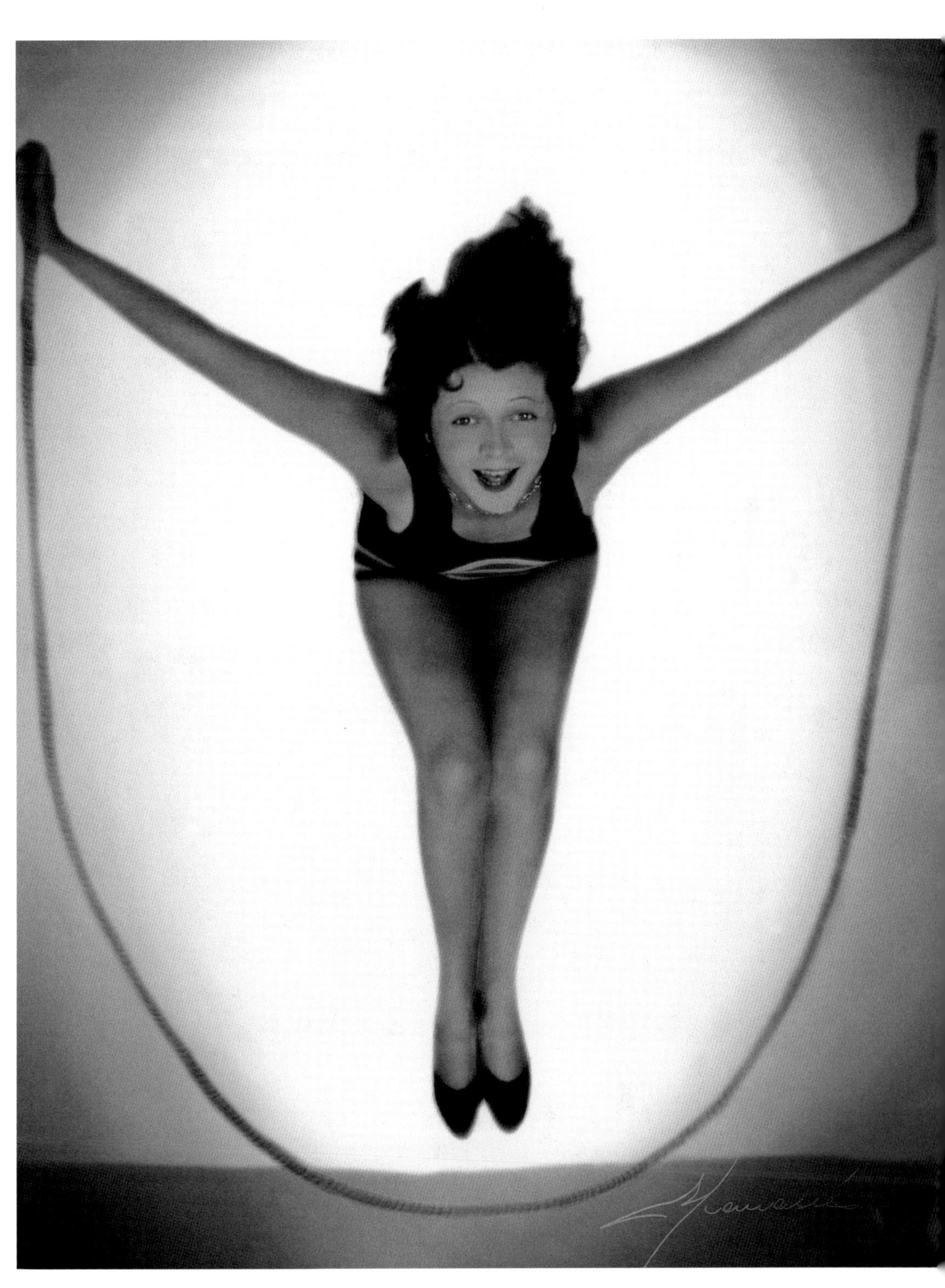

Ruth Gold, c.1928

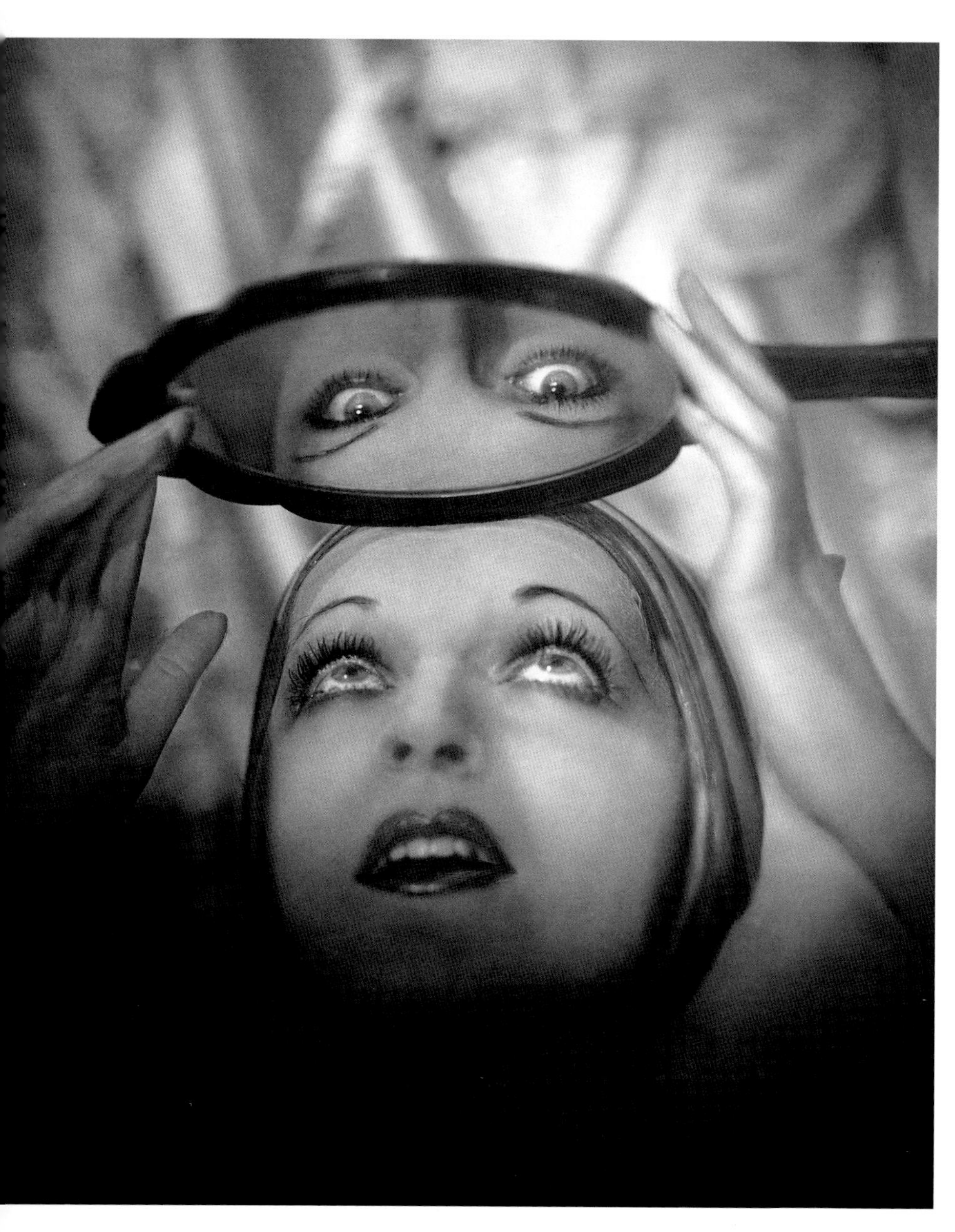

Study, c.1931; Study, c.1928; next two pages: Tala Birell, c.1928; 3 Postcards, 1922–1928

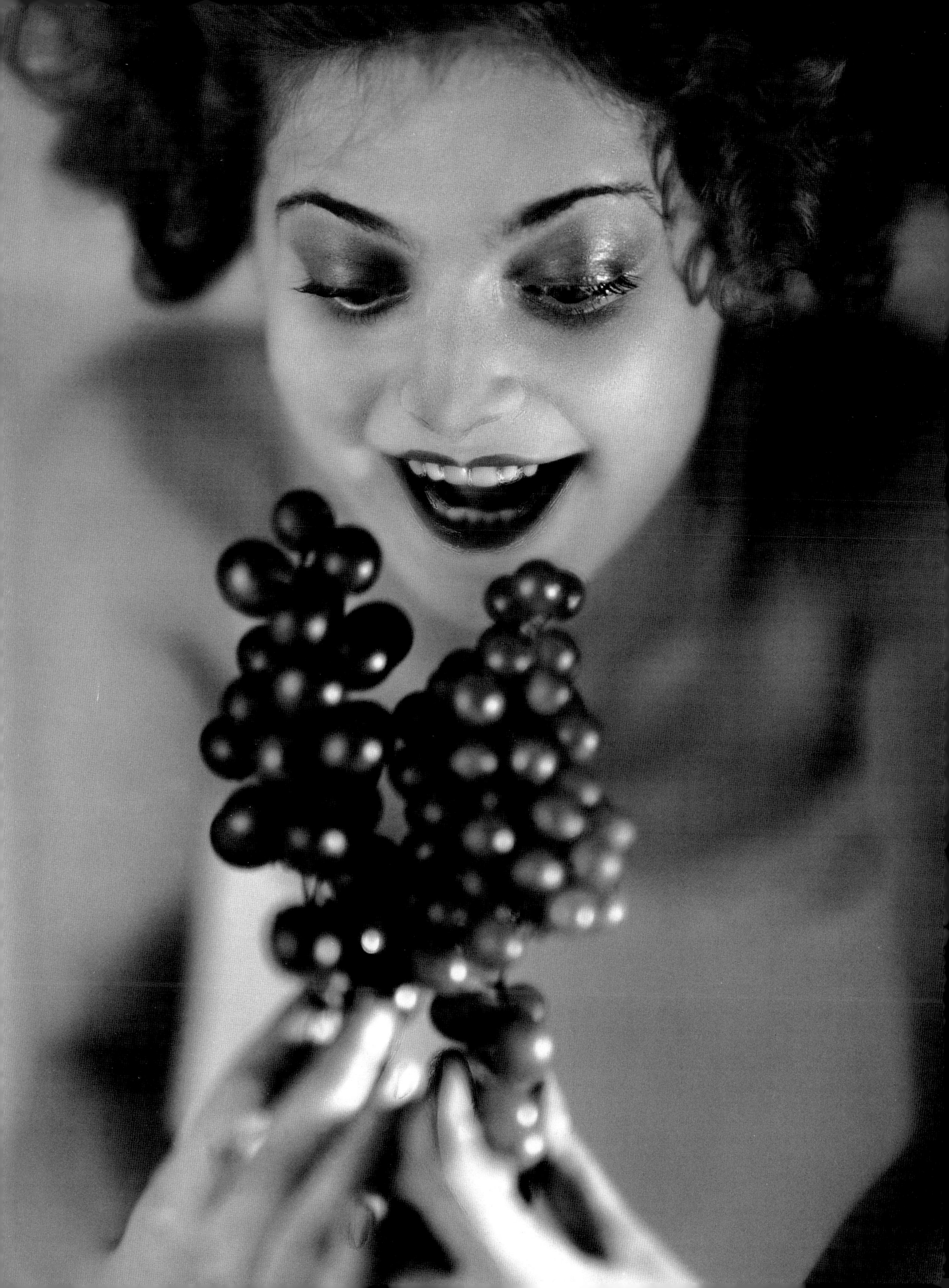

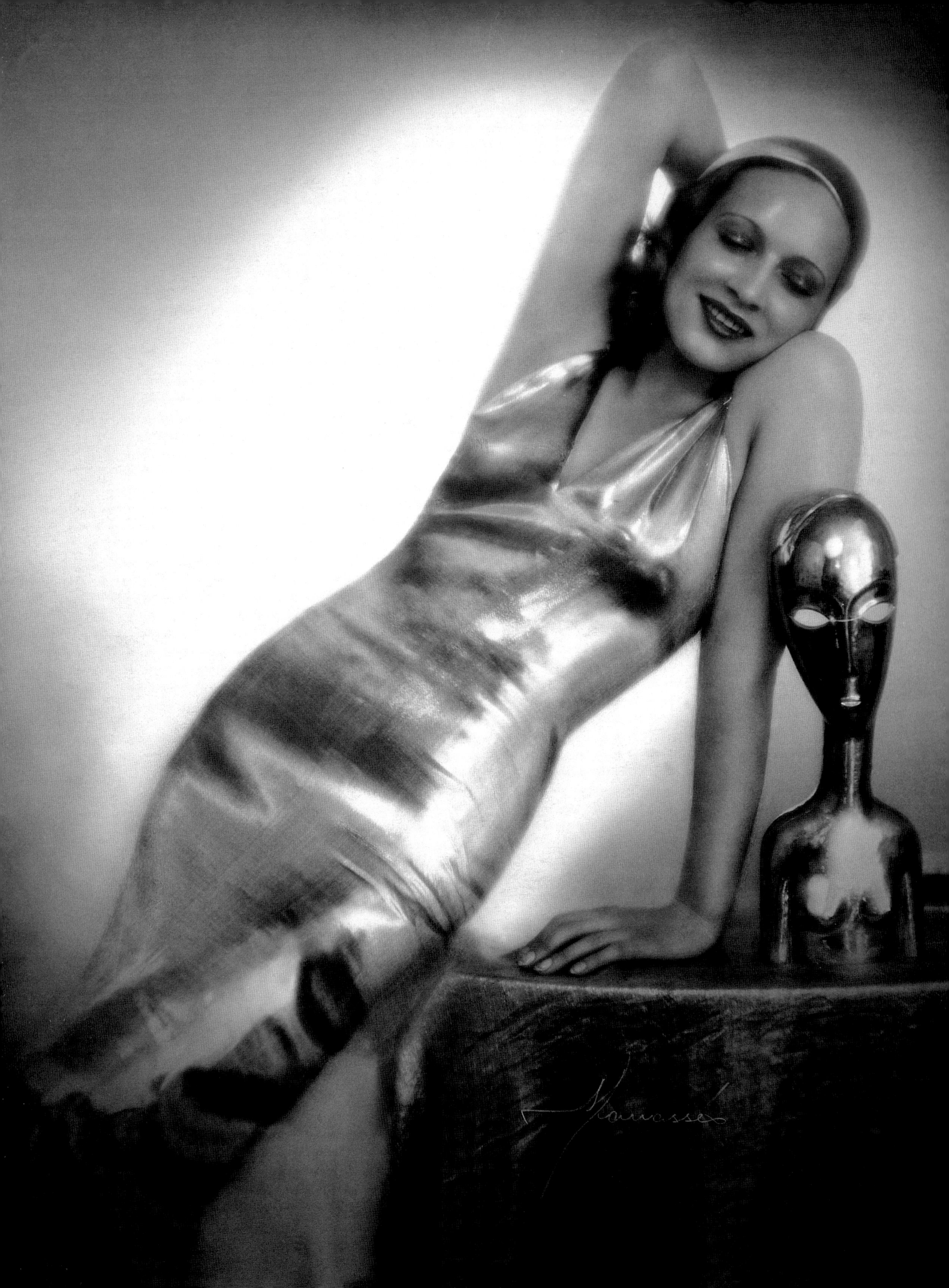
Manassé

THE FILM STAR IN FRONT OF THE PHOTOGRAPHER'S CAMERA

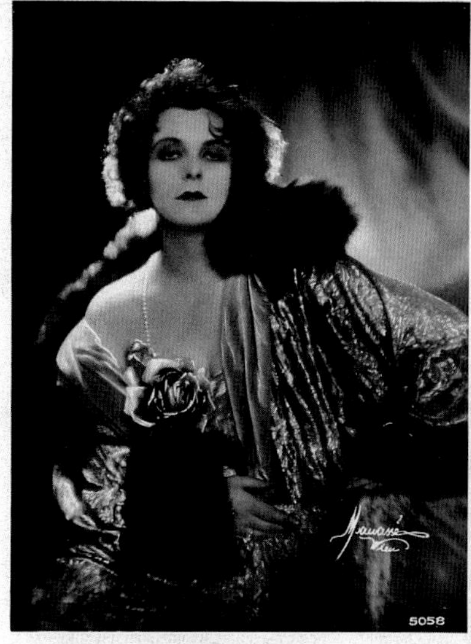
Ruth Weyher

„Iris Verlag"

Other important partners of the Manassé studio were Ross-Verlag in Berlin and the smaller Iris-Verlag in Vienna, which distributed portraits of stars in postcard format from a variety of sources throughout the German-speaking area. These postcards seem to have had an enormous circulation to judge from the frequency with which they turn up today at flea markets and in shops specializing in such items.

Among the earliest surviving photographs with the trademark signature *"Manassé"* are portraits of personalities from the world of film, theater, opera, and vaudeville. Among them are leading ladies from Sascha-Film productions: Magda Sonja (*Um ein Weib,* 1918), Lucy Doraine (*Sodom und Gomorrha,* 1922), Maria Korda (*Samsom und Delila,* 1922), and Lily Damita (*Das Spielzeug von Paris/*Red Heels, 1925)—and singers and dancers from the Vienna Staatsoper (Maria Nemeth, Hedy Pfundmayr). This list could go on and on over the years, with names of actors and actresses still well known today: Vilma Banky, Lil Dagover, Liane Haid, Hedi Kiesler-Mandl (who, as Hedy Lamarr, later became famous for one of the first nude appearances in film history), Anna May Wong, and Olga Tschechowa.

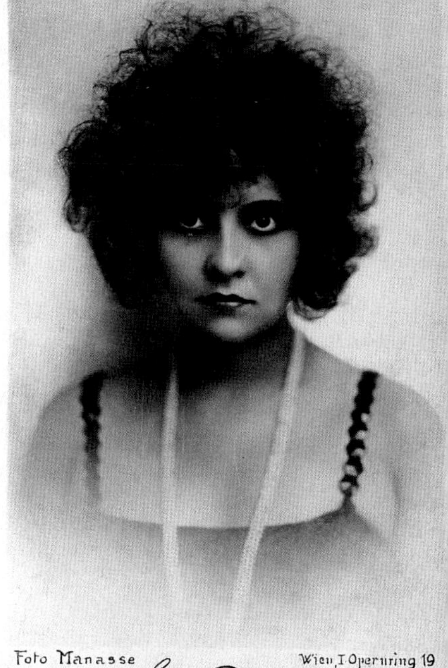
Foto Manasse Wien, I Operring 19

Lucy Doraine

We can only speculate about why and how the Wlassics were able to acquire so many clients from the film world. The most plausible answer seems to be that they benefited from the fact that their move from Budapest to Vienna in 1919–20 coincided with the departure of many other personalities who were leaving Hungary because of changing political conditions—first the Communist takeover by Béla Kun, then the Nikolaus Horthy regime. For several years, these people dominated filmmaking in Vienna before they moved on to Berlin and then to Hollywood or England. Among them were Michael Kertész (later Curtiz) and Alexander Korda, directors who turned the first clients of Studio Manassé into stars. There were also actors and actresses like Vilma Banky, Maria Korda, Michael Varkonji, and Béla Balázs, who began to work for *Muskete* as a film critic at the same time the first Wlassics photographs appeared.

Although Béla Balázs wrote the first aesthetic theory of motion pictures in 1924, he did not go as deeply into the subject of photography. Therefore, we will cite his somewhat younger colleague, Siegfried Kracauer, for a contemporary assessment of the effect of the star portraits. His text dates to 1927, the beginning of the heyday of Studio Manassé:

> "This is what a film star looks like. She is 24 years old and is pictured on the cover of an illustrated magazine [standing] in front of the Hotel Excelsior on the Lido. It's September. Looking through a magnifying glass, you can see the screen, the millions of dots that compose the star, the waves, and the hotel. But we are not referring to the network of dots when we speak of the picture; rather we mean the living star on the Lido. Time: the present. The accompanying text calls her demonic, our demonic star. Despite that she does not lack a certain expressiveness. The bangs, the seductive tilt of the

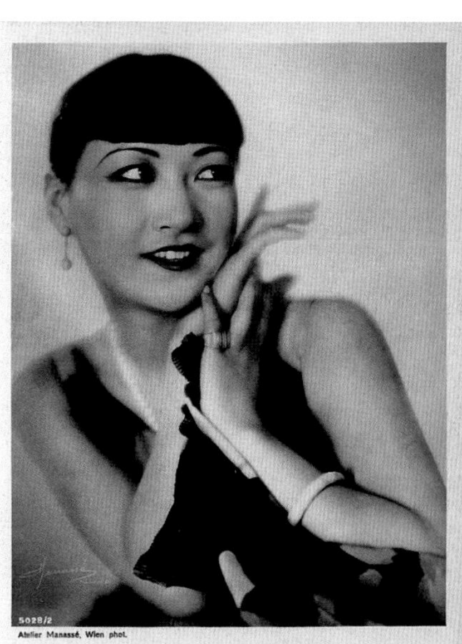
5028/2
Atelier Manassé, Wien phot.

Anna May Wong

„Ross" Verlag Reproduction verboten

Study, c.1936; Hella Gerth, c.1934; next two pages: Study, c.1934; Ossi Roudie, c.1925

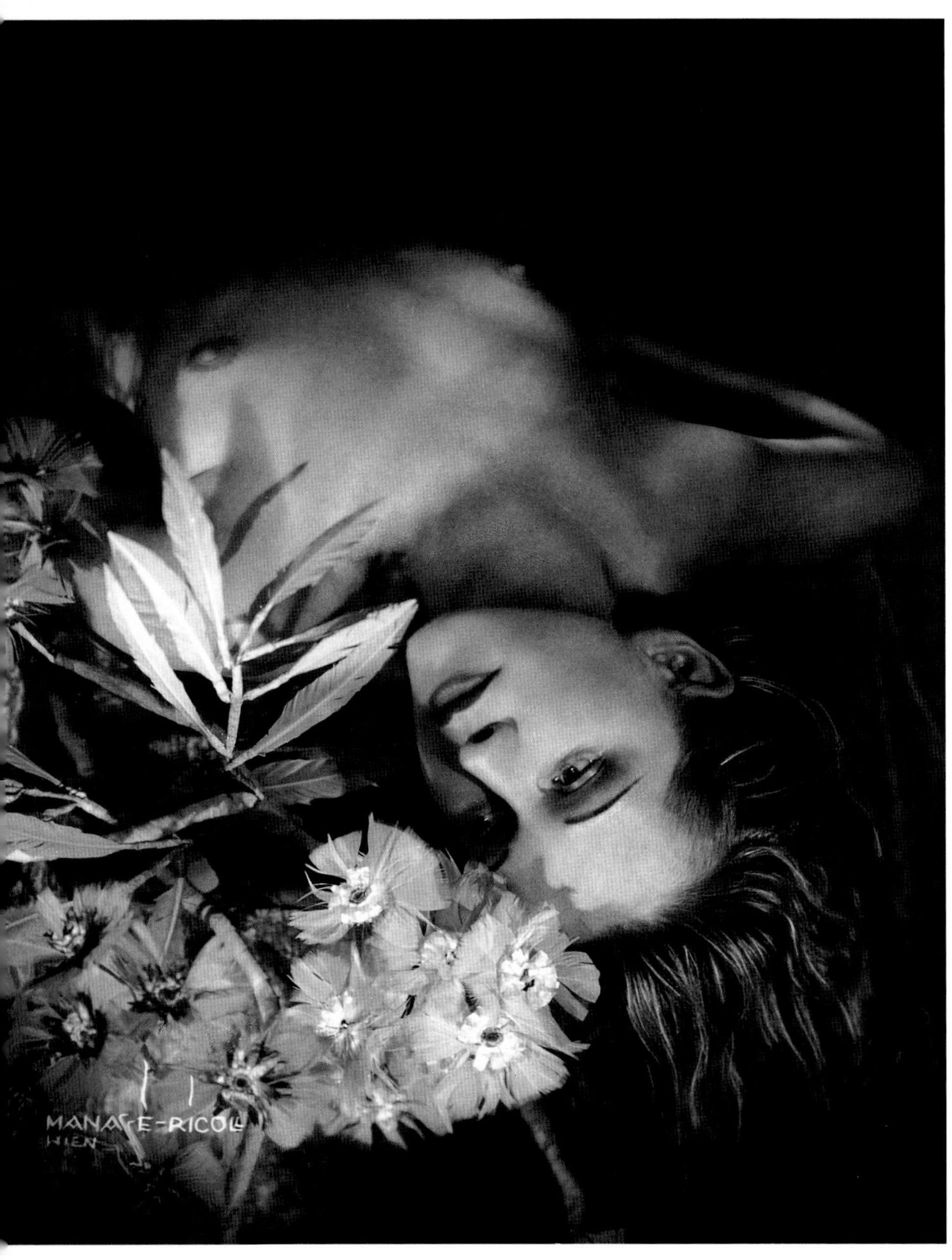

head, and the twelve eyelashes right and left—all the details conscientiously registered by the camera are properly placed in space, a vision. Everyone recognizes her and is charmed, for everyone has already seen the original on the [movie] screen. ... The contemporary observer believes that he is seeing the film star herself in the photograph, not only her bangs or the tilt of her head. Of course he cannot appreciate her just from the photograph. Luckily the star is alive, and the cover of the magazine serves to remind people of her physical reality. That is to say, current photography acts as an intermediary; it is an optical symbol for the star, for her essence. In the end one might have some doubts that her most prominent characteristic is demoniacal. The demonic however is less a statement by the photograph than an impression perceived by moviegoers who experience the original on the screen. They easily recognize it as a representation of the demonic. ..."

This description points up the projective nature of such pictures. The photo of the star and also the star herself are primarily symbols, syntheses of production and wishful thinking. Every visual perception consists, on the one hand, of elements of prior knowledge or expectation and, on the other, of the object itself within a certain context. This unique projection in a picture of what is intended, namely the synthetic "star" instead of a human being with certain characteristics, requires some clarification.

During the early years of filmmaking practically no actors' credits were given; filmmakers

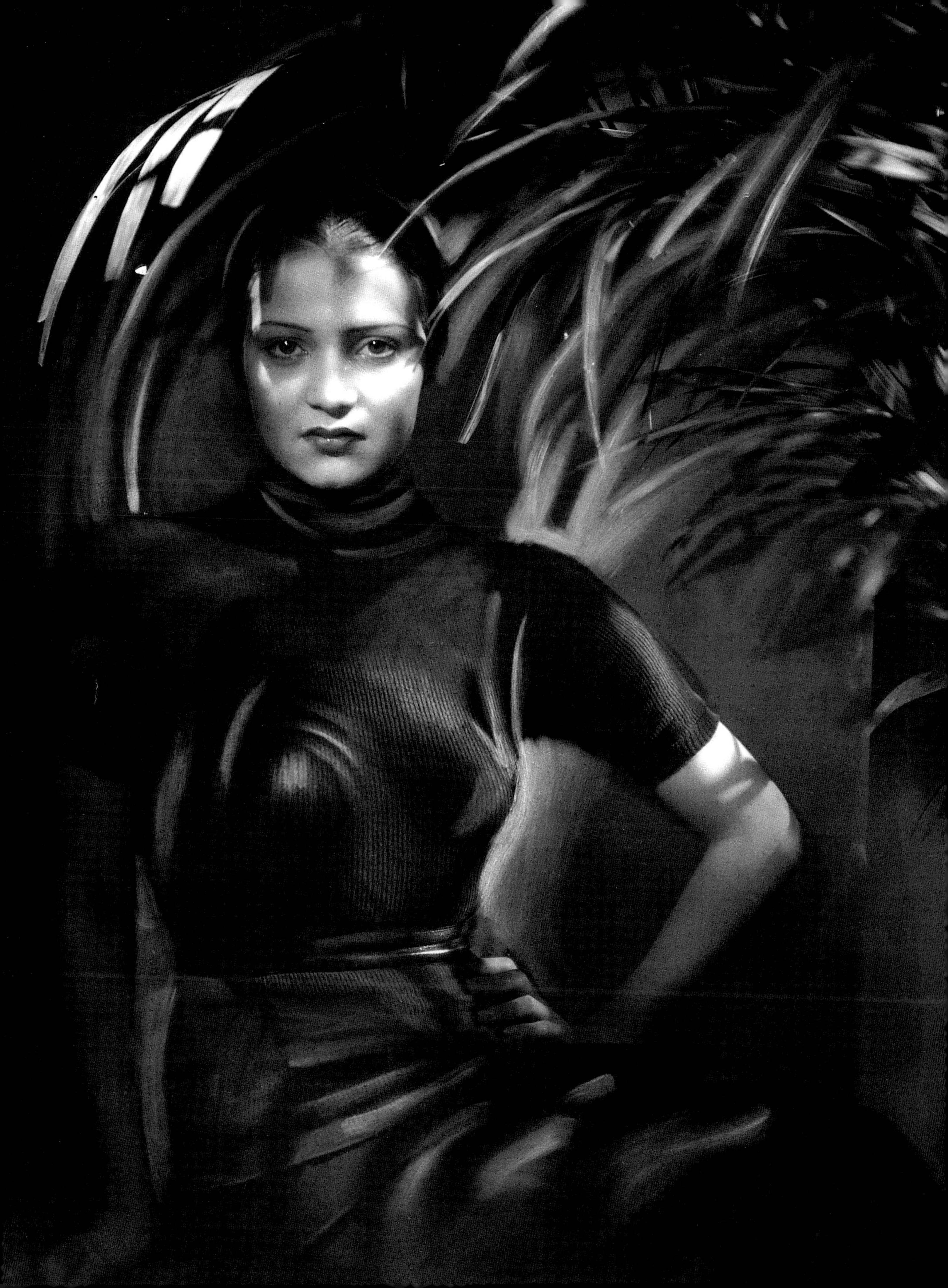

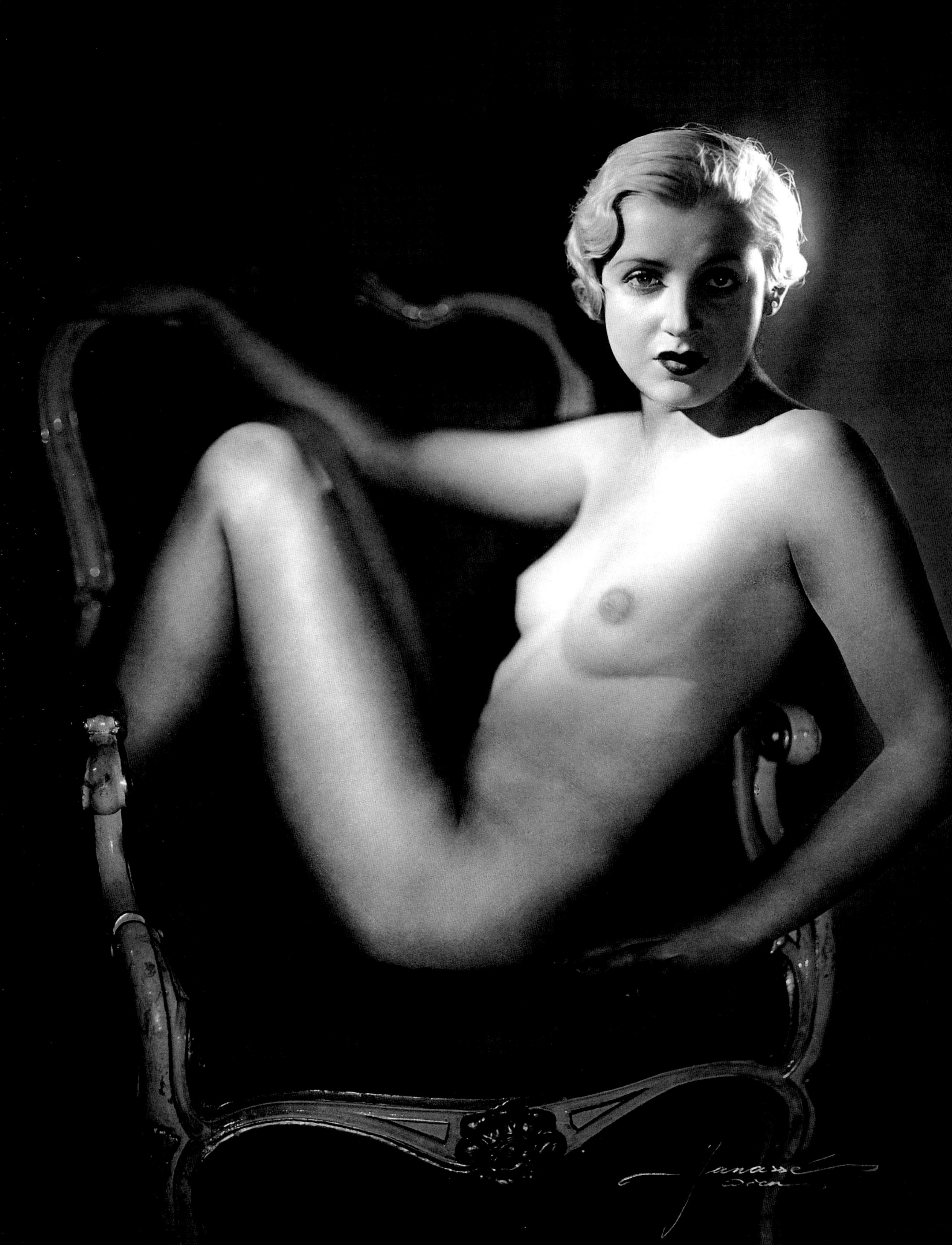

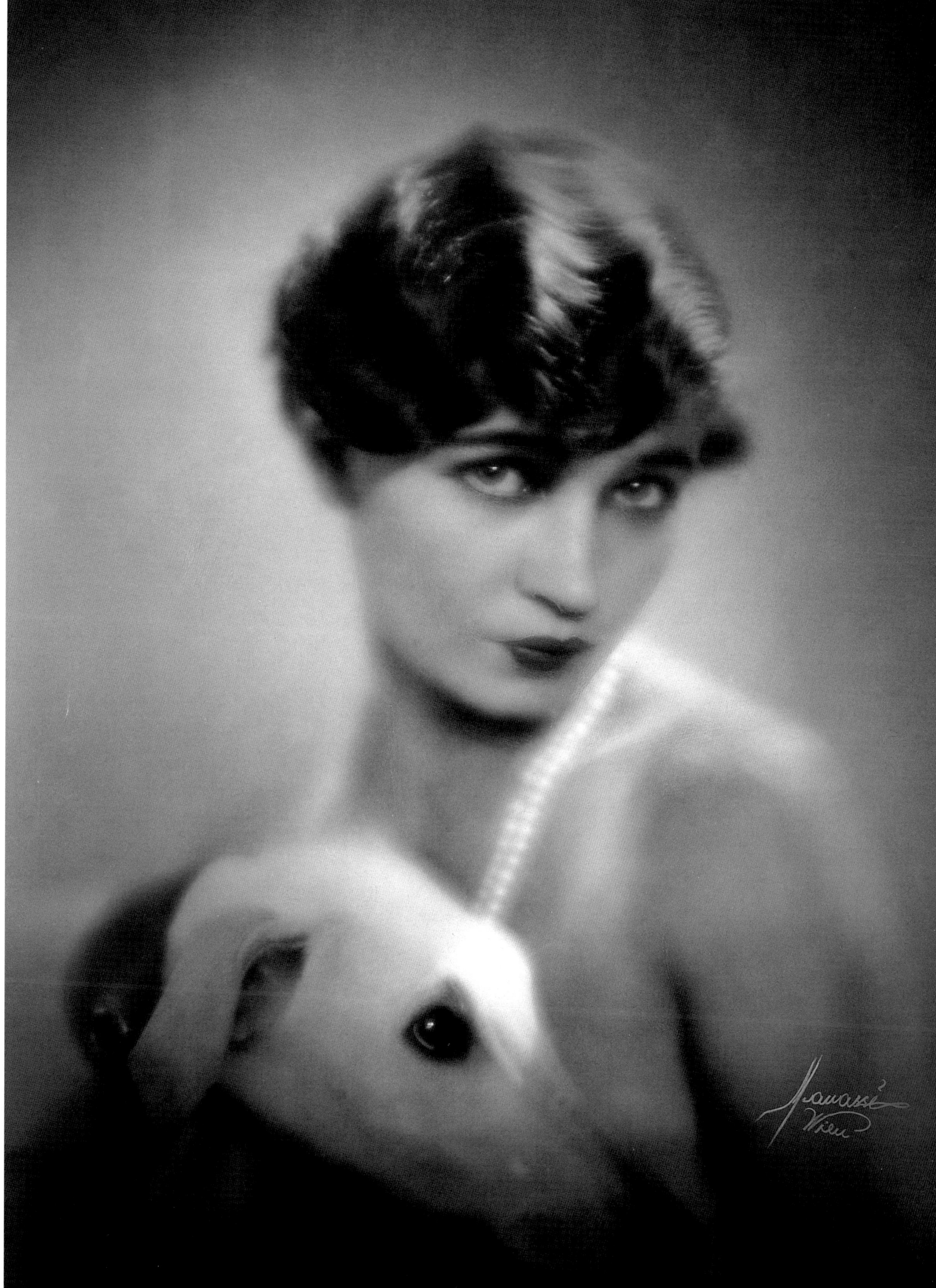
Manassé
Wien

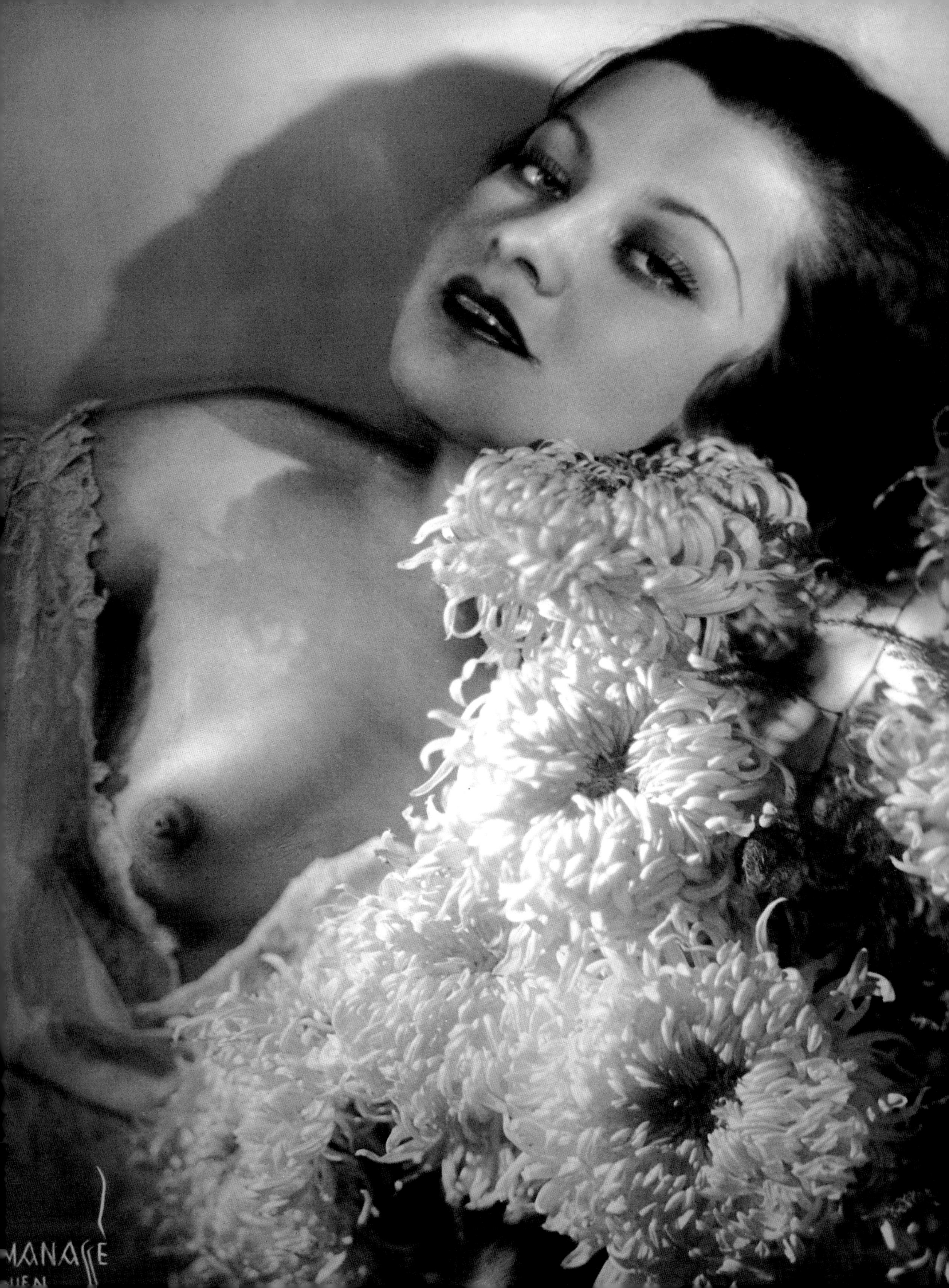
MANASSE

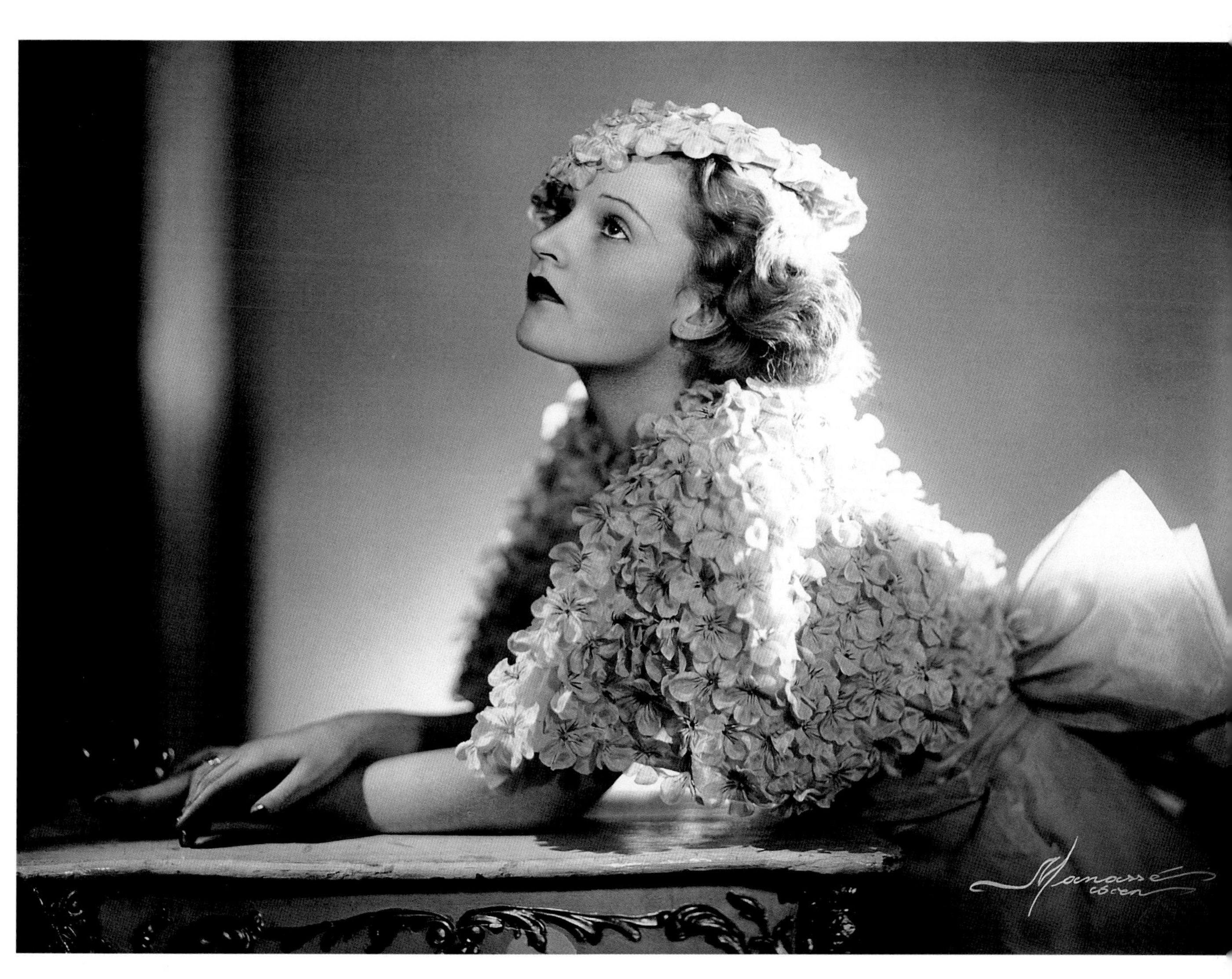

Study, c.1934; Sari Gabor, c.1933

Study, c.1931; Betty Bird, c.1926

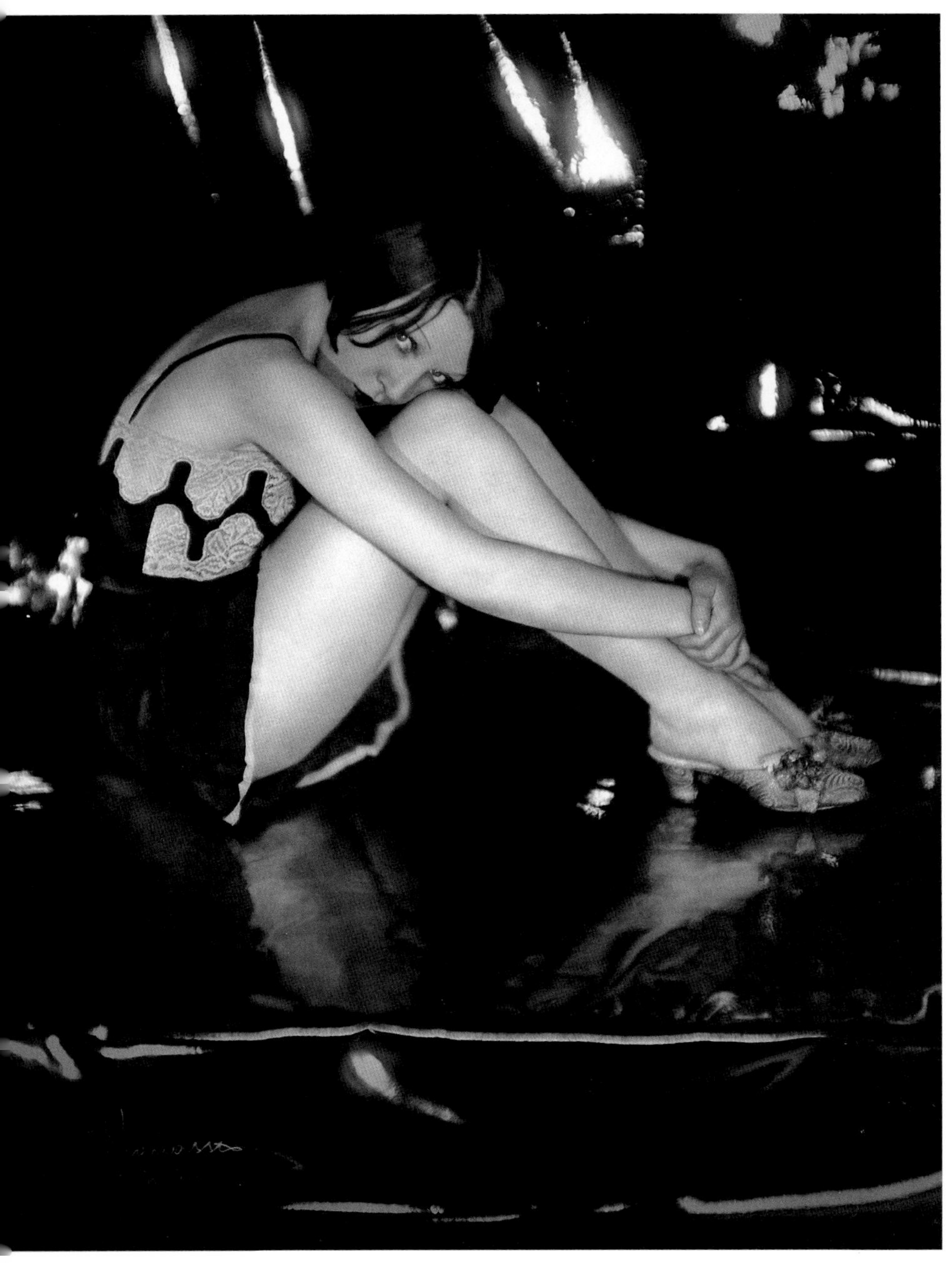

worked with "types" rather than with individuals. But the public—especially writers and journalists—who worshiped the Duse or Isadora Duncan as "divine artists" was not satisfied with anonymous performers. At the same time the first mimes became prominent in the young, still silent, medium; they knew how to act in the larger-than-life style appropriate to films. Theda Bara in the United States and Magda Sonja and Liane Haid in Vienna created role types—Bara's demonic-exotic vamp or Haid's sweet Viennese girl—that were very well received by the public and were used in film after film with only slight modifications. Thus as early as 1916, the United States film industry intentionally followed a policy of reinforcing the identification of performers with the particular stereo-types they embodied on the screen. Whether demonic or naive, funny or exotic, tomboyish or lady-like, the stars claimed as their own qualities from a successful film role and even carried these over into their private lives with the help of imaginative publicity releases and lavishly staged and retouched photographs.

The first photography departments were established in 1920 for this purpose exclusively by film studios in Los Angeles. In the course of a few years they developed a photographic style that quickly became identified with the idea of "glamour" and, like the silent films themselves, was understood on both sides of the Atlantic. This phenomenon of a visual language that was intended to have a wide influence and was used on an international scale differed essentially from all precedents in traditional visual culture. At least two components of different social dimensions were essential for its development: first, the radical political and social changes occurring in all of Europe in the first two decades of the twentieth century, and second, the fact that the world of print media, less inhibited by tradition than painting or the theater, broke with time-honored conventions and went out to explore new territory. At such a time of political change, the different visual cultures that crossed

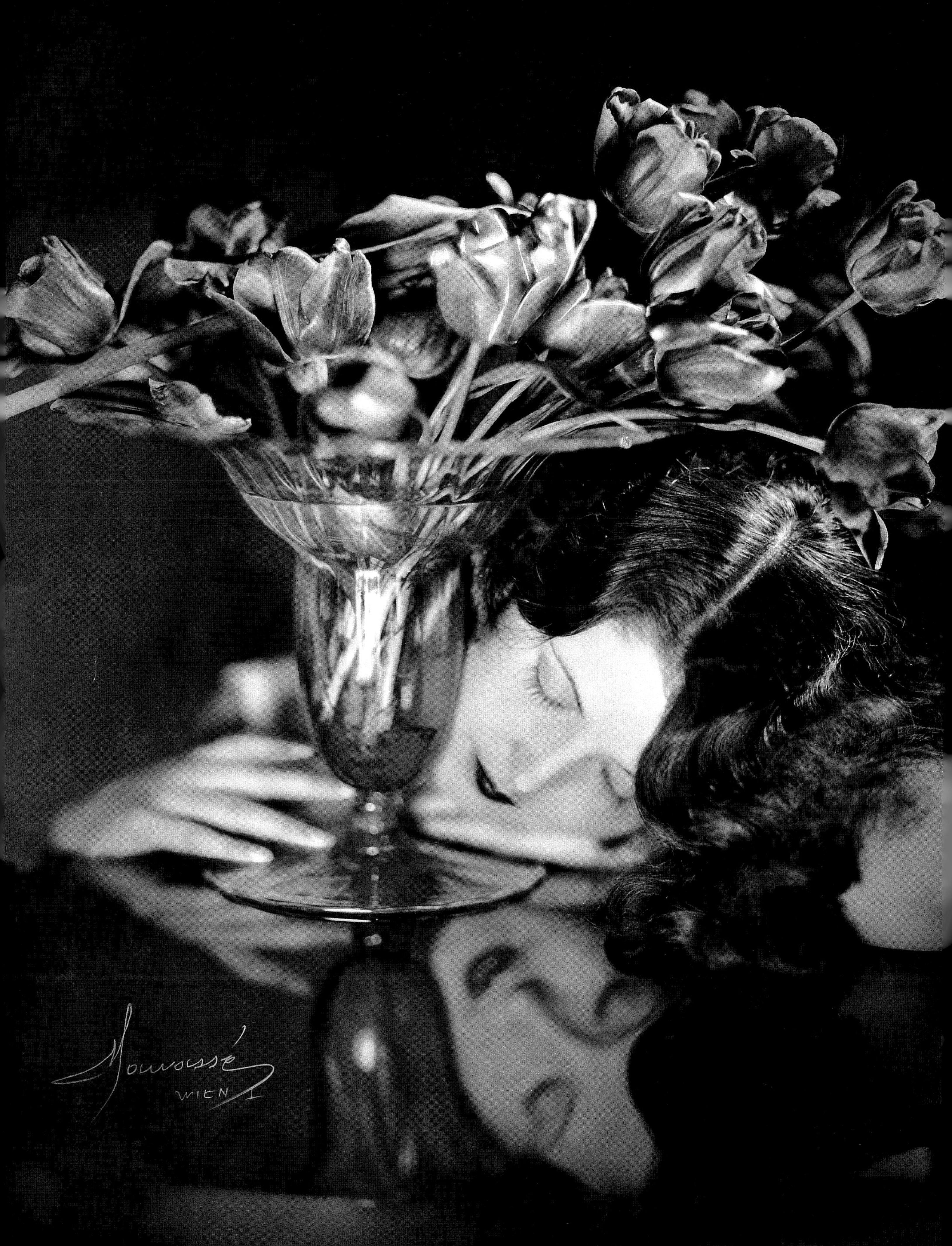
Manassé
WIEN I

Unknown photographer, Rudolf Valentino, c.1922; Ben Torren, c.1927; Tala Birell, the Viennese Greta Garbo, c.1927

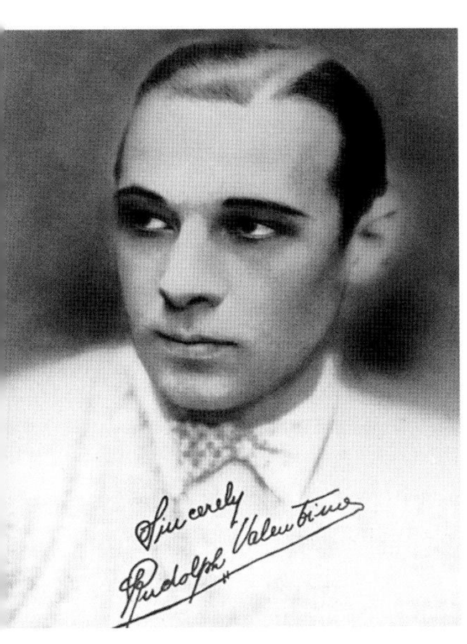

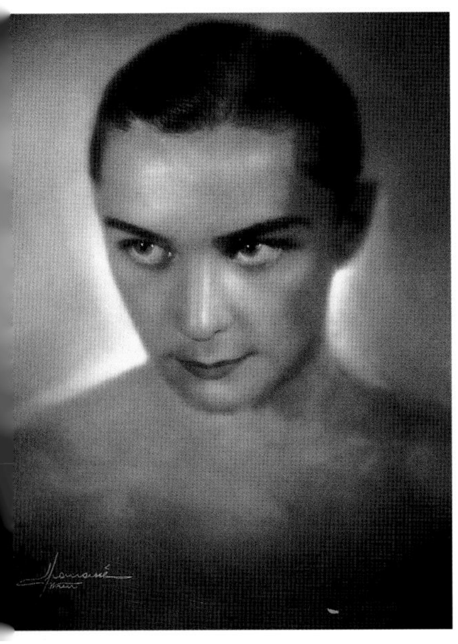

international borders strongly affected each other. The international nature of silent film was not simply due to the fact that the pictures could be understood by everyone, but rather was the result of a methodical international distribution of these pictures. "On the whole, silent films did not start out with an international vocabulary of visual impressions, they headed toward it," was how Siegfried Kracauer in 1931 described the peculiar relationship of pictures and motifs in the films of the previous decade. From the mid-twenties on, film distribution was, more and more, becoming contractually paved into a one-way street that led from Hollywood to Europe—a route to transport a new picture language. Distribution of films was not the only thing that functioned in this way. Photographs in magazines had their own reinforcing effect on the moving and, in a sensory way, more evanescent picture. In English-speaking areas during the late Victorian period there were already magazines dedicated in various ways to the cult of the stars. Content ranged from theater gossip to sanctimonious condemnation of the reported "permissiveness" of vaudeville performers and early film stars. All illustrated by photographs that were more or less "daring" for the times. In 1923, against the backdrop of a burgeoning film industry in Germany and elsewhere, F. W. Koebner imported this commercially successful publishing recipe-formula to Berlin. Within a few months his weekly, *Das Magazin,* had a circulation of 100,000 and was much imitated. With the advent of such magazines, glamour pictures made in the United States also found their way to Europe, with Austria a ready market. UFA (Universum-Film AG) engaged its own photographer, and several studios in major cities where films were being produced and magazines published—Berlin, Prague, and Vienna—now served the growing market of the star cult.

In concert with actresses, photographers, and magazines, and surely with the approval of the film industry, a dual strategy of imitation was followed. Stars and aspiring stars patterned their dress, hairstyles, and poses on famous, mostly American, models. Along with this purposeful agreement in motifs there was also an attempt to transmit certain already molded star types, so-called standards that lent themselves to variations. First Rudolf Valentino, later Greta Garbo and Marlene Dietrich—the big stars—got their "doubles." It was not even important for the viewer to make the connection between the original and the copy. This connection was often mentioned directly in the caption. During repeated photo sessions over the years in the Manassé studio, Tala Birell, "the Viennese Greta Garbo," kept looking over and over again into the camera with veiled eyes and an expression of melancholy on her lips. She worked hard to obtain her title.

Film roles not only formed peoples' ideas about the behavior and character of certain performers, but also brought across (in Kraucauer's sense) many new formulations or reformulations of old picture concepts. Béla Balázs had already mentioned this phenomenon in 1924 in his book *Der sichtbare Mensch oder Die Kultur des Films* (The Visible Person or The Culture of Film). Thus many motifs of the waning nineteenth century—symbolism, decadence, and the beginnings of expressionism—developed into a variety of long-running themes in filmmaking. Such themes were exploited, from the myth of the femme fatale and the subjects of popular romantic paintings by Hugo Höppener, to the new enthusiasm for antique and exotic objects from the

Near or Far East. Many films were made with an extravagance in both expenditure and effect unknown up to that time. Similar styles of dress, poses, and accessories were also reflected in the still photos and studio portraits of the stars. One of the most famous photos of Garbo, used to promote the film *Mata Hari,* shows not only the actress wearing her exotic costume, but also in the background a huge Asiatic statue, which today seems more like a late-expressionist sculpture. The effect of this threatening demonic male figure is not so much that of an incidental piece but rather that of the possessive companion of the exotic slender-boned dancer, a contrast that brings to mind innumerable associations. This theme—a more or less naked woman with a larger-than-life-size male sculpture—also found its way into some Studio Manassé photographs, but here the subliminal aggression is played down. Instead of dynamism there is ornamentation of the motif. Thus one of the decisive factors in the "harmlessness" of these Manassé pictures lies in the emphasis on the contrast between the apparently live woman and the wooden idol. In the Studio Manassé photos, the women were retouched to look like dolls, linking them with the Hollywood pictures of the time. Recently published anthologies, based on extensive American archives, suggest that the "period style" in the pictures as well as in the images of actors was more a product created by their distributors—the studios themselves as well as the editors of magazines—than by the models and photographers.

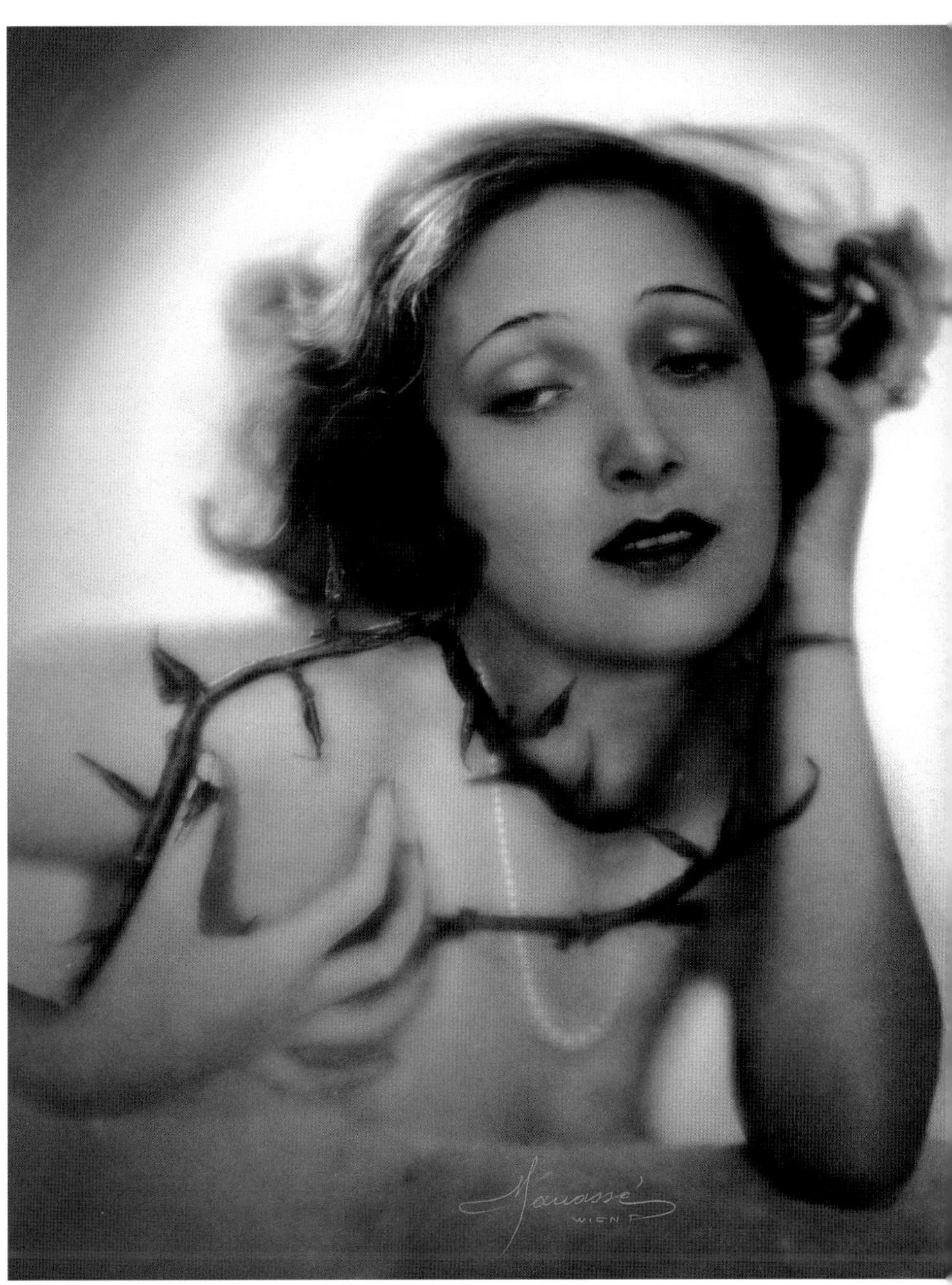

Similarly, the selection in this volume of Manassé pictures is the product of a changed esthetic interest. As far as these pictures are concerned, part of the change resulted from the fact that many illustrated magazines revised their layouts in the early thirties. Pictures that were dropped into the text in an optically exciting position on facing pages displaced the "classic" pattern of photographs surrounded by white borders. At the same time there

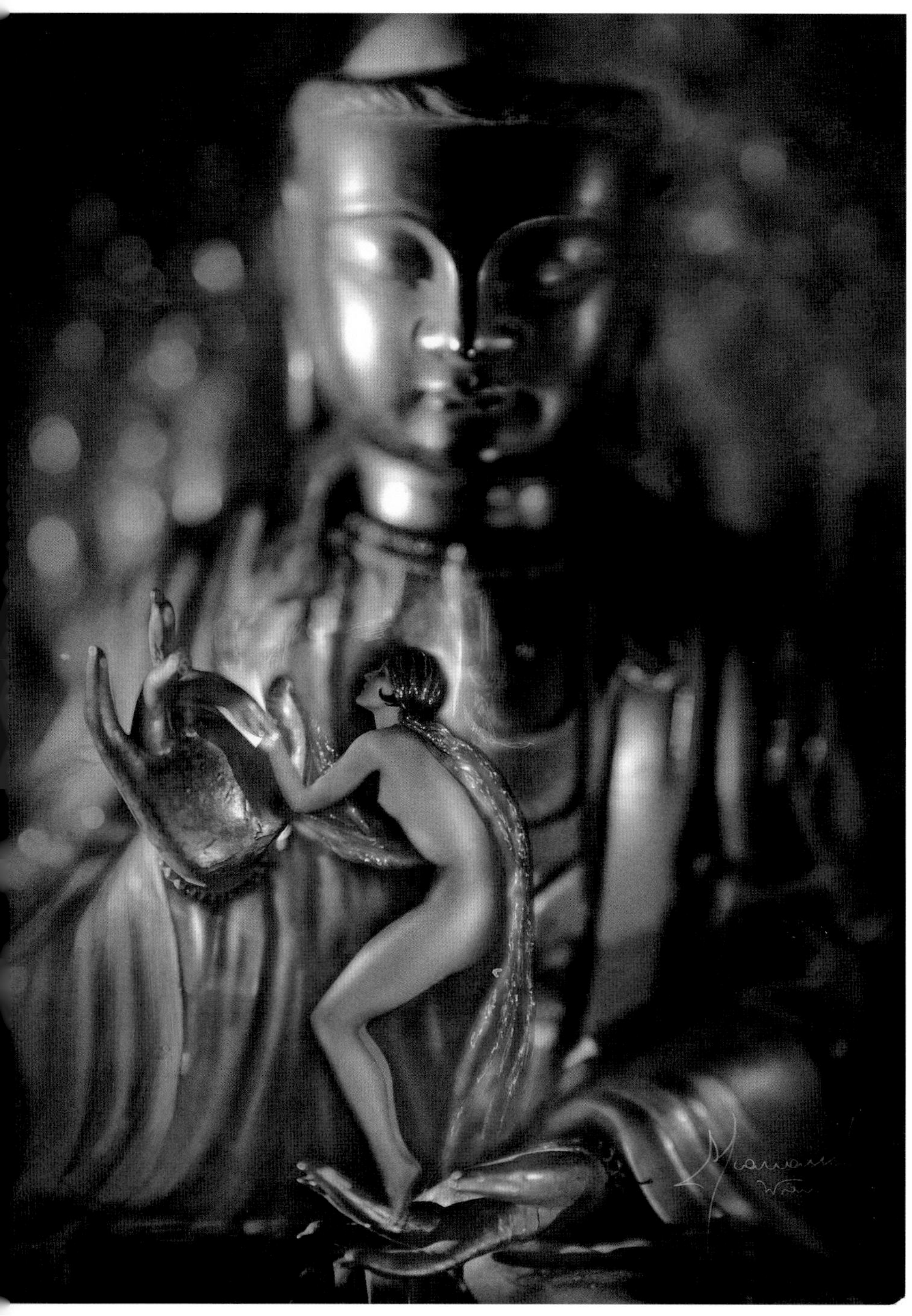

were more close-up shots with heads often filling the entire page, and in photographs of nudes there was often fragmentation of the body. These changes may be seen as an emulation of avant-garde tendencies in photography and also the result perhaps of lessening interest in the narrative and informative aspects of illustrations in favor of visual variety.

Ariman Banu, c.1931; Study, c.1931; next two pages: Study, c.1933; Study, c.1934

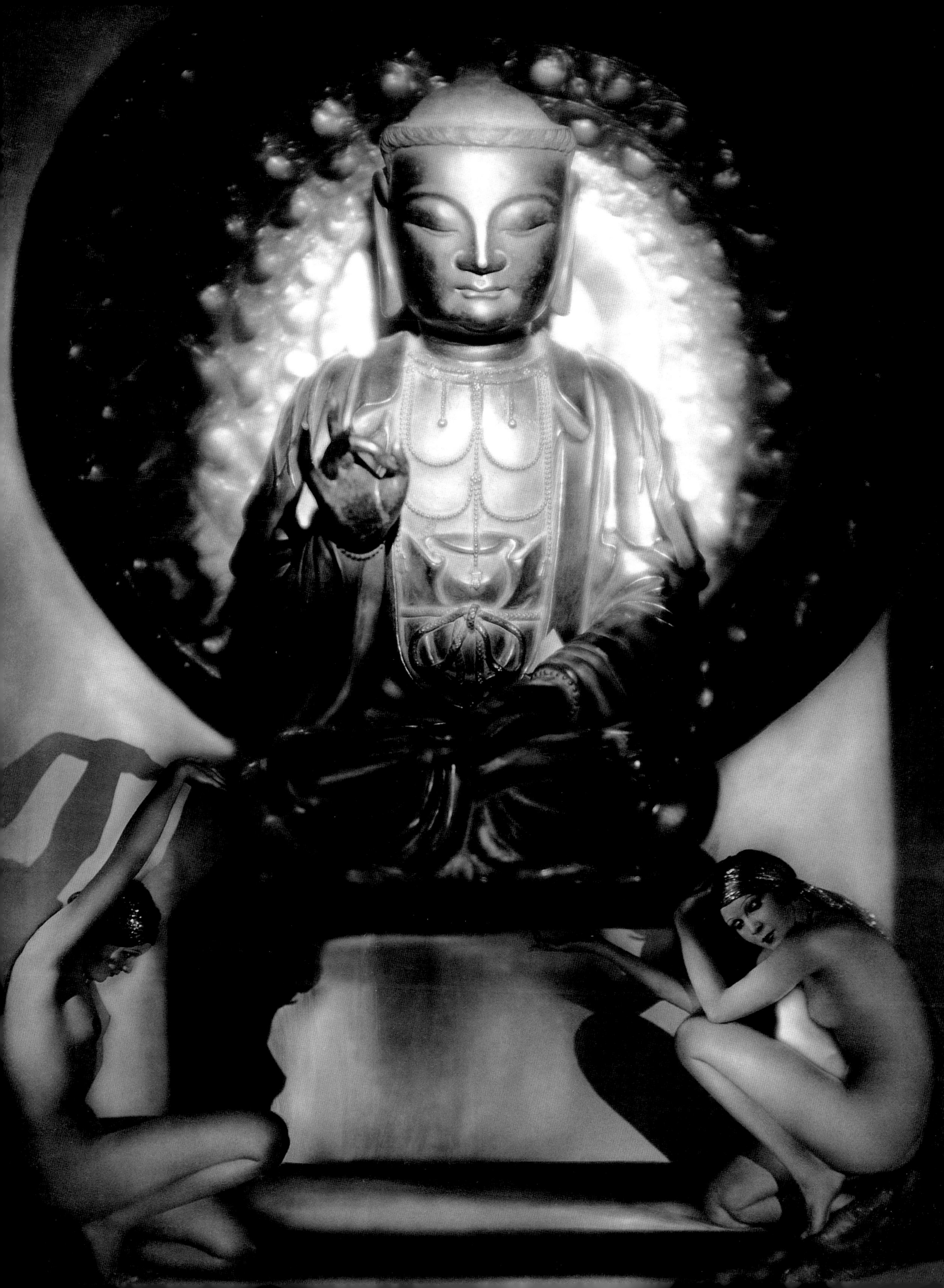

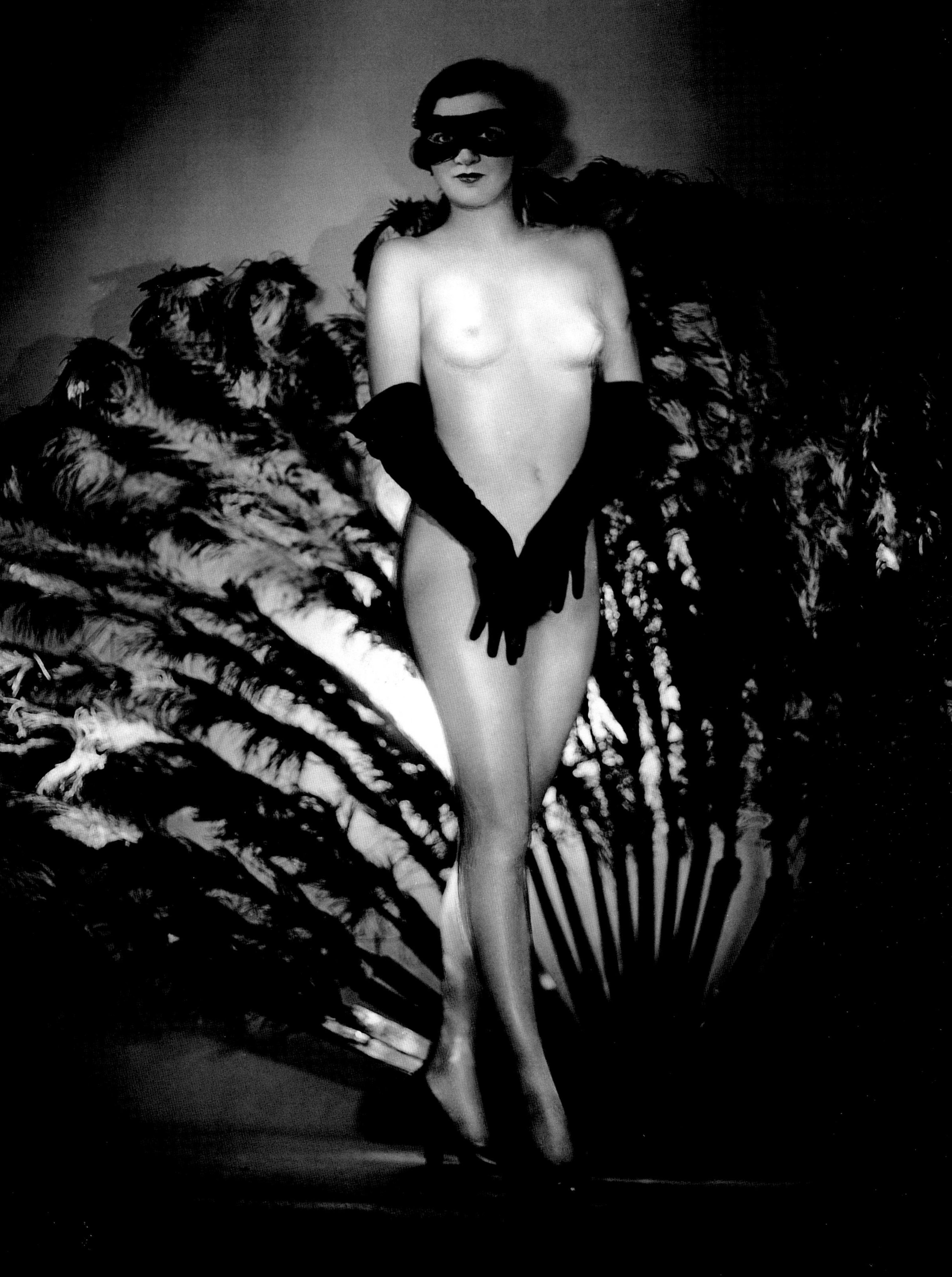

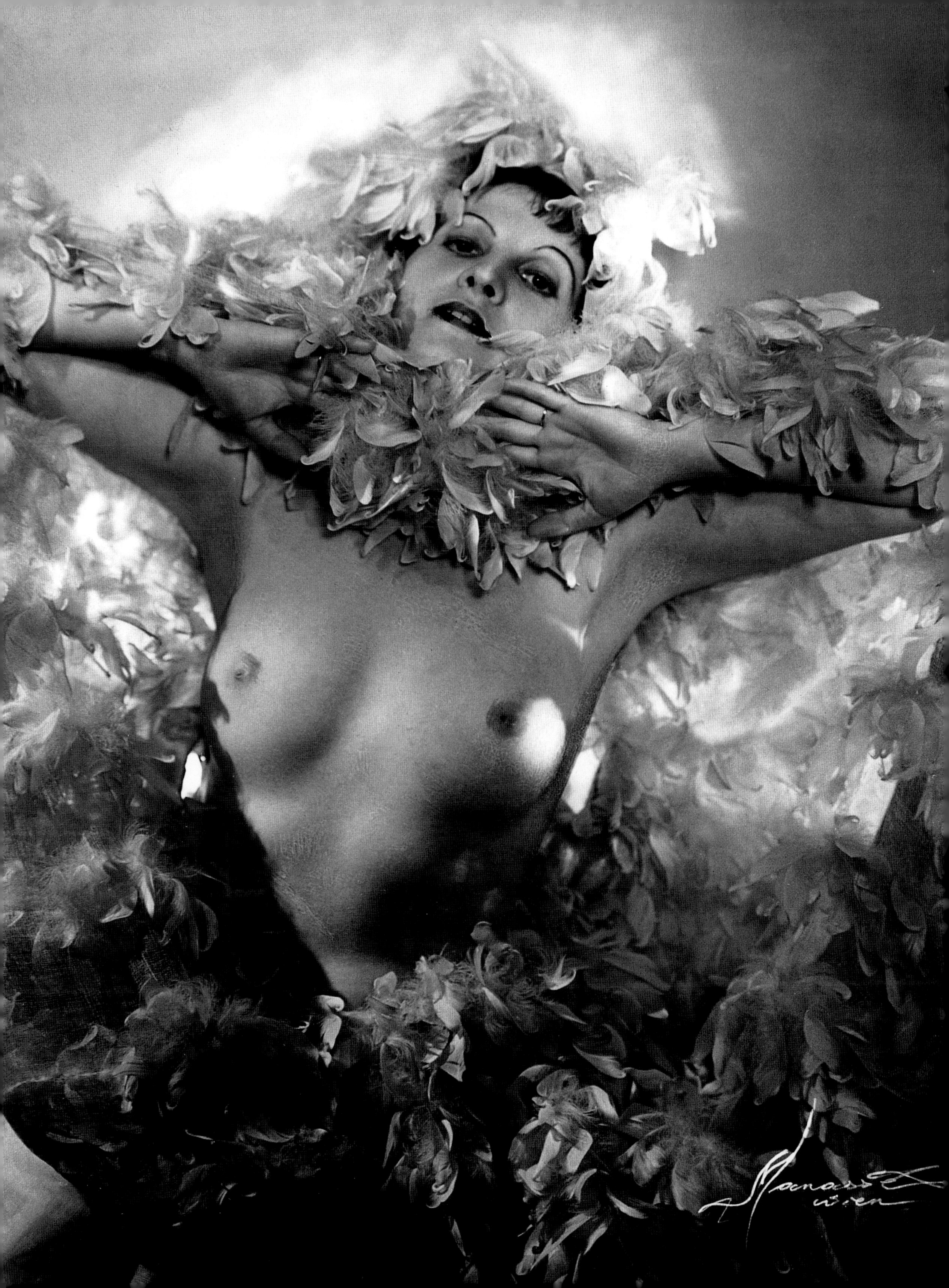
Manasse
Wien

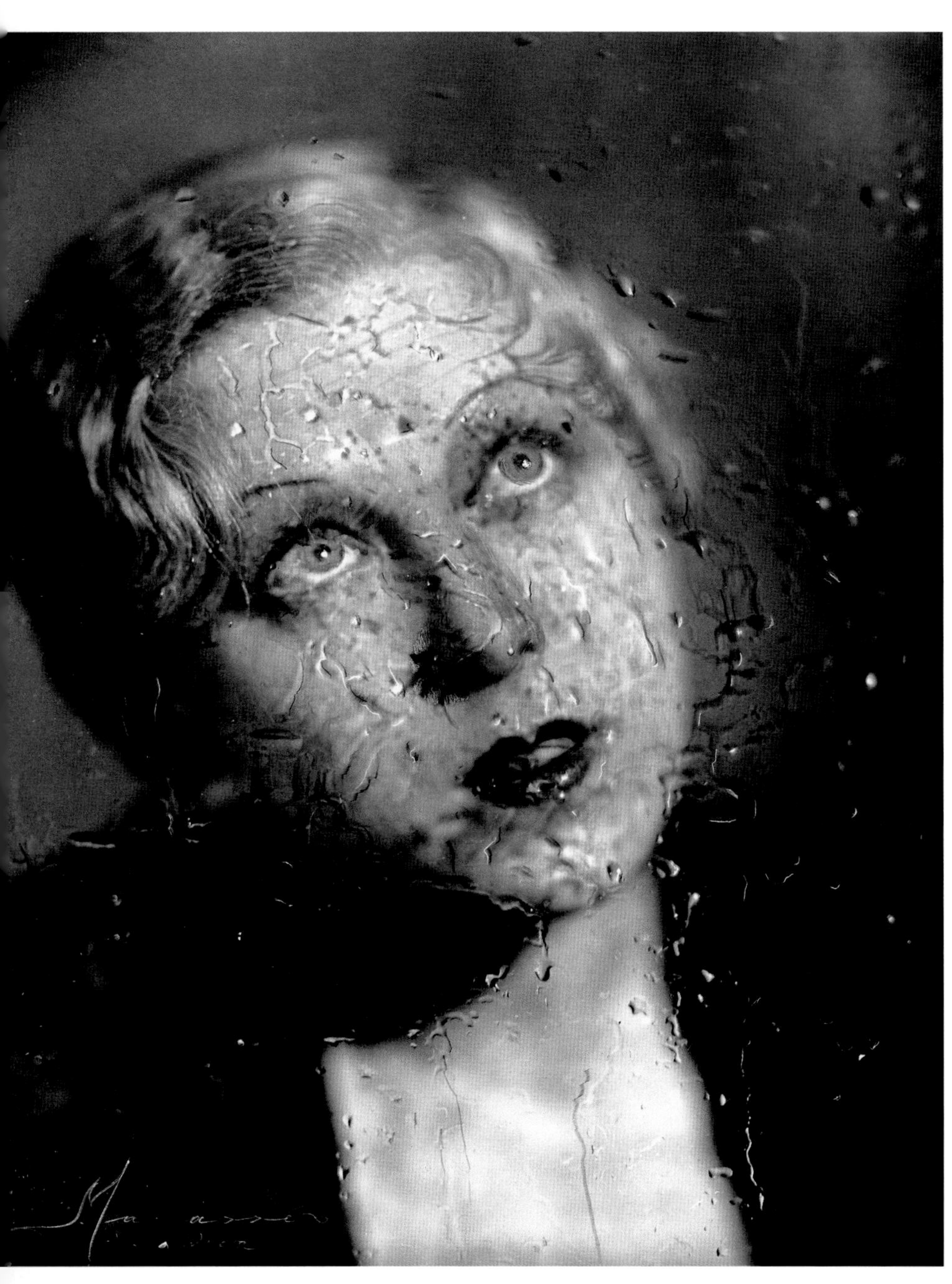

Christiane Delyn, c.1931; Study, c.1935; next two pages: Study, c.1934; Study, c.1928

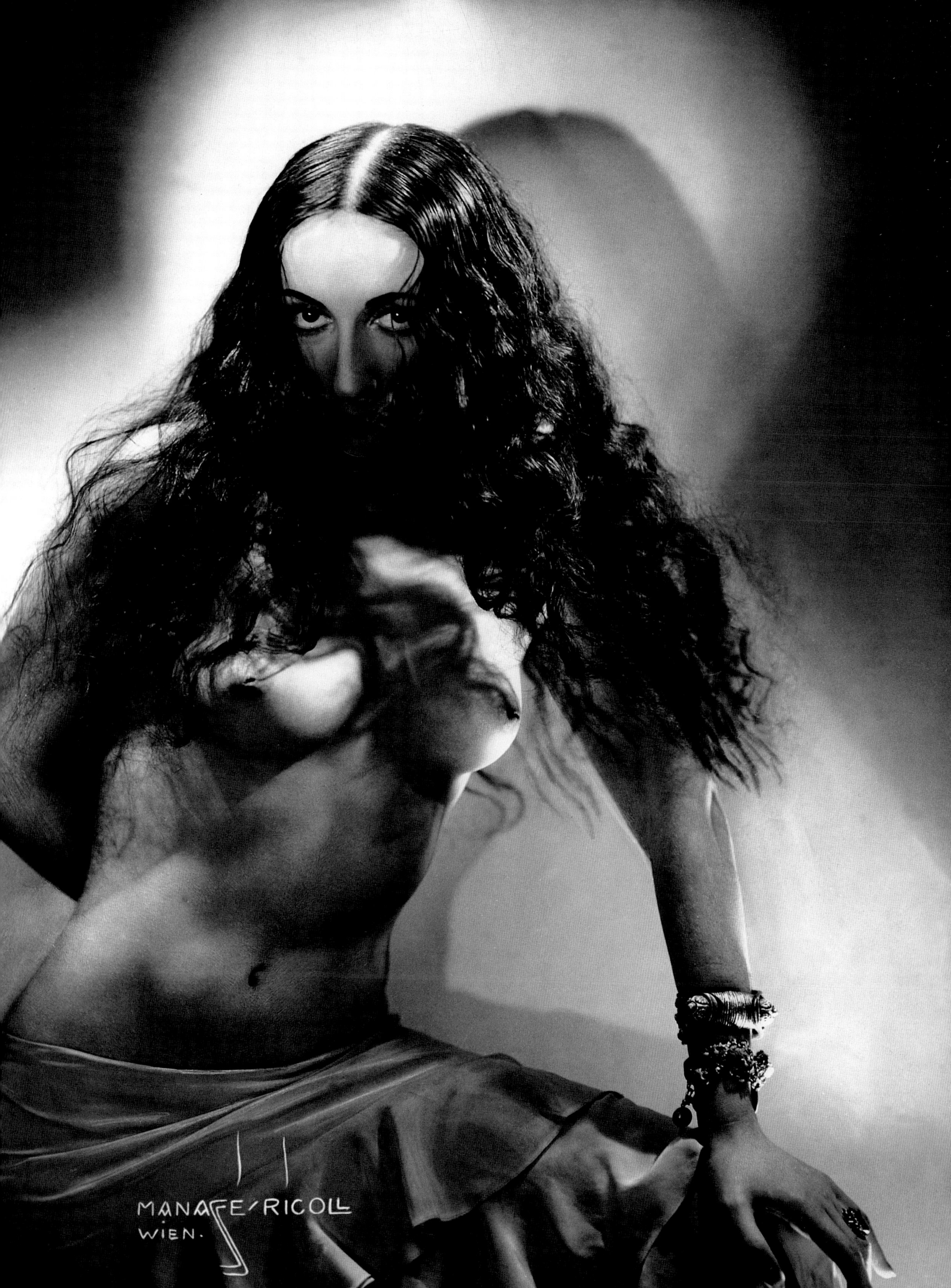
MANASSE/RICOLL
WIEN.

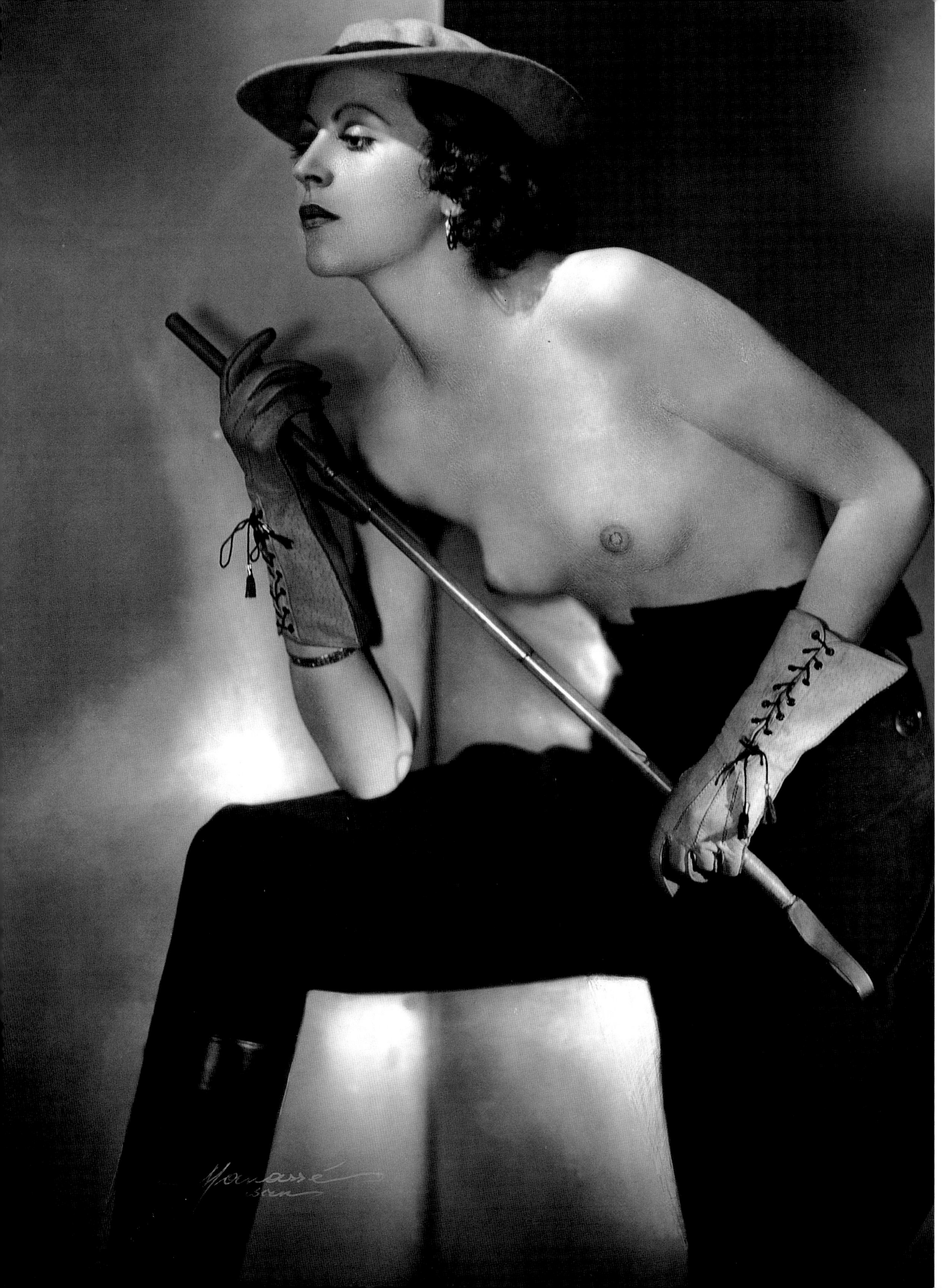

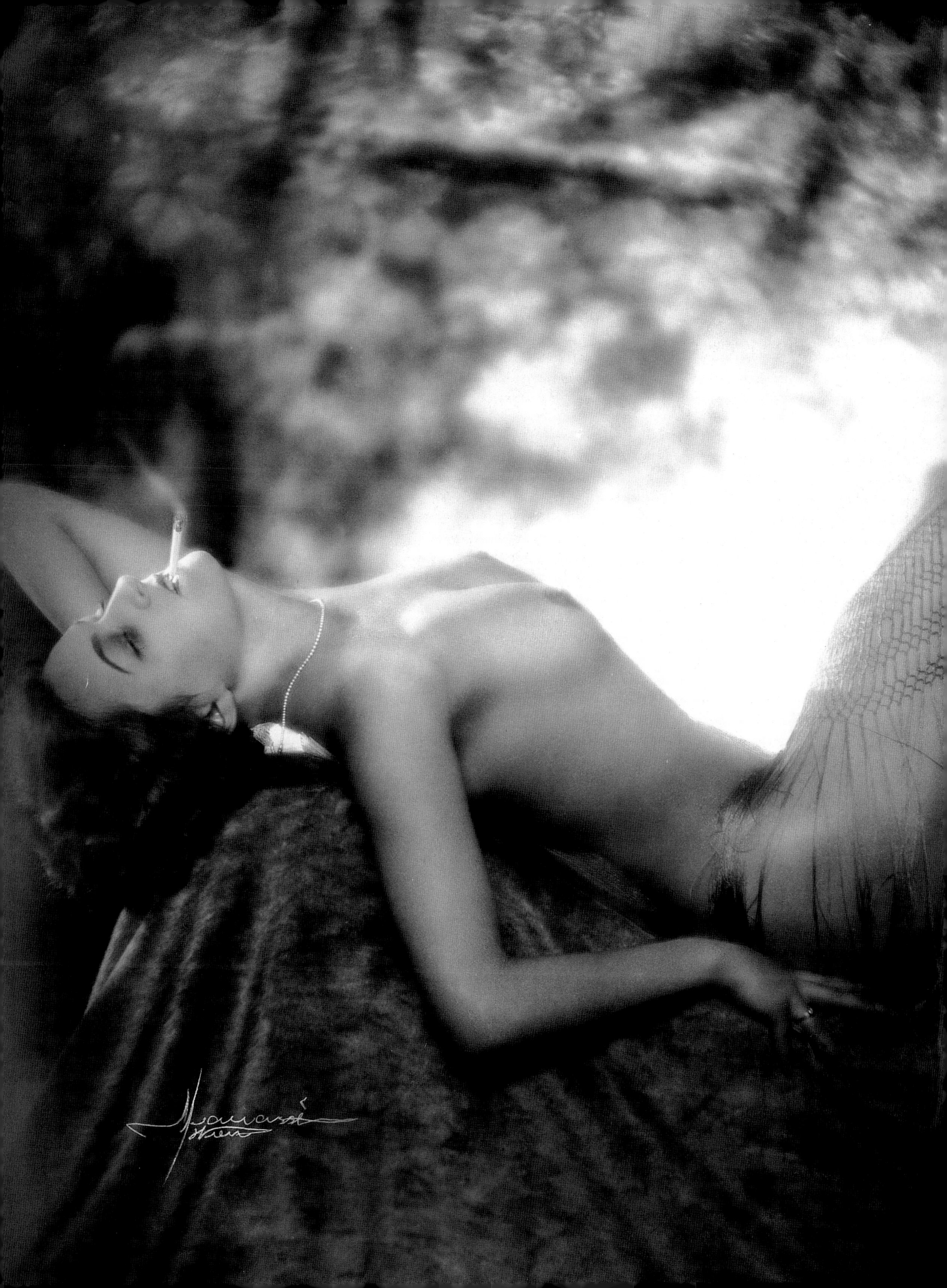

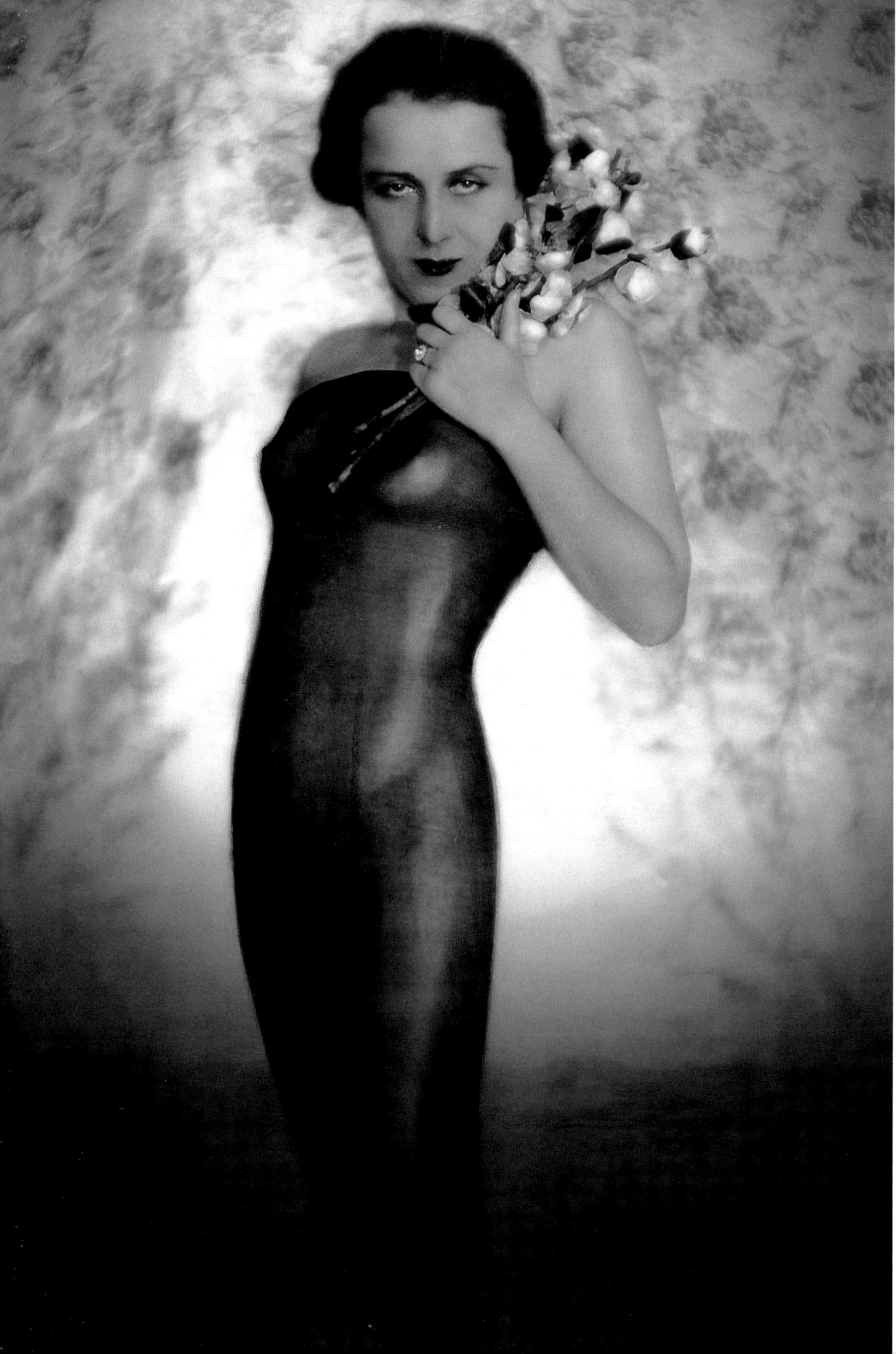

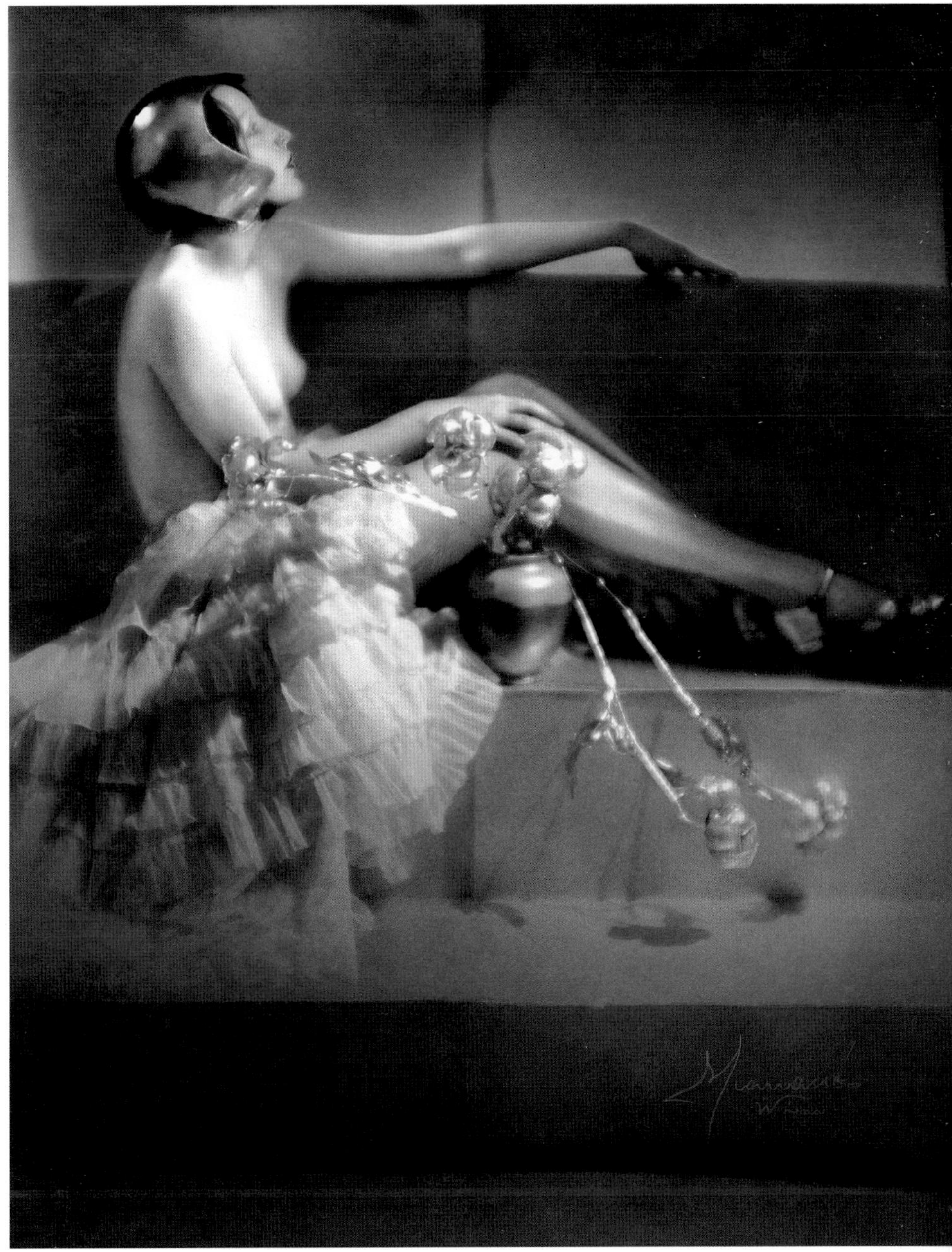

Bill Walling, an executive at MGM Photo Studios in the thirties, explained the most important task of Hollywood photographers as follows: "One must try to capture the look that they (the stars) ascribe to themselves and which the public wants to see. This has nothing to do with their real personality." And this look, photographed in Hollywood style, resulted in the required "glamour." "By glamour," Walling continued, "I mean merely what one expects from a fascinatingly beautiful woman, those women you can never approach in real life, of whom one can only dream on the screen." Thus "glamour" signifies radiance and inaccessibility per se; women presented in this way do not remind the viewer of his own "real" experiences. "Their skin doesn't even have any pores through which they could breathe. But then, gods are immortal. Their skin—like marble and alabaster—displays a transparent gleam in which the fantasies of the viewer appear as in a mirror," noted John Kobal, perhaps the most avid collector of such photographs. "As soon as film actors became famous, they not only changed but also discarded their rough shells and turned into transparent luminous images. Anyone who entered a portrait studio left it without having changed externally. Yet she (or he) left behind a trace, a trace with which she had no further connection, but which existed because of her and was abstracted by the photographer and captured by the camera. The resulting crystallization was a work of art—flowing lines à la *Jugendstil*, gigantic dimensions shared with Mount Rushmore—moist lips seductively open; eyelids shiny with cream, lowered in a blasé look; hands provocatively placed on hips or tousling elaborate coiffures, carelessly emphasizing the bosom—creatures of light, marble, glass. ... These pictures have no subtlety; they were created, like icons, to be worshipped; they want to be desired, to be collected like works of art."

Study, c.1931; Study, c.1931

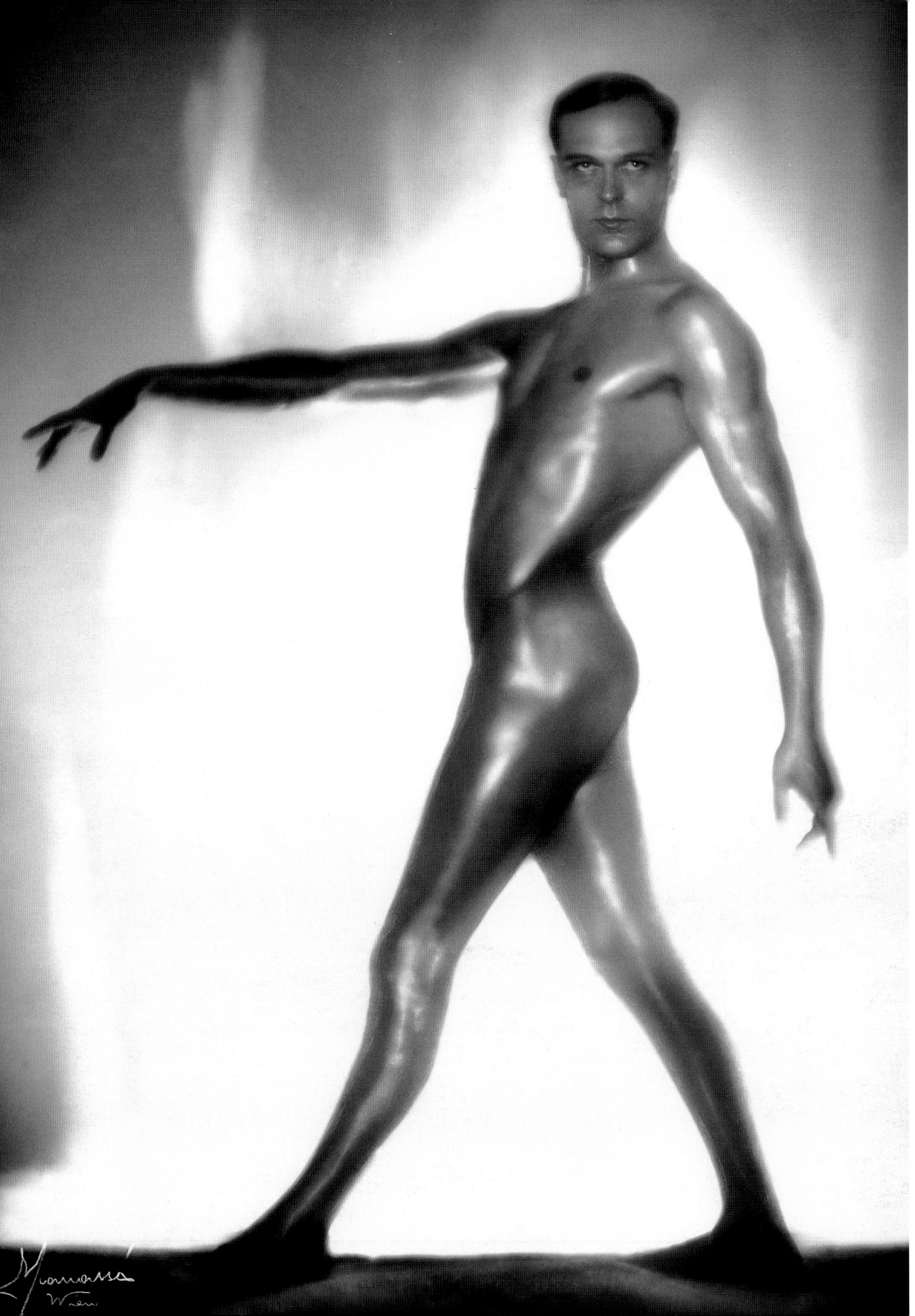
Manassé
Wien

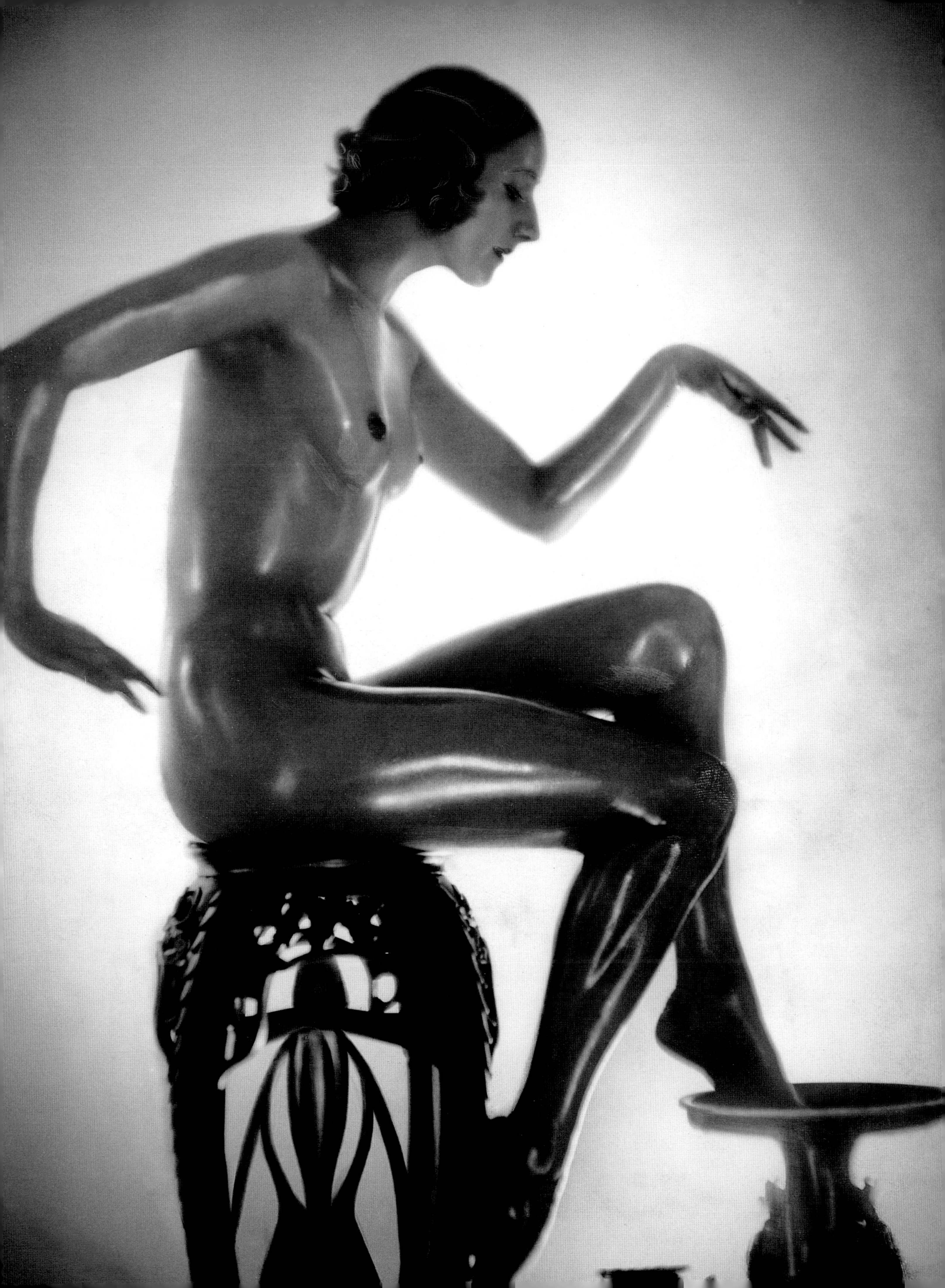

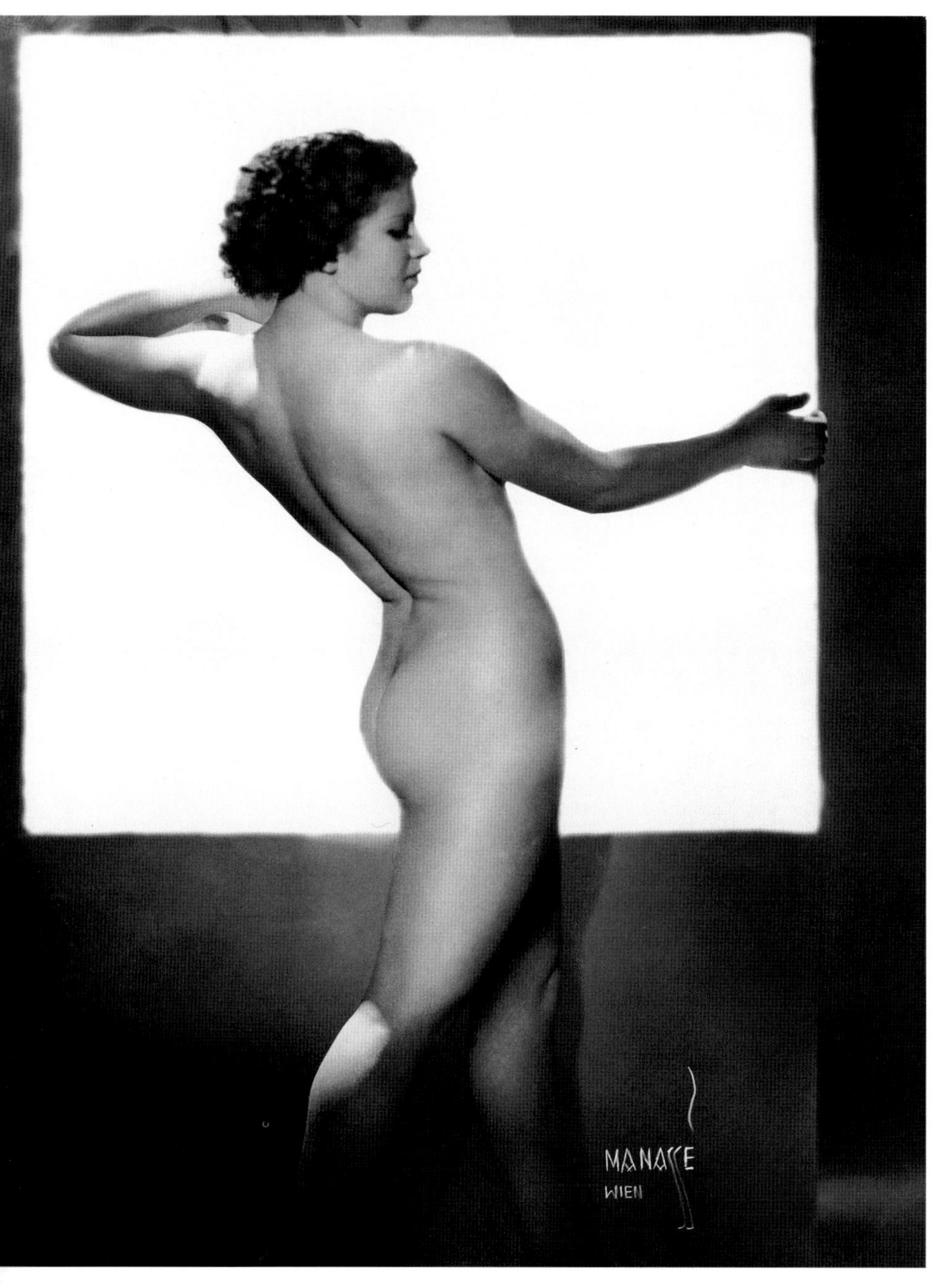

These "works of art" were in fact the products of a costly process, with model and photographer often supported by an extensive staff. On both sides of the Atlantic in the early twenties, flair and uniqueness in portraits were achieved through lavish use of the tried and proven soft-focus lens, which was available in all the better studios. Soon, however, more clever and more sophisticated methods were developed, including experiments with various backgrounds and accessories and, above all, with clever lighting. One should not forget that magazines in those days were printed on poor-quality paper, very unlike the glossy products we are accustomed to today. Thus concise line and clear drawing of portraits were particularly important. Backgrounds with too many small details had to be avoided, so that the model would stand out. One of the most popular ways of achieving this was to use a spotlight to create a more or less uniform background. The light surrounded the figure like an aureole, brought it forward, and lifted it up into that sphere that is traditionally occupied by an aura. This spot of light was also used in vaudeville to pick up the performers in their acts and follow them as long as they are on stage, while the rest of the visual field fades away, at least temporarily.

But background lighting of the star photo was equally important, for it assured a clear outline of the body, an outline that had to comply with one of the key requirements of the era, the slender figure. Hollywood introduced and promoted this ideal of the girl-like woman who, dressed or not, never gives the impression of voluptuous womanhood. However, this image was never pursued there as consistently as when it began its triumphal march through European studios. Until 1935 almost no Studio Manassé photographs existed in which the models' legs, arms, and especially hips were not trimmed down and reduced to a uniform slimness. (Later more "natural" shapes came into vogue, but that only meant that a different kind of

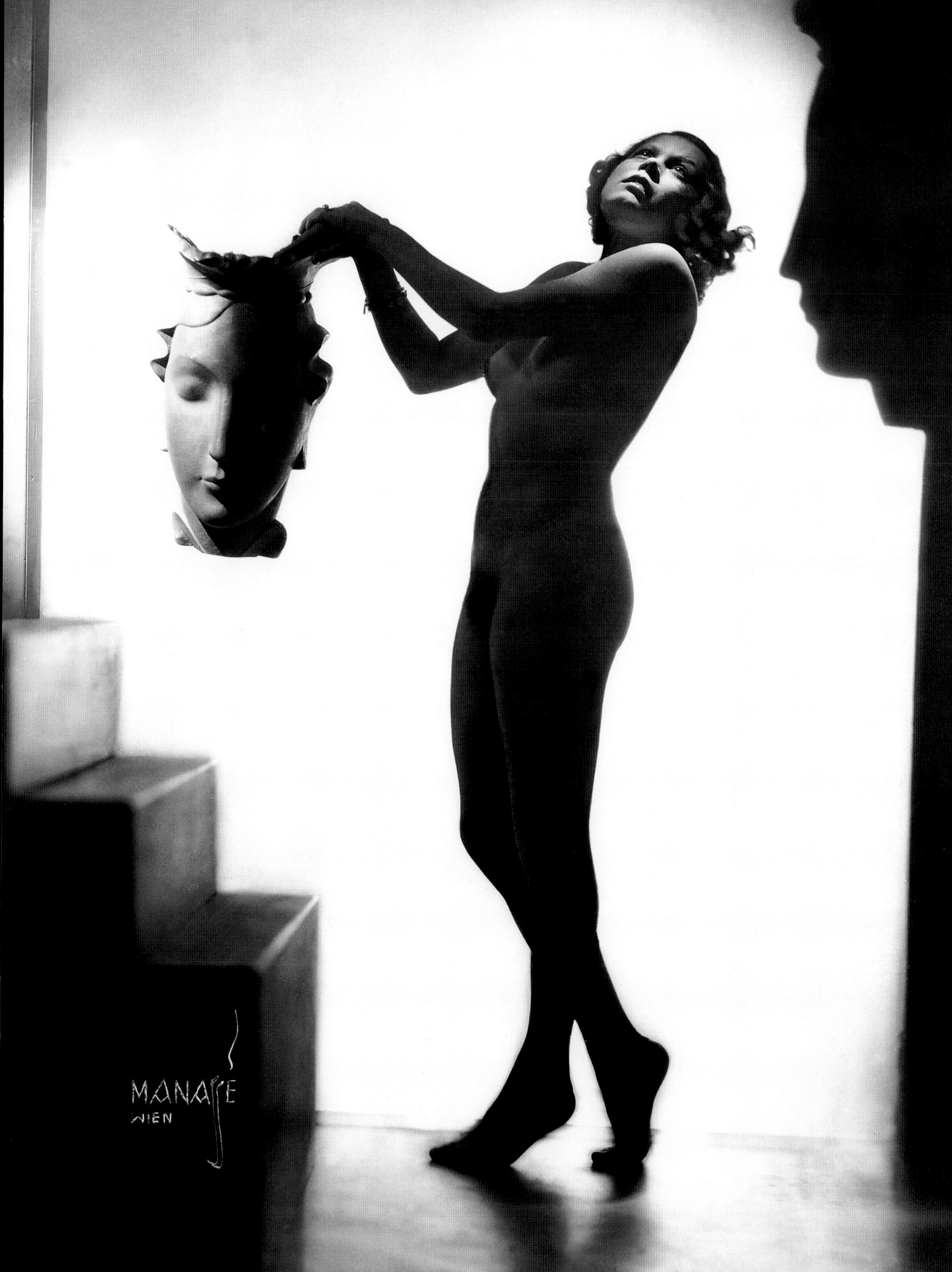
MANASSE
WIEN

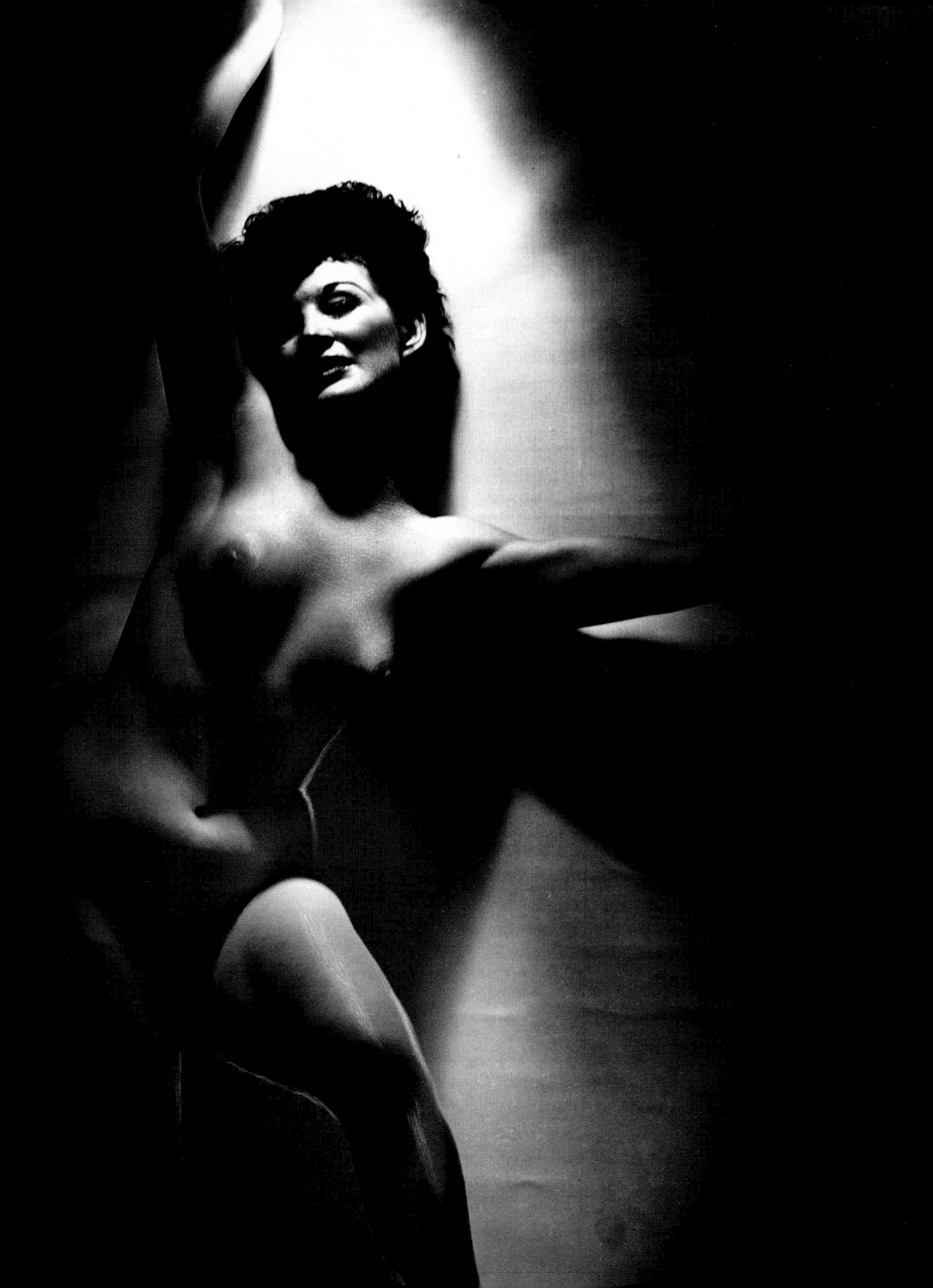

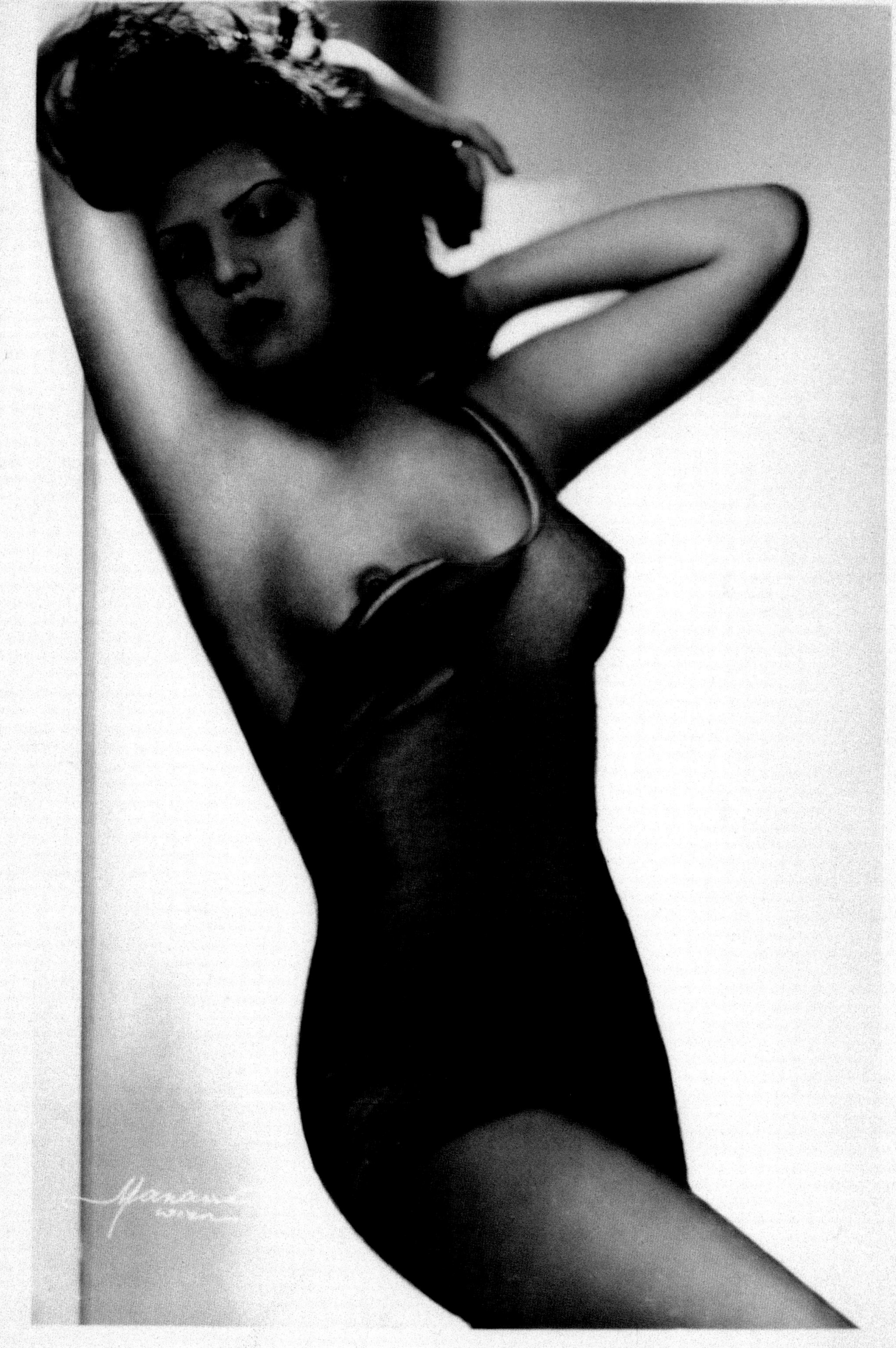

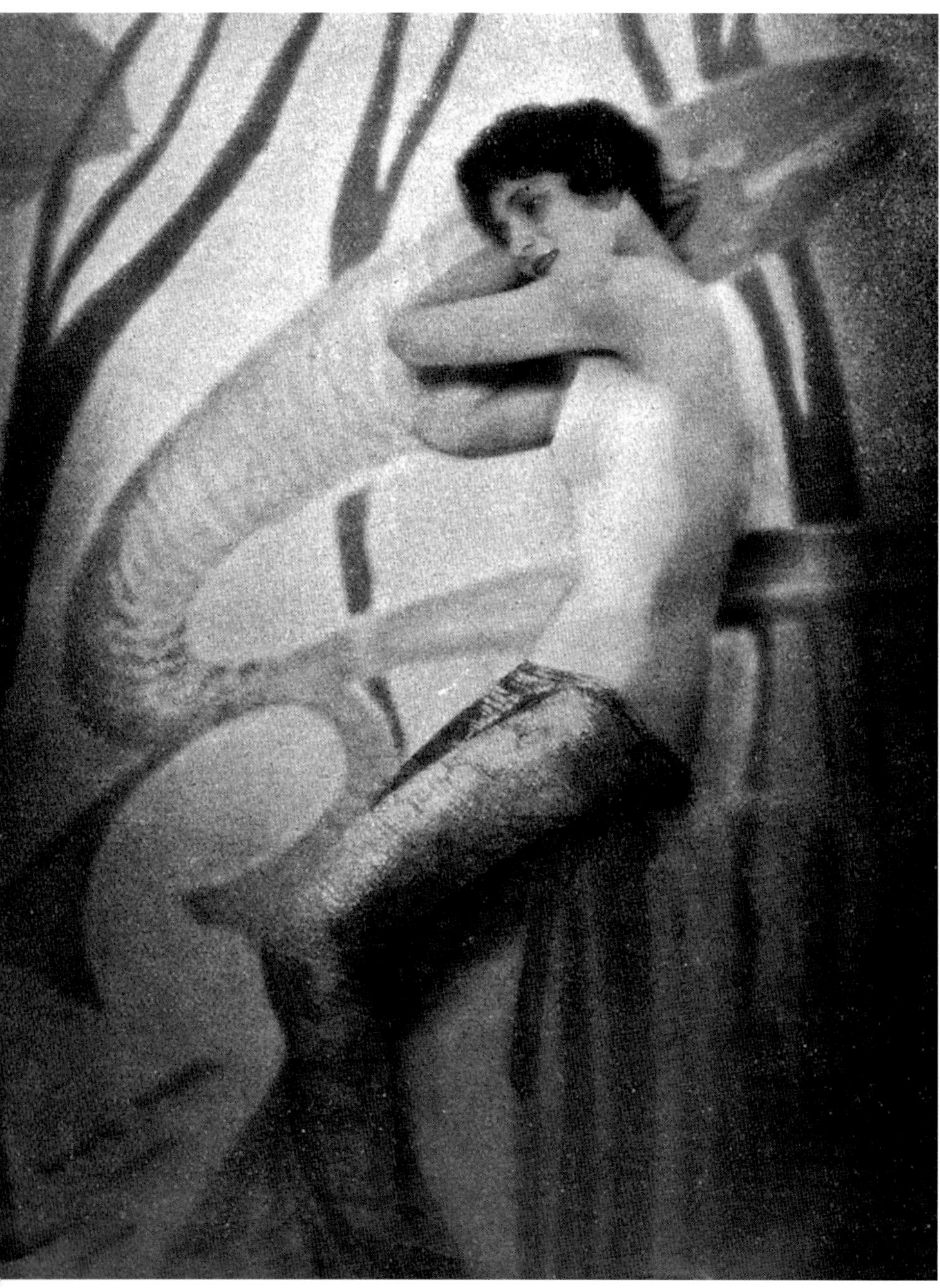

artificiality came to the fore, one oriented to the athletic and at the same time chaste ideals of German art of the time.)

The association of these slender artificial body outlines of the late twenties with those of the body of a fish is not confined just to a later view of these photographs. Olga and Adorján Wlassics themselves commented on it. In their picture *Auch am Meeresgrund hat man sich für die schlanke Linie entschieden* (The slender figure is prefered, even at the bottom of the ocean), they replaced the usually retouched garment with a mermaid body and decorated the background with seaweed and fish motifs painted in on the negative. However, these streamlined creatures have nothing in common with the exotically resplendent sensuality of Gustav Klimt's *Water Snakes*. Doll-like, smooth, and without any hint of personal features, they remind us of the Tiller or Ziegfeld girls of those days, who were chosen according to standardized body measurements and made up to look as uniform as possible. (Members of both of these dance groups were among the clients of Studio Manassé.)

Although it seems to conflict with the effect and purpose of the spotlight, the Wlassics made use of veils, both graphically and symbolically. In this case too it is possible that they took as their models the work of American photographers Edward Steichen and George Hurrell. The owners of Studio Manassé must have had an enormous supply of transparent and diaphanous textiles on hand. Although always draped in different ways, the same patterns turn up over the years in various applications: Here, the material is gathered up impishly short so that it scarcely covers the model's hips (again retouched to be slender); there, it flows in luxuriant lines like a bridal veil. It may appear as an extravagant costume *(The Princess)* or torn and tattered *(Victim of an Assault?)*. Sometimes it serves to hinder the view, elsewhere to break up the light, which then falls in fanciful decorative shadows upon the model.

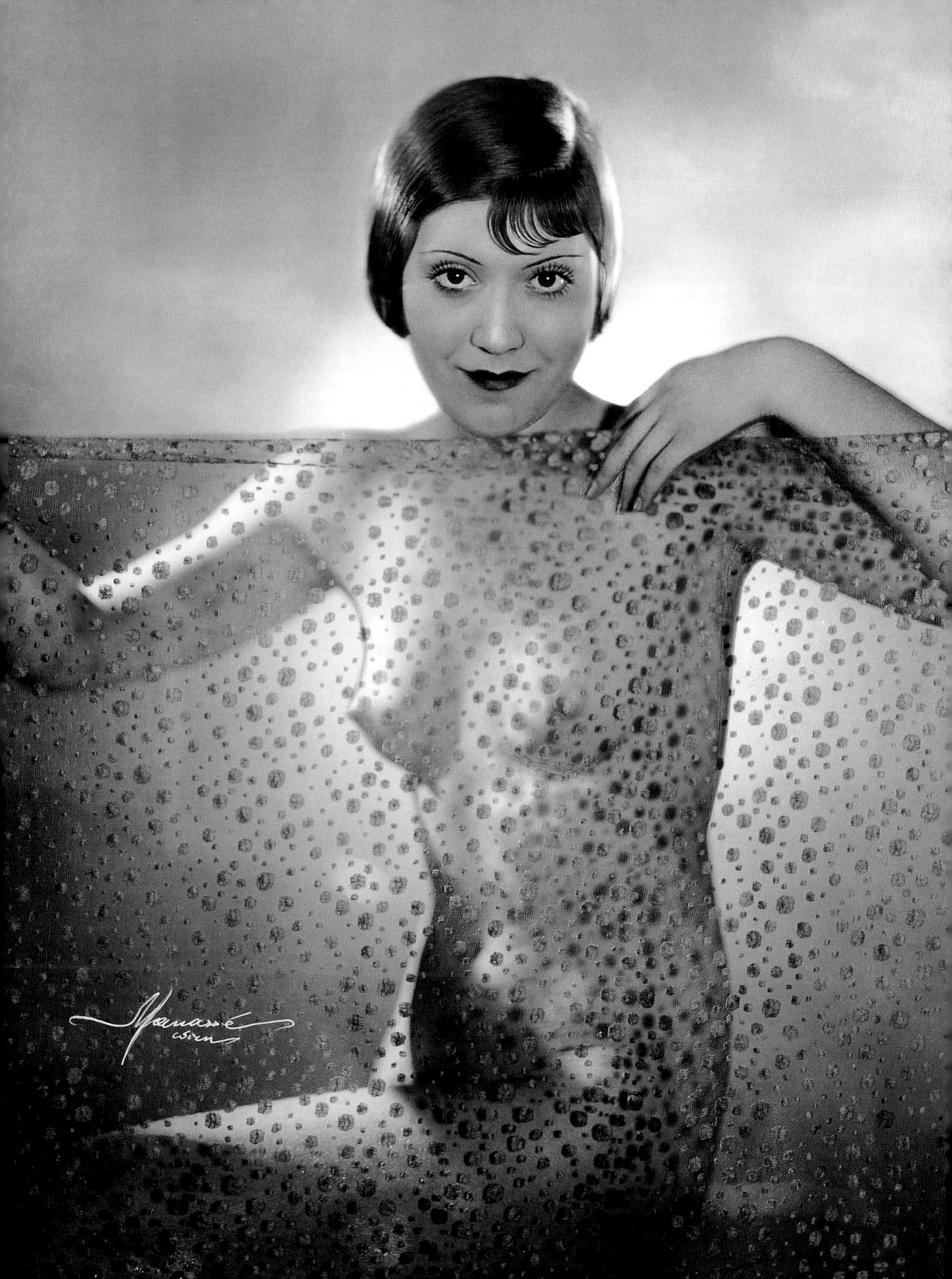
Manassé
Wien

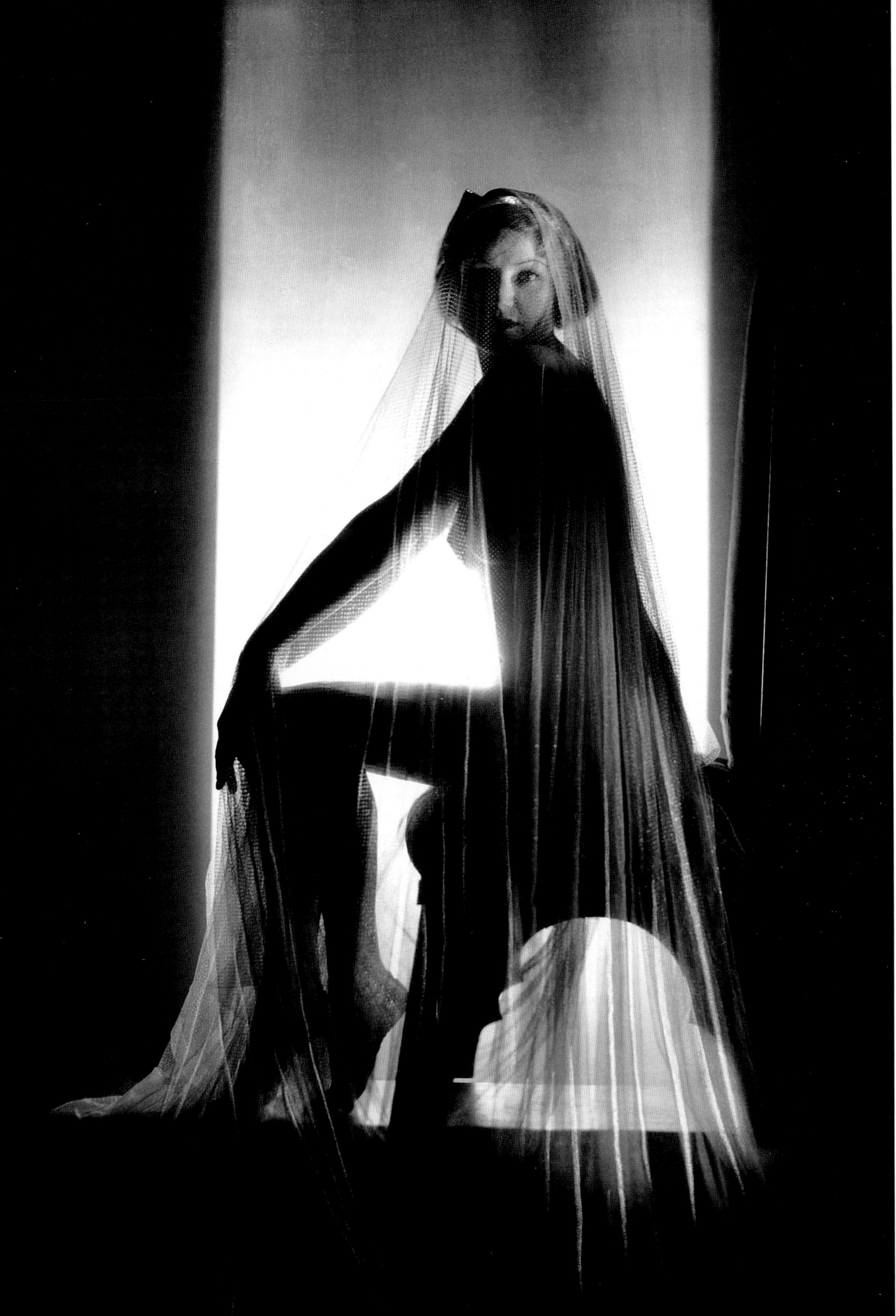

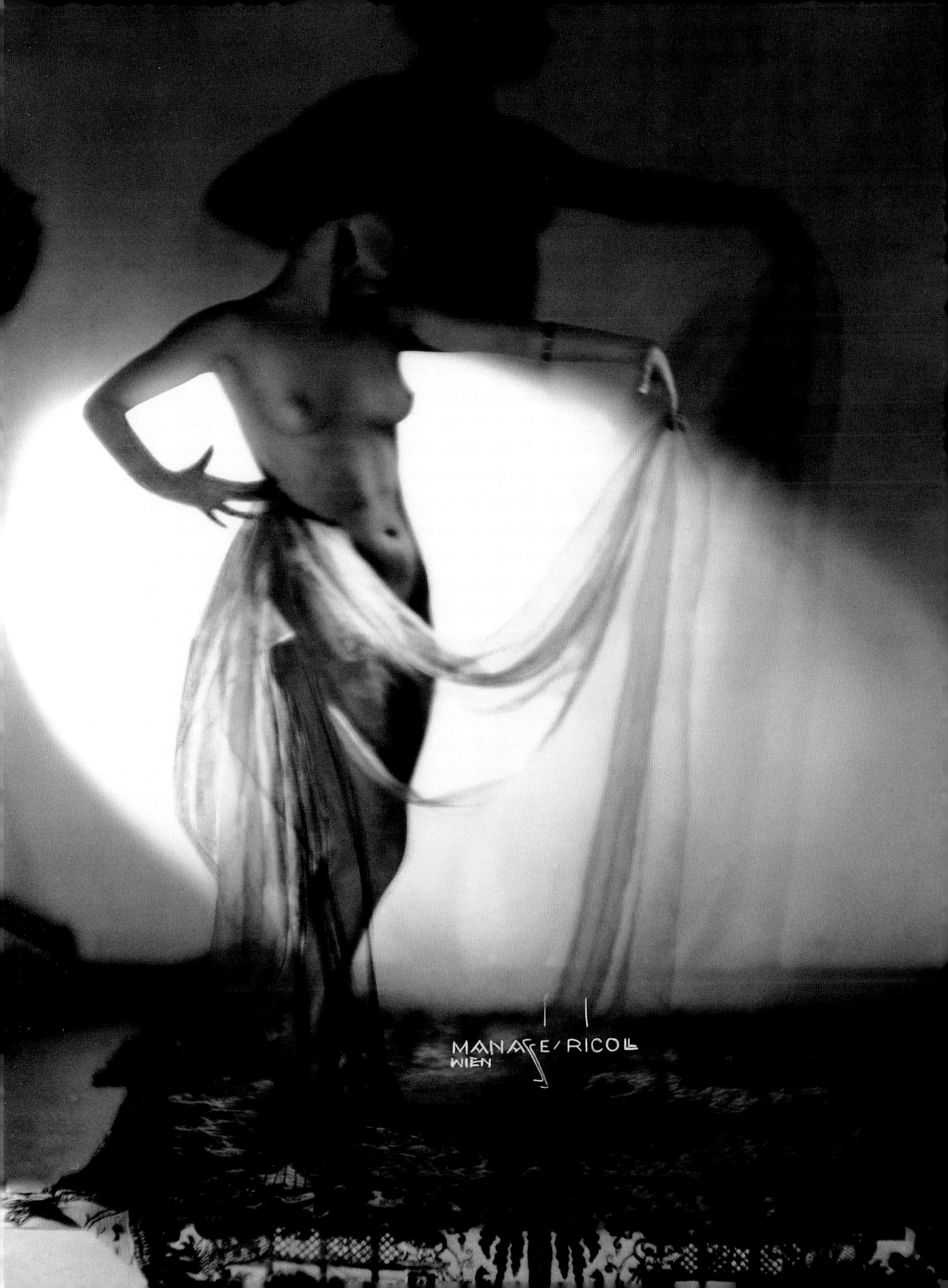

MANASSE / RICOLL
WIEN

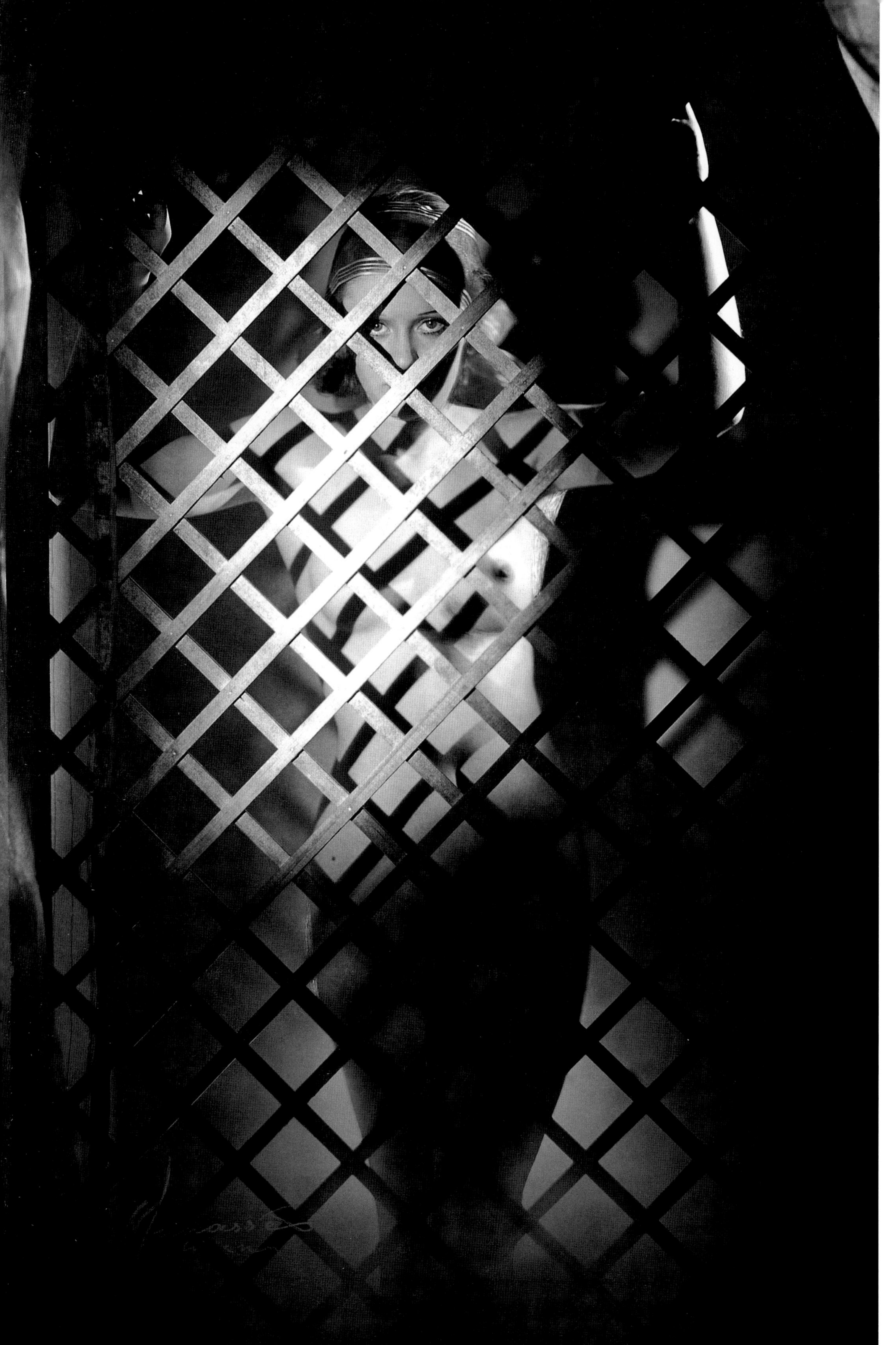

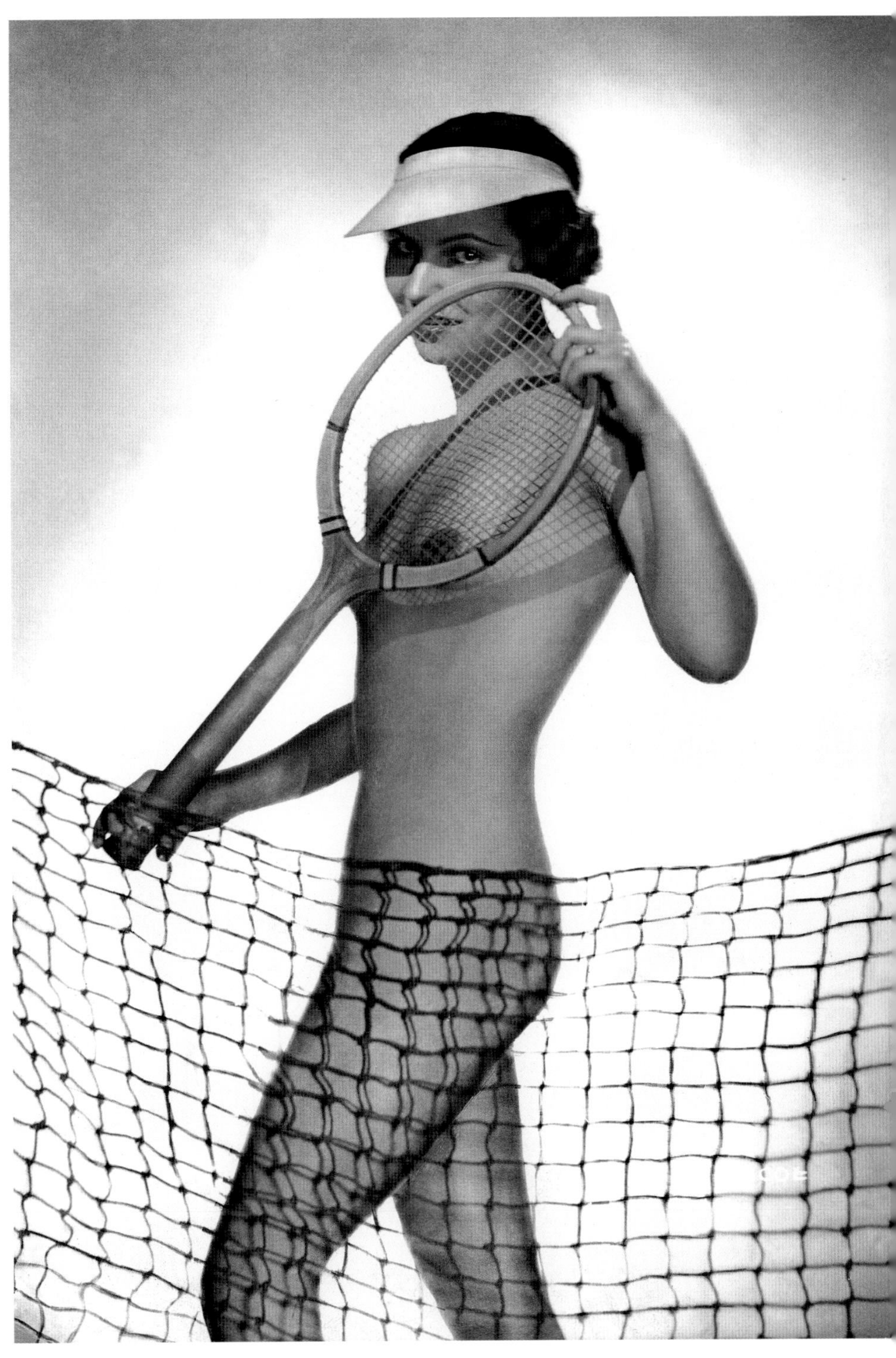

The previously mentioned poor print quality of the magazines concealed all evidence of the "improvements" that were made to the shapes of bodies, but the original photographs from the Manassé studio give an idea of how much retouching was done. The extraordinary quality of the pictures from Hollywood is due in part to the fact that all corrections were made so as to leave no traces of them in the copy that was sent out. About 20 employees at MGM were employed exclusively to "doctor" negatives. "They helped turn the dream into reality," said Eric Carpenter, one of the Hollywood studio photographers who considered retouchers the true artists in this business. They removed everything that was undesirable on the large-format negatives from skin blemishes and superfluous body fullness to occasional dust and surface irregularities in the props. They also added whatever was expected, which John Kobal described as "a process that was often so extensive that another set of negatives had to be made because the first one was already so scratched up, punctured, and scraped that no further retouching was possible. To achieve an alabaster look in close-up photos they often worked with spray paint; on the original negatives practically the entire face is covered with very delicate traces of retouching." This description agrees with evidence found in the few surviving Manassé negatives.

Standard procedures for the star portrait were also applied to portraits of those who were not as beautiful, successful, or famous. From members of the ensemble performing in the Femina Bar in Vienna to those ladies of society who liked to push themselves into the limelight, imitating the model *from* the media provided a picture that was all the more suitable *for* the media.

Josef Pesci, Montage, c.1930; Study, c.1927

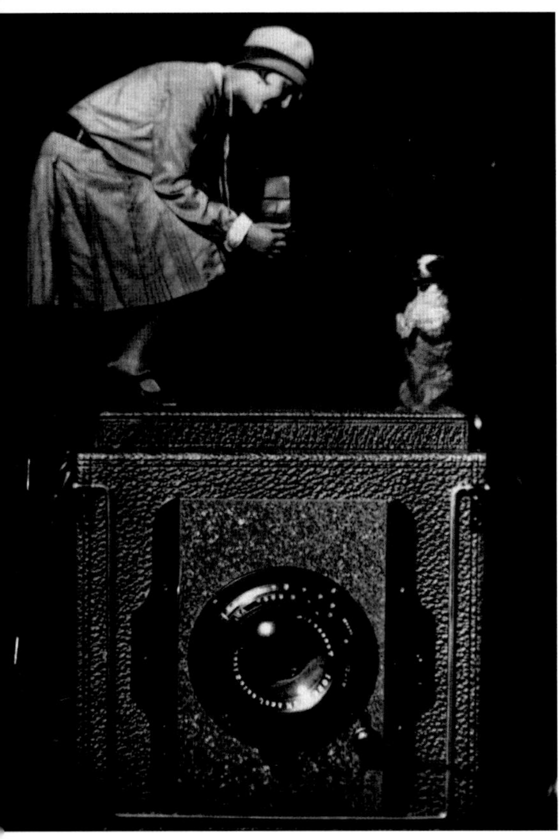

Olga and Adorján Wlassics made use of all the techniques of make-up and retouch, employing them as diligently as their colleagues in Hollywood did. In an article accompanied by pictures in the Berlin *Revue des Monats* they wrote: "Women in particular demand more of us photographers than mere pictorial representation. They want to appear in the picture the way they would like to look; but only a few women really know themselves. Most have a fantasy picture of themselves and are disappointed when the photograph made by the photographer does not correspond to their ideal." But the remedy was at hand; they "triumphed over time and space with photographic art," according to a 1929 article Adorján wrote for the same publication. Here the banality of his words indicates a naivete that some of the surviving photographs also suggest. Olga and Adorján were not mere "snapshot takers," a subject that they and some of their colleagues used as pretext for a joke photo: She stands facing us legs akimbo, the camera held up to one eye, her finger on the shutter release, and the camera bag covering her genital area—a naked beauty, accompanied by a shadow, her "free" eye open in wonderment, leaving the door wide open to possible erotic associations. While in this instance the theme is looking and being looked at, Josef Pecsi, a Hungarian photographer whom the Wlassics might well have known personally and with whom they had much in common, explored the theory that the camera reduces the picture of reality, a theme that we also encounter in many Manassé montages.

Among the portraits, there are two Manassé photographs, which are probably not self-portraits, that show a female and a male painter at work, each with identical palettes. The woman—once again undressed—stands facing us and apparently paints on a clear surface that is between her and the camera. Interpreted figuratively, she stands in front of a mirror (the camera lens) and paints (over) her reflection. The man is working on a female nude photograph with a brush. *She* corrects her own picture; *he* corrects the reproduction.

Just as retouching of negatives and positives was common procedure in Studio Manassé, so was painting over of photographs. Most of the pictures used on the cover of the *Wiener Magazin* are not direct reproductions of photographs but of paintings, their origins as photographs practically unrecognizable. The same thing applies to many of the illustrations in the book, *Die Erotik in der Fotografie*. It is uncertain whether it was the publisher's desire to have colored pictures available or Adorján and Olga Wlassic's "artistic" streak that was responsible for the overpainted photographs and the fact that not just "straight" photographs were used. Other publications in Austria and Germany—magazines, advertising brochures, etc.—were also illustrated with this sort of painting done by others.

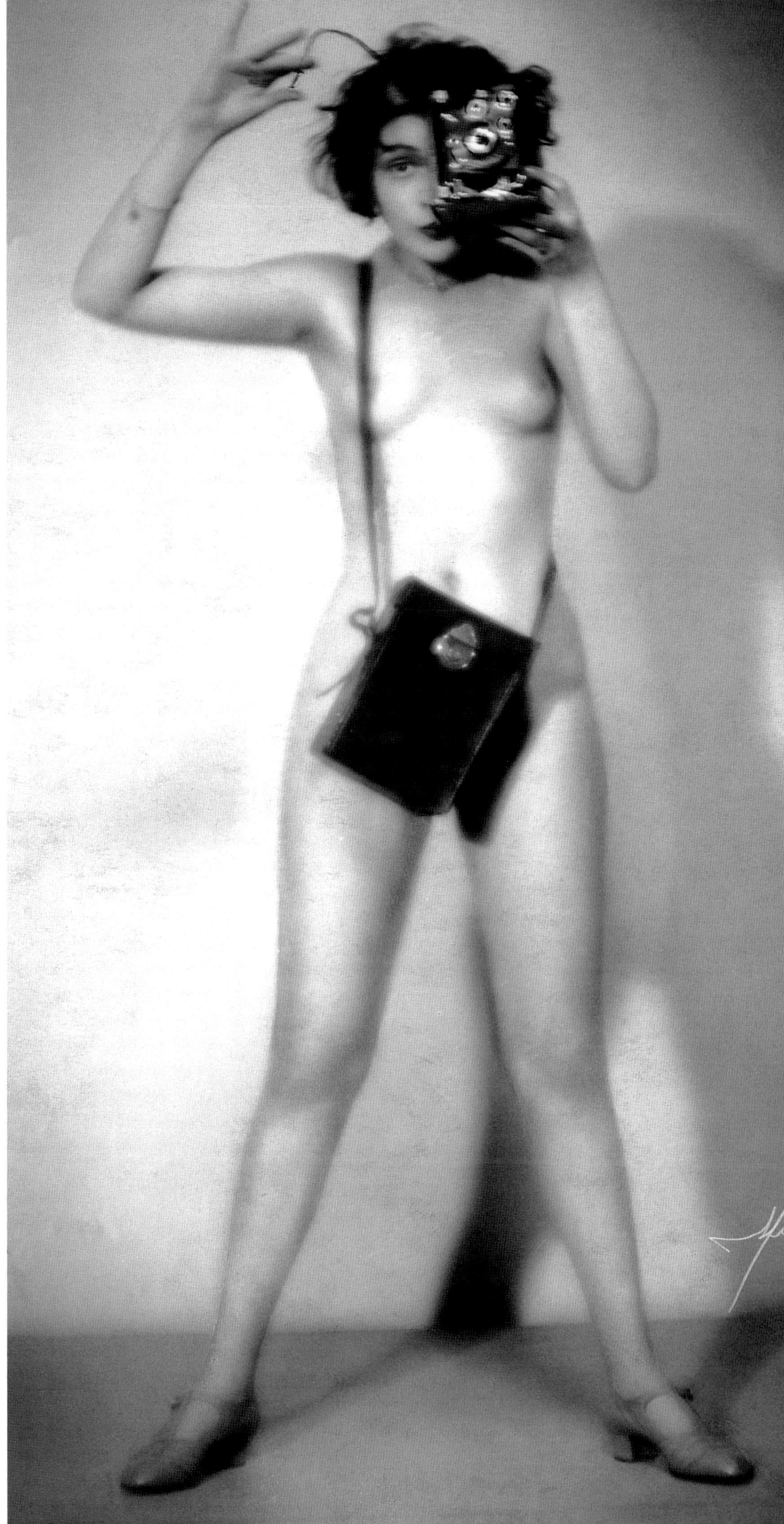

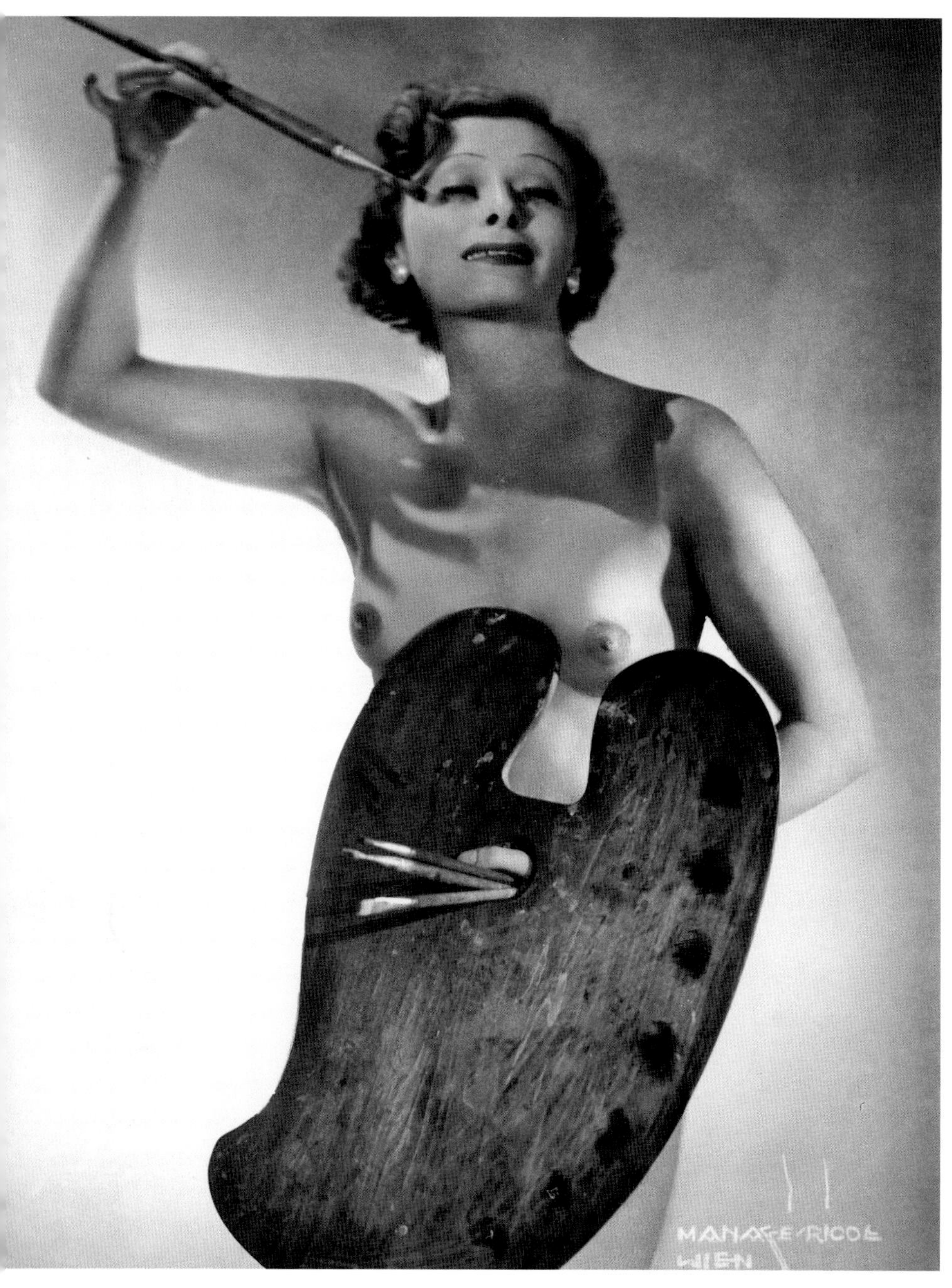

The two photographs showing the painters at work can also be interpreted in a figurative sense. The artistic "correction" of the picture of the woman to make it correspond with male ideals may be viewed as a symptom—or symbol?—of the constant adaptation of woman's role to the requirements of a changing patriarchal society. Again, as is so often the case in Manassé pictures, the dedication of the painter to his work can be interpreted in two ways: matter-of-factly, as simply the presentation of an actual situation, or satirically, as the artist painting an artificial beauty. The uncertainty in judging the so-called "new woman"—an alternative to the male-determined woman—and her picture, whether in the media or in the minds of her contemporaries was a frequent subject in light fiction and magazines of the twenties and early thirties. Whether it was D. H. Lawrence *(Give Her a Pattern)* or Robert Musil in an article in a volume of collected pieces *Die Frau von Morgen, wie wir sie uns wünschen* (Tomorrow's Woman as we want her to be), serious writers of that time grappled in one way or another with the problem of women's emancipation. They oscillated between a satirical representation of men being made insecure by the disappearance of conventional role divisions and a complete lack of understanding of the true wishes of the women's movement. If we extrapolate from these two essays, Musil and Lawrence could only understand the woman painter, who is working on her own picture in accordance with the pattern she has chosen for her life, if she were to act more in accordance with the new post-war role projected upon her by men. This would be a correction in the sense of her adapting to such new circumstances that, in turn, have been laid down by men.

Study, c.1931; Study, c.1940; next two pages: Bimini-Figure, c.1932; Maria Salvoty, c.1927

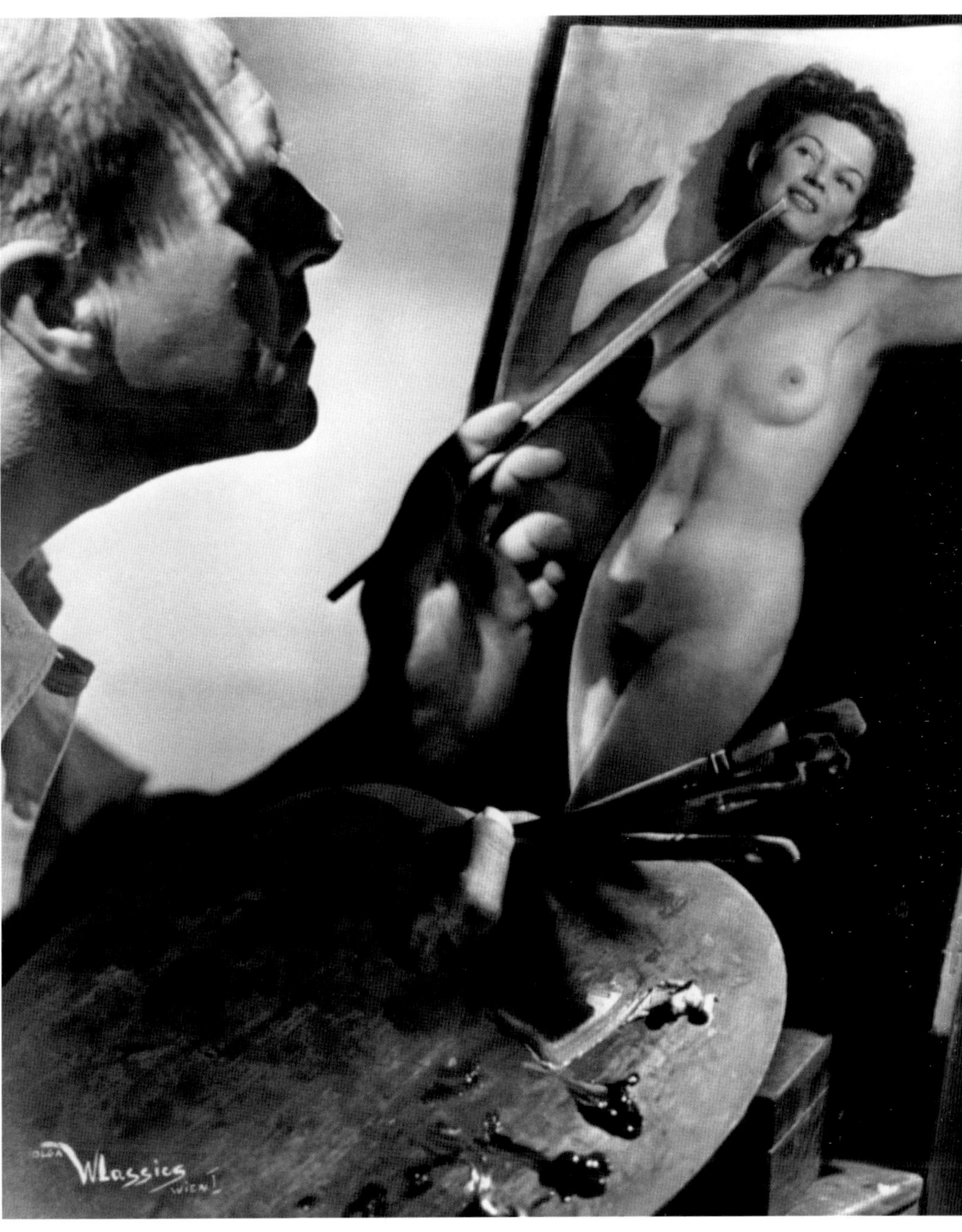

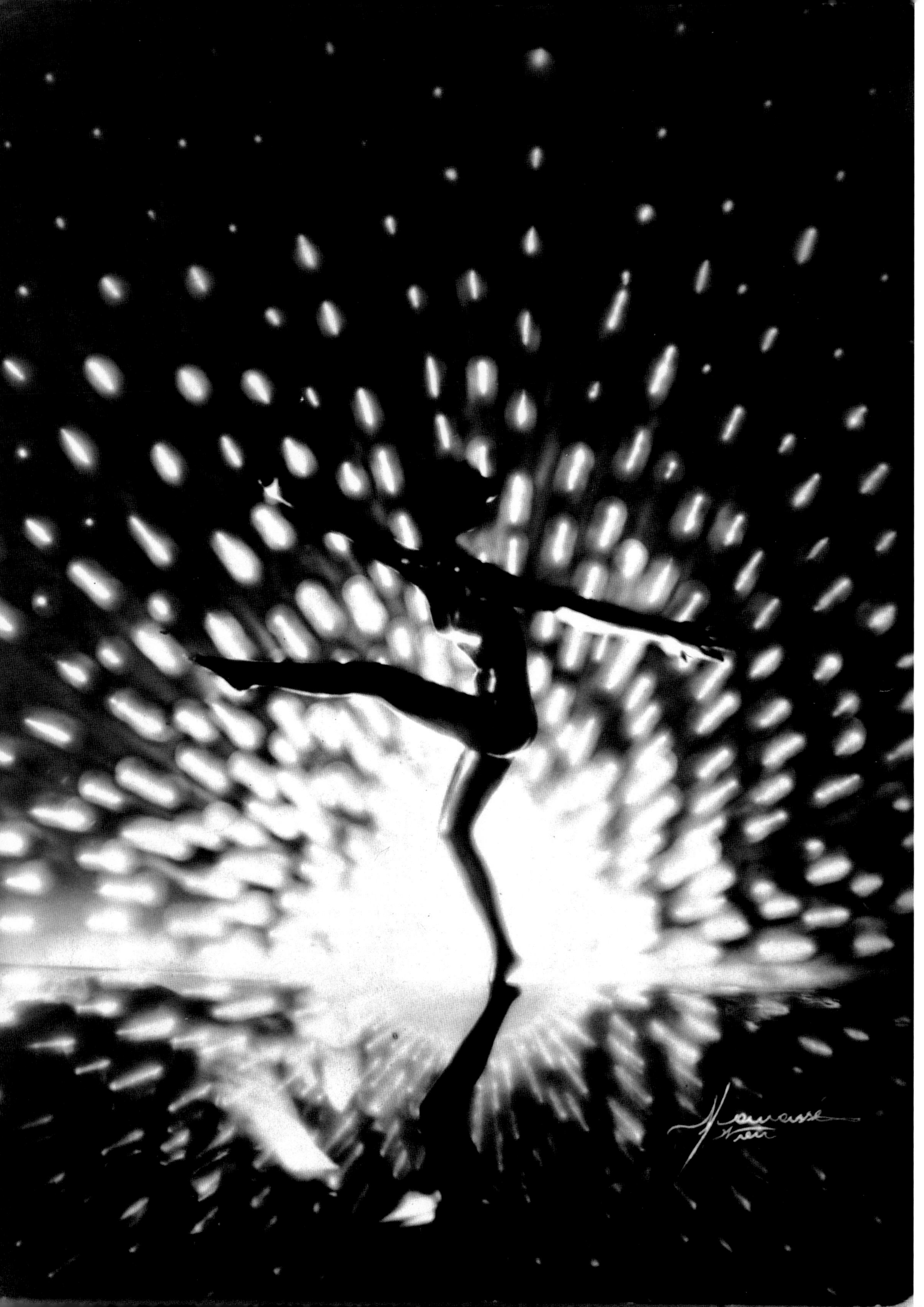

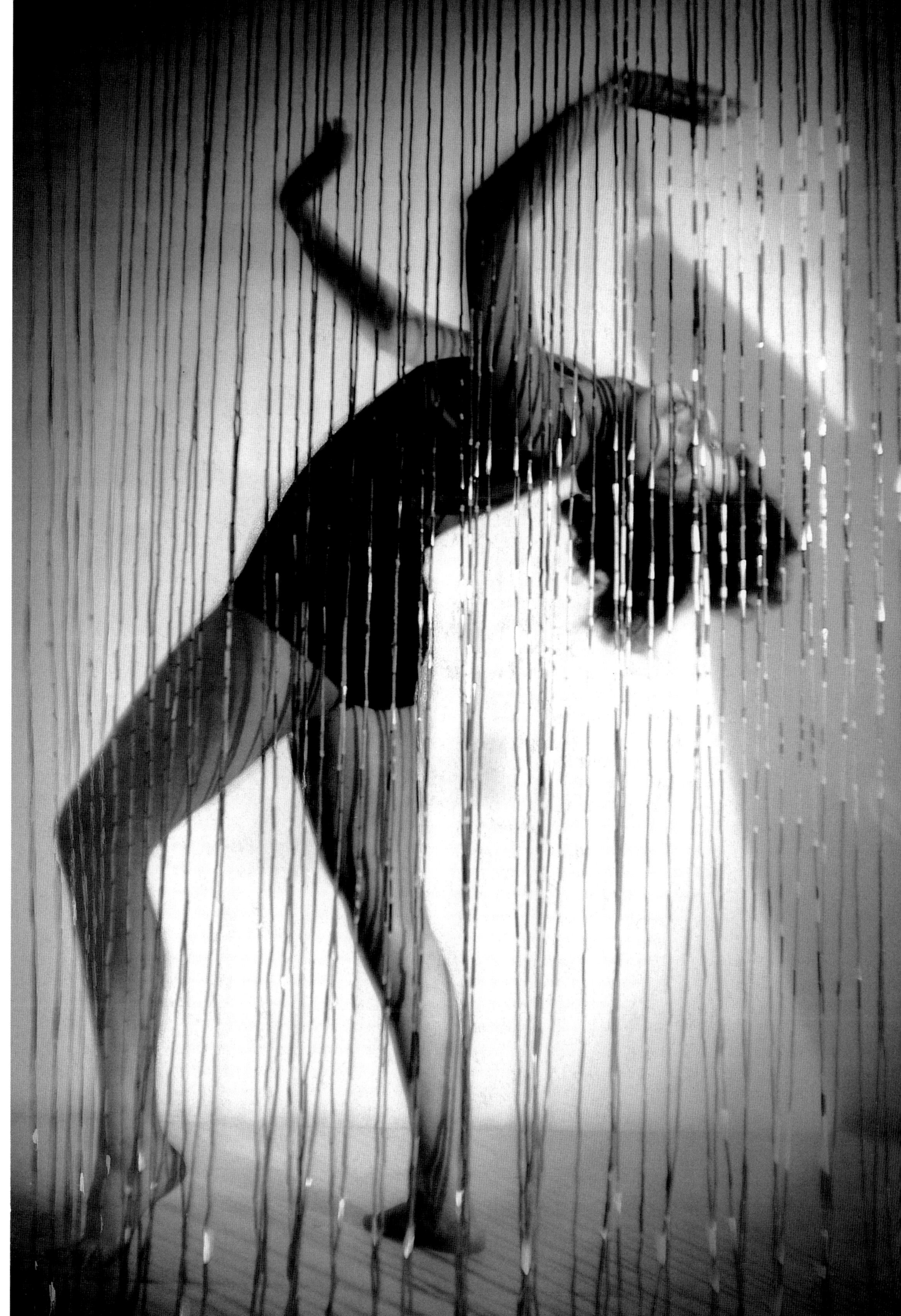

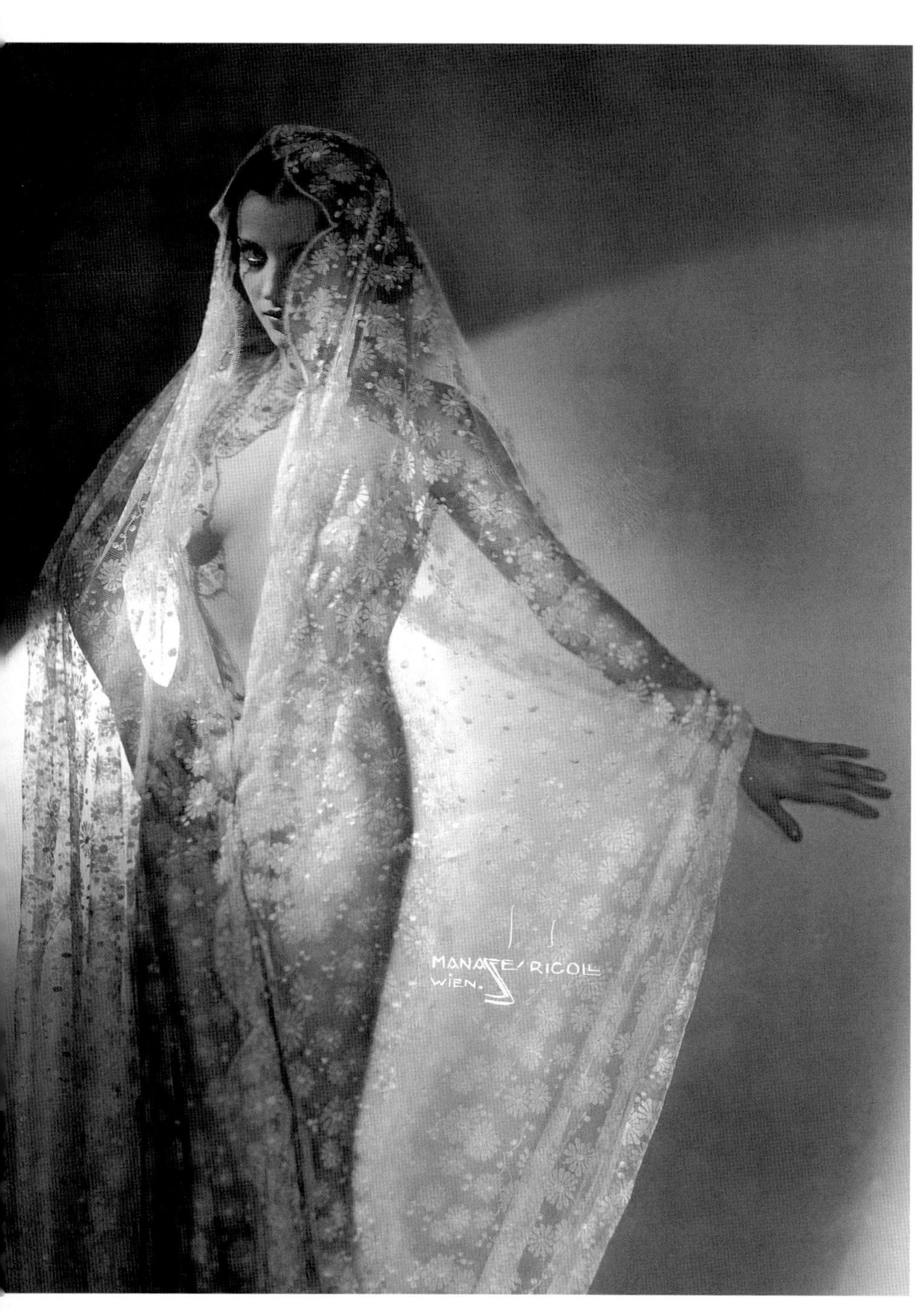

Study, c.1934; Study, c.1931; next two pages: Study, c.1935; Study, c.1935

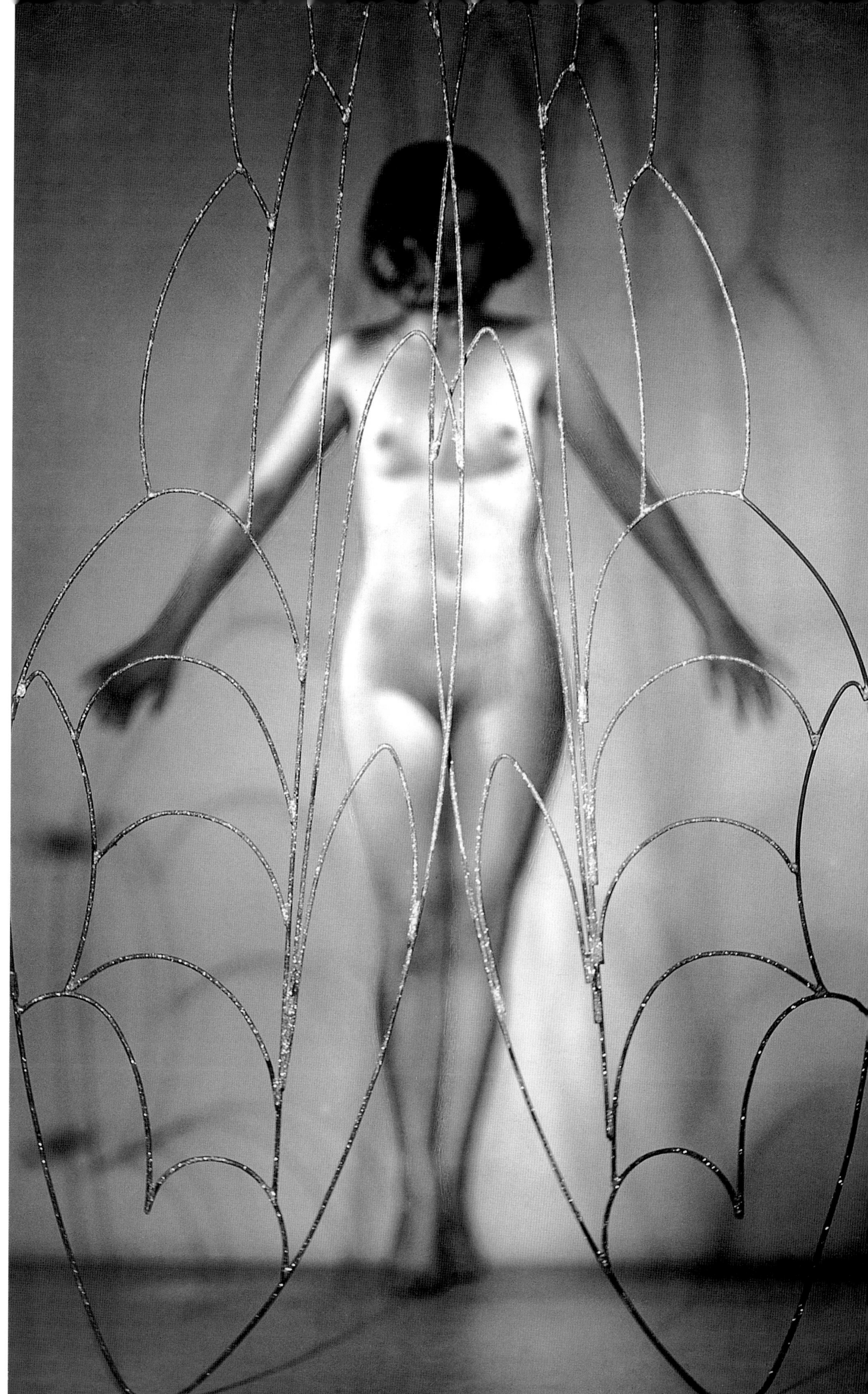

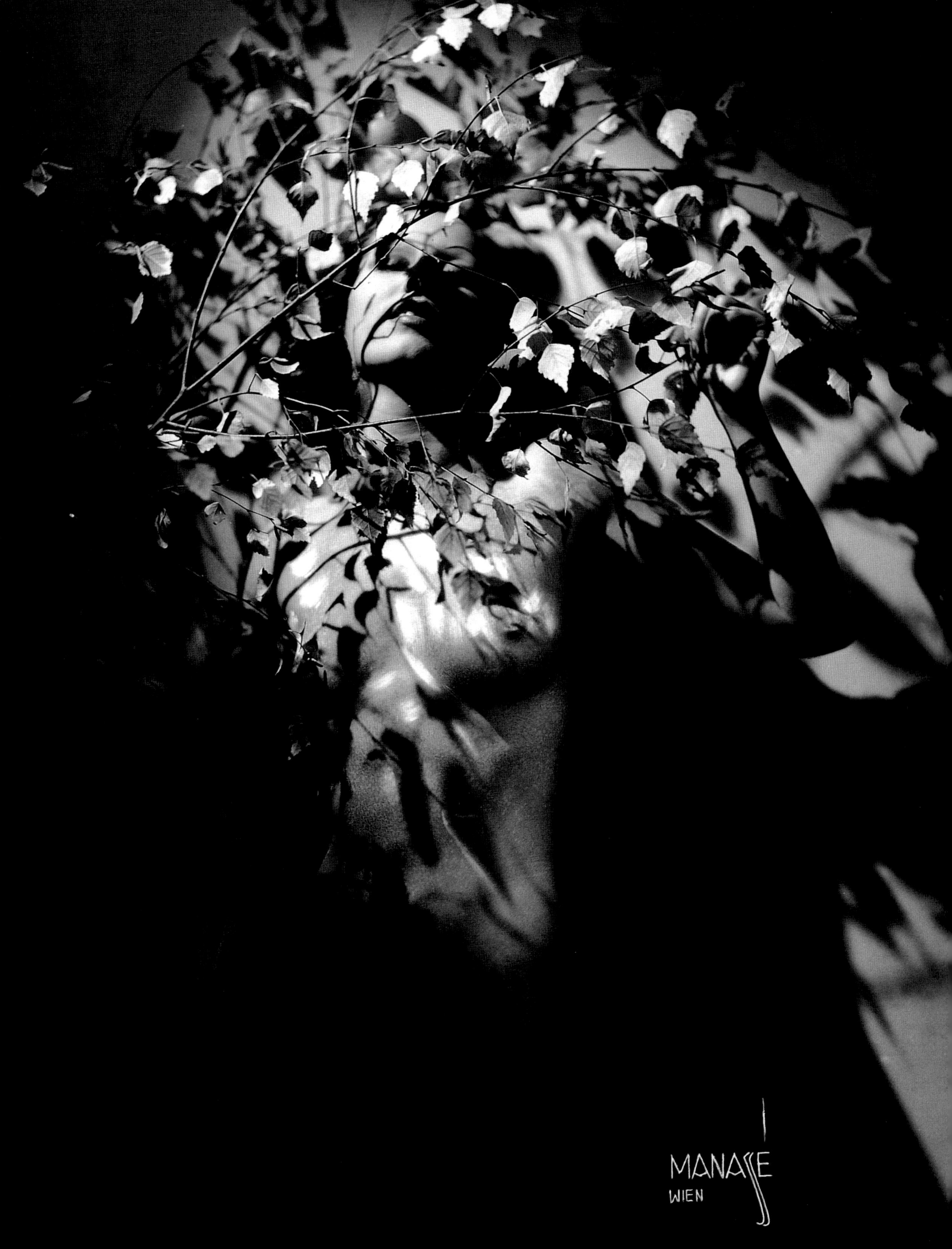
MANASSE
WIEN

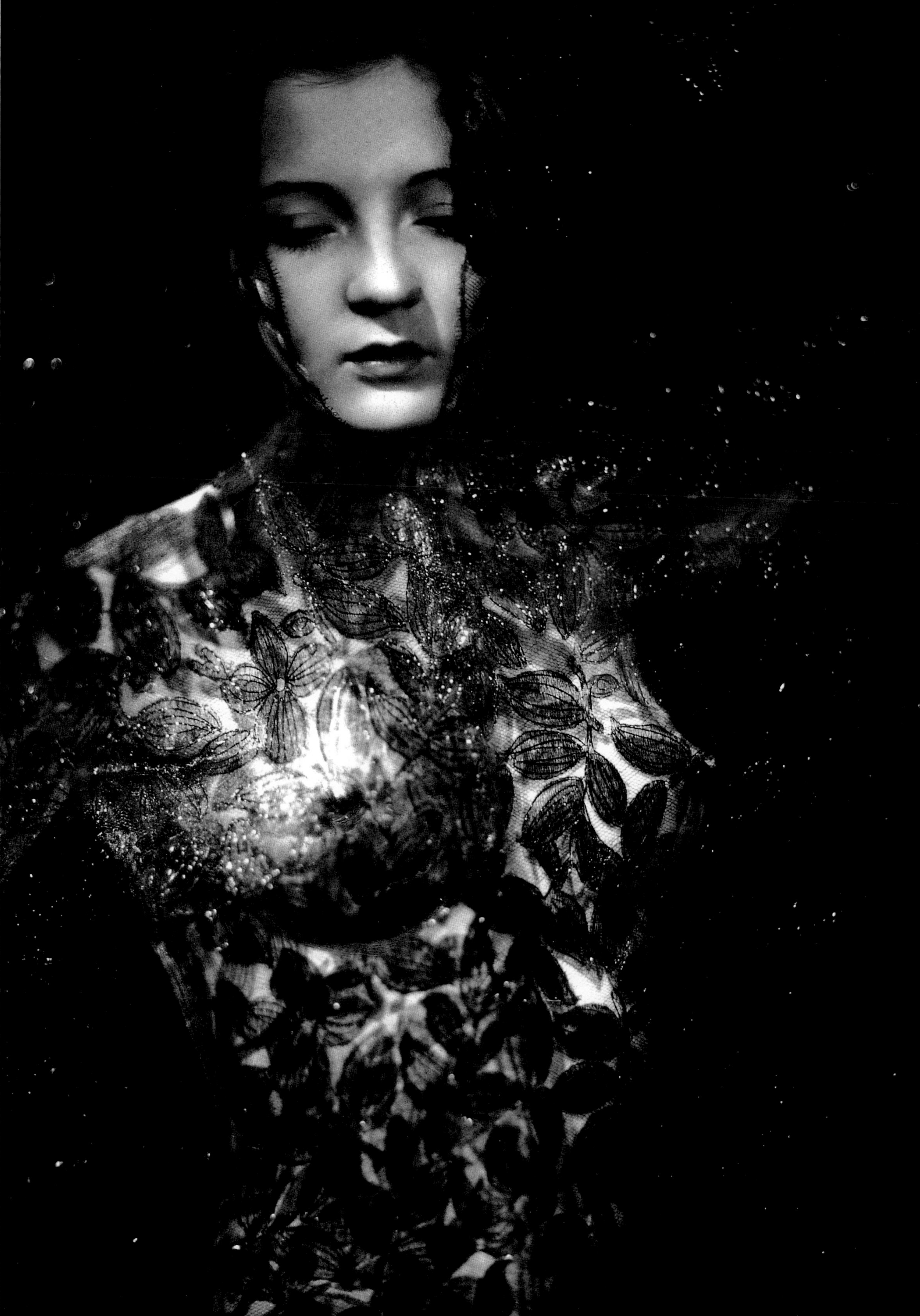

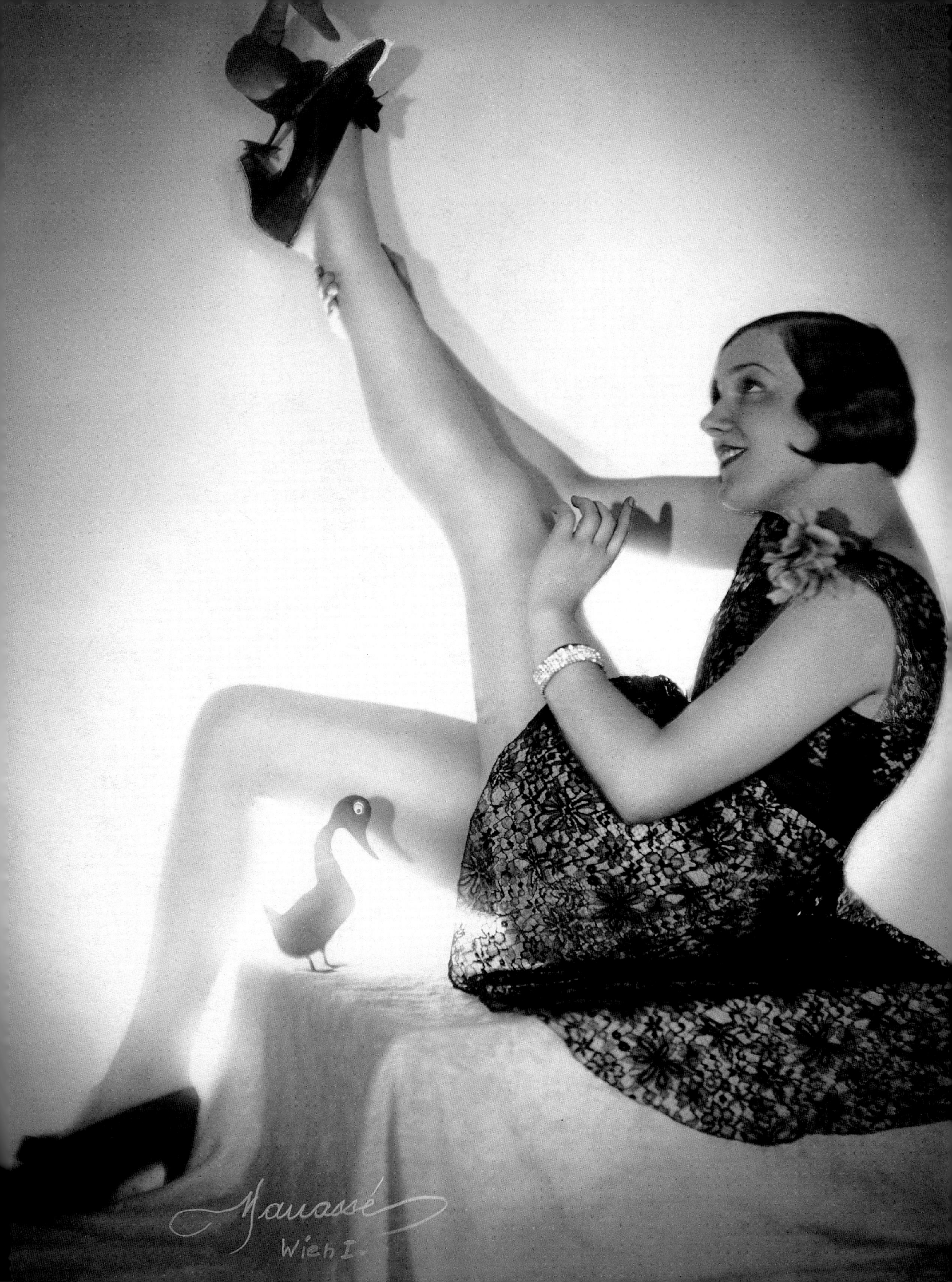
Manassé
Wien I.

"HUMOROUS PICTURES AND GROTESQUE PHOTOS"

According to Hans Frank and Peter Dressler, both of whom had contact with former assistants of the Wlassics, there was actually a division of labor in Studio Manassé. The photographic work, the staging in the studio and the photographing itself, was handled by Olga Wlassics. The final finishing, retouching, overpainting (above all on the countless covers for *Wiener Magazin* and on colored insertions in *Die Erotik in der Fotografie* in which almost no remnant of the photograph was visible), and the montages were the domain of Adorján. Judging exclusively by surviving documents, one would conclude just the opposite: Only Adorján's photography business license has been preserved, and the studio in Vienna, until it was moved to Berlin, was registered in his name, while Olga's membership in an association of artists is documented.

The couple's "artistic" streak played an especially important role in works that were described by the Schostal Agency as "humorous pictures and grotesque photos," called "photographic jokes" by some publications. These pictures, which had nothing but the models in common with the star portraits previously described, deal with very diverse subjects. They are alike in only one way: They are even farther removed from everyday life than the glamour photos by the absolute artificiality of their settings. However, there is no intention to create a dream of beauty and elegance, but rather to provoke laughter. Both genres of photography represent escape from the routine and commonplace. Both kinds of pictures stand in contrast to an unsatisfying reality. In the production of the glamour photo, the art of the studio consists in making the fantasy picture as believable as possible. The "photo joke," on the other hand, works in the opposite way, making the improbable and the artificially created clearly recognizable for what it is. This is how the photo joke differs from humorous snapshots such as those by Henri Cartier-Bresson, the appeal of which lies in the photographer's quick grasp of a comic situation.

This genre of photography and its wide publication in magazines of all sorts seem particularly unusual to the present-day observer because the photo joke has more or less fallen by the wayside. In the twenties and thirties it was dealt with on many different levels, either routinely or even as an aspect of the avant-garde. László Moholy-Nagy, in his forward-looking Bauhaus work of 1926, *Malerei, Fotografie, Film* (Painting, Photography, Film), classified the areas of application of the new medium: "Hyperreality, Utopia, and humor (here is the new joke!)" A few years later, a book entitled *Foto-Humor* appeared, which provided amateurs with detailed instructions on how to imitate the popular comical pictures.

Artists, professional photographers, and amateurs were able to fall back on a lively tradition of humorous iconography. The Wlassics, too, industriously mined this lode of witty erotic picture postcards from the second half of the nineteenth century. Whether they were risqué or corny, surreal or earthy, painted, drawn or photographed, these small mass-produced cards offered all the themes of the comic films of early days, and of many surrealistic collages and montages, plus jokes that actually originated in Studio

Hilde Thiele, c. 1927

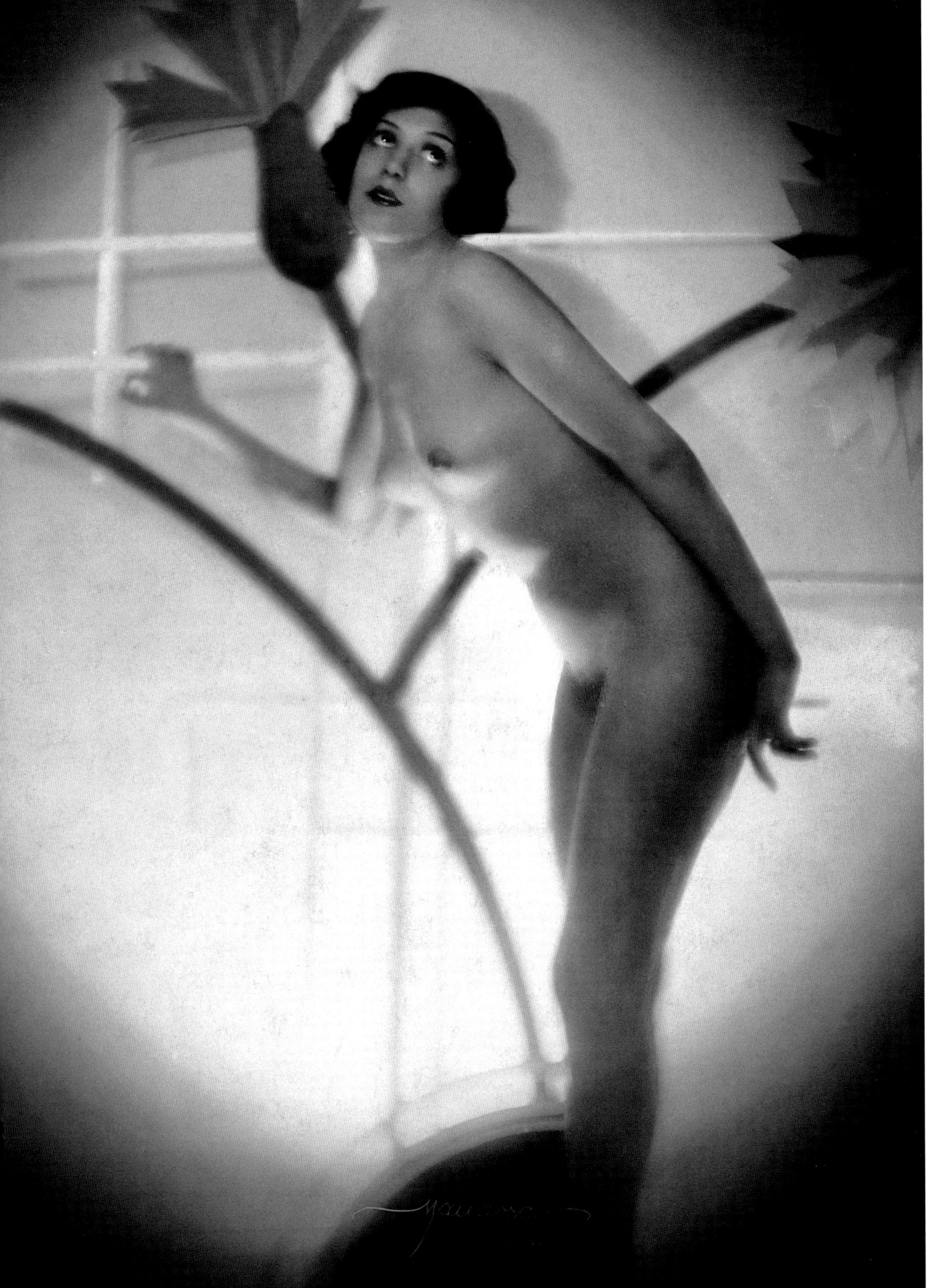

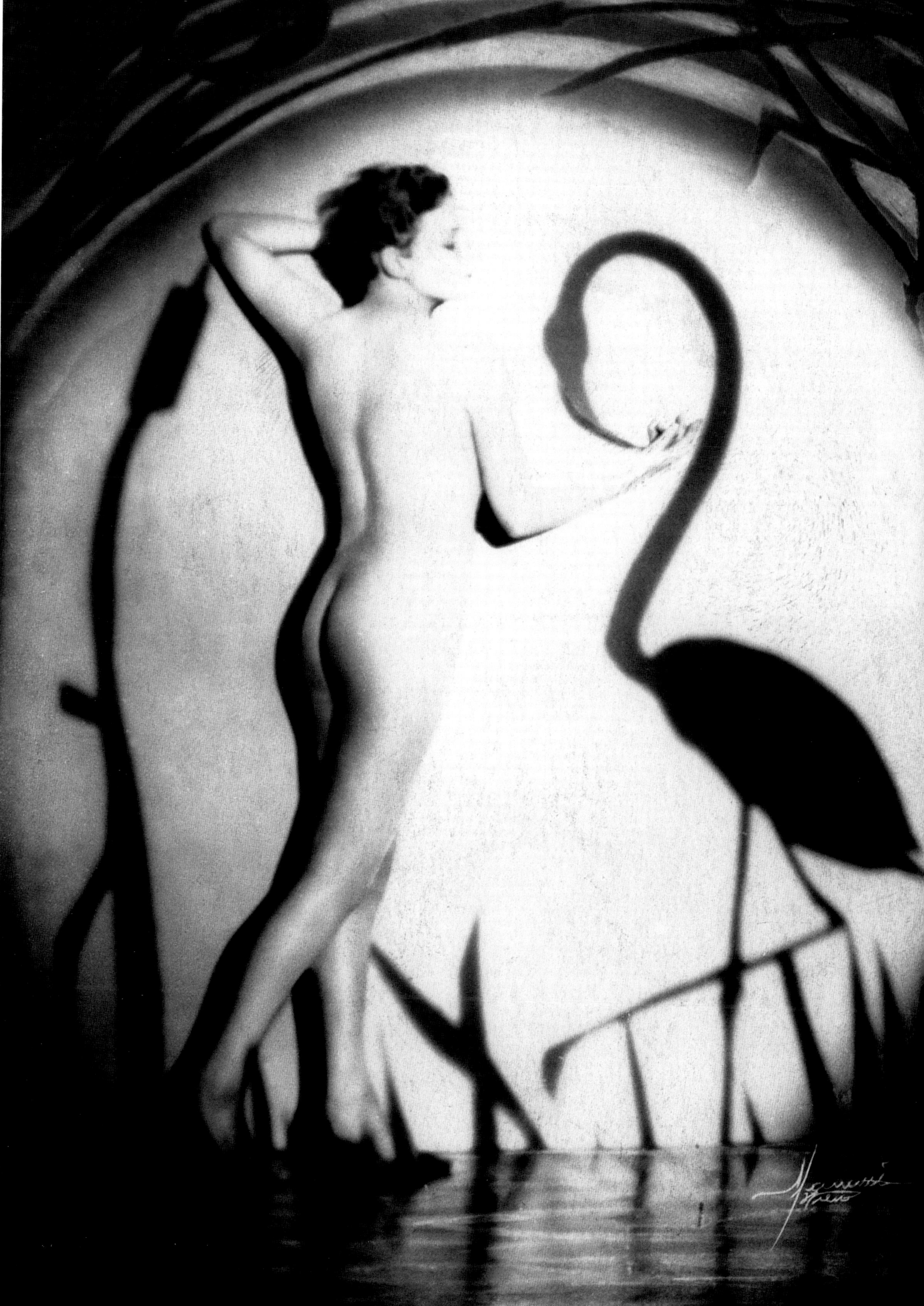

Previous two pages: Study, c.1927; Study, c.1926; these pages: Eva Verbee, c.1926; Study, c.1928

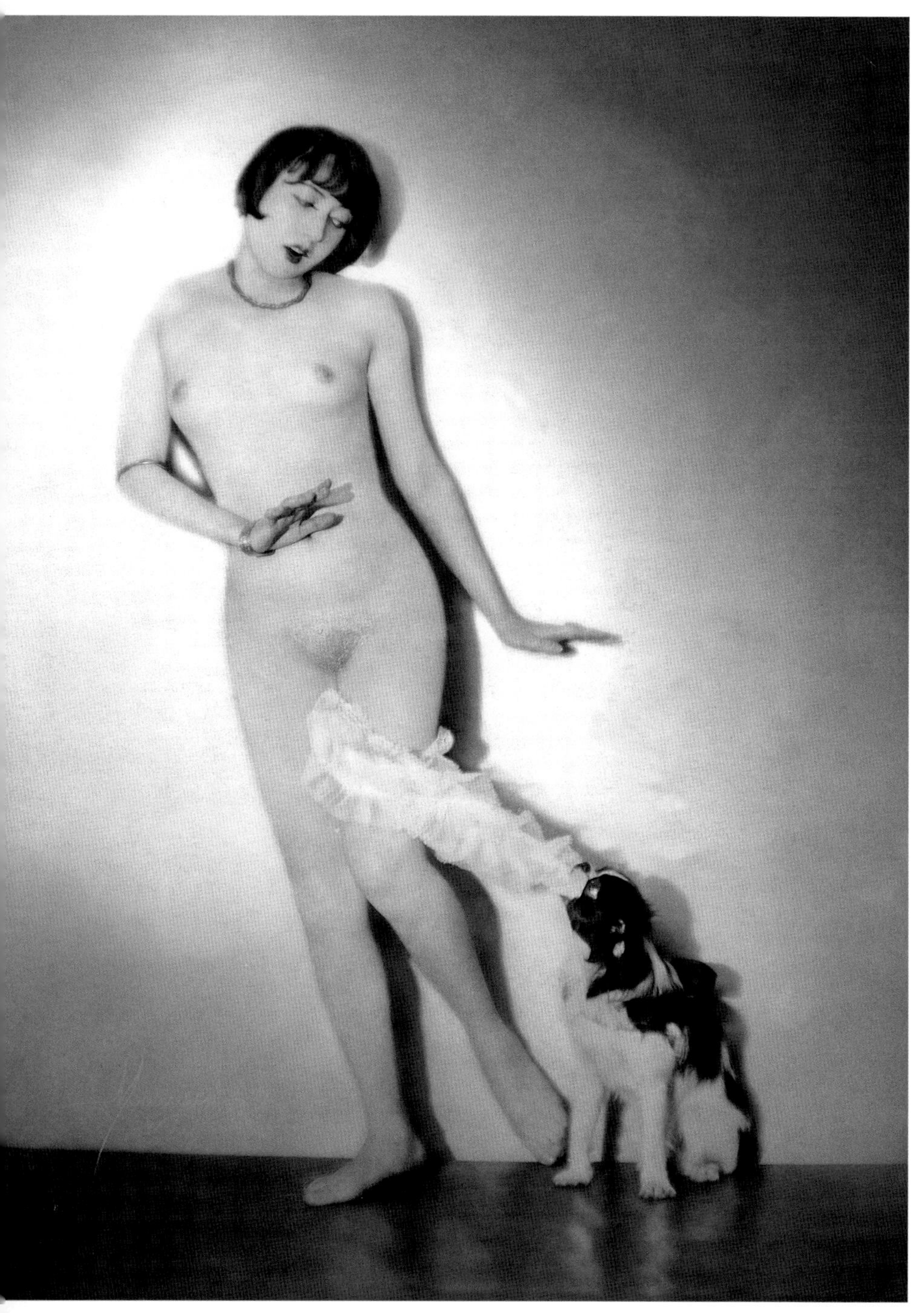

Manassé. Paul Eluard introduced almost 50 examples of these cards in 1936 in the surrealistic magazine *Minotaur* under the title *Les 100 plus belles cartes postales* (The most beautiful postcards). Eluard wrote, "All of it is only a pretext to show female nudity."

The prudish Victorian era—a parallel period in the area where German was spoken, which was under the rule of the no-less prudish emperors Franz Joseph and Wilhelm, was called *Gründerzeit*—acted like a hothouse for all sorts of fancies that either found ways around the strict rules of moral conduct or at least vegetated at the edge of respectability. Photographs and drawings of naked women could be distributed only under the pretext that they had artistic value and then only in a very limited way, subject to repeated interference by the censors. (The exceptions were humorous photographs.) It was no coincidence that nude studies, described as "artists' photographs," were marketed on a huge scale in the nineteenth century. Presumably, these were bought by painters and sculptors as substitutes for doing studies from life. Indeed, the earliest pin-up photographs in the United States were printed in magazines that, in name at least, were dedicated to "art photography."

These postcards—and also the pictures derived from them, which appeared in humorous magazines ranging from *Vie Pariesienne* and *Jugend* to *Muskete*—used all the prototypes that had been developed for caricatures and pictorial jokes in the course of a long tradition: exaggeration of physical features, distortion of size relationships, exaggeration of clumsiness or mishaps, "errors" in the pictorial medium itself (such as wrong perspective), combinations of people or things that were absurd because in reality they were impossible, etc. The material could deal with wordplay and puns, as well as references to fairy tales, myths, or any well-known subjects or excesses in everyday life. Common clichés might be grossly

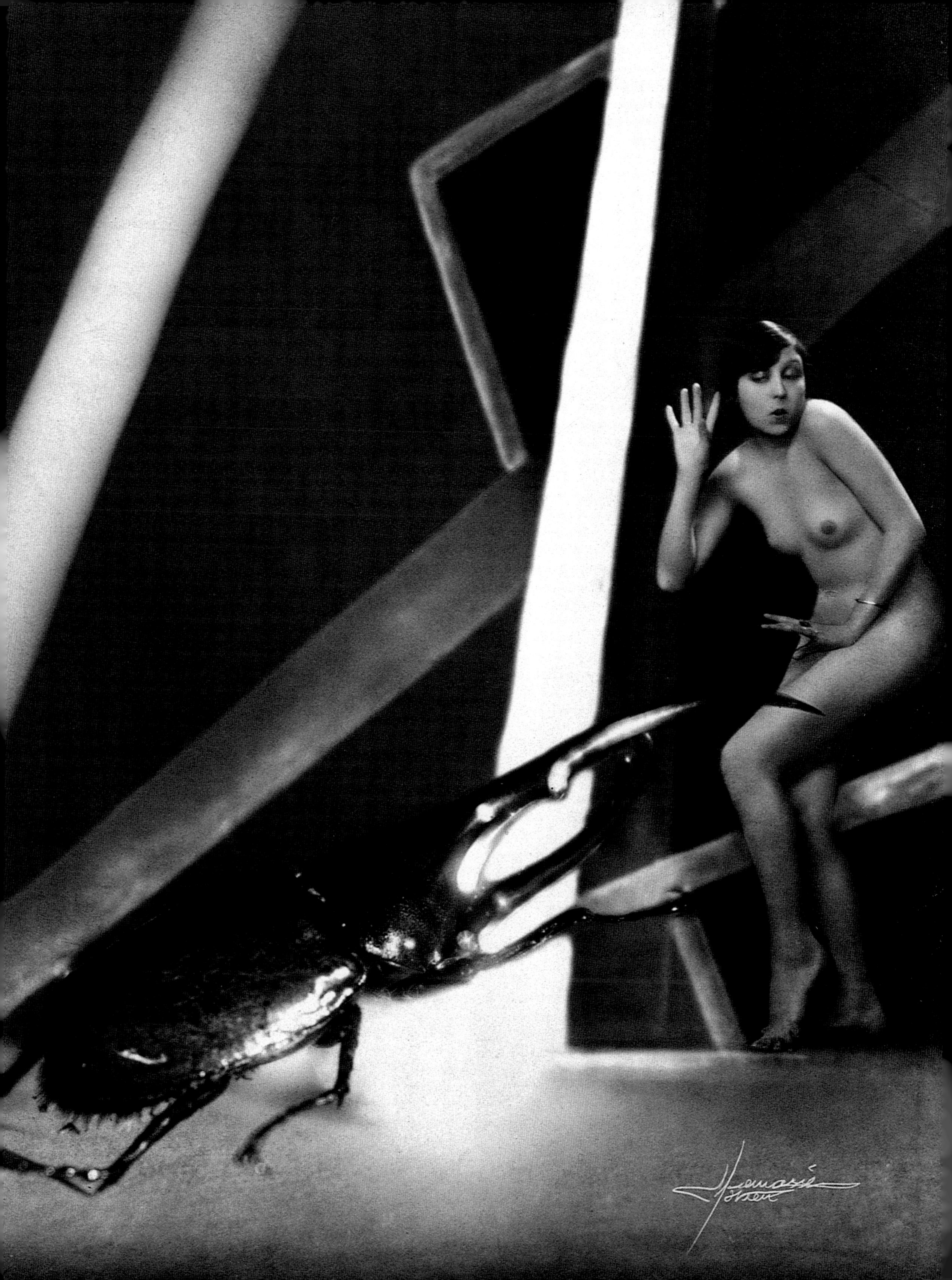
Manassé
Wien

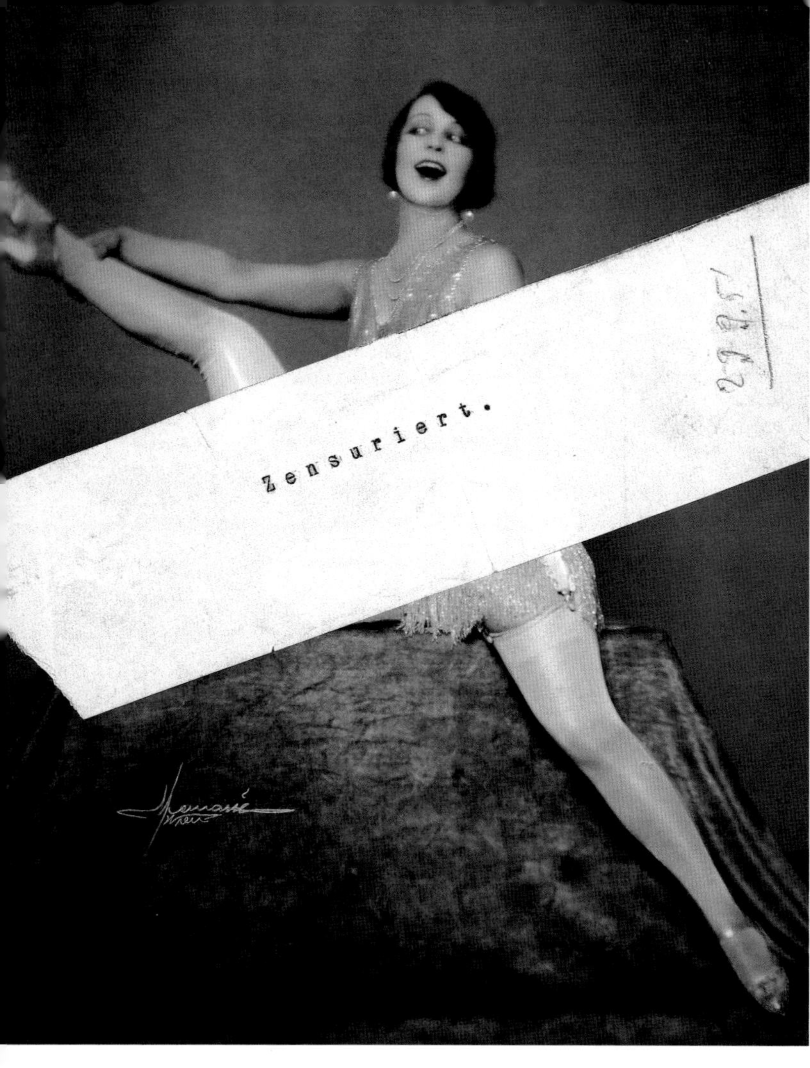

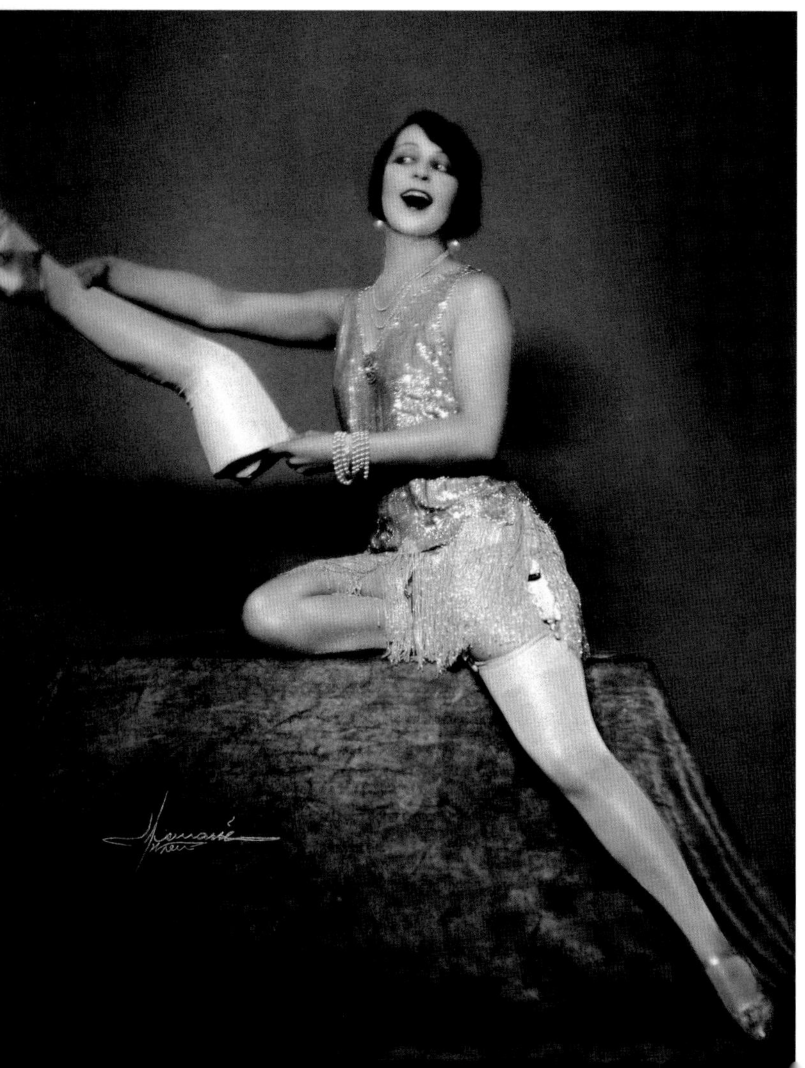

exaggerated or might be made ridiculous by switching them around into their opposites. Photography added a twist to things that were already funny in a drawing. The reference to reality immanent in these media derives from the technical process of their production, coupled with the manipulations which made the creation of a "joke," in whatever form, possible in the first place. This lends the presentation an ambivalent effect—it is basically artificial since it hasn't been taken from an existing reality. As early as 1924, Béla Balázs compared the differences between the same imaginative motif used in a textual narrative and in film: "A fairy tale miracle can never be taken seriously in film despite the fact that film technology makes any illusion possible. Or precisely because of that fact. Because the public has an *awareness of film technology,* and the most spine-chilling fantasy tale amuses us as an ingenious technological trick." Or to descend from the level of the theoretical to a more naive but surely no less widely held interpretation of the handling of this problem, here is a 1934 quotation from one of the previously mentioned sets of "Instructions" for creating joke photographs from *Lichtbildner,* a Viennese amatuer photography magazine: "One doesn't quite know whether it's a trick or not; for the whole thing is obviously a photograph and therefore conceivably a believable proof for existing facts, which one would not ordinarily dare to doubt." The article continues, "One of the basic reasons for the comic effect lies in this unconditional belief in photography; it is one of the chief tricks of photo humorists."

The same article is illustrated with Carlheinz Albrand's photo montage entitled, *Das Kaffeebad* (The coffee bath), which has a close affinity with some of the joke pictures from the Manassé studio, ranging from *Mein Zuckerl* (My Sweetie) in the mid-twenties, to *Sie stolpern über Schritt und Tritt über die schönsten Frauen* (At every step they trip over beautiful women), which was reproduced in 1936 in *Muskete*. However, it also reveals the gulf between the harmless cleverness of this amateur product by Albrand and the professional irony present in the Wlassics' montages. The methods used are identical.

The *Lichtbildner* article goes on to analyze and explain what actually happens: "What is the source of the amusing, baffling effect? It is in the fact that photos which really have nothing to do with each other have been melded into *one* picture, and moreover not in the usual scale of the photograph, but in part as *enlargement* and in part as *contact copy*. In this way the comic situation is created. ... The components must be very meticulously cut out. To make cutting edges and picture lines invisible or to complete broken lines, one takes white and black watercolors, mixes them, and applies them with a fine, pointed retouch brush. ... The finished photo montage is then photographed again; on the surface, the reproduction gives the illusion of being a genuine photograph."

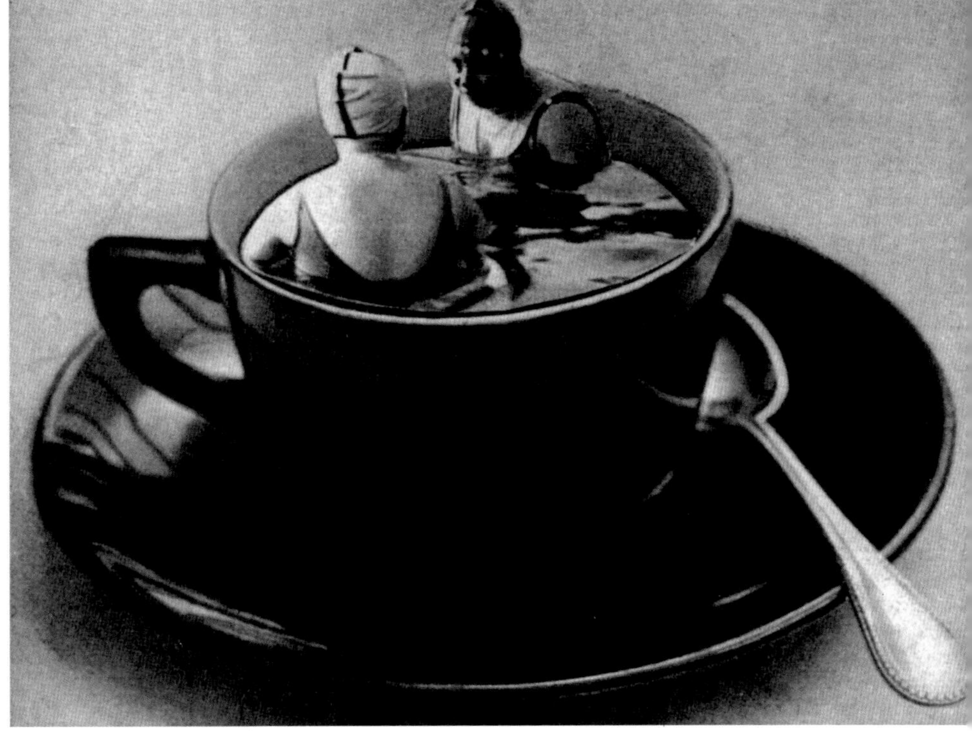

Both in Albrand's and in the Wlassics' pictures the figures of people either shrink to tiny dimensions in relationship to the objects surrounding them, or the objects grow to enormous proportions. As in *Gulliver's Travels* one can conceive of either change in scale and project the pictures into it. Women can bathe in coffee cups, they can fit into a spoon, a mousetrap, a champagne glass, or a cigarette box. In the Albrand pictures the dwarf women merely stand in a baffling relationship to a commonplace household item, but in the Manassé pictures there is always a connection between a tiny naked woman and a huge, always fully clothed man. The man's wishes are served both by the item pictured, which corresponds to his size, and also by its tiny occupant. For example, the dwarfed woman sweetens his coffee, she turns up in a gemstone, hangs on the Christmas tree as an ornament, or is fed inside a birdcage. She is a pleasant accessory constantly available to the man, who is often, but not always, directly visible in the picture. Today's viewers, sensitized by feminist discourse since the 1970s, are certainly not the first to be aware of the misogynism in such representations, which have their roots in male fantasies based on a latent fear of the other sex. Even in 1933, *Muskete,* one of the magazines that published such montages, printed a self-mocking piece: "Using a patented process, an American researcher has finally succeeded in making women as small as men would like them to be. In

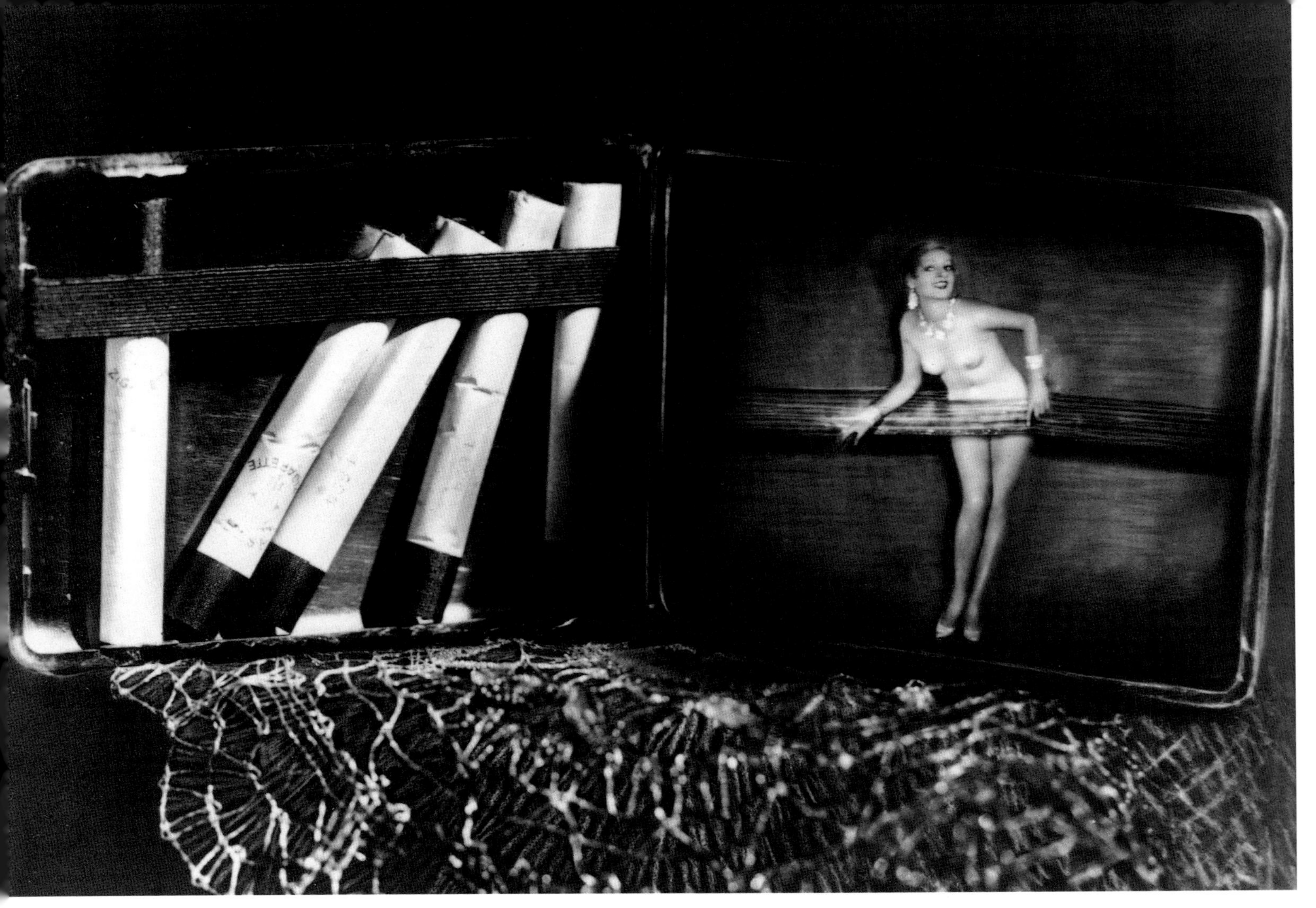

photos made available to us, he presents us with some of his results." For once these photos were not from Studio Manassé; they were anonymous pictures. A number of other commercial studios had published such montages, but I know of none that had as many as Studio Manassé. Among these studios were Residenz-Atelier, Willinger, and d'Ora-Benda in Vienna, Walther Jäger and Studio Binder in Berlin, and Josef Pecsi in Budapest. Pecsi discussed the method of photo montage in his 1930 book, *Photo und Publizität* (Photos and Publicity) and illustrated it with appropriate examples.

In 1927, before *Muskete* published the first Manassé workshop montages based on the above principle, there had already been a whole series of covers done by various artists who presented this kind of joke in drawings and relied almost entirely on postcard models. Many magazines during the period between the wars remained undecided as to whether to give preference to drawn or photographic versions of jokes. The first photographic illustrations appeared in *Muskete* in 1924; after that there was a marked increase in their use, but they never quite supplanted the drawings. One of the reasons for this was that it offered variety to the male reader. (Women were probably not targeted readers.) There was also another completely different reason: In 1934 an entire issue of *Muskete* was confiscated by the censor because of a nude photo from Studio Manassé (!) in which the retouch did not quite meet requirements. Merely the hint of pubic hair or even the traces left by the retouch brush in the process of completely eliminating it, brought an immediate condemnation of the picture as "obscene." A ban on the sale of that particular issue followed. However, the next month, the confiscated edition of *Muskete* was republished in identical form, the only difference being that the Manassé photo was again retouched, this time properly! (I mention this just in passing to give an idea of the "timeless" nature of this type of magazine.)

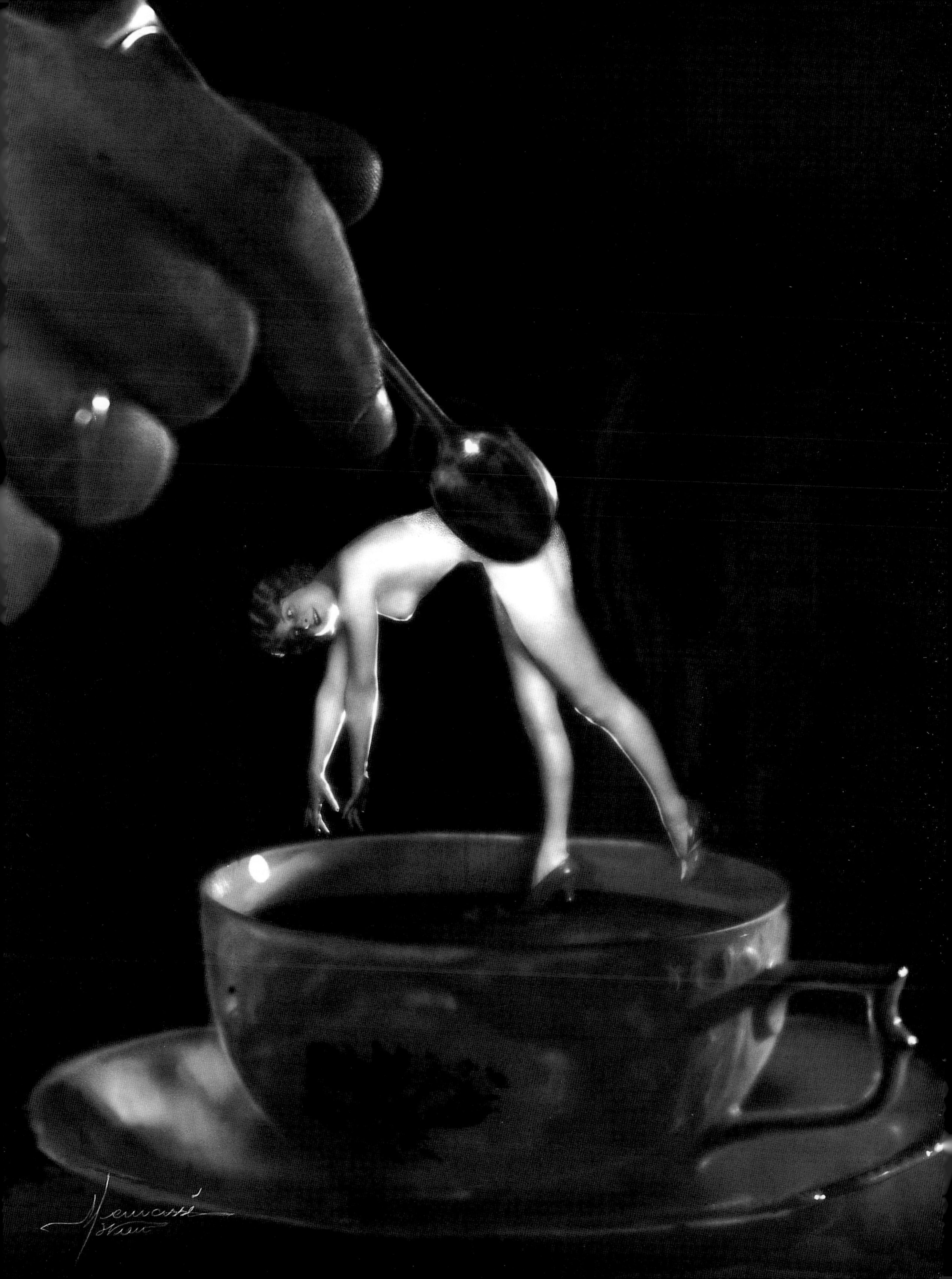

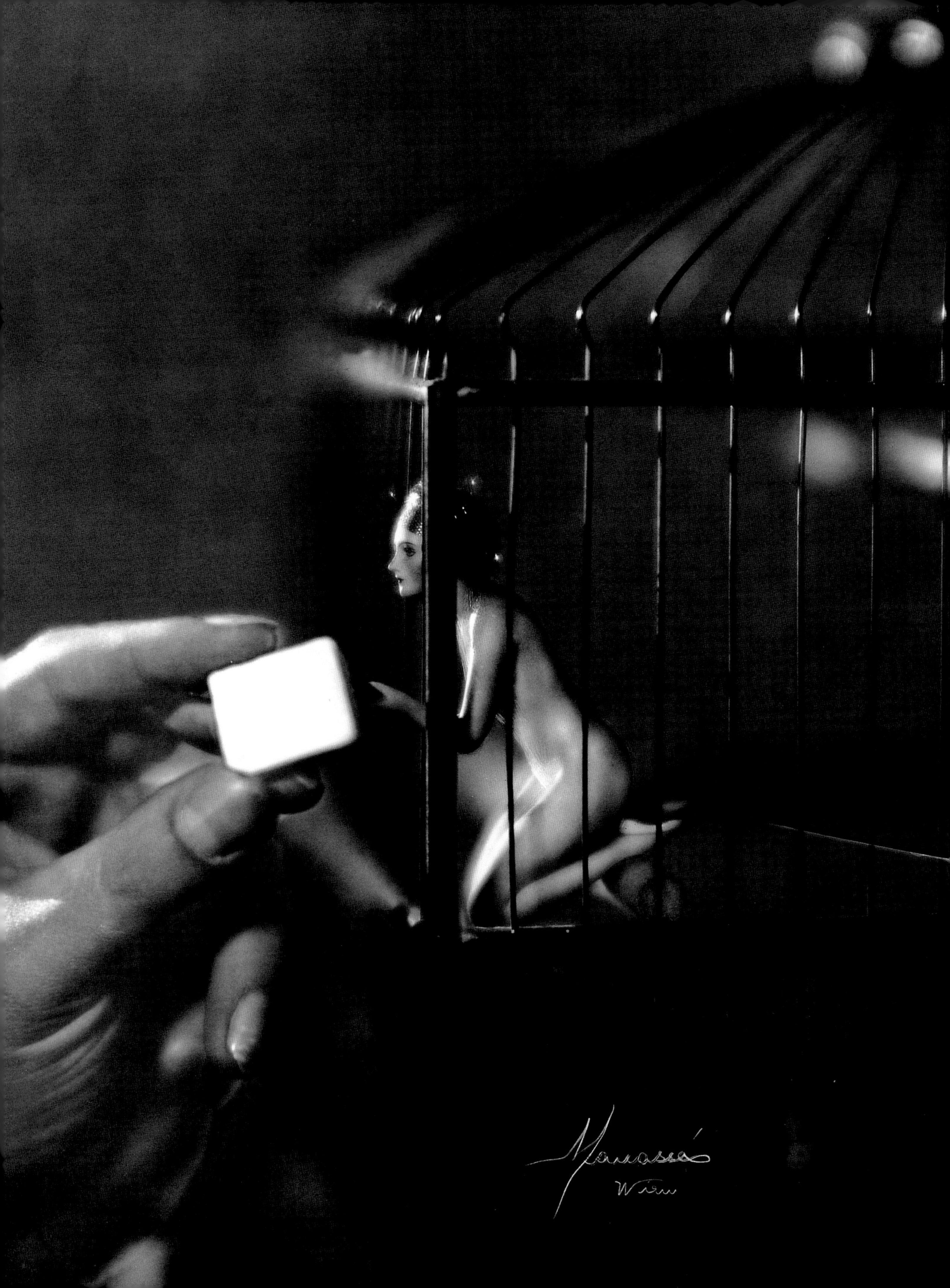
Manassé
Wien

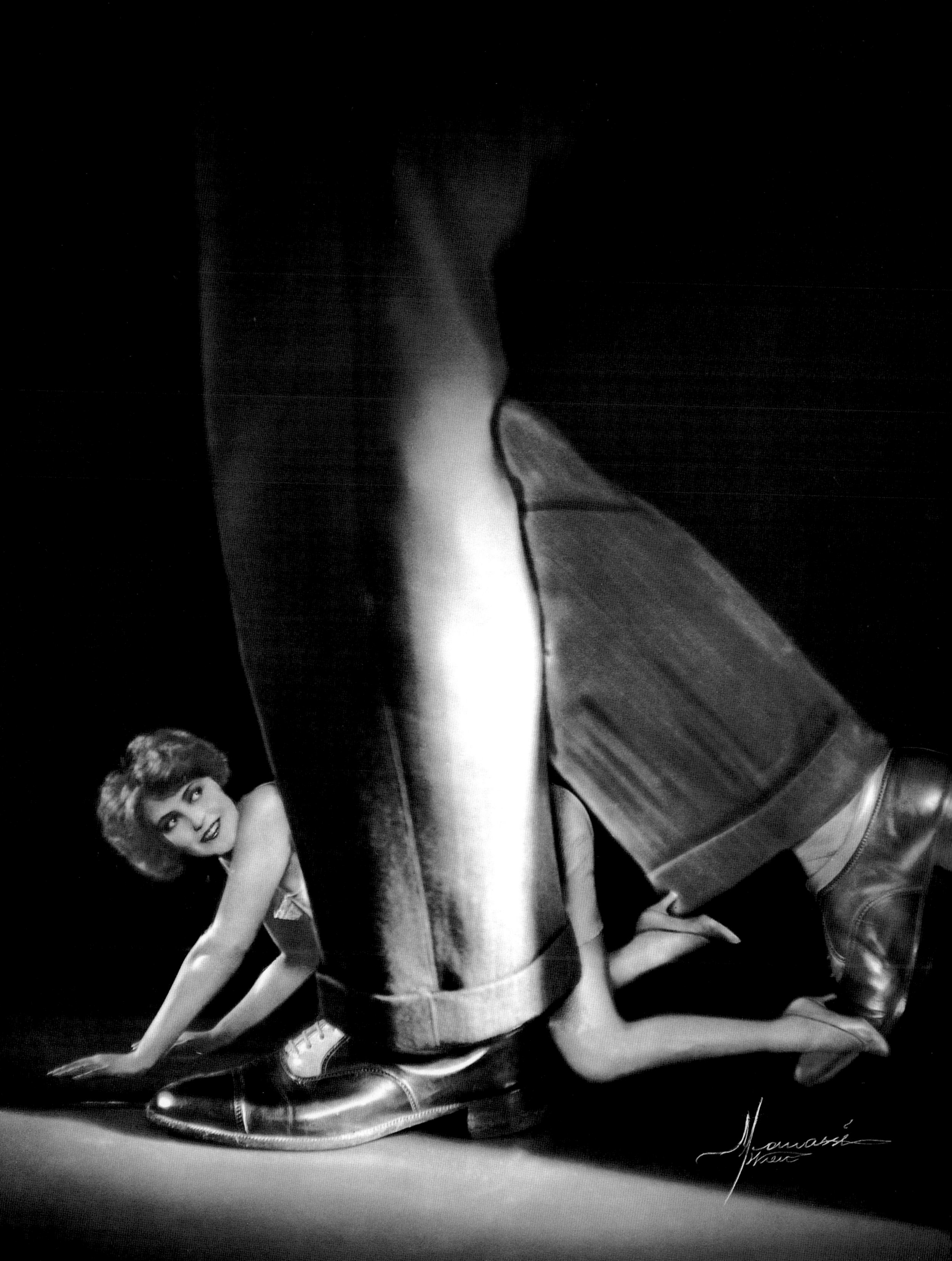
Manassé
Wien

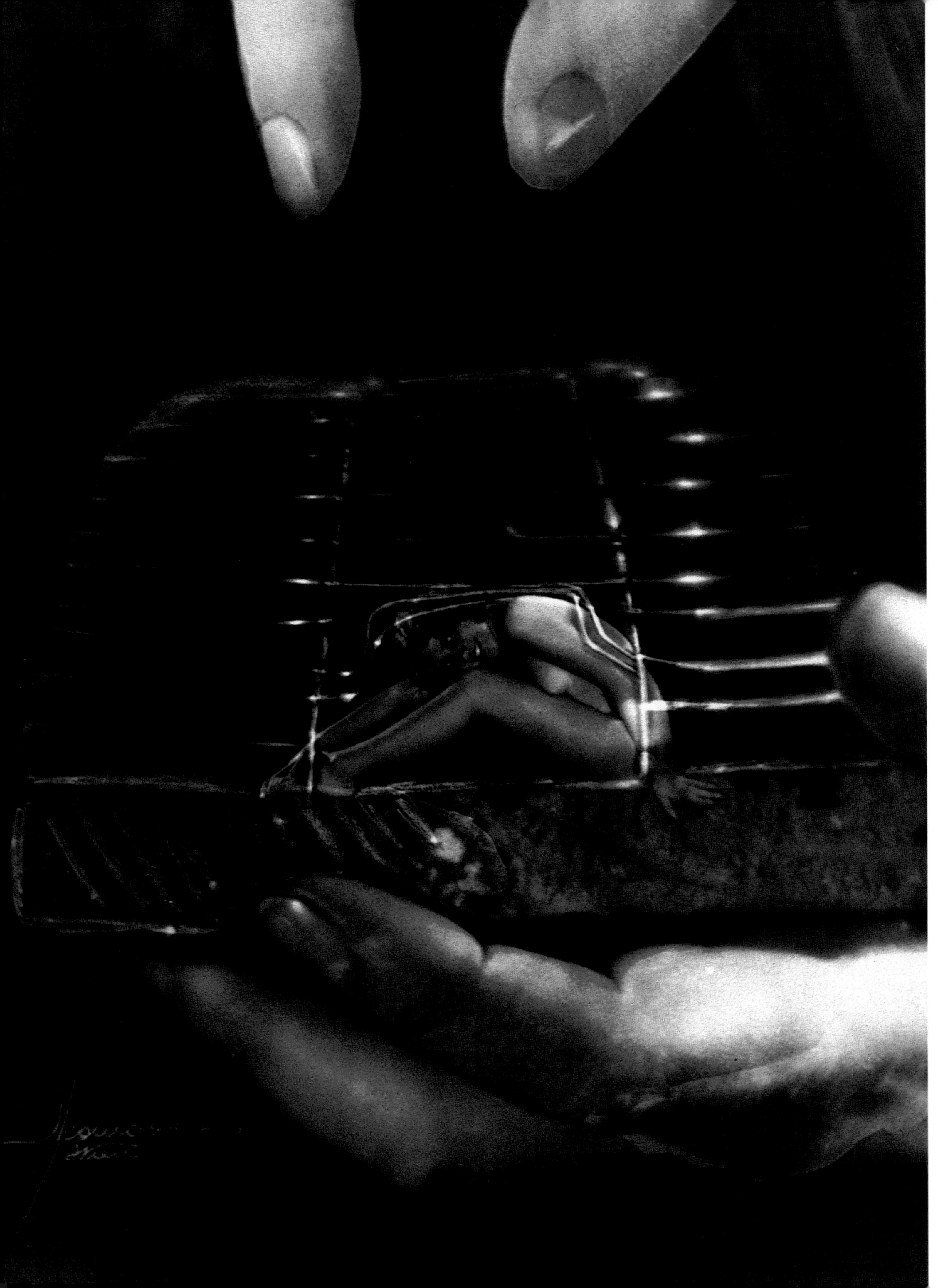

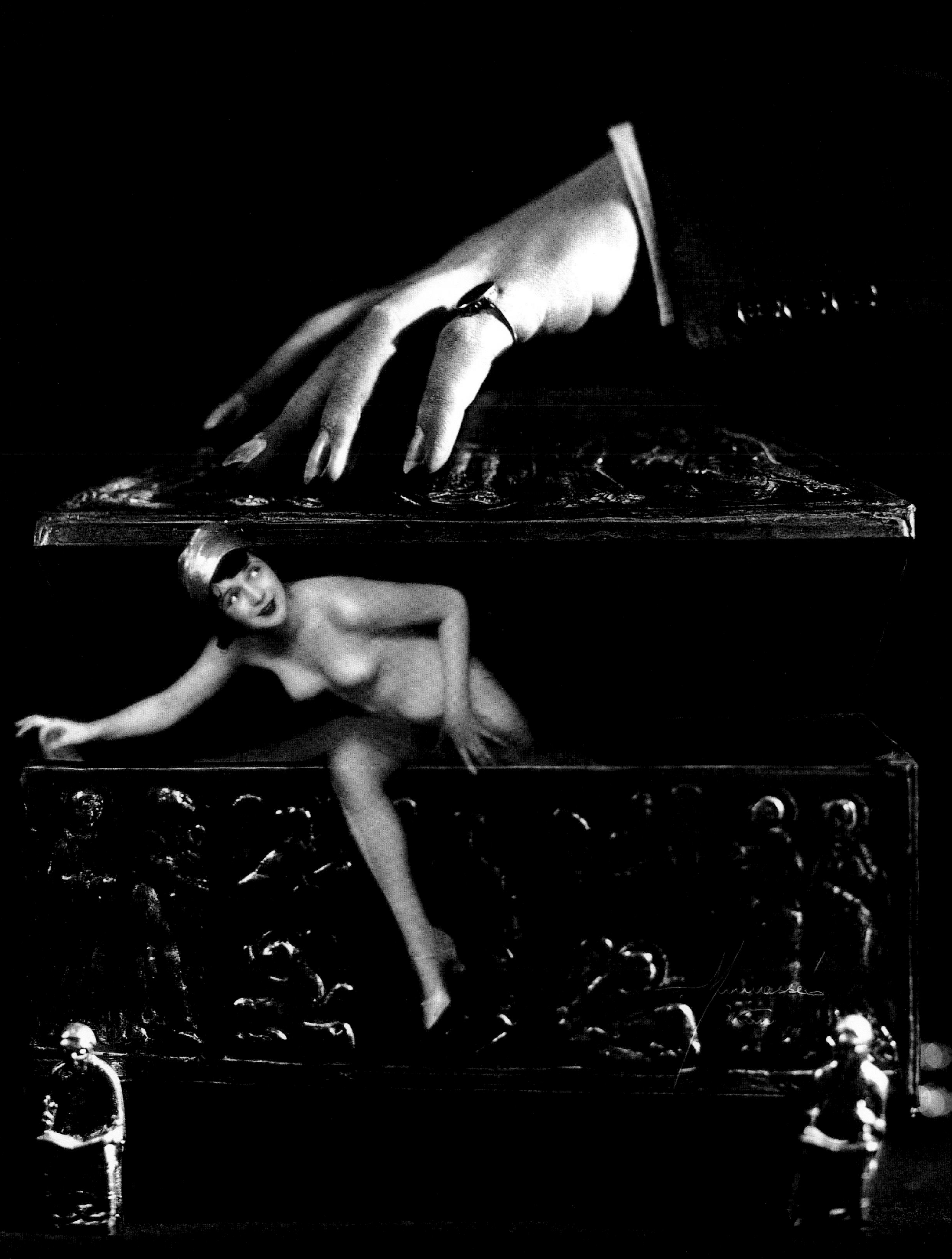

Previous two pages: My Little Bird, c.1926; My Kitten, c.1926; My Little Mouse, c.1928; Study, c.1926; these pages: Study, c.1933; My Dear, c.1926

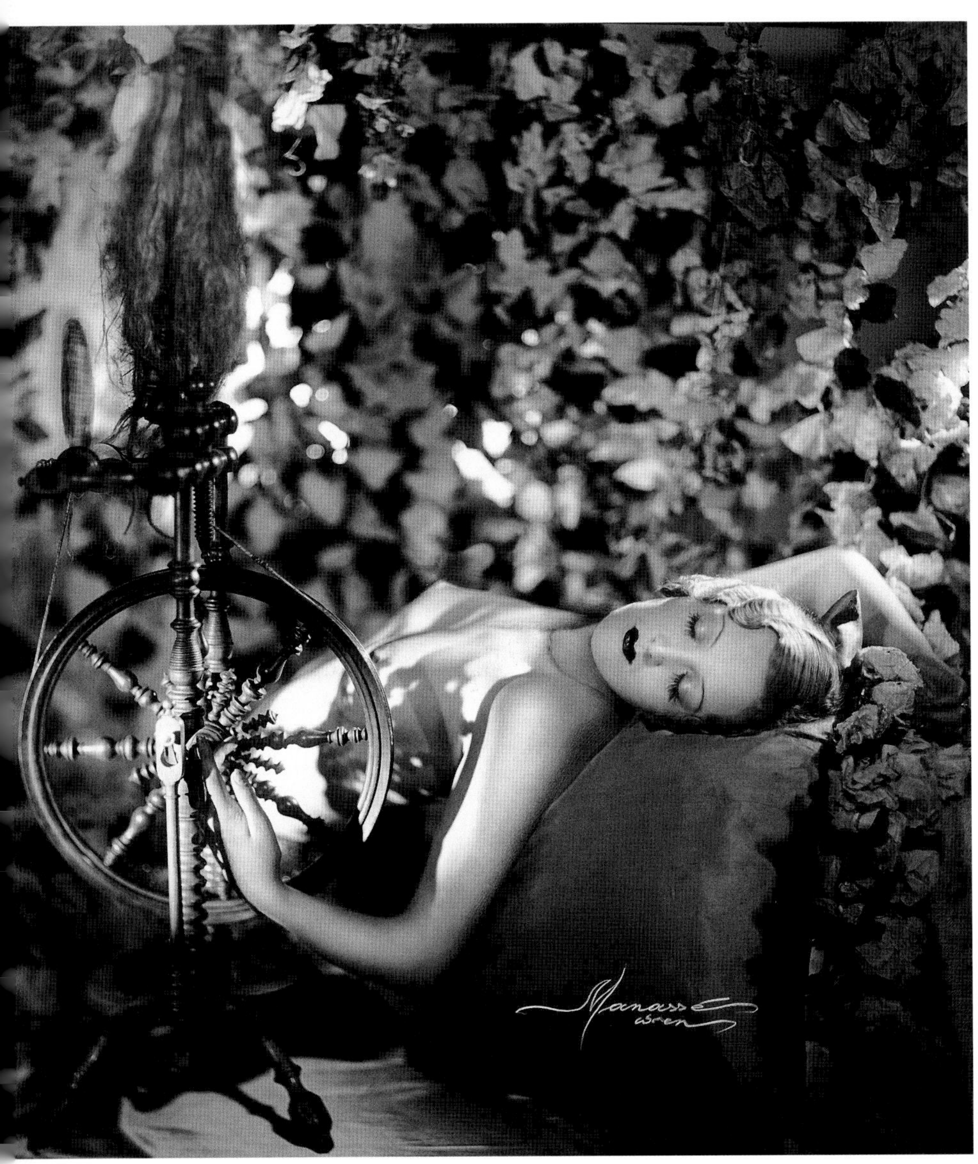

It would be a mistake for us to see a shortcoming in the failure in those days to refer to the sociopolitical reality of the time. This fade-out of reality did not happen by accident; it was planned. Indeed it may seem remarkable today, but it was all actively related to the fairy-tale world that was cultivated in *Muskete*. In 1923 the magazine filled an entire issue with contemporary illustrations of *1001 Nights*, a resource that was familiar and popular with the Wlassics too, much like the well-known stories of the Grimm brothers. In addition to producing a fairy-tale-like character by using a montage of photographs, Manassé also used the technique of staging completely fantastic scenes in the studio: The set, featuring the usual skimpily dressed leading lady, was furnished with standard props, which ranged from garden dwarfs, fake trees, and plastic frogs to carnival masks. Then with the use of backdrop projections, clever lighting, and retouching, the desired effects were achieved. It wasn't obligatory to follow the plot of the familiar fairy tale in all respects: Contradictions were popular ("something like a fairy tale, but certainly not puss-in-boots," fig., p. 6). Just a hint of the tale, a tiny motif, was enough to awaken desired associations in the viewer, to maintain the state of suspense between the realism of the photograph per se and the lack of reality in the individual representations. In some of these scenes where the naked woman is seen in front of silhouettes of flowers, animals, or body parts, shadows thrown on the background play a unique role. Are we perhaps confronted here with a visual stand-in or double for the phenomenon of a viewer's thoughts being projected into a picture, without which all the pictures mentioned would lack any meaning? If so, an ambivalence would arise in the pictures comparable to a form of satire used in literature and drama: The criteria of a certain genre—in this case pin-ups and jokes—are fulfilled. Then, however, the product itself indirectly caricatures the consumer/reader/viewer. In the grotesque photos of Studio Manassé, the extreme exaggeration of the role

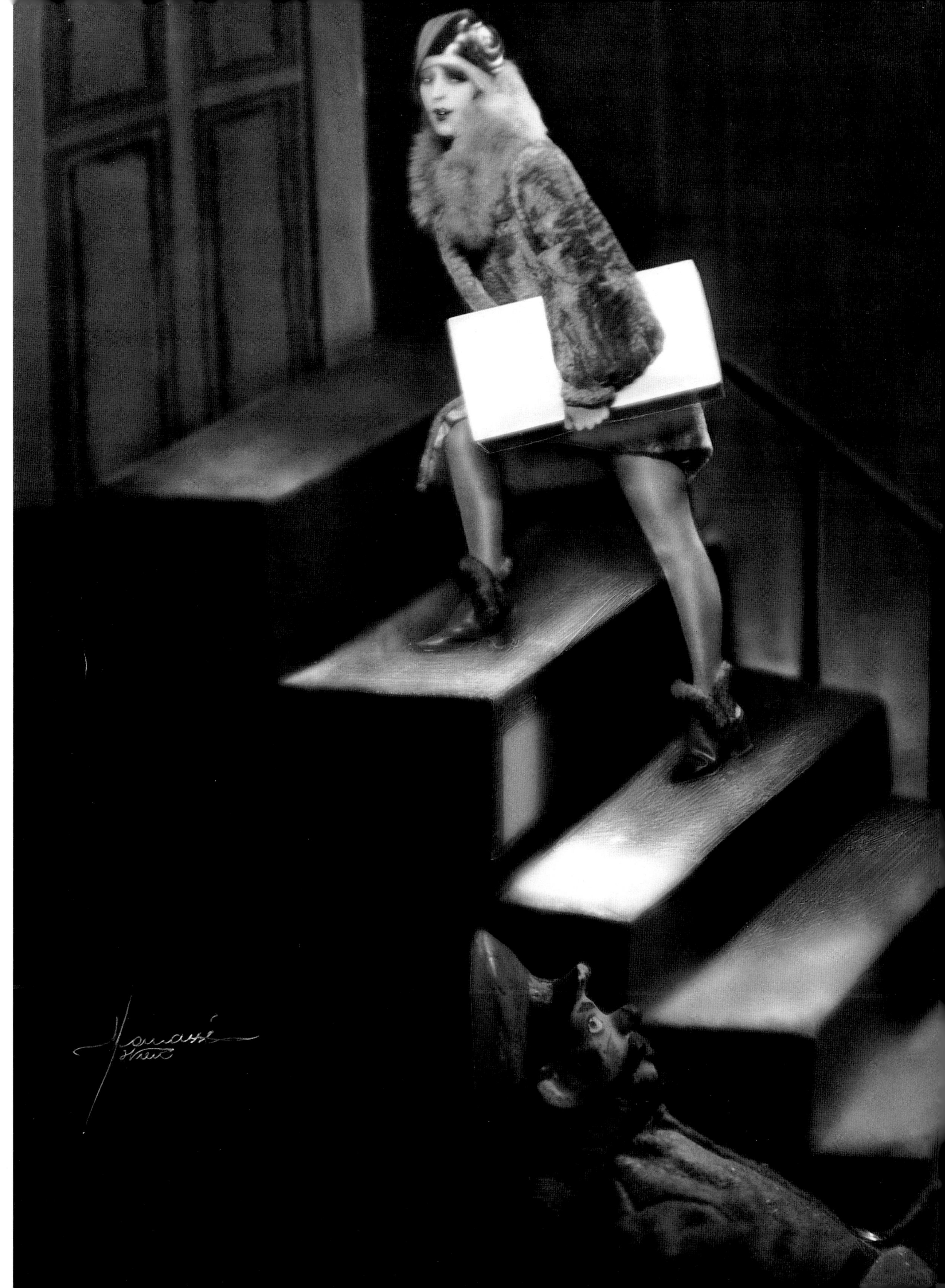

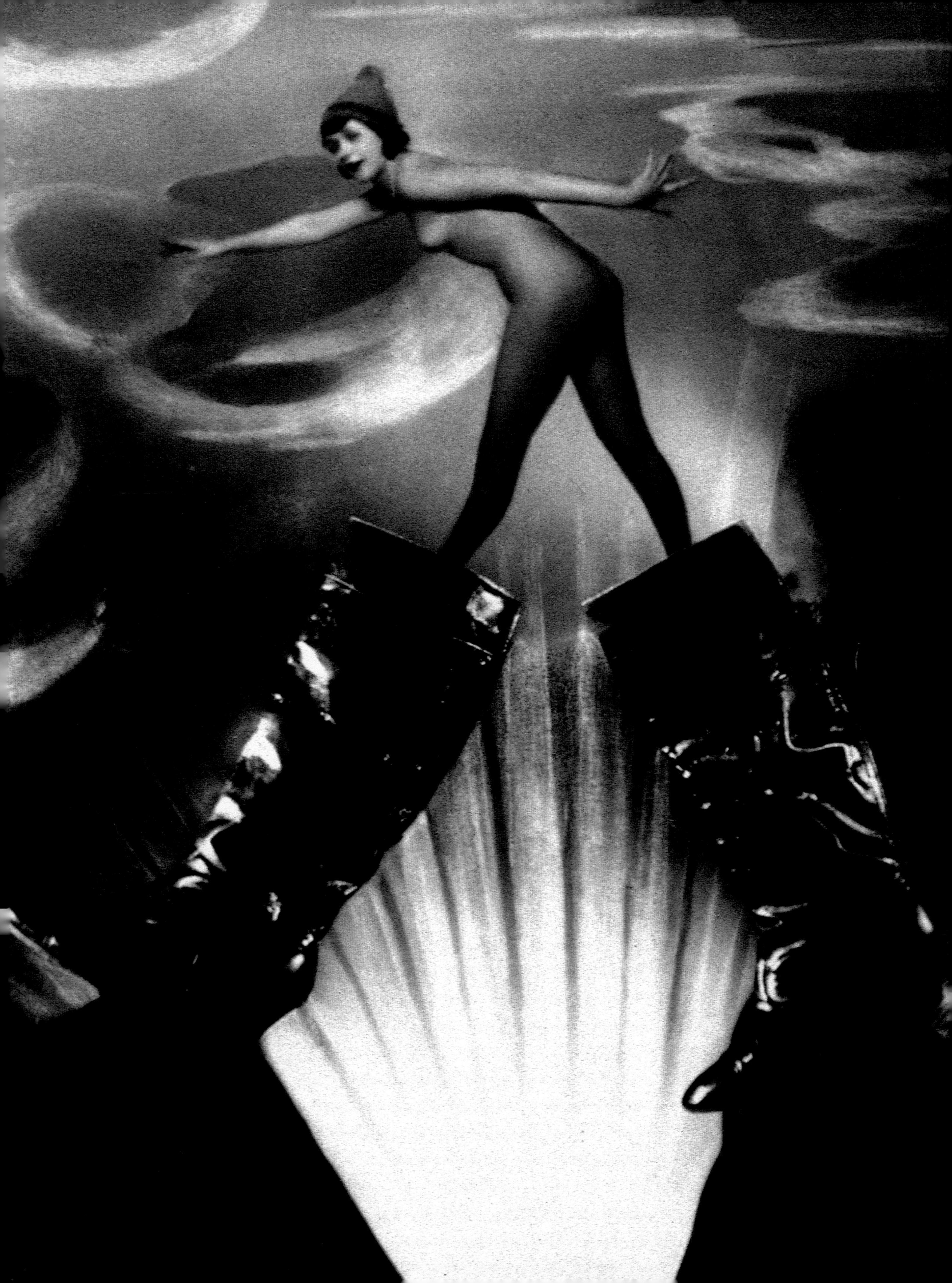

of the woman as a freely available object of male desires or as mirror and projection screen of fantasies reveals the viewer as an object of ridicule. Is this the *Entstellung zur Kenntlichkeit* (Distortion of reality in order to make it recognizable) that Brecht demanded for the theater?

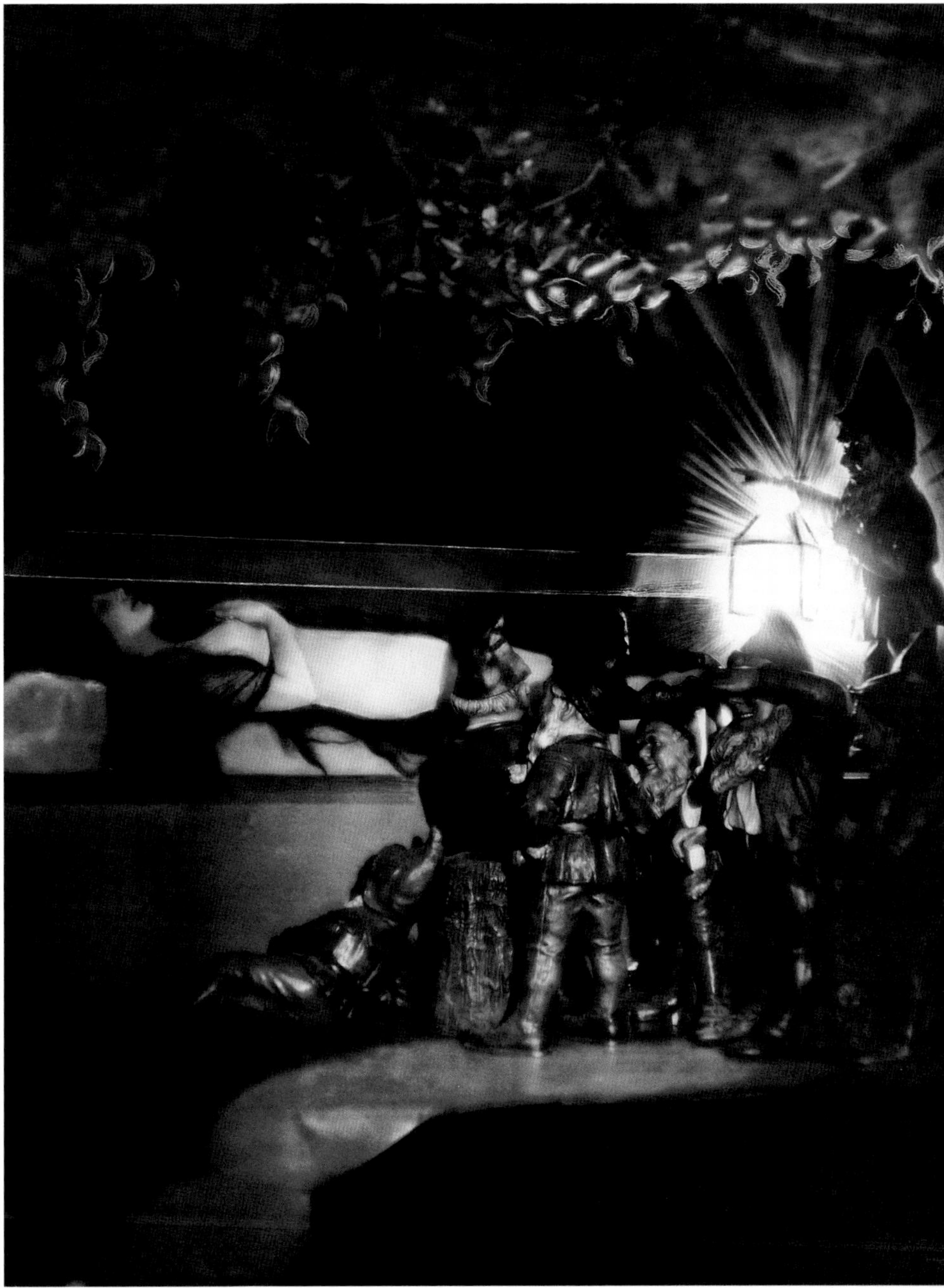

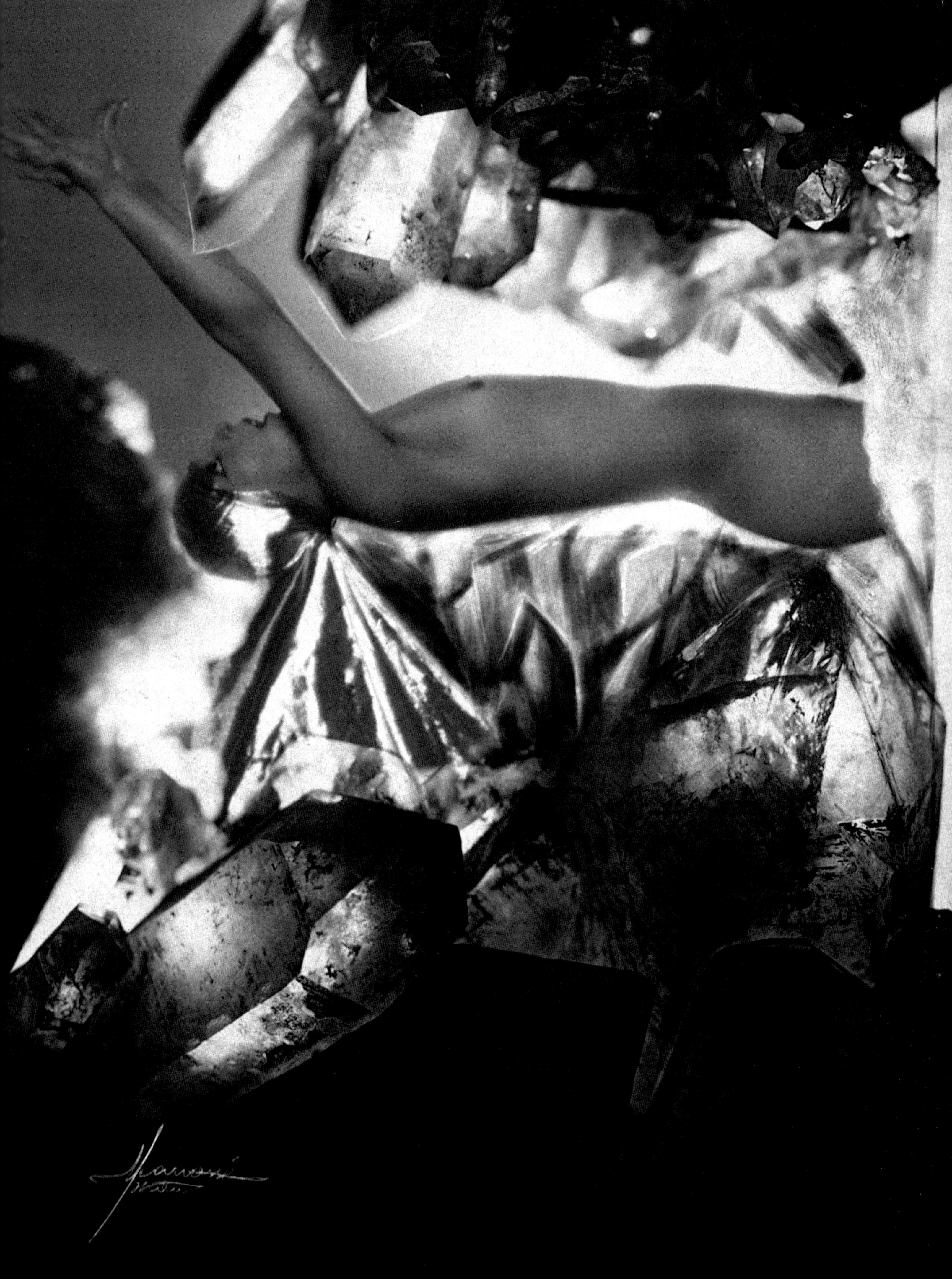

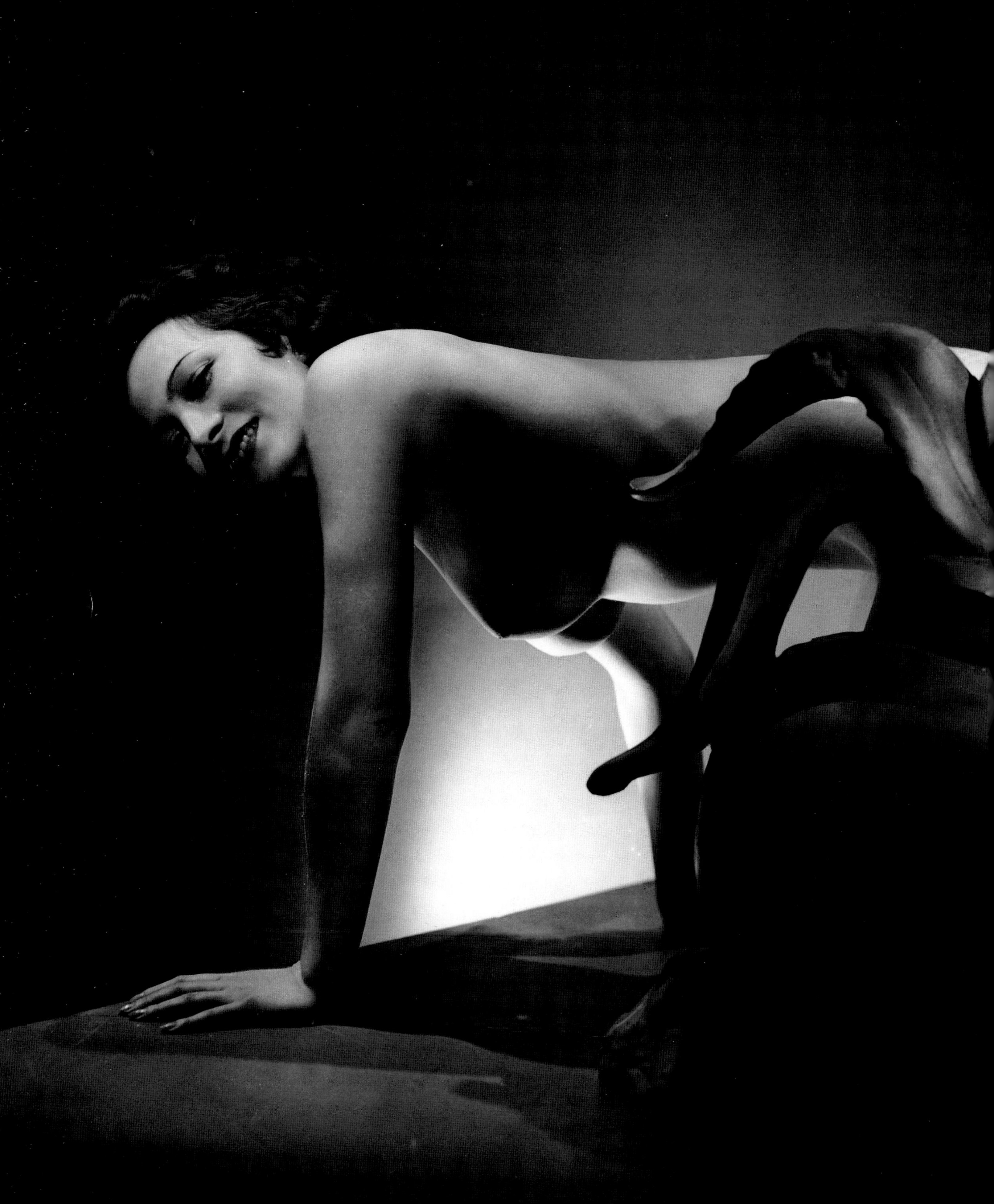

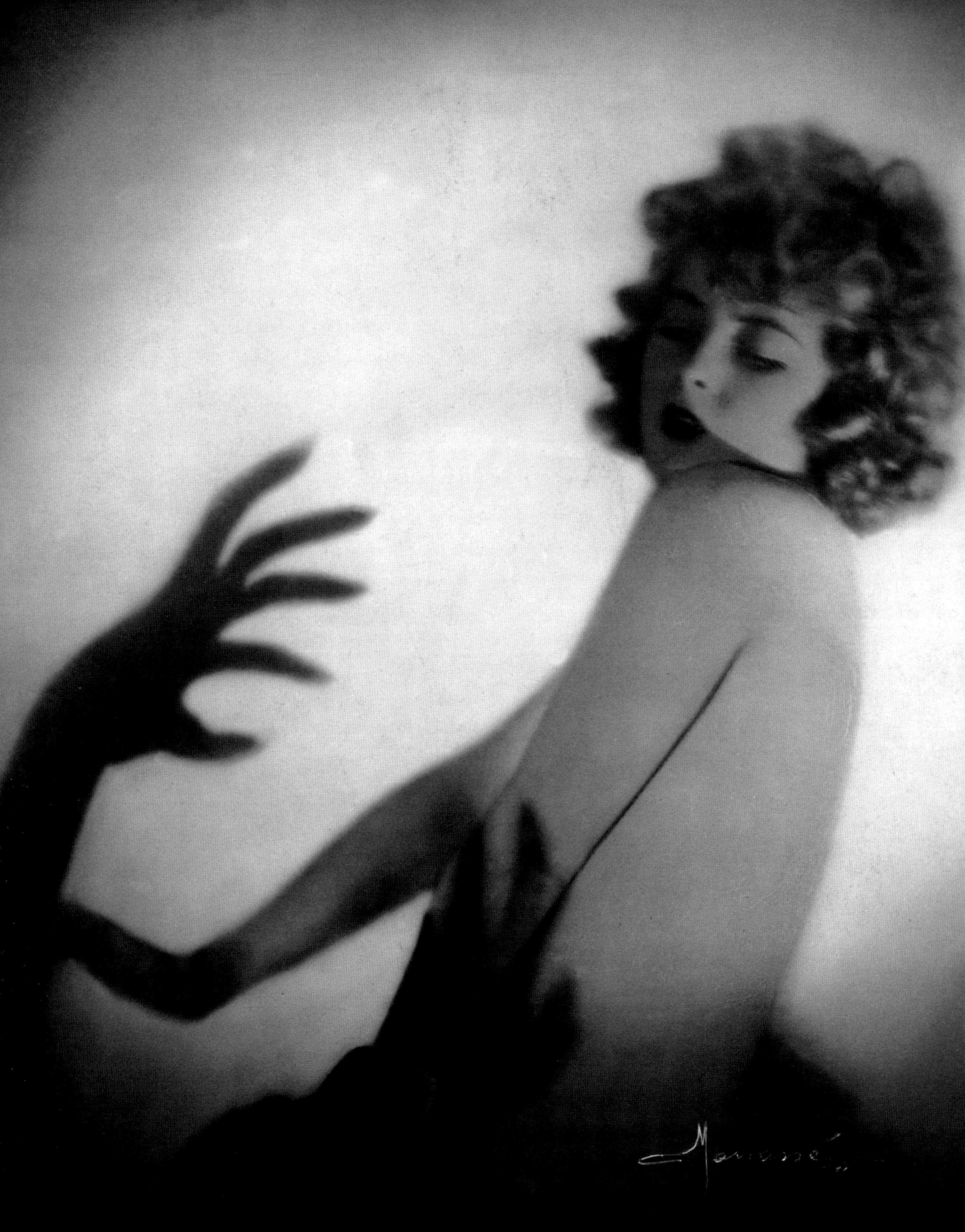
Manassé

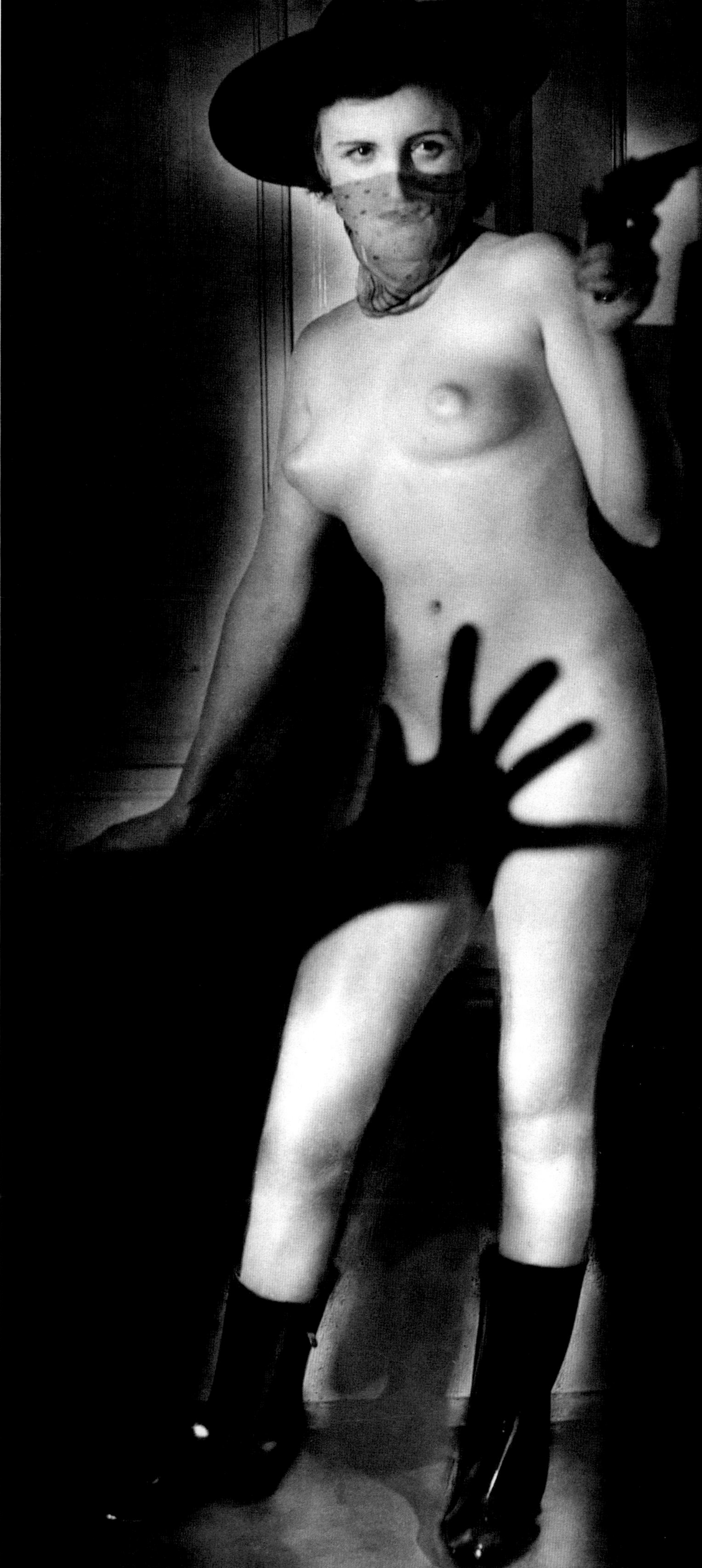

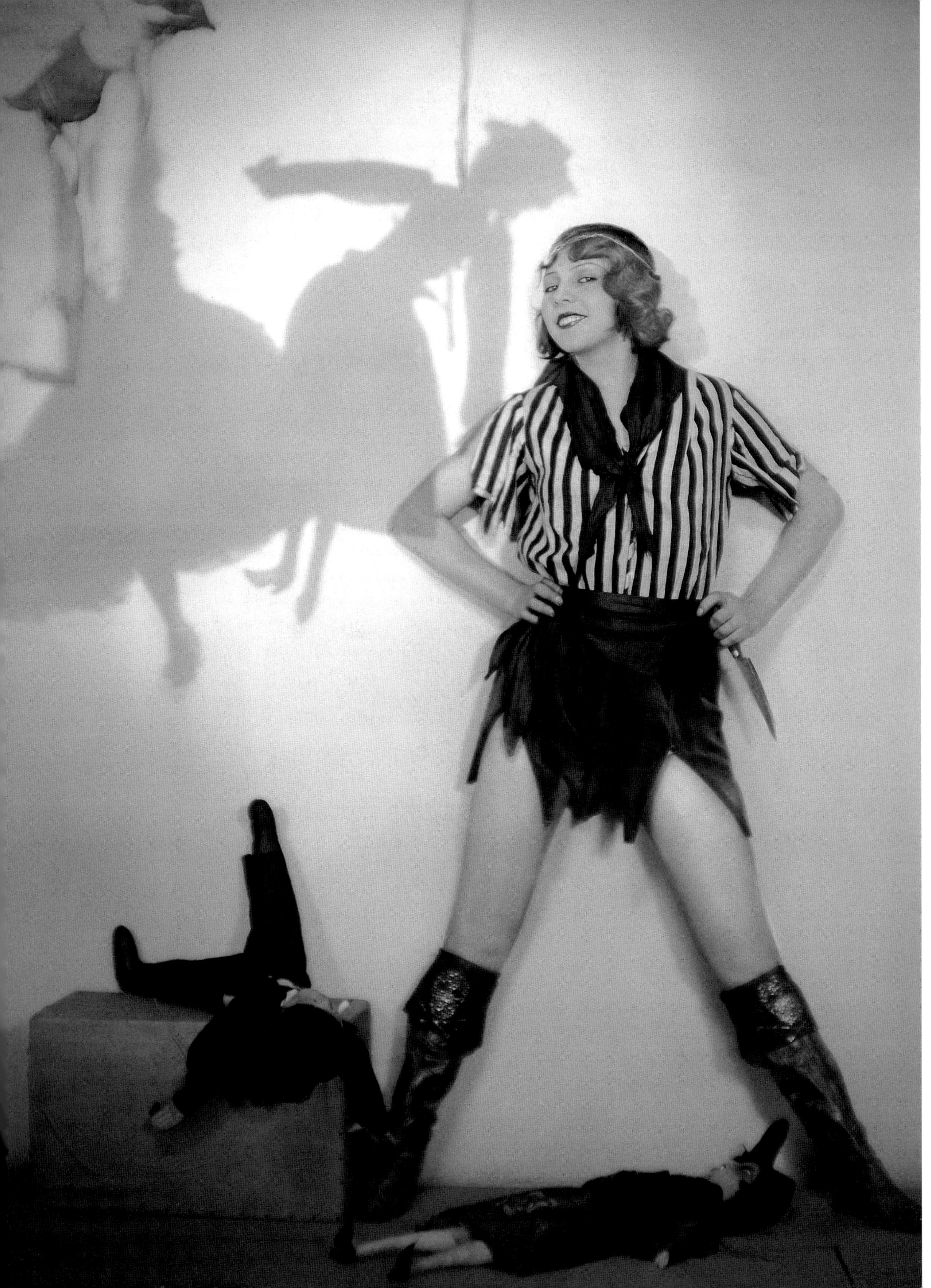

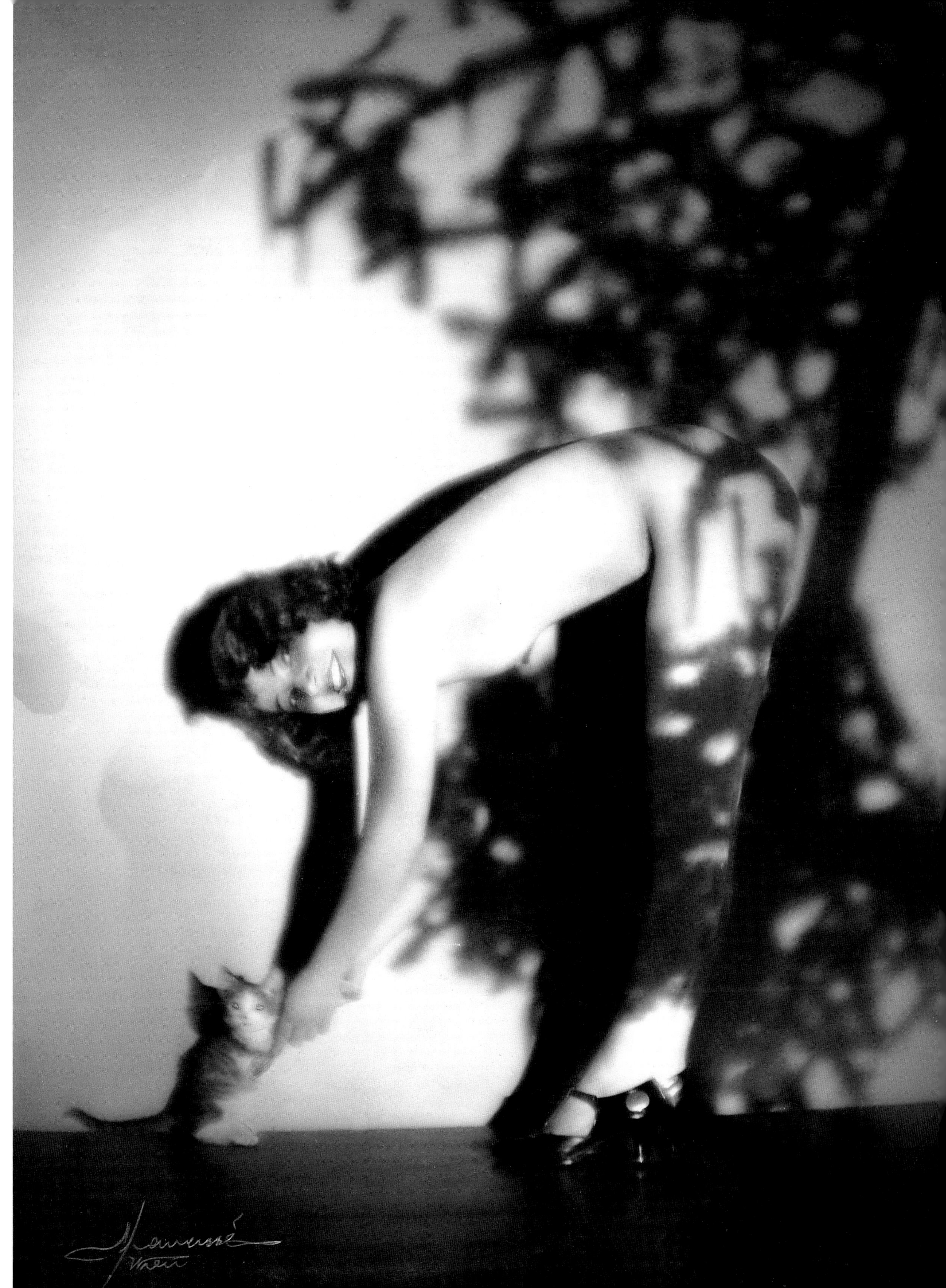

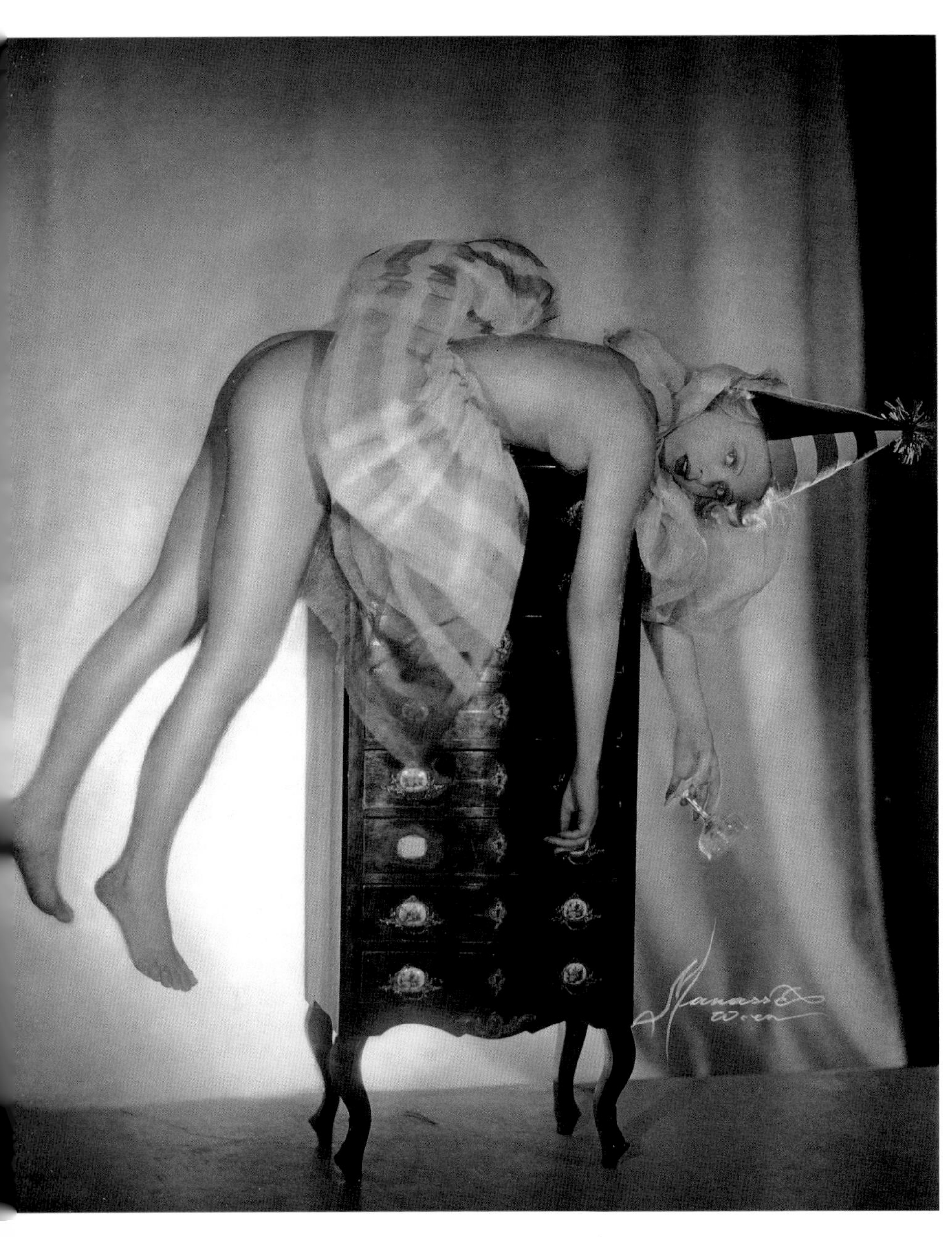

Previous four pages: Study, c.1928; The Black Hand, c.1947; Elly Werner, c.1927; Study, c.1926

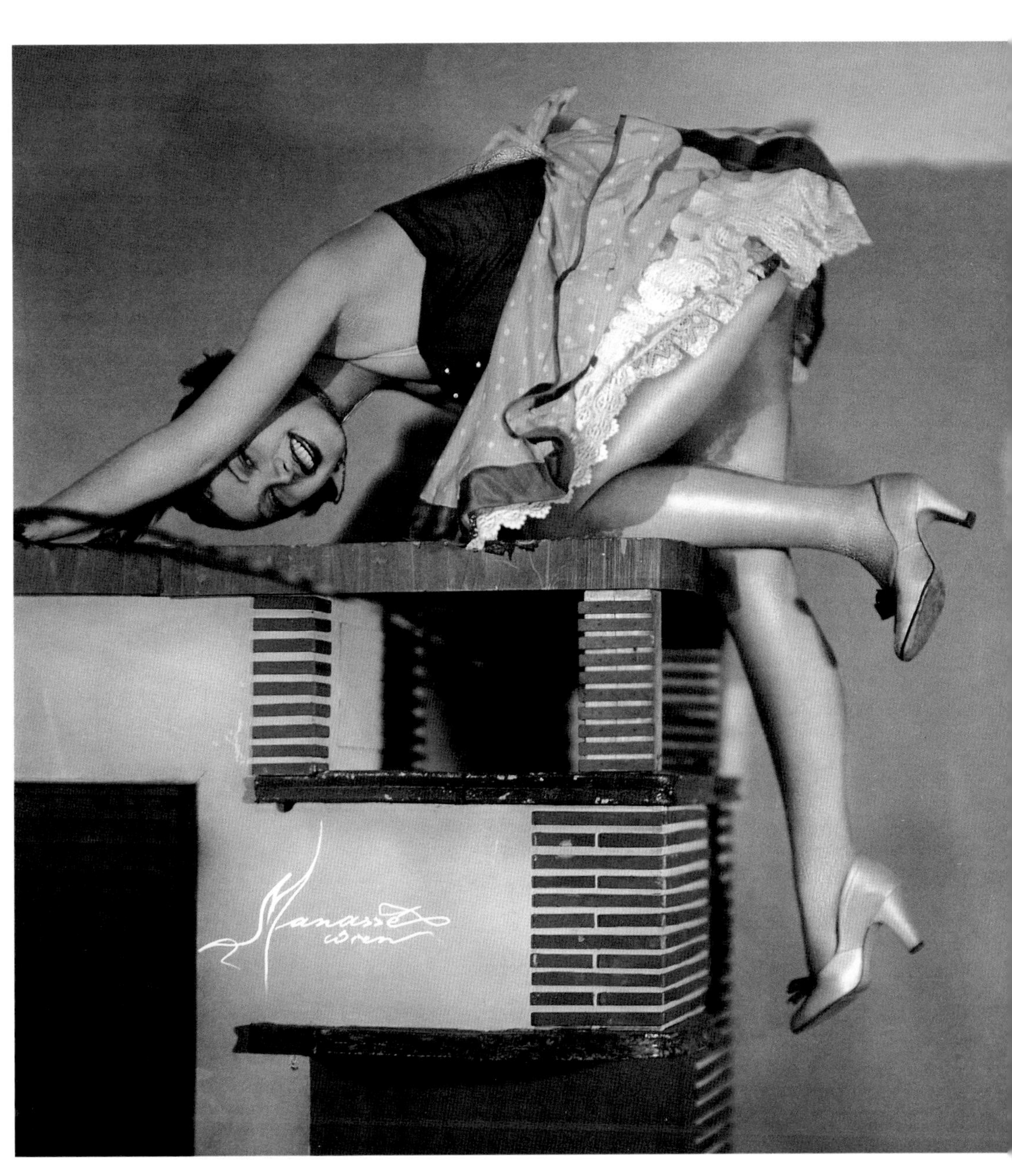

Study, c.1933; Susie Lanner, c.1933

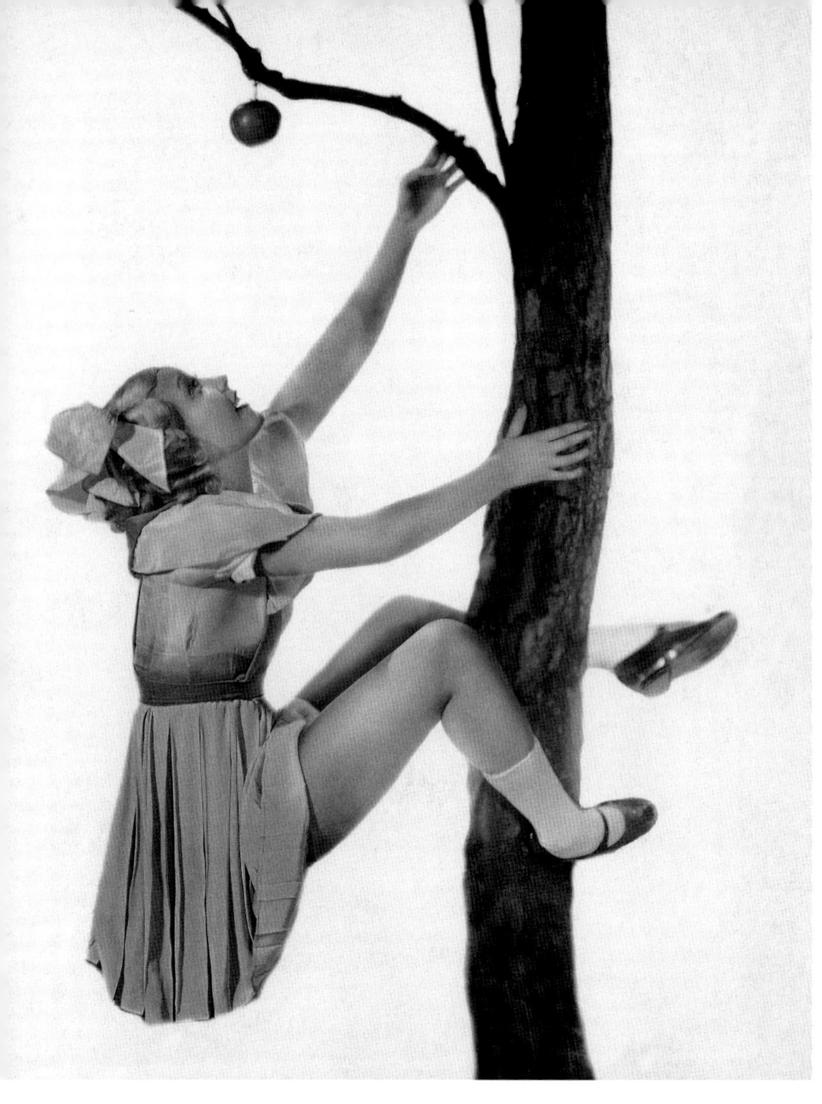

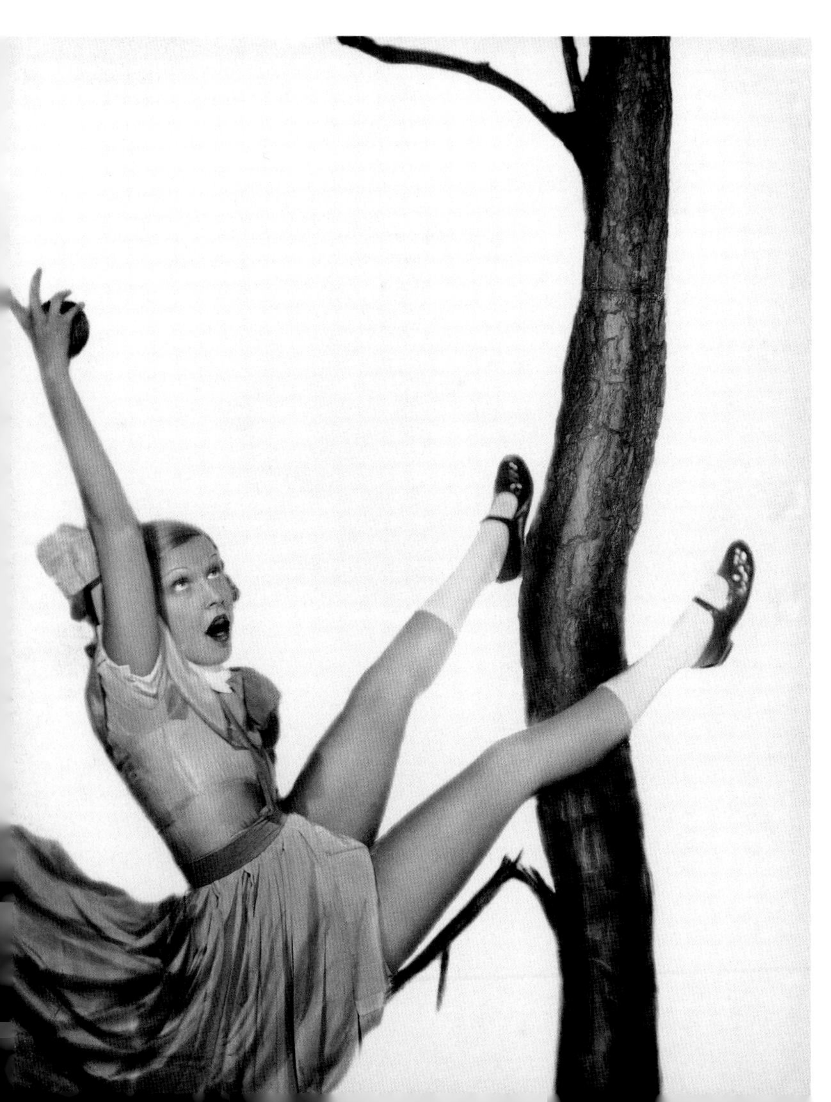

Rosy Csikos, c.1933; Edith Zeisler, the World Champion of Tap Dance, c.1931

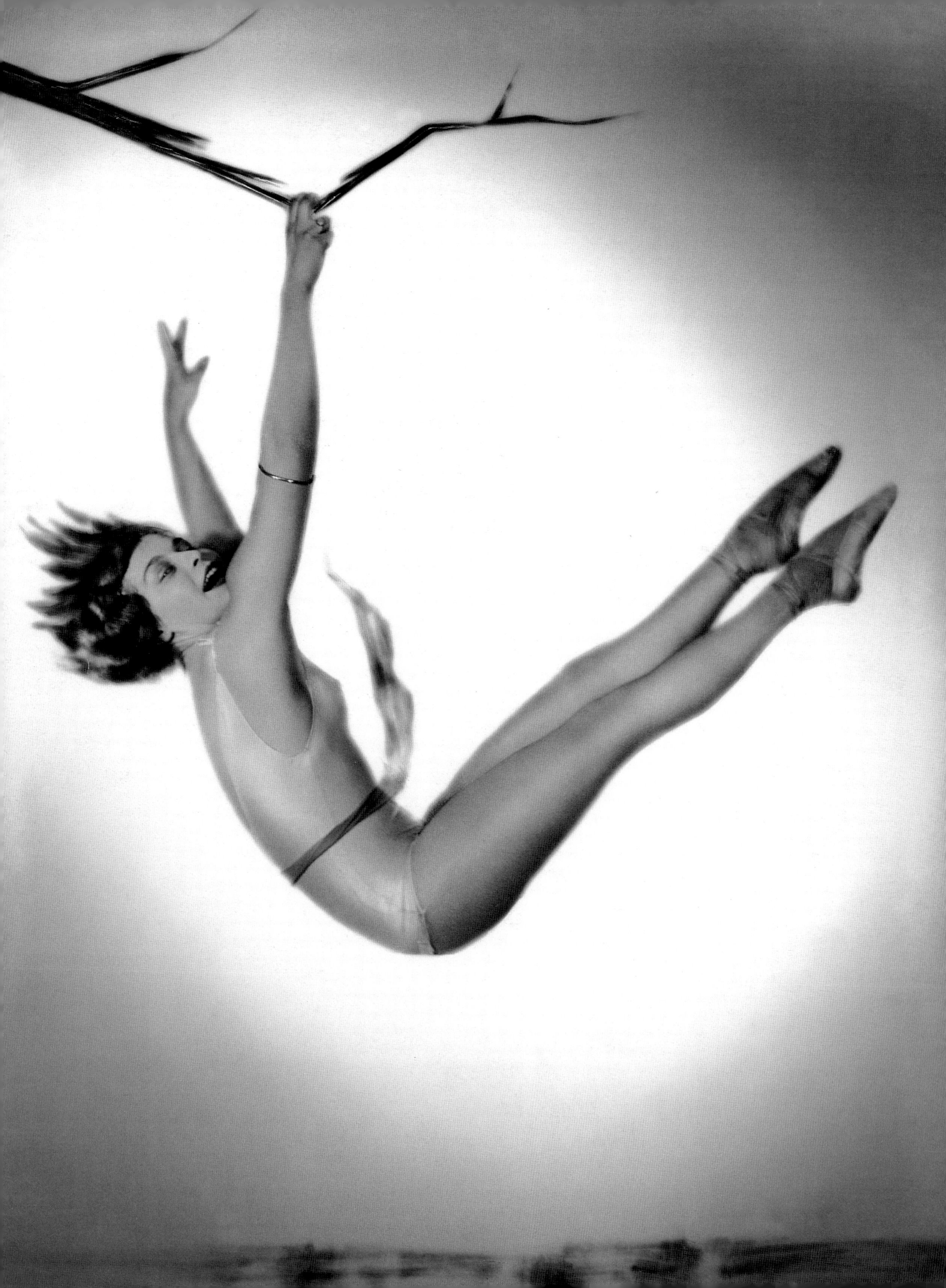

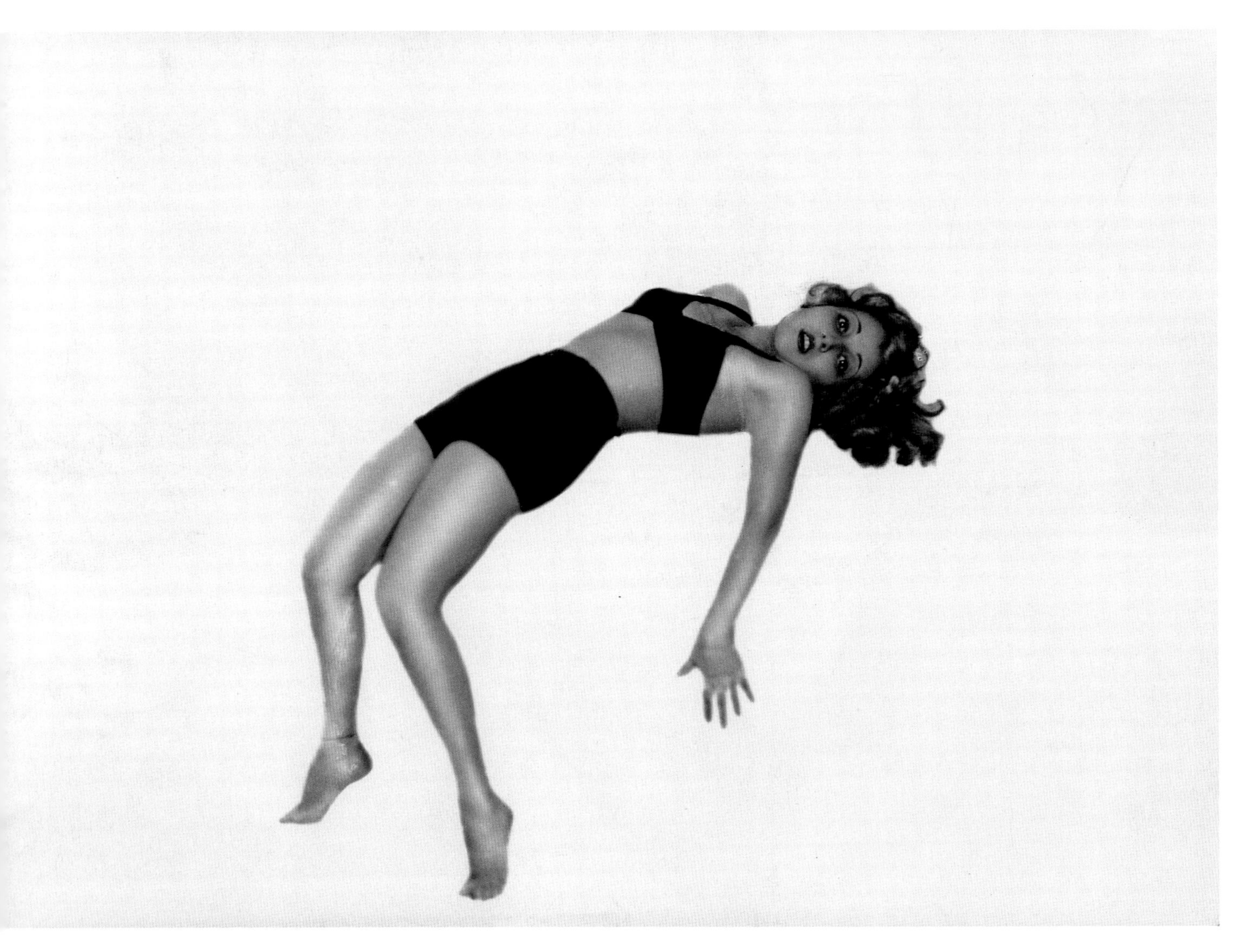

Anny Schwarz, c.1931

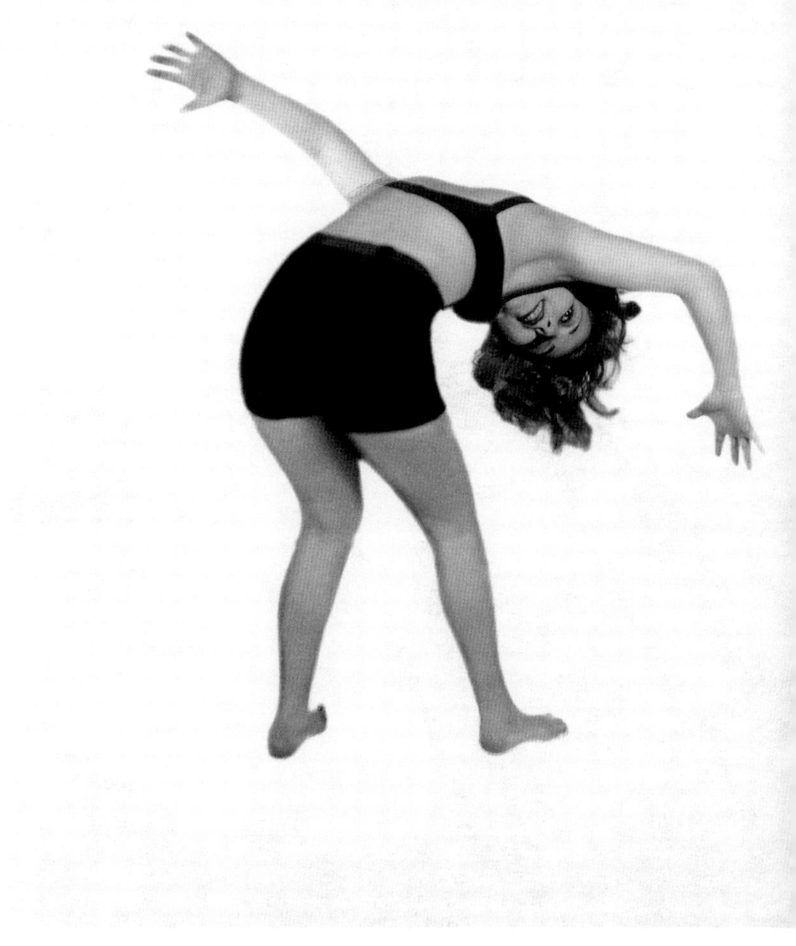

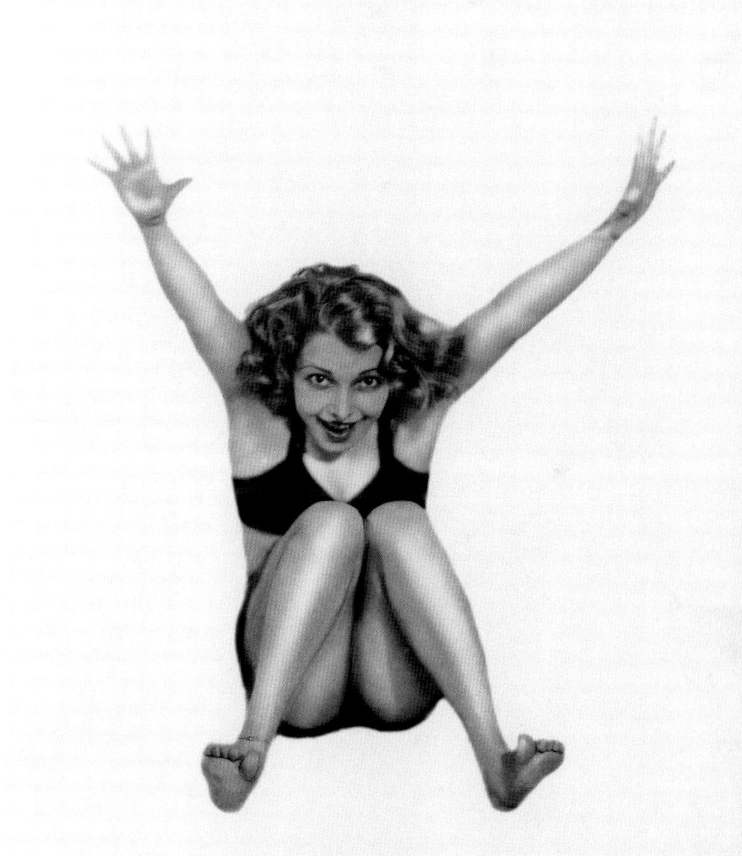

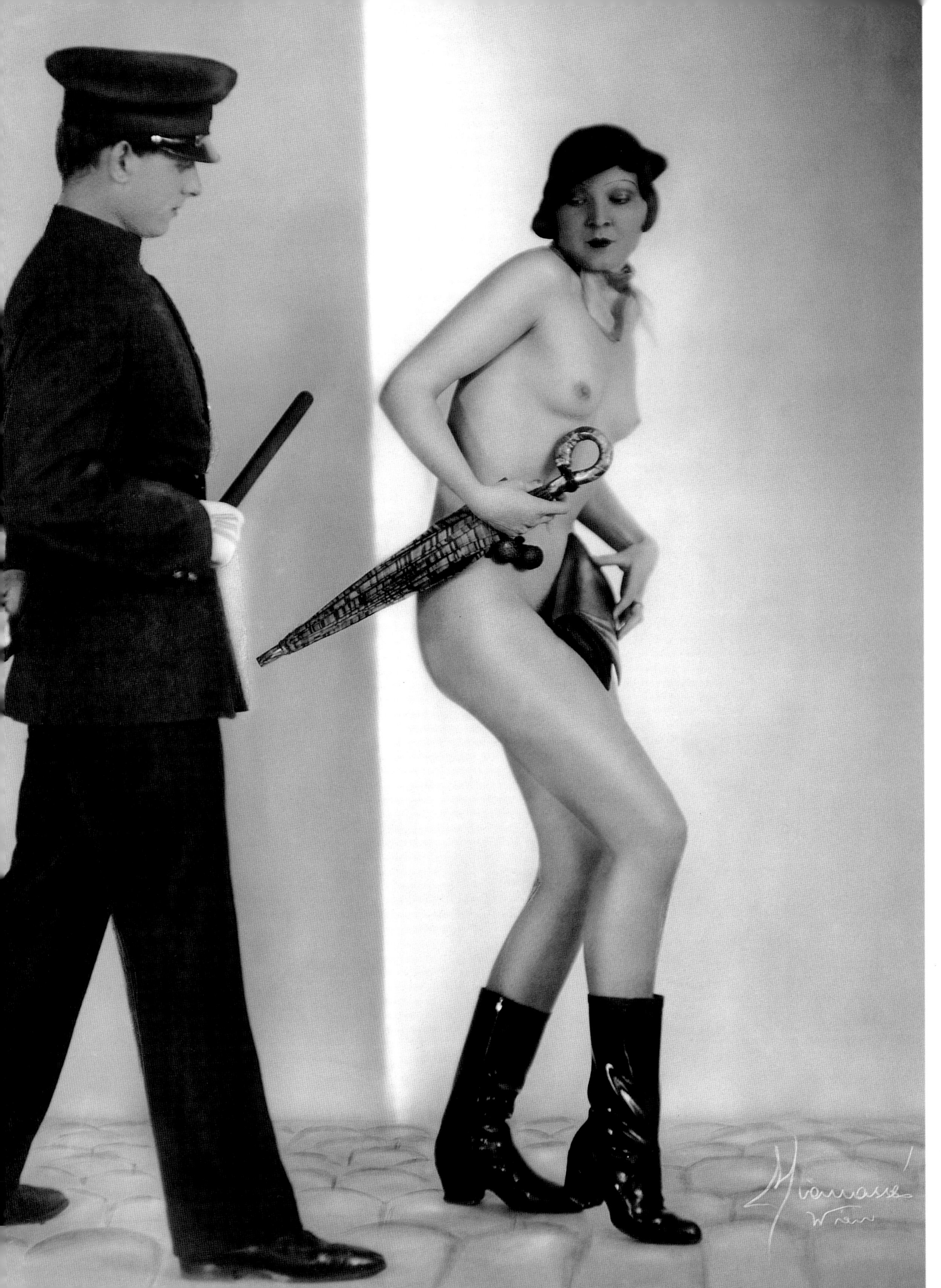
Manassé
Wien

MALE FANTASIES AND THE "NEW WOMAN"

Eclectic manipulation of various set pieces and motifs by Olga and Adorján Wlassics in producing their montages and photo productions can be compared most directly with the techniques and stylistic means used in vaudeville and film. In our discussion of this subject, we shall have to simplify these comparisons, which must start at different levels of production and perception: Continuity and breaks in dealing with visual conventions on the one hand reflect social reality; on the other, they contribute to the creation of modified or new role models, which, in point of fact, are seen by society as real.

In 1921, in the *Neue Freie Presse,* Hugo von Hofmannsthal, quite obviously impressed by expressionist films, commented on the multiplicity of visual sources used by filmmakers right after the war: "... but in film meanwhile an entire literature flies by, torn to shreds; no, a complete chaos of literatures, of vestiges of characters from thousands of plays, novels, crime stories; historical anecdotes, the hallucinations of people who see ghosts; accounts of adventurers; but at the same time also beautiful creatures and transparent gestures, faces, and looks, from which the whole soul bursts forth." Here we differentiate between subjects rich in tradition that were picked to set up the plot so that it would be generally understood or to advance the action, and silent film, which offered a genuine possibility to create beings on the screen by using exaggerated acting techniques. During the twenties not only did films themselves change, but also those who commented on them. Thus Siegfried Kracauer, already much less friendly in his comments, wrote about the same problem in 1924—that is, about using myths and older subjects in the big films: "Instead of evoking the old epics visually, they turn myth into cheap trash and spectacle that isn't even exciting." Why were these old epics constantly retold or at least quoted? Why, even in films that take place in the present were abstractions or simplifications used behind which one could glimpse archaic models? Here we come up against an uncertainty about the present and its social as well as its visual expression that reminds one of the beginnings of historicism in the nineteenth century. Curtiz's (Kertész) and Korda's biblical monster productions remind me of a train station paneled in Gothic style—if in the latter, courage to employ the appropriate style was lacking; then in the former there was no courage to grapple with an up-to-date subject. In such films the identification of the female stars with their roles produced, via the star portrait, an imaginary picture of women (man-eating vamp, mysterious exotic, naive blonde, helpless princess) that had already had its day or had never actually existed.

Western women proved during World War I that they were able to handle daily life without help from men. For that they were greatly encouraged by and applauded in illustrated magazines, of which there were fewer than there would be ten years later. Then, even before the return of soldiers to their homes and traditional jobs, the mood changed: these same women were emphatically reminded of their conventional place within the family. Their independence, which had often been forced on them by circumstance, was branded a danger to society as a whole. The male fear that this independence would be continued must have worried those who had profited from the status quo.

Study. c.1931

Study, c.1931; Study, c.1931; following two pages: Ly Fassig, c.1933; Study, c.1934

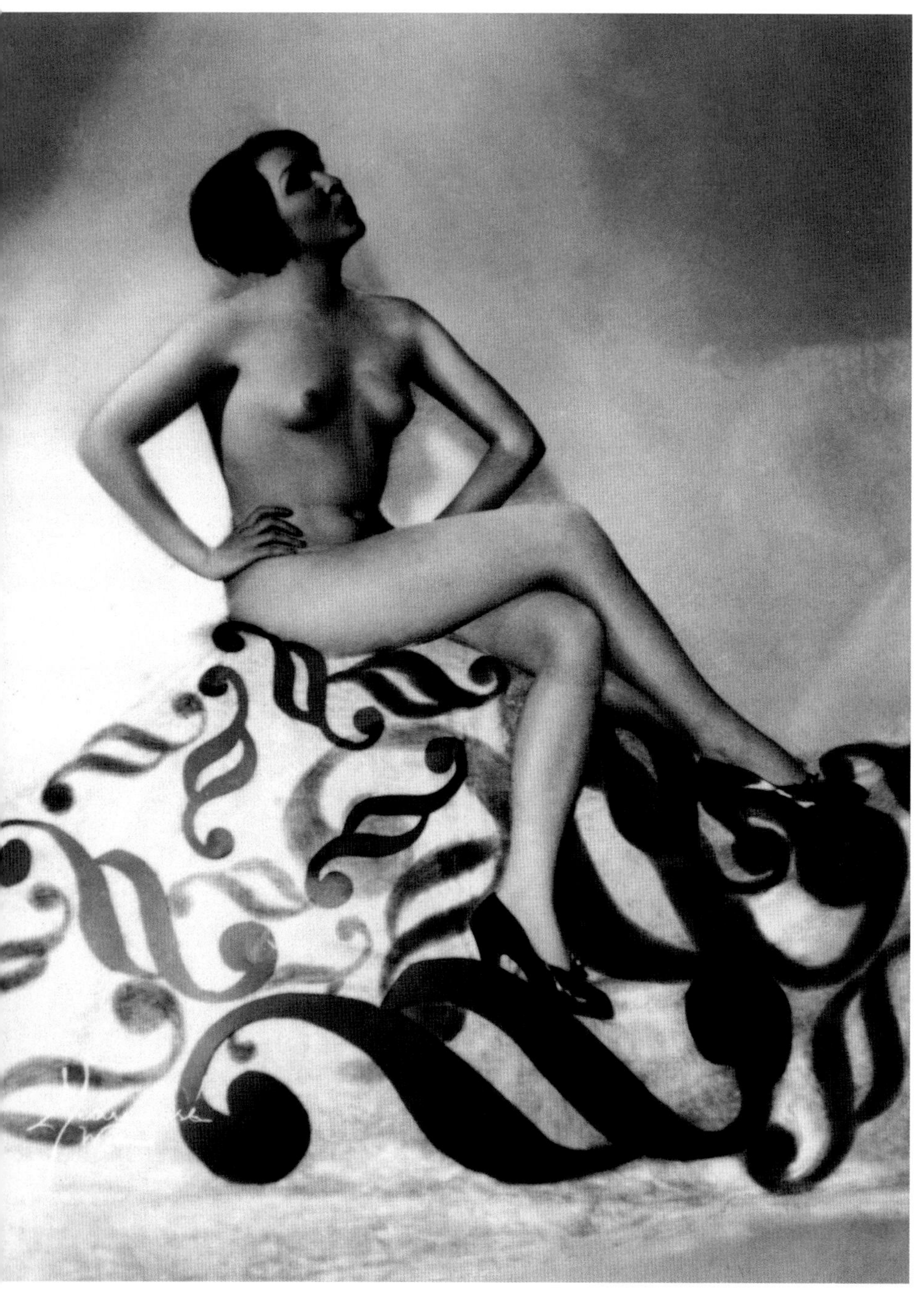

It must have disturbed them as deeply as the dissolution of the monarchy at the end of the war. In his study, *Männerfantasien* (Male Fantasies), Klaus Theweleit has exhaustively examined the role of women, particularly as it was influenced by the First World War and its aftereffects. Not surprisingly, his research has shown many themes that were often depicted in the twenties, in the star cult as well as in the pin-up picture—two areas that represented an escape from reality. Descriptions of female roles in Germany, such as those by Hedwig Dohm around the turn of the century, and those later elaborated by Elsa Herrmann and Alice Rühle-Gerstel in the twenties and early thirties, dealt with the "new woman" and represented contrasting types who were striving for liberation from imposed traditional roles. They in turn led into new concepts of the self and of the other, which found expression in the mass media of the time. The fact that women wanted to determine their own fates and that they were working to gain a new theoretical and practical understanding of their own gender-specific behavior could not be denied, even though it was viewed with skepticism by many. Contributing to a 1929 anthology, *Die Frau von Morgen, wie wir sie uns wünschen* (Tomorrow's Woman As We Want Her to Be), Robert Musil wrote with evident annoyance: "Woman has become tired of being the ideal of a man who no longer has the strength for idealizing, and she has taken charge of thinking of herself as her own ideal. ... A woman doesn't want to be idealized at all any more but rather to form ideals, to contribute to her education as men do, though for the time being she is not having any success."

The "new woman" as depicted in the mass media between the wars actually seemed to be torn between completely different role models. Attempts at emancipation were often joined

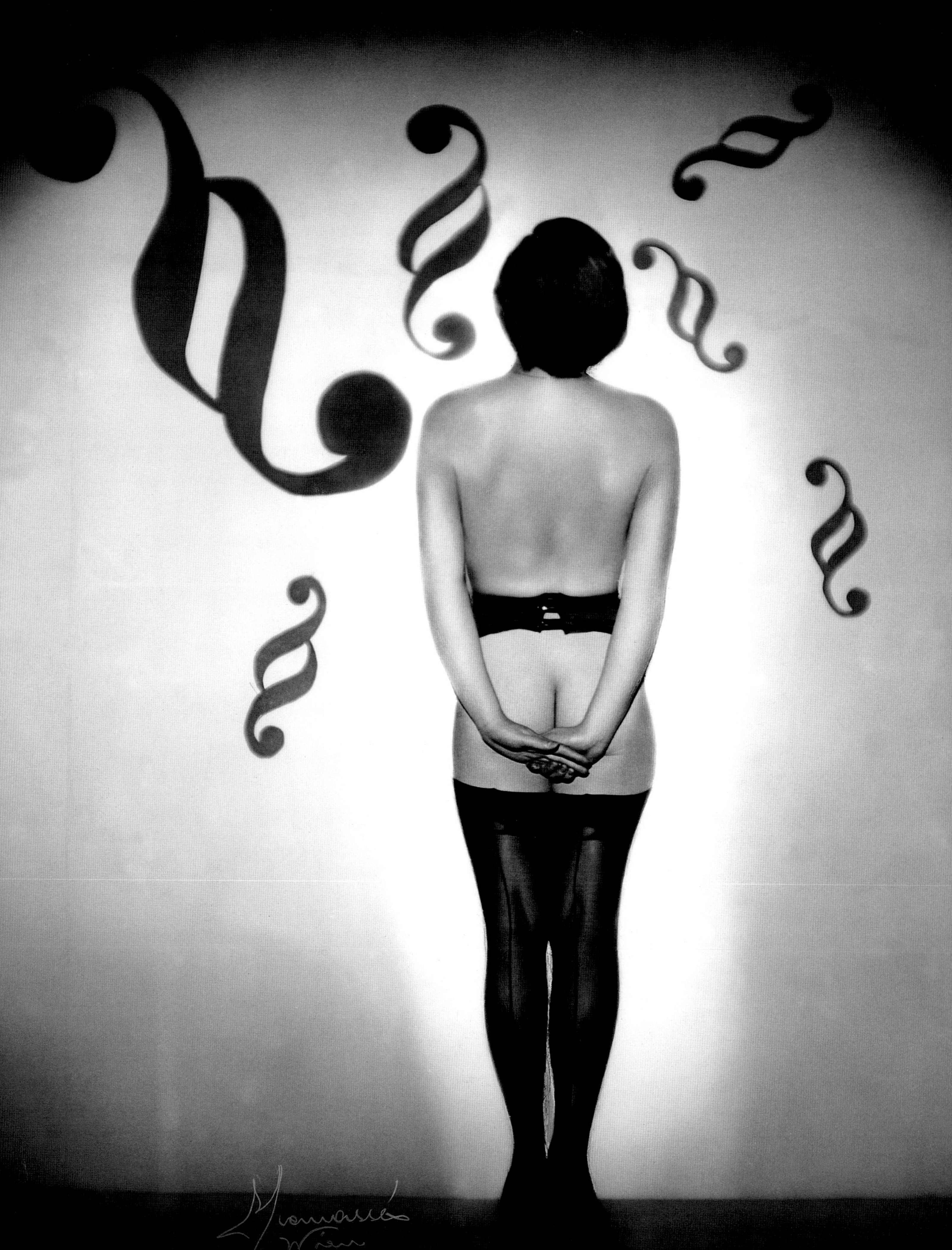
Manassé
Wien

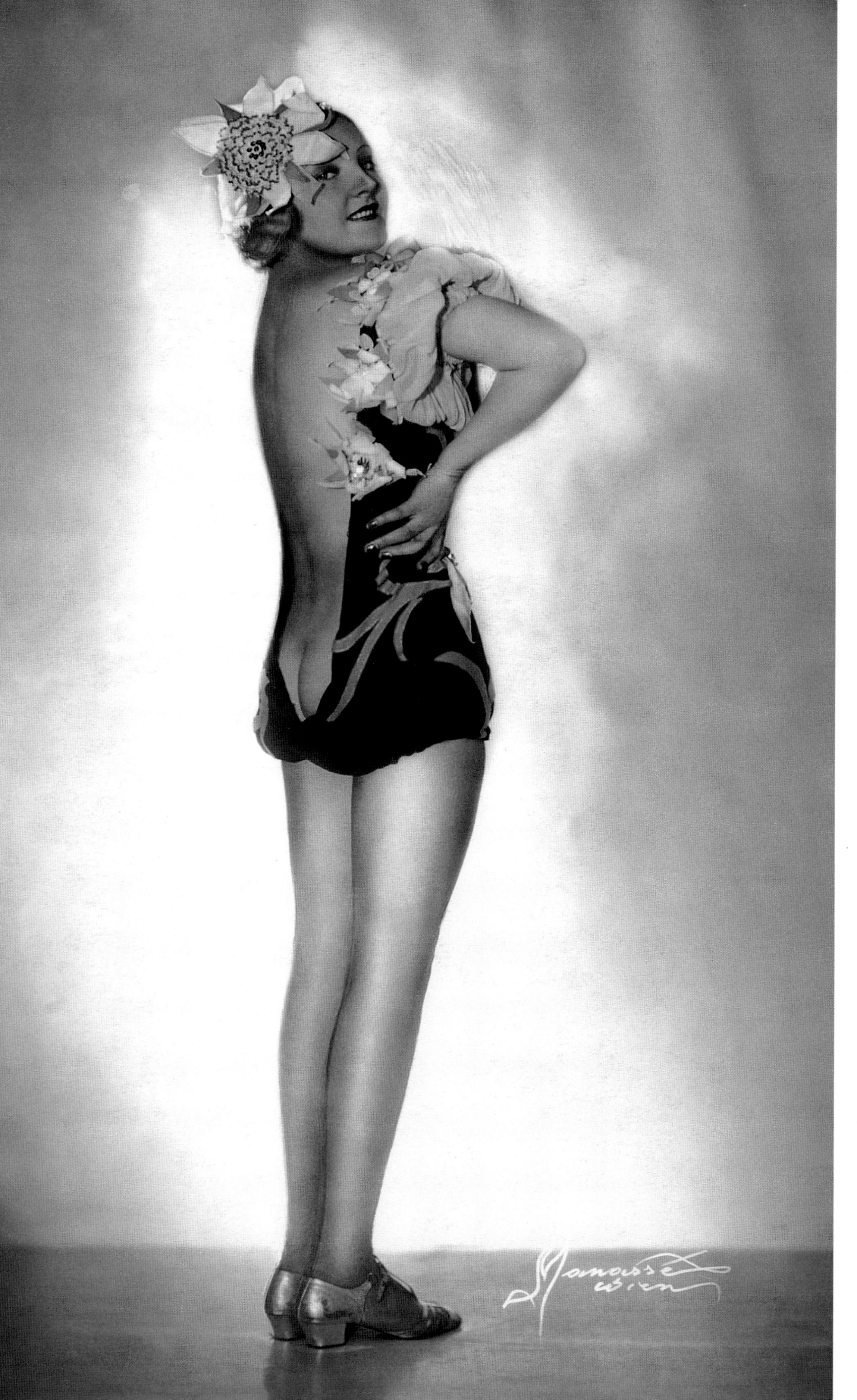
Manassé
Wien

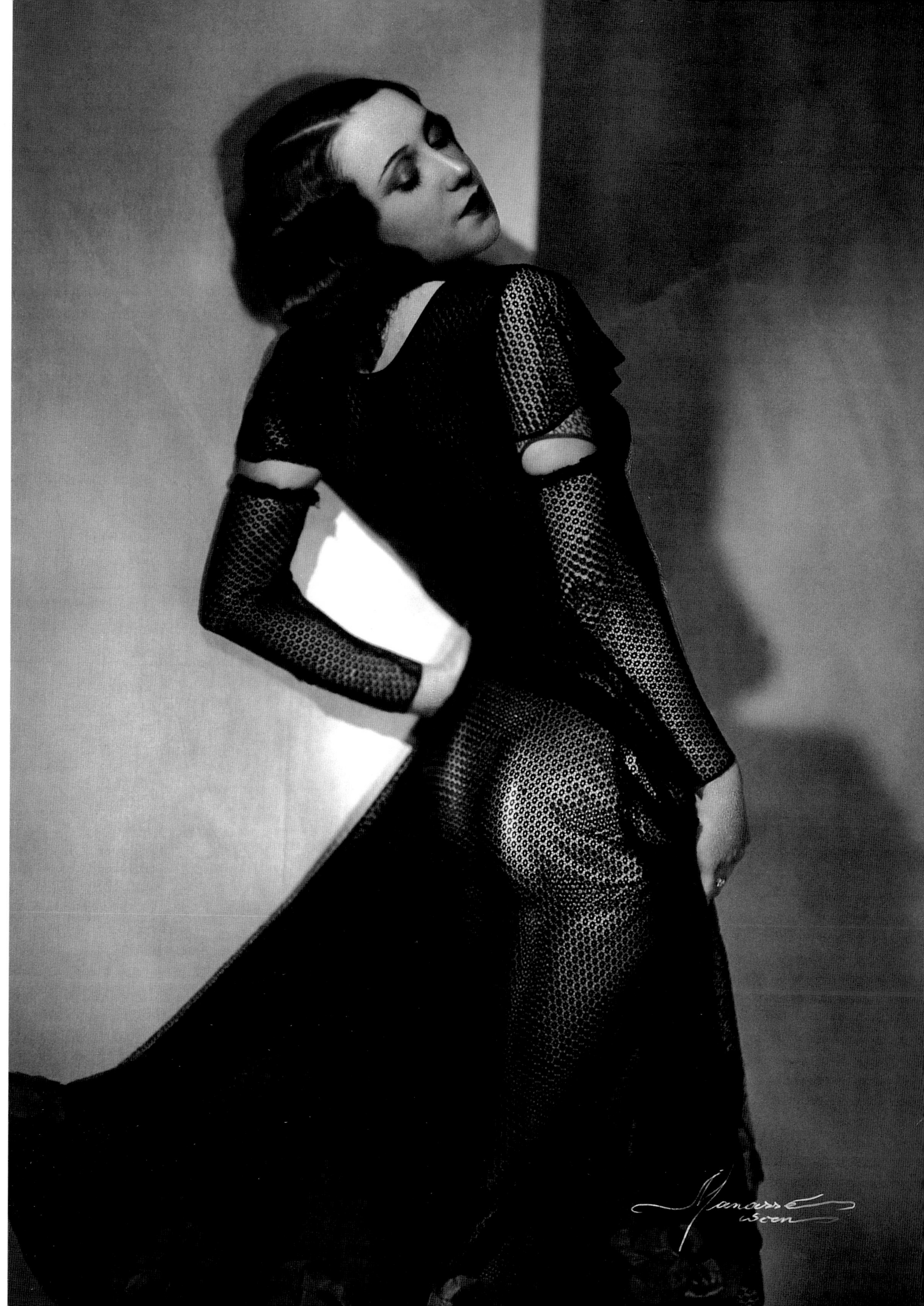
Manassé
Wien

Anny Schwarz, c.1931; Hilde Lassl, c.1932

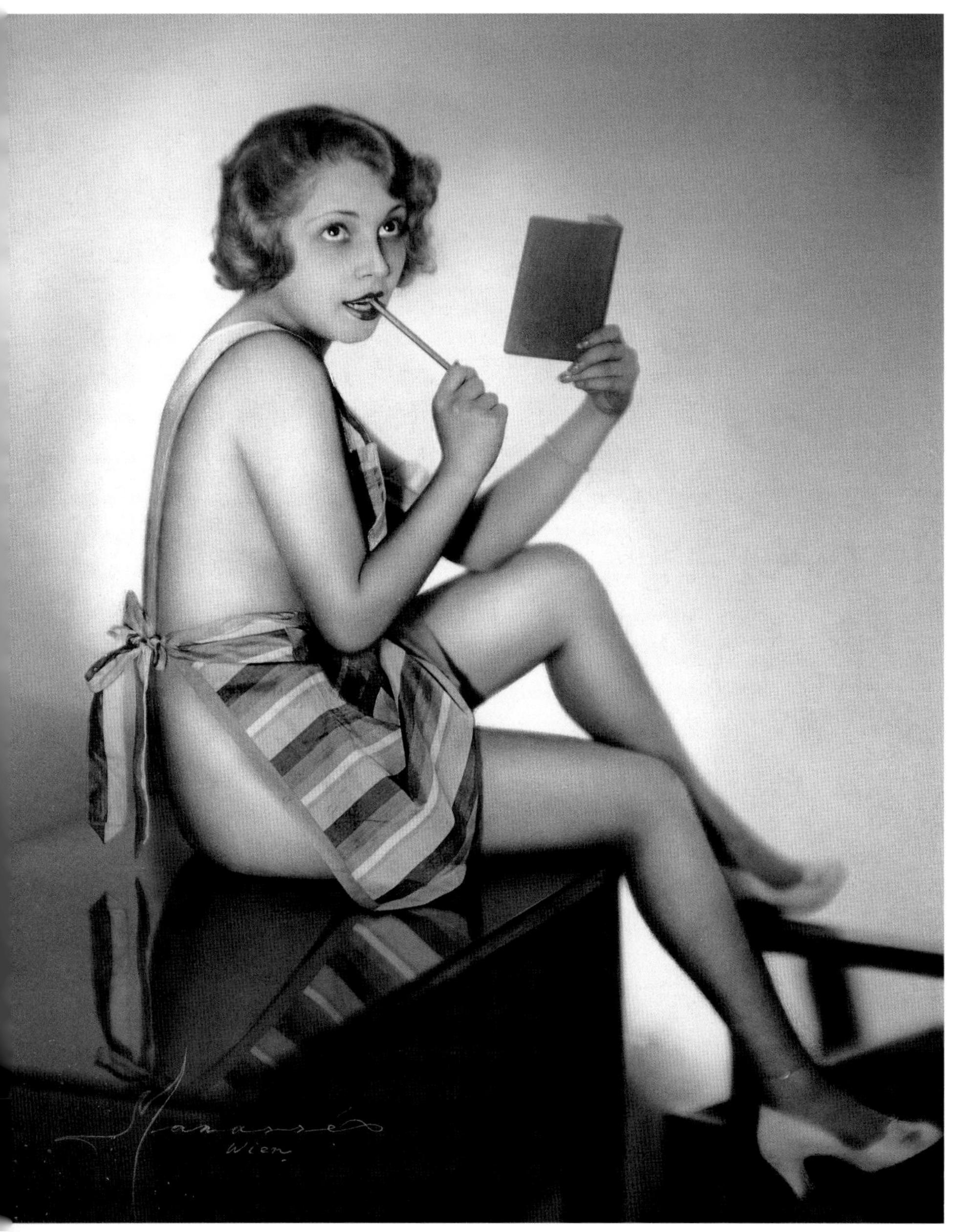

with fantasies of social advancement and power, which were directly influenced by ready-made patterns. The pictures of Studio Manassé should be seen in this context of oppositions of male desires and fantasies, some—but certainly not all—of these pictures when looked at carefully reveal conflicting concepts. Icons of availability, the women are seen in provocative poses, enthralled or naive-dumb, waiting for the man to look at them, for him to act. They are presented in traditional roles that have been so enormously exaggerated that cynicism turns into humor. There are also pictures in which the men are demoted to puppets that are now at the disposal of the women. Even if one can find models for these later photographs in popular genres, such as the man tied to a woman's apron strings or the sophisticated man-eating woman of the fin de siècle, the Manassé pictures never quite fulfill these clichés. The naked woman holding a sword and standing in front of a row of dolls' heads, which are clearly recognizable as trophies, seems almost shy (fig., p. 140); she doesn't hold her weapon aggressively but presses it to her body as if ashamed. It is more a caricature of this type of picture than a satire of the woman in a role not inherent to her nature. However, models in Manassé pictures play the same unhappy role as the "bathing beauties" in the films of Mack Sennett. Much as the Senett girl parodied the role of the woman as sex object, she could not help being one. Simply caricaturing the traditional role doesn't create a new identity. Magazines that featured Manassé photographs were not the place to head in this new direction—toward self-determination. Rather they lent themselves to remarks like this by D. H. Lawrence: "The real trouble about women is that they must always go on trying to adapt themselves to men's theories of women, as they always have done. ... We shall see the changes in the woman-pattern follow one another fast and furious now, because the young men hysterically don't know what they want. ... Men are fools. ..."

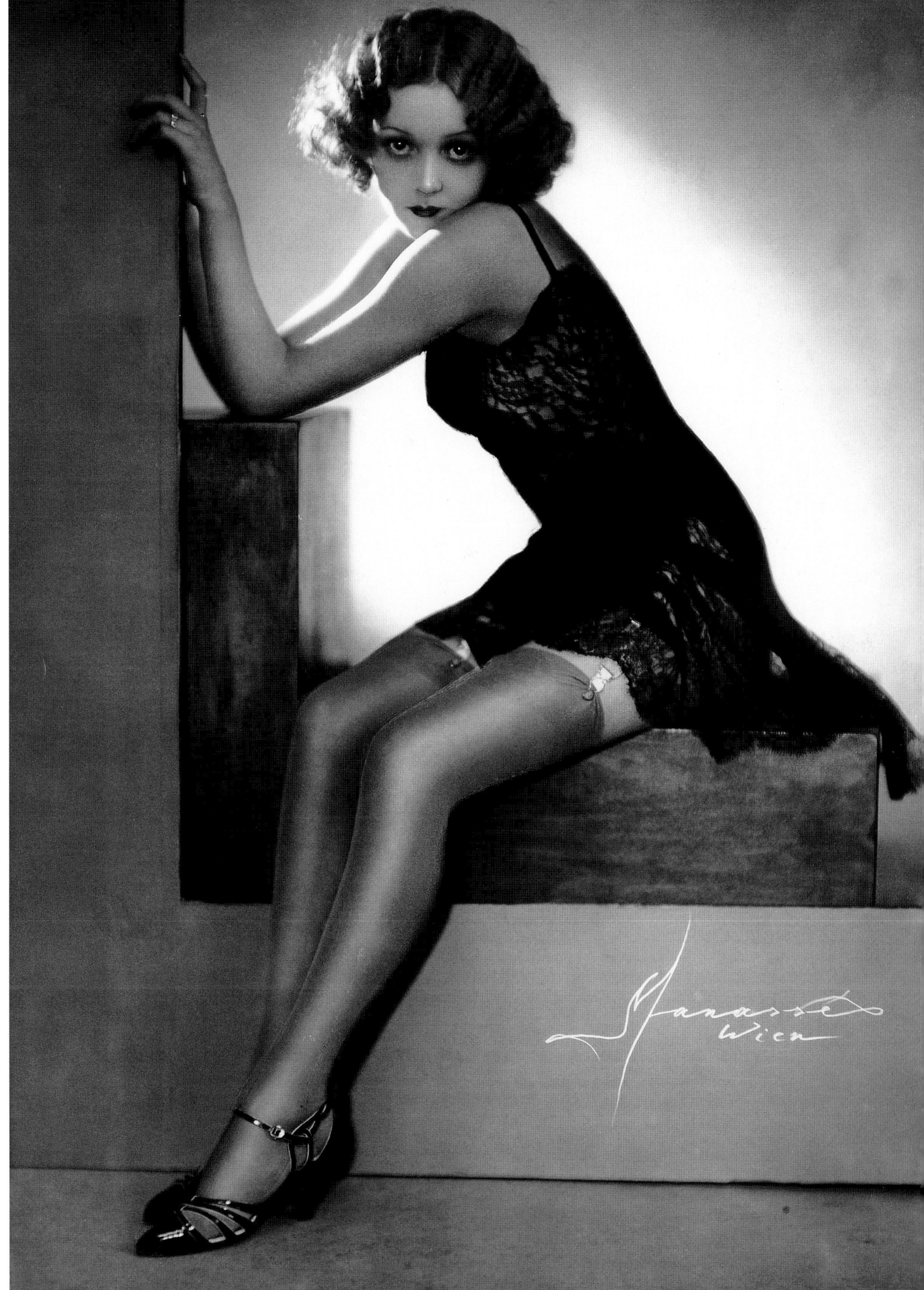
Manasse
Wien

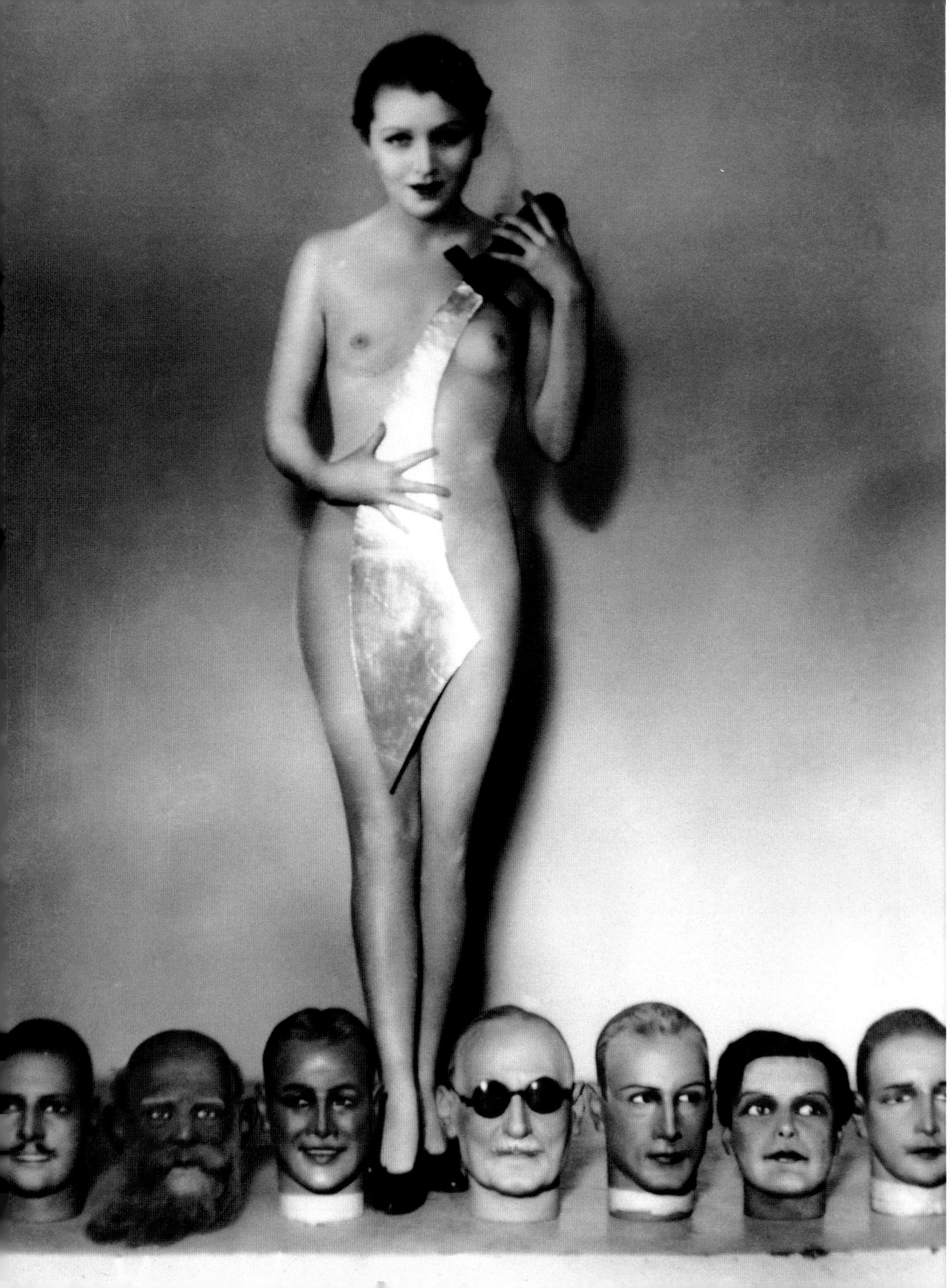

Not only did women's role models change during the decades under discussion, but the political situation in Europe was also in upheaval. After the 1934 revolt by the Austrian socialists and country's annexation by the German Reich in 1938, Olga and Adorján's work and their aesthetic sense no longer seemed suited to the time. They opened a new atelier in Bucharest, then later in Berlin. Why? We don't know. The fact that Manassé pictures continued to be published in Austrian magazines during the 1930s suggests that business considerations were not the primary reason governing the couple's decisions. However, for years, Austrian film production had been declining, and perhaps this made Berlin seem a more promising base of operations. Why not Hollywood? Probably they felt their inability to speak English would prove a barrier to their success. On the other hand—although we have no proof of this—they may have felt a certain sympathy for the regime in Berlin. The WOG studio was not perceptibly harmed during those years. Yet the magazines that continued to publish increasingly became an arm of National Socialist propaganda, and the Manassé pictures found no receptive audience in their pages. Olga and Adorján's ideal of beauty, a beauty based on charm, had gone out of style, and they never embraced the Nazis' typical male-fantasy image of women as 'comrades' and 'mothers.'

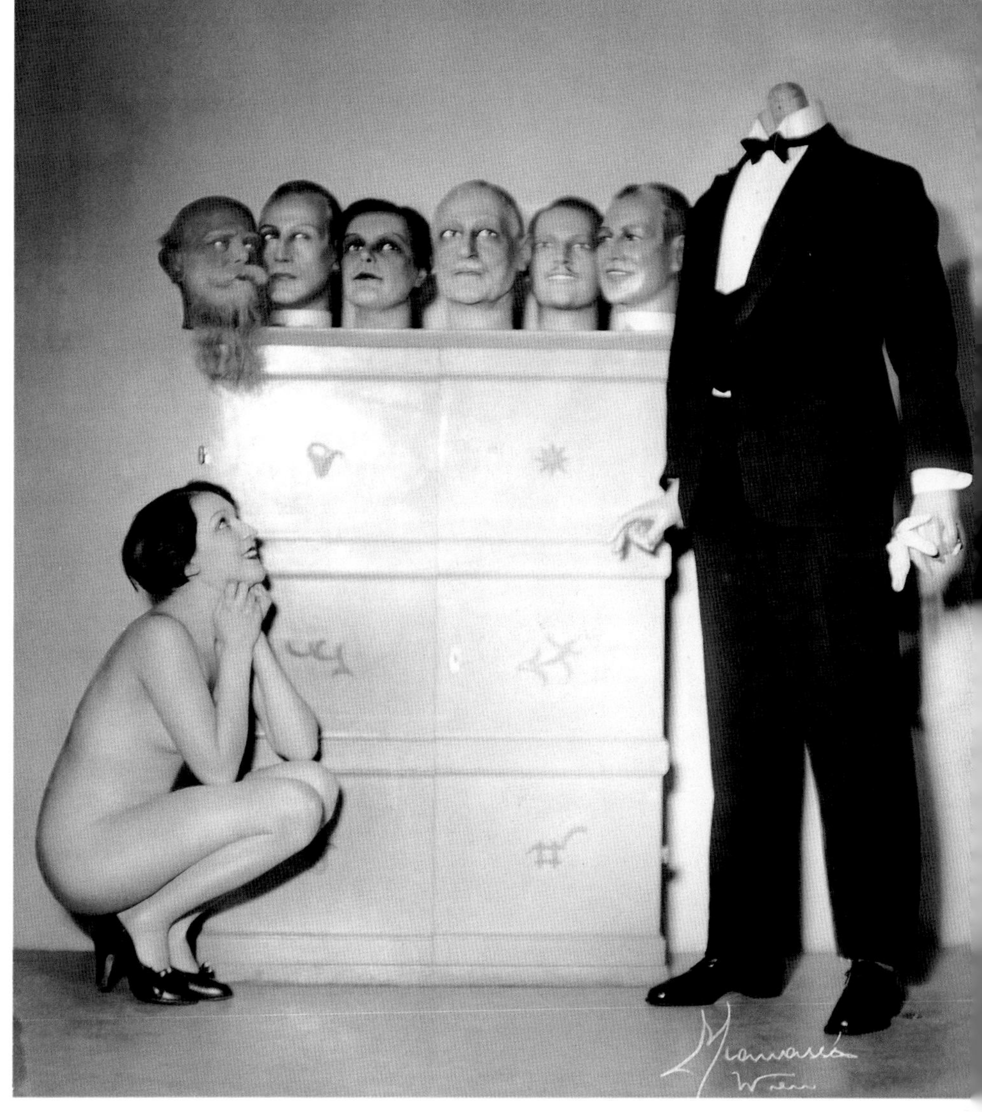

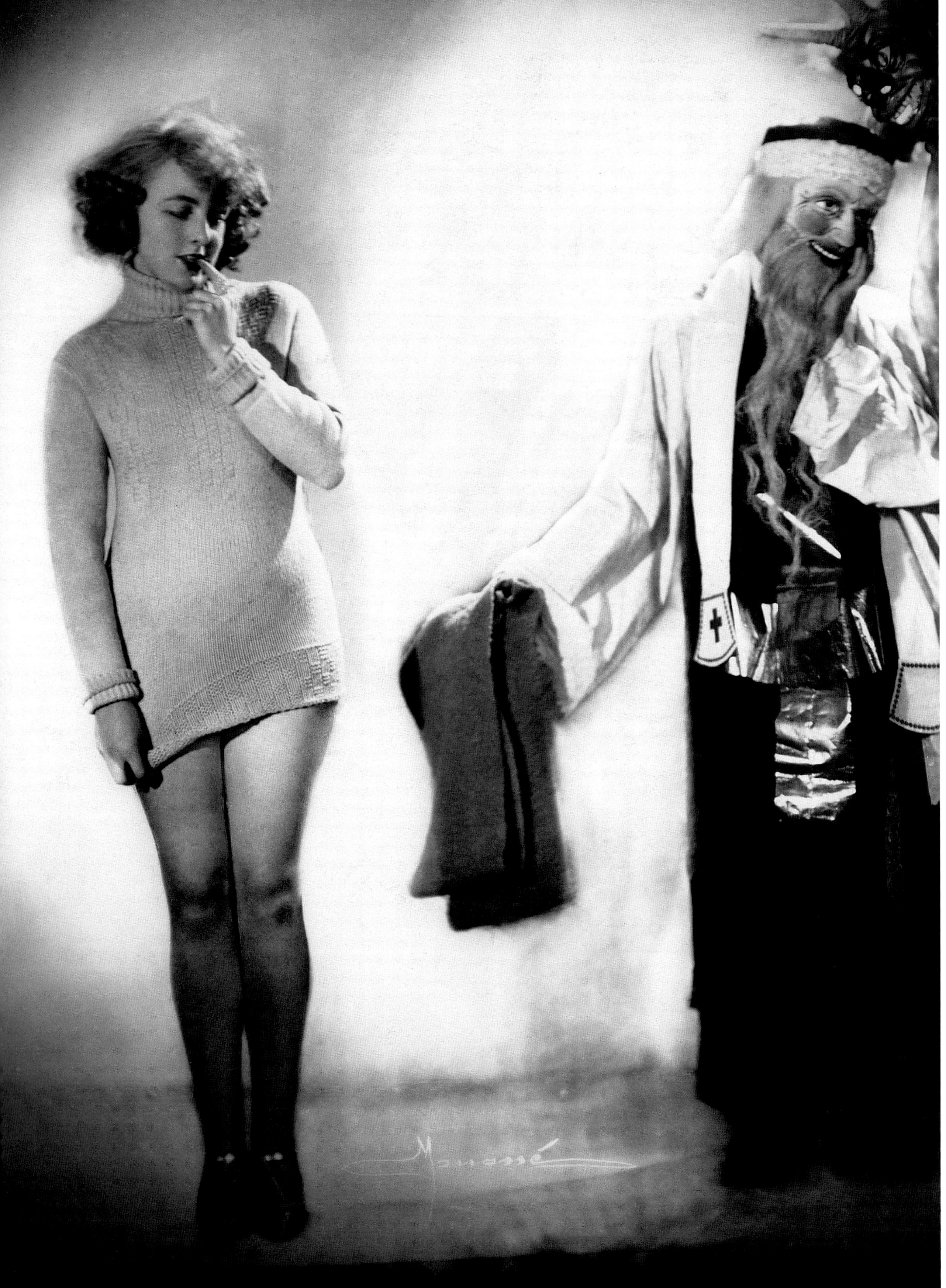
Manassé

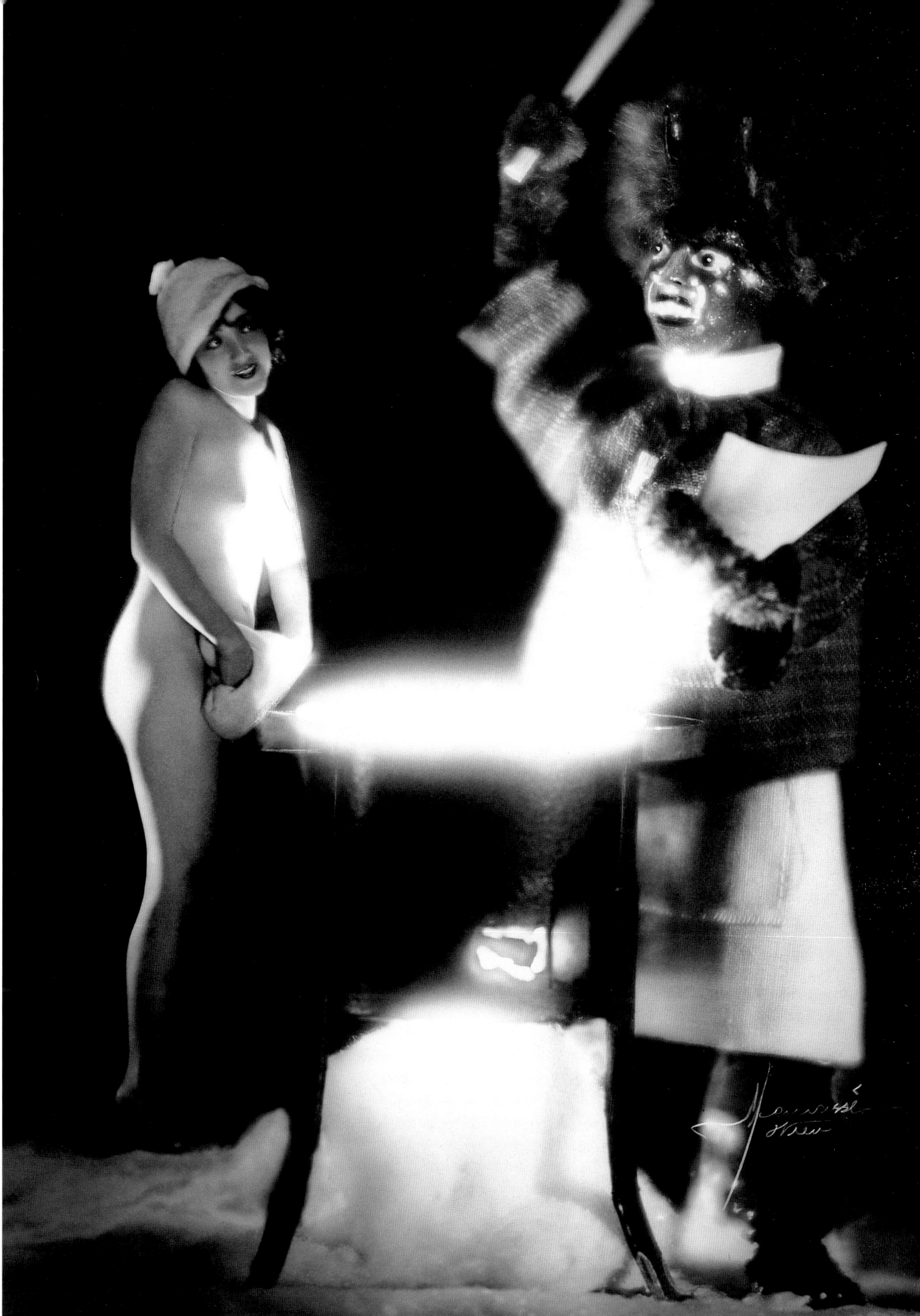

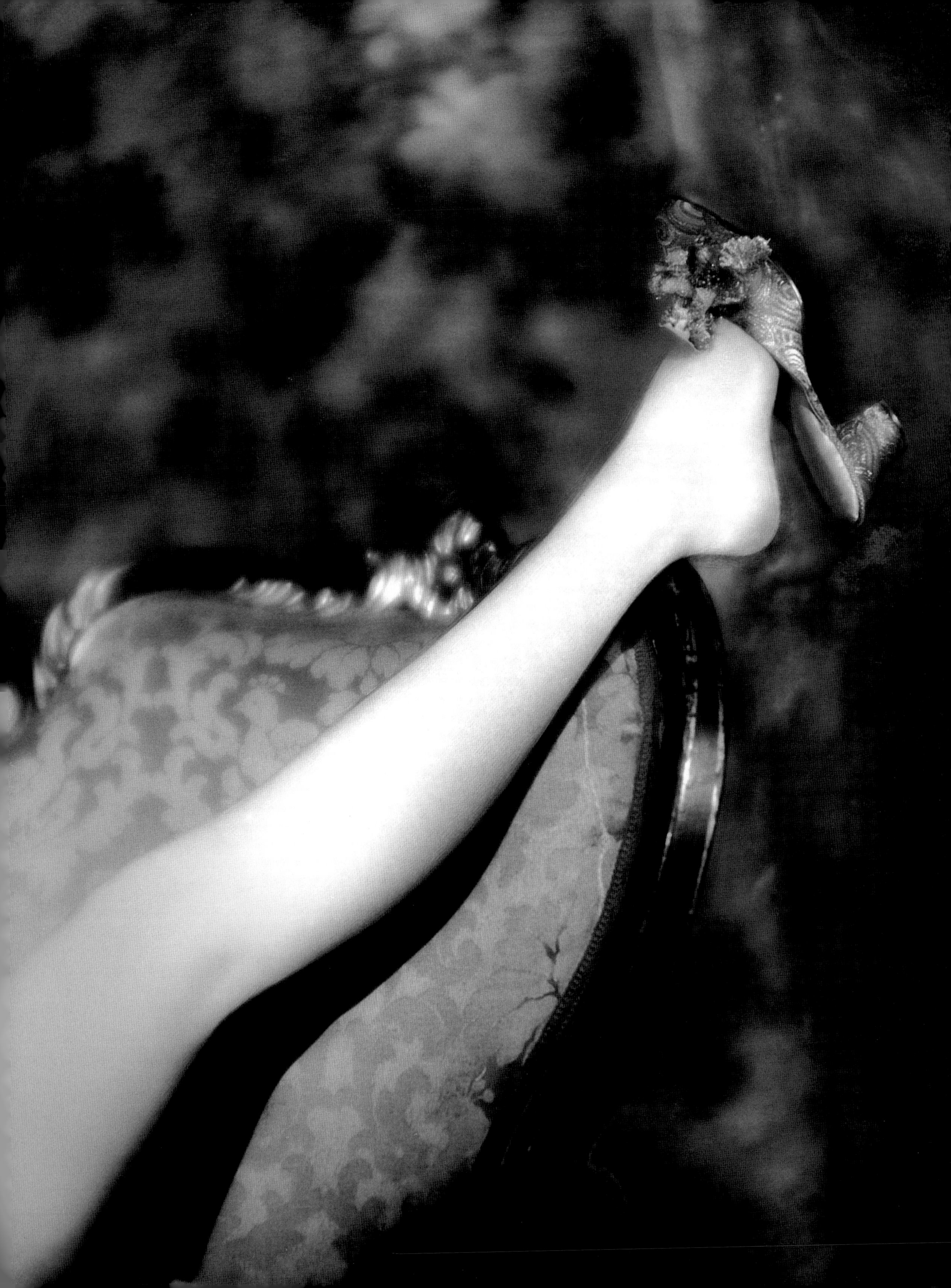

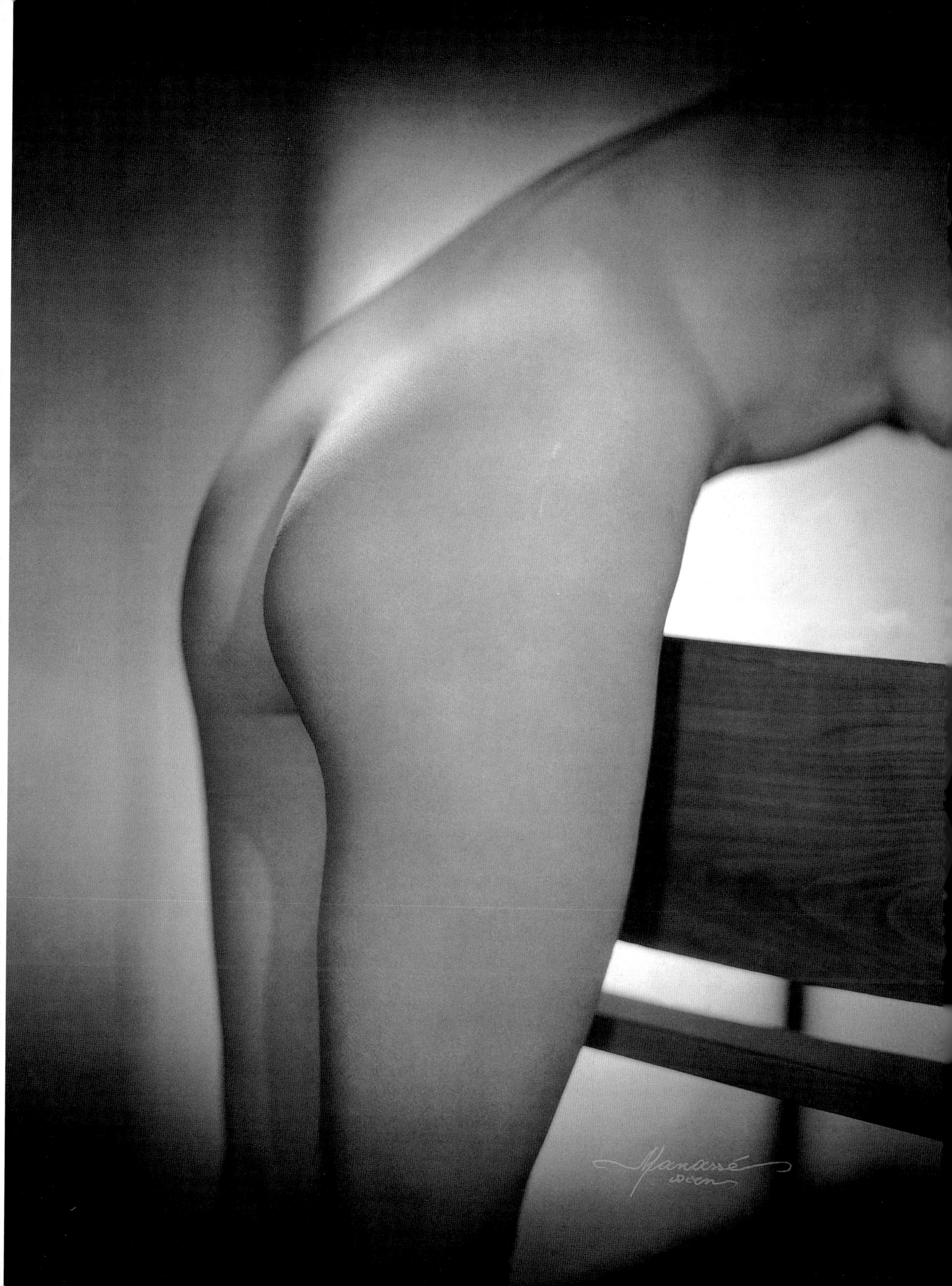
Manassé
Wien

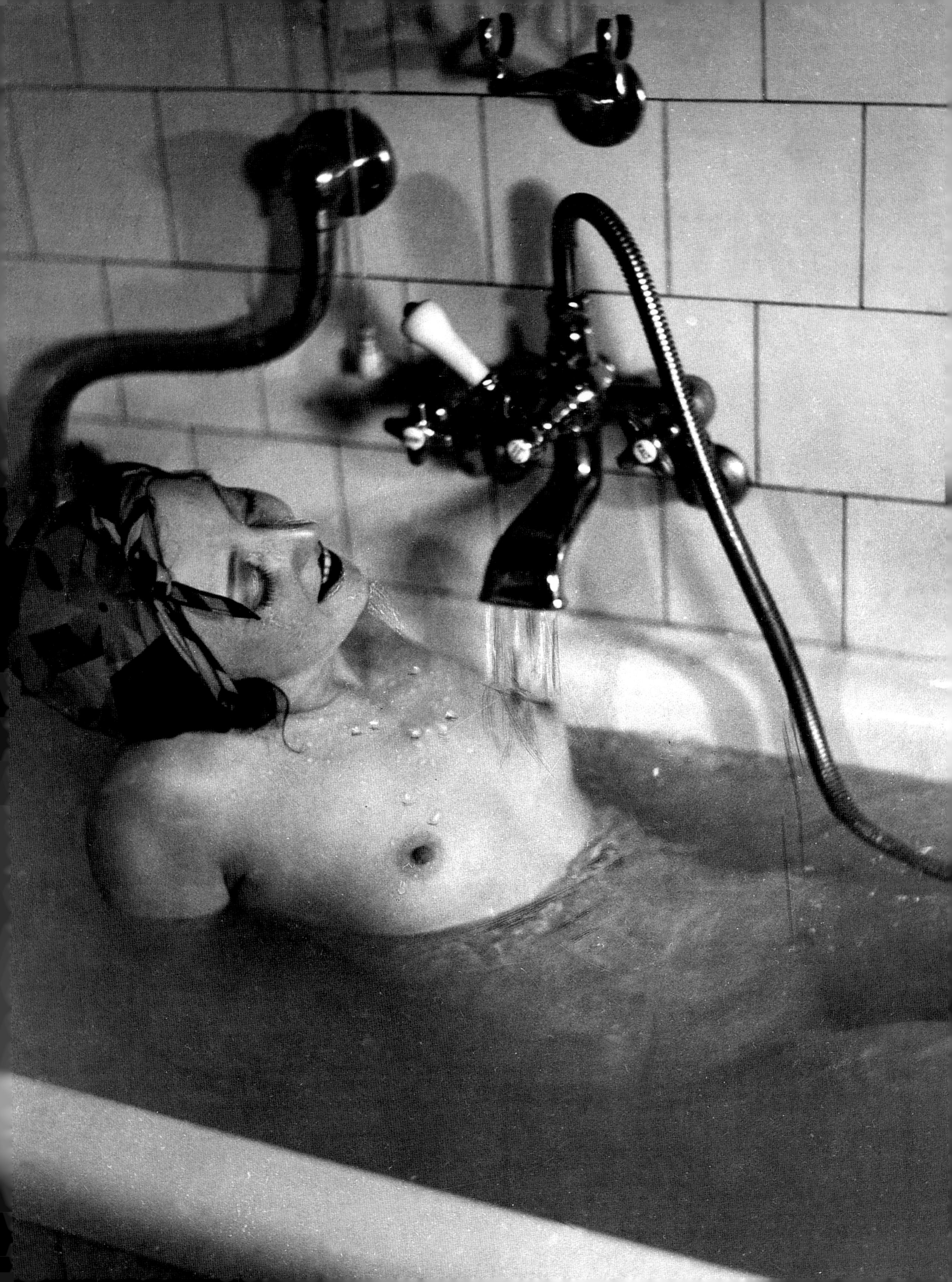

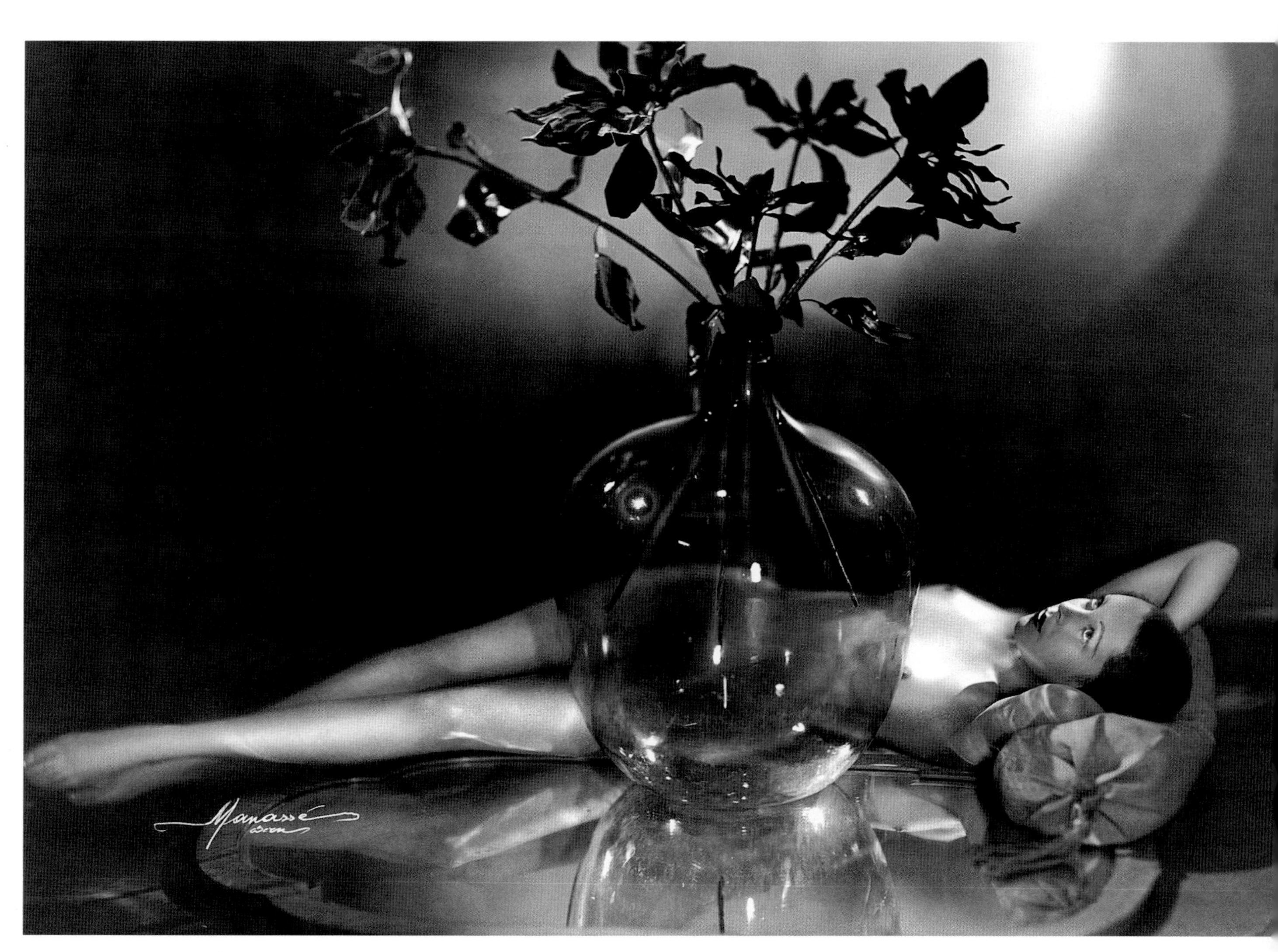

Previous two pages: Study, c.1931; Study, c.1934; these pages: Study, c.1931; Study, c.1935; next two pages: Study, c.1933; Bee Jackson, c.1930

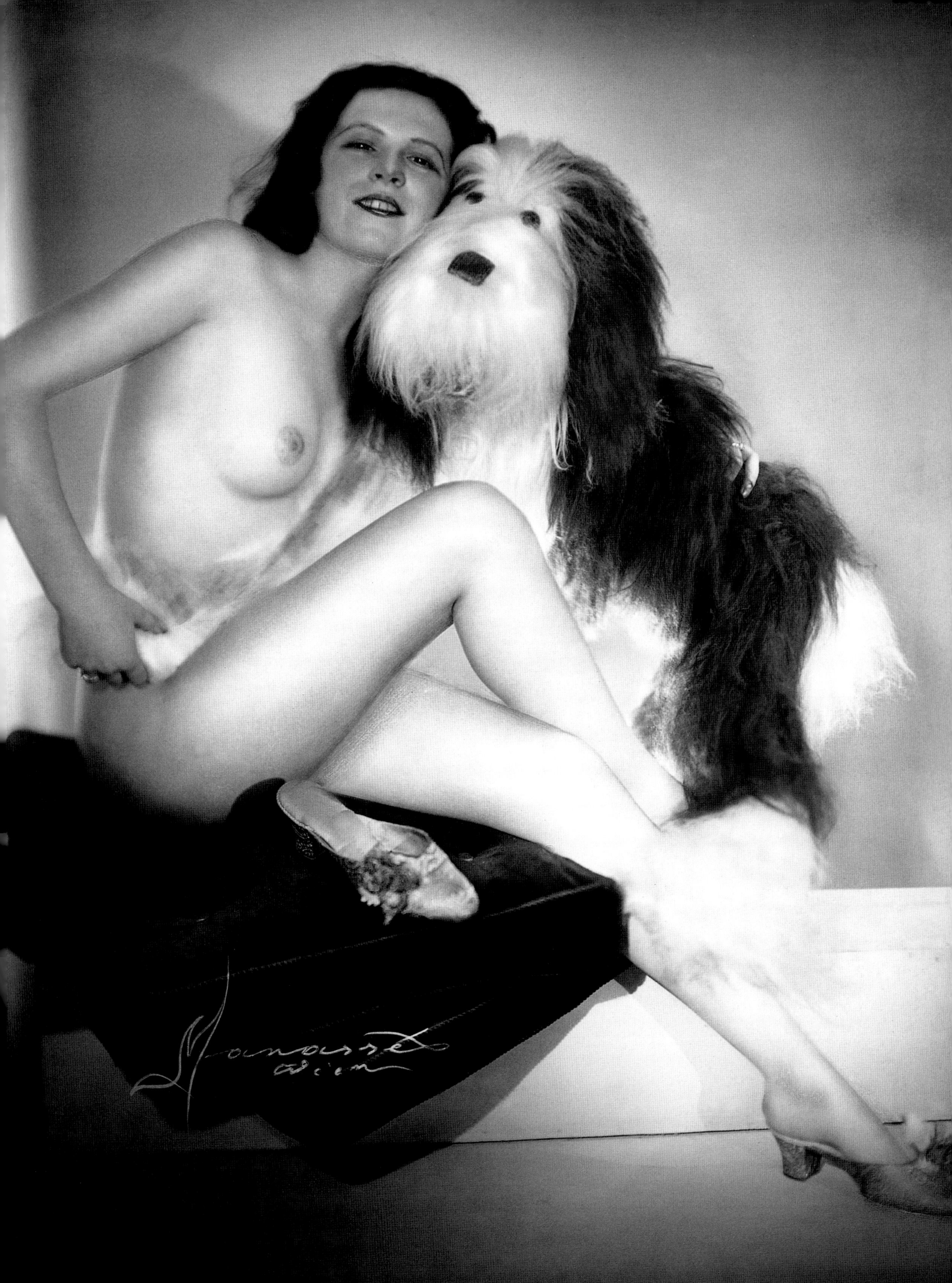
Manassé
wien

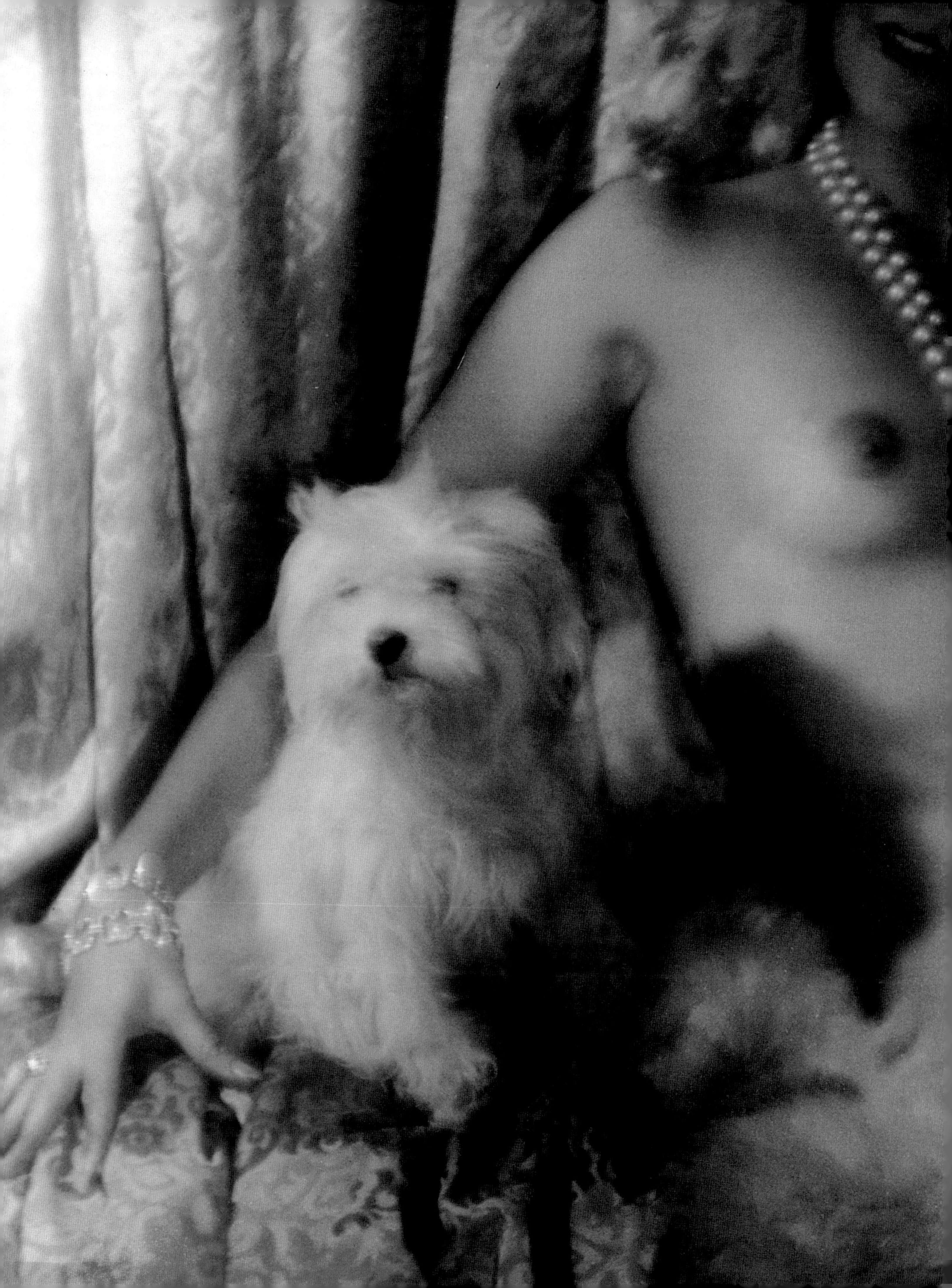

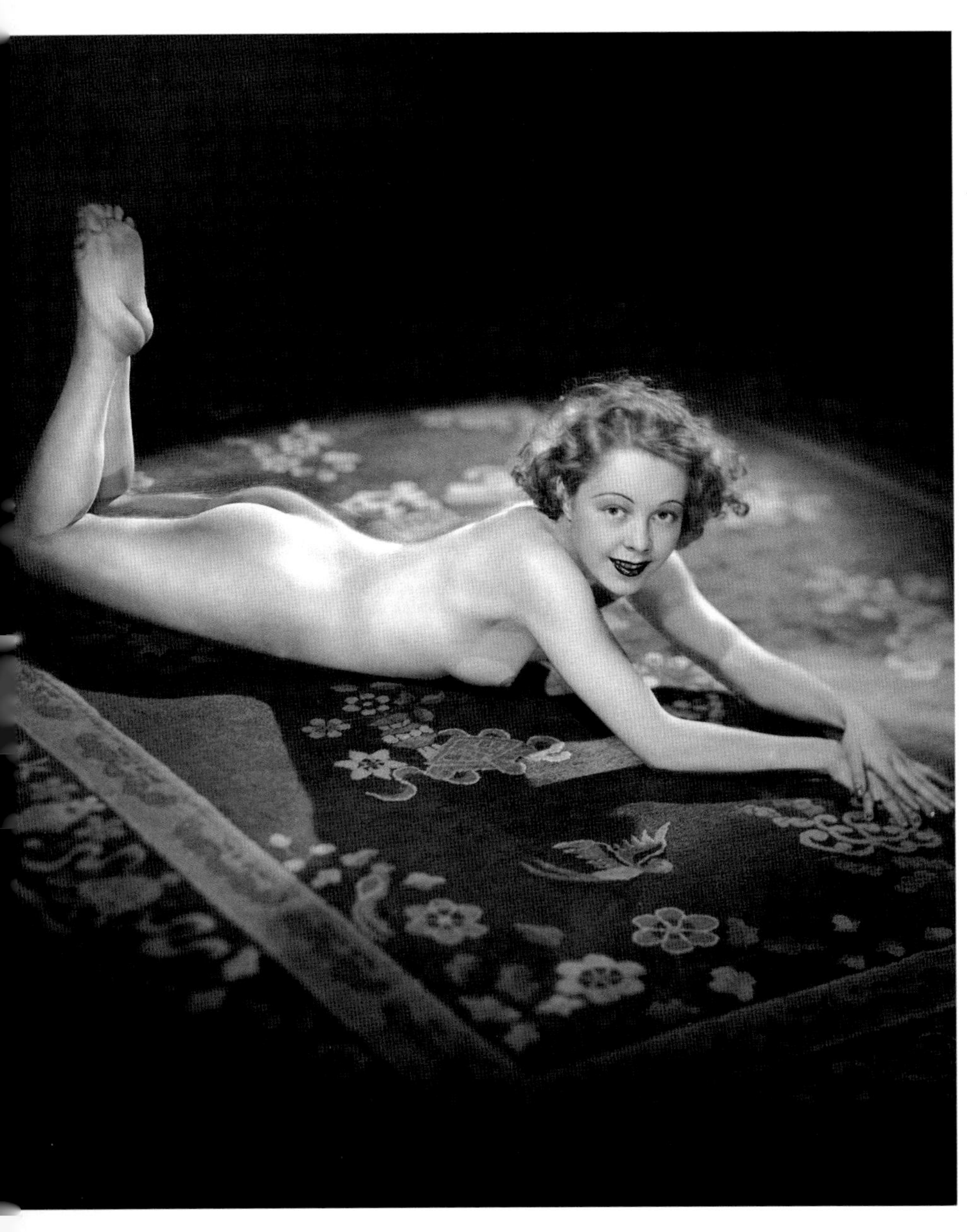

Study, c.1934; Study, c.1926; next page: Study, c.1930

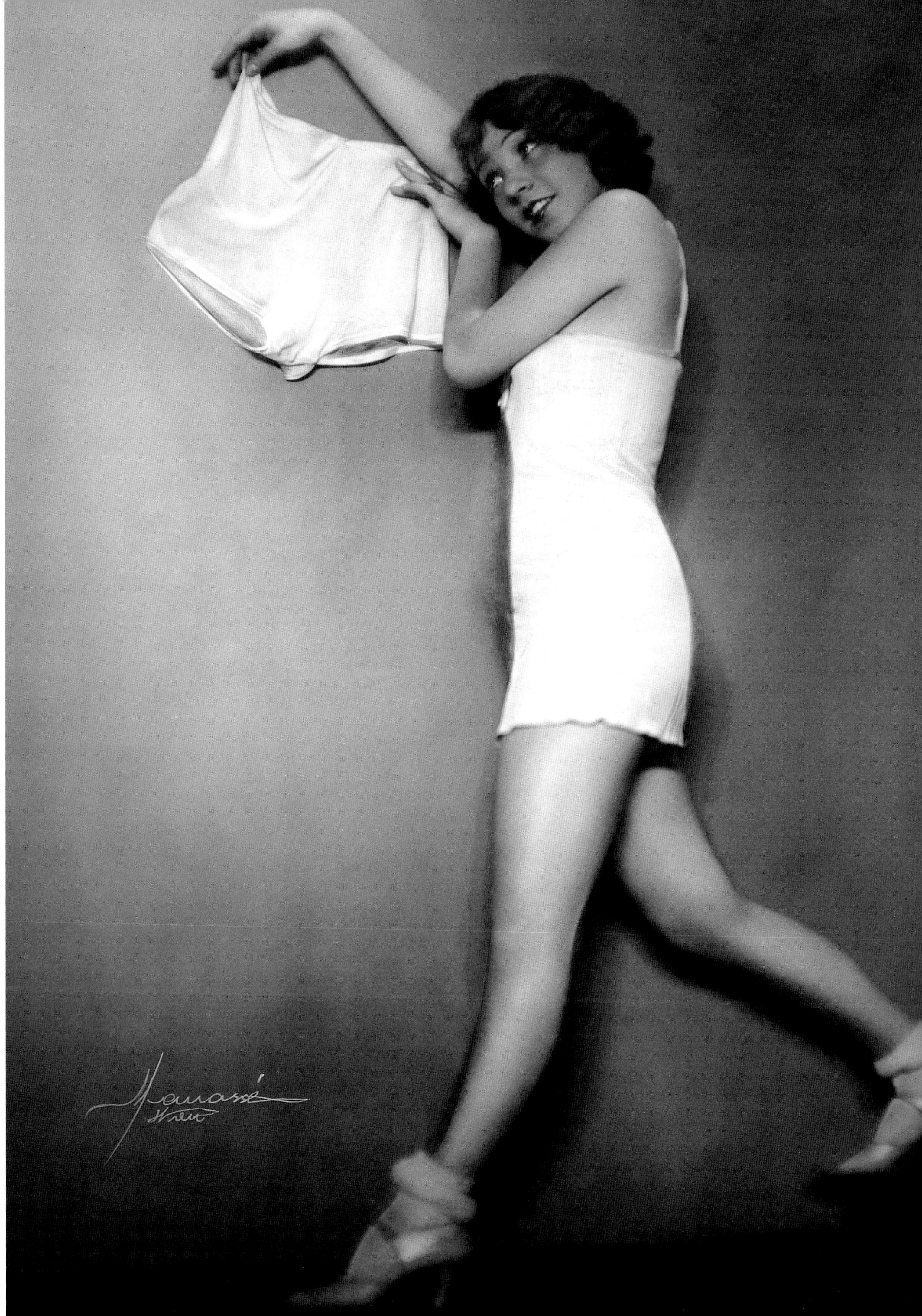
Manassé
Wien

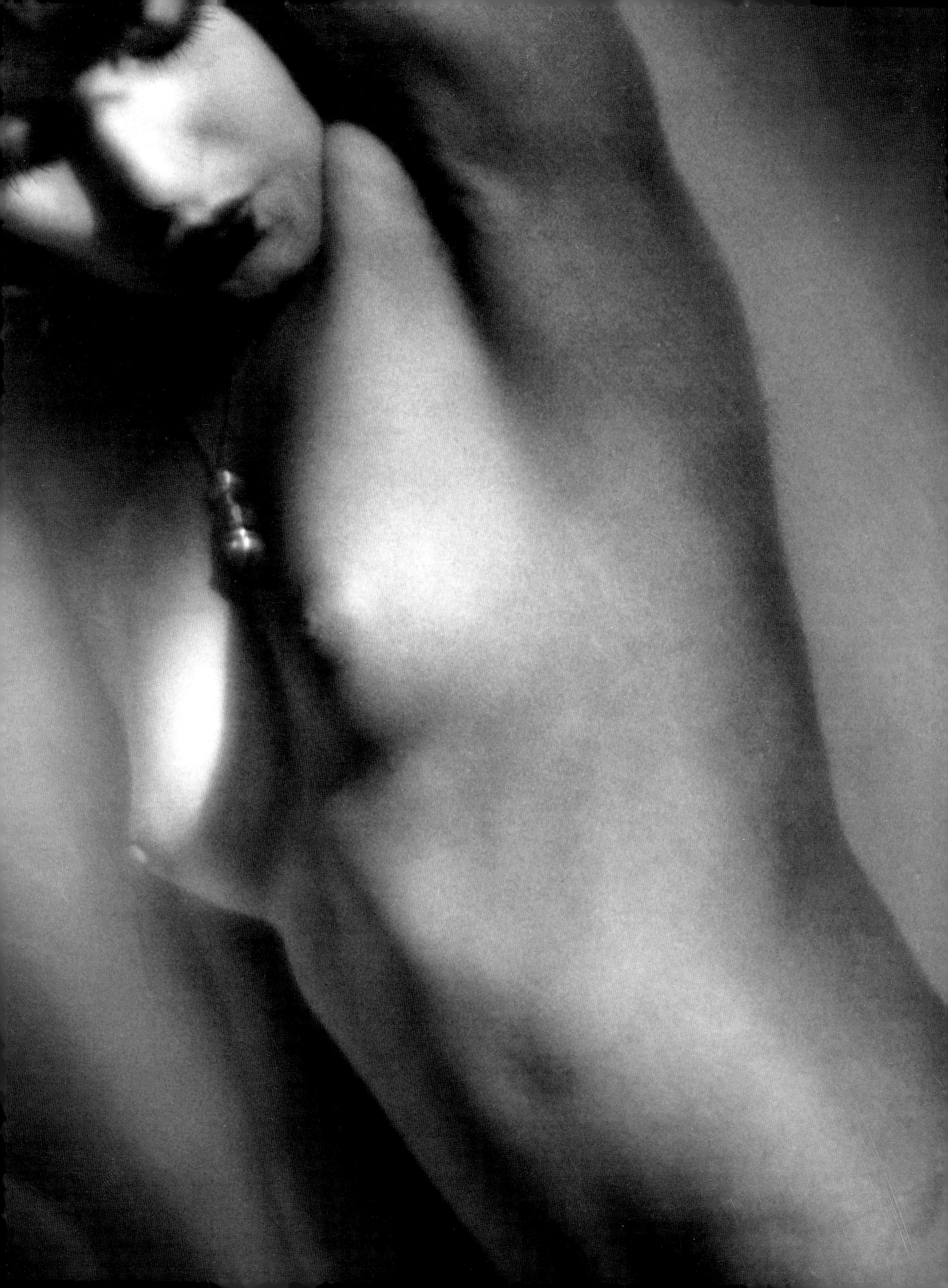

LIST OF FIGURES

Unless otherwise noted all illustrations reproduced here are c. 22 x 16 cm silver bromide prints from the archives of the Schostal agency, Vienna, Paris, Milan. These photographs all carry the stamp—in its various forms—of the agency and of Studio Manassé; often the negatives are also signed "Manassé Wien." In addition, there are some prints made from photographs taken between 1931 to 1936 with the notation "Manassé-Ricoll," but these were published with this notation only between 1935 and 1939. In 1937 the inscription "A. von Wlassics" was also used. Between 1938 and 1943 some pictures carrying the signature "WOG" were published in Austrian magazines. This was the name of the studio in Berlin and stands for "Wlassics/Olga/Geschke". From 1947 on there were some signed "Olga Wlassics"; these are identified as such in the list that follows.

Titles in quotation marks and without any additional comment replicate the handwritten remarks on the back of the photo in question. These pictures were often given other titles when they were published in periodicals. In the captions for many of these pictures, we have used shortened versions of these titles. In all other cases we have given the publication dates. The four-five digit numbers refer to the Studio Manassé numbers on the negatives; these were also marked on the backs of the prints in the Schostal archive and in the Seemann Collection.

37 Advertisement for Studio Manassé in *Wiener Magazin,* designed by Hermann Kosel; appeared in all issues of the monthly magazine of 1930 and 1931

38 "Some advice for women who, in spite of the long skirts, want to show their legs," about 1931, neg. 15,930

39 "Gerty Gert, actress," about 1932, neg. 17,779

40 "Member of Viennese society: Mrs. Olly von Wlassics," reproduced from *Wiener Magazin,* April 1928

41 "Study," about 1931, neg. 15,272

42 "Gry Dorescu, dancer," about 1928, neg. 10,699

43 "Study," about 1930

44 Unknown photographer: advertising photo reproduced from Wulffen et al., op. cit.
"Study," about 1934, neg. 19,302C (detail) with typed text: "The series, Eros as head of advertising. An advertisement for stockings seems always also to be an advertisement for beautiful legs, as our picture clearly demonstrates."

45 "Study," about 1930, neg. 13,792, private coll.

46 "Hansi Prinz, dancer. The last bottle," about 1932, neg. 17,581

47 "Anita Knauer, dancer," about 1932, neg. 17,562

48 Ball bearings, 1933 (relief etching from a folder of advertisings from the A. Krampolek Art Institute, Vienna IV), Seemann Coll., Vienna.

49 "Darmora, dancer," about 1927, neg. 10,285

50 Studio WOG, brochure, *Kunst und Anmut* (Art and Charm), Berlin, about 1940, self-published by the studio, private coll., Vienna
"Passion," reproduced from *Wiener Magazin,* December 1932.

51 "Study (Little Red Riding Hood)," about 1928, neg. 9,459, private coll.

52 "Study," about 1931, neg. 15,279, reproduced in *Muskete,* March 1936

53 "Study," about 1926, neg. 7,901

54 "Hildegard Thiele, actress," about 1928, neg. 9,869

55 "Ruth Gold, dancer," about 1928, neg. 11,943

56 "Study (Bee Jackson)," about 1931, neg. 15,975, private coll.

57 "Study," about 1928, neg. 11,622, private coll.

58 "Tala Birell, film actress," about 1928, neg. 11,391

59 "Ruth Weyher," about 1922, postcard, Iris-Verlag, Seemann Coll., Vienna
"Lucy Doraine," about 1922, postcard, Seemann Coll., Vienna
"Anna May Wong," about 1928, postcard, Ross-Verlag, private coll., Vienna

60 Manassé-Ricoll, "Study," about 1936, neg. 24,916

61 "Hella Gerth, film actress," about 1934, neg. 21,822

62 "Study," about 1934, neg. 19,537, private coll.

63 "Ossi Roudie, dancer, Stadttheater Wien," about 1925, neg. 4,133

64 "Study," about 1934, neg. 21,220T

65 "Sari Gabor, dancer," about 1933, neg. 18,920

66 "Study," about 1931, neg. 15,282

67 "Betty Bird, film actress," about 1926, neg. 7,870

68 Unknown photographer: Rudolph Valentino, about 1922
"Ben Torren," about 1927, neg. 9,757

69 "Tala Birell, the Viennese Greta Garbo," about 1927, neg. 10,230

70 "Ariman Banu, Indian Dancer," about 1931, neg. 15,744

71 "Study," about 1931, neg. 15,745, private coll.

72 "Study," about 1933, neg. 20,612

73 "Study," before 1934, neg. 20,033

74 "Christiane Delyn, Palais Royal, Paris," about 1931, neg. 16,775 (similar to cover picture used for *Wiener Magazin,* April 1933)

75 Manassé-Ricoll "Study," about 1935, neg. 24,696

76 "Study," about 1934, neg. 19,548, private coll.

77 "Study," about 1928, private coll.

78 "Study," about 1931, neg. 14,788

79 "Study," about 1931, neg. 15,281, reproduced in *Wiener Magazin,* June 1932

80 "Fridi Grubbe," about 1927, neg. 9,780A

81 "Teresa Paoly, dancer," about 1926, neg. 7,181, reproduced in *Wiener Magazin,* September 1928 under the title "Bronzeplastik" (Bronze Sculpture)

82 "Study," about 1935, neg. 23,000C
83 "Study," about 1935, neg. 23,125, a cropped version was reproduced in *Wiener Magazin,* November 1938
84 Olga Wlassics: "Light and Shadow," neg. 305-2, about 1947, Seemann Coll., Vienna
85 "Study," about 1932, Scheid Coll.
86 "The slender figure is preferred, even at the bottom of the ocean," reproduced from *Wiener Magazin,* April 1928
87 "Study," about 1934, neg. 20,607
88 "Study," about 1935, neg. 23,145
89 Manassé-Ricoll: "Study," about 1931, neg. 16,300B
90 "Study," about 1933, neg. 18,360D
91 "Study: Nude Tennis Player," about 1935, neg. 23,322
92 Josef Pecsi: montage, about 1930, reproduced from Josef Pecsi, *Photo und Publizität (Photo and Advertising),* Berlin 1932 (reprinted Basel 1989)
93 "Study," about 1927, neg. 8,846, private coll.
94 Manassé-Ricoll: "Study," about 1931, neg. 16,300
95 Olga Wlassics: "Study," about 1940, reproduced from *Dr. Faustus, Künstlerische Aktfotografie* (The Art of Nude Photography), an undated brochure with photographs from Arthur Benda, Manassé, Rothen, Wlassics, and WOG studios, Vienna about 1947, private coll, Vienna. There is also a (laterally inverted) print in existence marked "WOG"
96 "Bimini Statue," about 1932
97 "Maria Salvoty, great-grandniece of Heinrich Heine," about 1927, neg. 10,752, reproduced in *Wiener Magazin,* June 1930
98 Manassé-Ricoll: "Study," about 1934, neg. 20,420C
99 "Study," about 1931, neg. 16,921
100 "Study," about 1935, neg. 22,126
101 "Study," about 1935, neg. 21,676
102 "Hilde Thiele, dancer," about 1927, neg. 9,471, reproduced in *Wiener Magazin,* April 1930
104 "Study," about 1927, neg. 9,814
105 "Study," about 1926, postcard, neg. 7,536
106 "Eva Verbee, dancer," about 1926, neg. 7,769
107 "Study," about 1928
108 "Photographic Joke," about 1926, neg. 7,938, private coll.
109 Carlheinz Albrand: "The Coffee Pool," reproduced from Carlheinz Albrand, *Foto-Humor, Fotomontage: Scherz, Ulk und Trick,* Halle/Saale 1933.
110 "Study," about 1928
111 "My Sugar," about 1926, neg. 7,914
112 "My Little Bird," about 1926, neg. 7,913
113 "My Kitten," about 1926, neg. 7,911, published in *Muskete* 11/1936 under the title "At every step I meet the most beautiful women," private coll.
114 "My Little Mouse," about 1928
115 "Study," about 1926, neg. 8,801, private coll.
116 "Study, not for Italy," about 1933, neg. 18,615
117 "Study, My Dear," about 1926, neg. 7,909
118 "Study," about 1926
119 "Snow White," about 1927, neg. 8,805, private coll.
120 "Study," about 1935
121 Manassé-Ricoll: "Study," about 1936, neg. 24,912
122 "Study," about 1928, postcard, Seemann Coll., Vienna
123 Foto Wlassics, Vienna: "The Black Hand," about 1947, neg. 361-26, Seemann Coll., Vienna
124 "Elly Werner, actress: The sixth most beautiful woman in Vienna," about 1927, neg. 10,983
125 "Study," about 1926, neg. 7,890, private coll.
126 "Study," about 1933, neg. 19,341
127 "Susie Lanner, Film Actress," about 1933, neg. 18,929
128 "Rosy Csikos, dancer," about 1933, neg. 18,578 and 18,580
129 "Edith Zeisler, World Champion Toe Dancer," about 1931, neg. 15,528
130 "Anny Schwarz, actress," about 1931, neg. 16,601
131 "Anny Schwarz, actress," about 1931, neg. 16,606 and 16,002

132 "Study," about 1931, neg. 14,214, private coll.
134 "Study," about 1931
135 "Study," about 1931, neg. 14,219, private coll.
136 "Ly Fassing," about 1933, neg. 18,983, reproduced in *Wiener Magazin,* June 1934.
137 "Study," about 1934, neg. 19,050
138 "Study: Anny Schwarz," about 1931, neg. 16,796
139 "Hilde Lassl, dancer," about 1932, neg. 17,175, reproduced in *Wiener Magazin,* January 1933
140 "Madame Bluebeard," about 1931
141 "The ideal way to choose a husband," about 1931, neg. 15,941
142 "Study," about 1924, neg. 4,065
143 "Study," about 1926, neg. 7,888, private coll.
144 "Study," about 1931, neg. 14,284, appeared in a montage with other photographs from the Manassé studio in *Muskete,* September 1936; in the montage it was used horizontally, but the original is captioned vertically
145 "Study," about 1934, neg. 21,290
146 "Study," about 1931, neg. 14,270, private coll.
147 "Study," about 1935, neg. 21,534
148 "Study," about 1933, neg. 18,025
149 "Bee Jackson," about 1930, neg. 13,996
150 "Study," about 1934, neg. 21,532
151 "Study," about 1926, neg. 7,886
152 "Study," about 1930, neg. 13,335, reproduced in *Revue des Monats,* July 1931, with the title "The Amulet," private collection
157 "Anny Schwarz, actress," about 1931, neg. 16,602

Anny Schwarz, c. 1931

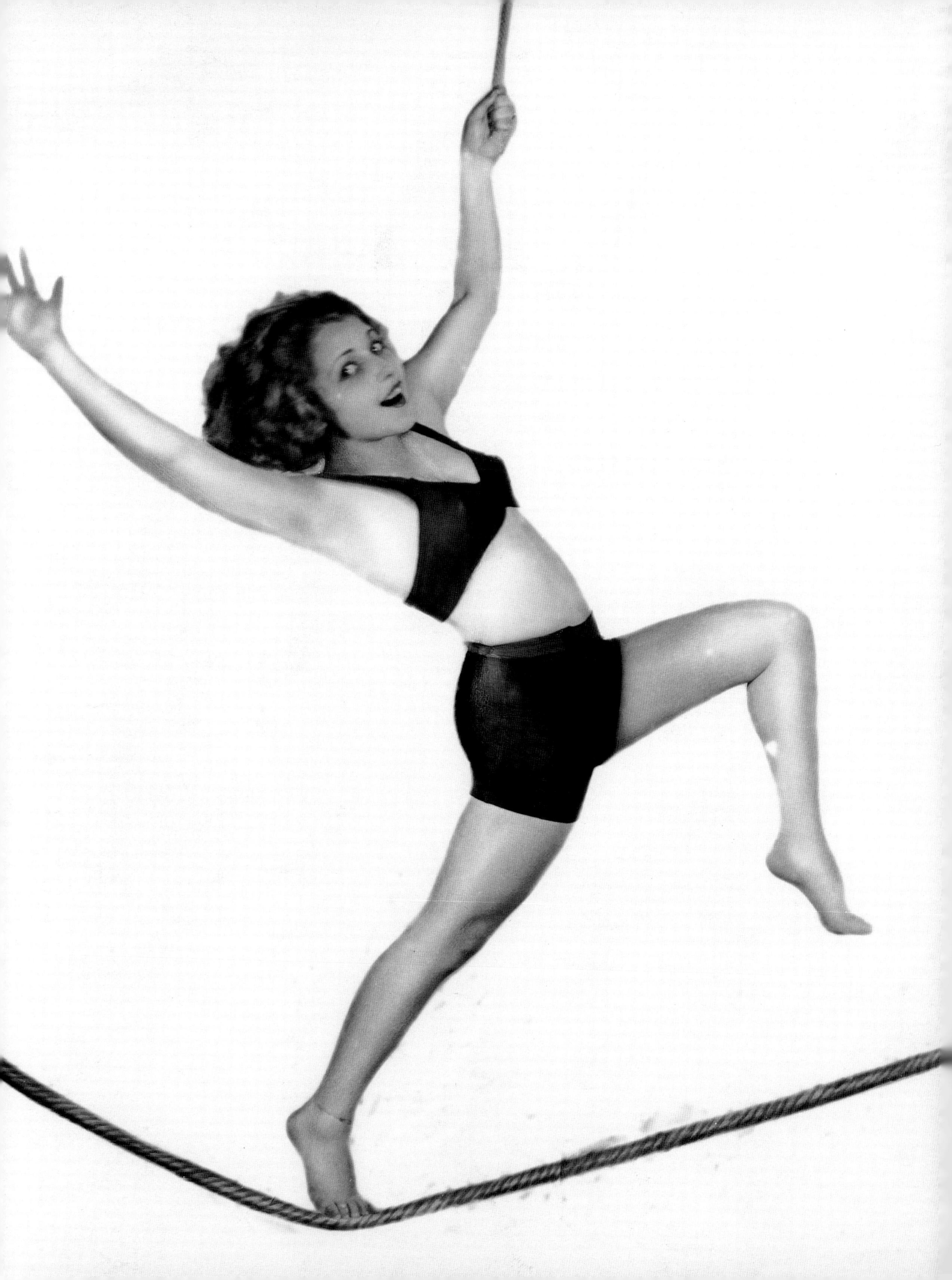

BIBLIOGRAPHY

Carlheinz Albrand, *Foto-Humor. Fotomontage. Scherz. Ulk und Trick.* Halle/Saale 1933

Béla Balázs, *Der sichtbare Mensch oder Die Kultur des Films.* Wien—Leipzig 1925

Ilsebill Barta, Zita Breu, Daniela Hammer-Tugendhat, Ulrike Jenni, Irene Nierhaus and Judith Schöbel, *Frauen: Bilder. Männer: Mythen.* Berlin 1987

Bertolt Brecht, *Augsburger Theaterkritiken.* Augsburg 1928

Bran Dijkstra, *Evil Sisters: The Threat of Female Sexuality and the Cult of Manhood.* New York 1996

Mary Ann Doanne, *Femmes Fatales: Feminism, Film Theory and Psychoanalysis.* New York 1991

Ilja Ehrenburg, *Die Traumfabrik.* Berlin 1930

Paul Éluard, "Les plus belles cartes postales". *Minotaure,* 2. Paris 1936, p. 85 ff.

Monika Faber, *Die montierte Frau: Aktphotogaphien des Atelier Manassé aus den 20er und 30er Jahren.* Wien 1988

Christian Ferber (ed.), *Der Querschnitt: Magazin der aktuellen Ewigkeitswerte.* Frankfurt/Main—Berlin 1981

Hans Frank, Die Photographie in Österreich: zwischen Handwerk und Kunst. In: *Alte und moderne Kunst,* 123/1972, p. 24 ff.

Walter Fritz and Gerhard Tötschinger, *Maskerade. Kostüme des österreichischen Films: Ein Mythos.* Wien 1993

Walter Fritz, *Im Kino erlebe ich die Welt: 100 Jahre Kino und Film in Österreich.* Wien—München 1997

Frivol. Erotische Fotografien aus der Kollektion Uwe Scheid. Text by Reinhold Mißelbeck. Heidelberg 1994

René Fülöp-Miller, *Phantasie-Maschine.* Berlin, 1931

Mark Gabor, *Die Geschichte des Pin-up.* München 1975

Fritz Giese, *Girl-Kultur.* München 1925

Ernst Günther, *Geschichte des Varietés.* Berlin 1978

Murray G. Hall, Franz Kadrnoska, Friedrich Kornauth and Wendelin Schmidt-Dengler, *Die Muskete: Kultur- und Sozialgeschichte im Spiegel einer satirisch-humoristischen Zeitschrift 1905–1941.* Wien 1983

Friedrich Huebner (ed.), *Die Frau von Morgen, wie wir sie uns wünschen.* Leipzig 1929

Annemarie Hürlimann and Alois Martin Müller (eds.), *Film Stills: Emotions made in Hollywood,* Exhibition Catalogue. Zürich 1993

John Kobal, *Hollywoods Ruhm und Schönheit: The famous „John Kobal Collection". Die hohe Kunst der Glamour-Fotografie.* München 1983

Siegfried Kracauer, *Von Caligari zu Hitler: Eine psychologische Geschichte des deutschen Films.* Frankfurt/Main 1995 [first published 1958]

Siegfried Kracauer, *Das Ornament der Masse: Essays.* Frankfurt/Main 1977

Siegfried Kracauer, *Kino*, ed. by Karsten Witte. Frankfurt/Main, 1974

Dieter Krusche, *Reclams Film-Führer*. Stuttgart 1982

László Moholy-Nagy, *Malerei, Fotografie, Film*. Mainz 1967 [first published 1925]

Francette Pacteau, *The Symptom of Beauty*. London 1994

Josef Pecsi, *Photo und Publizität. Photo and Advertising*. Berlin 1932 [Reprint Basel 1989]

Patrice Petro, *Joyless Streets: Women and Melodramatic Representation in Weimar Germany*. Princeton 1989

Stefan Riesenfellner and Josef Seiter, *Kuckuck: Die moderne Bild-Illustrierte des Roten Wien*. Wien 1995

Heide Schlüppmann, *Unheimlichkeit des Blicks: Das Drama des frühen deutschen Kinos*. Basel—Frankfurt/Main 1990

Helfried Seemann and Christian Lunzer, *Das süße Mädel und die erotische Photographie im Wien der Jahrhundertwende*. Wien 1994

Georg Seeßlen, *Klassiker der Filmkomik: Eine Einführung in die Typologie des komischen Films*. München 1976

Diana Souhami, *Greta & Cecil*. San Francisco 1994

Timm Starl, *Berufsfotografen als „Knipser"*. In: *Fotogeschichte*, Vol. 6, 1982, p. 22

Katharina Sykora, Annette Dorgerloh, Doris Noell-Rumpeltes and Ada Raev (eds.), *Die Neue Frau: Herausforderung für die Bildmedien der zwanziger Jahre*. Marburg 1993

Tanz: 20. Jahrhundert in Wien, Exhibition Catalogue, Österreichisches Theatermuseum. Wien 1979

Klaus Theweleit, *Männerphantasien*. 2 Vols. Frankfurt/Main 1977

Joachim Welzl, *Das Weib als Sklavin: Die Frau in gewollter und erzwungener Hörigkeit, das brutalisierte und mißhandelte Weib, die Sexualpsychologie der Masochistin*. Wien 1929

Andrea Winkler-Mayerhöfer, *Starkult als Propagandamittel? Studien zum Unterhaltungsfilm im Dritten Reich*. München 1992

Adorjan von Wlassics, in: *Revue des Monats*, September 1929, p. 1144 ff.

Jack Woody, *Lost Hollywood*. Altadena, 1987

Erich Wulffen, Erich Stenger, Otto Goldmann, Paul Englisch, Rudolf Brettschneider, Gustav Bingen and Heinrich Ludwig, *Die Erotik in der Fotografie*. 2 Vols. Wien—Berlin—Leipzig 1931

First published in the United States of America in 1998
by UNIVERSE PUBLISHING
A Division of Rizzoli International Publications, Inc.
300 Park Avenue South
New York, NY 10010

98 99 00 01 02/ 10 9 8 7 6 5 4 3 2 1

Printed in Austria

Library of Congress Catalog Card number: 98–61072